Spring Roo in Action

Spring Roo
in Action

KEN RIMPLE
SRINI PENCHIKALA

MANNING
SHELTER ISLAND

Manning Publications Co.
20 Baldwin Road
PO Box 261
Shelter Island, NY 11964

Development editor: Sebastian Stirling
Technical proofreaders: Alan Stewart, Andrew Swan
Copyeditors: Benjamin Berg, Bob Herbtsman,
Tara McGoldrick Walsh
Proofreaders: Katie Tennant, Alyson Brener
Typesetter: Dottie Marsico
Cover designer: Marija Tudor

ISBN 9781935182962
Printed in the United States of America
1 2 3 4 5 6 7 8 9 10 – MAL – 17 16 15 14 13 12

To my wife, Kris,
and my children, Drew, Miles, Jayna, and Justine

— *K.R.*

To my parents, Siva Reddy and Lakshmi

—*S.P.*

brief contents

contents

ix

foreword

Java has been the world's most popular programming language for well over a decade. You can find it running everywhere: on super computers, servers, set top boxes, PCs, phones, tablets, routers, and robots. There are millions of expert engineers fluent in it, libraries for every conceivable purpose, and unparalleled tooling and management capabilities.

Despite Java's success, few people consider it highly productive for quickly developing enterprise applications. Indeed, if we step back to the year 2000, the mainstream model revolved around a standard called EJB 2. It promoted patterns that are unthinkable in the modern era, including vast deployment descriptors, code that was virtually impossible to unit test, confusing lifecycle methods, meaningless layers, excessive redeployment delays, and so on.

These problems would not remain unchallenged. In the early 2000s, Spring introduced a vastly more productive approach that quickly replaced EJB 2 for new applications. It also significantly popularized the use of open source within traditionally conservative organizations that had previously only allowed vendor-endorsed products. Today, most developers enjoy considerable latitude in their ability to use liberally licensed open source software.

Convention-over-configuration web frameworks started to gain traction by mid-decade. Ruby on Rails in particular exploited a range of dynamic language capabilities to further raise the bar of enterprise application development productivity. Grails delivered similar benefits on the JVM by combining Spring's solid enterprise foundations with Groovy's dynamic language capabilities.

Implementing a convention-over-configuration web framework for Java was challenging because of its static typing model, so I designed an incremental active code generator that would emit mixins. This allowed multiple compilation units to be woven into a single class file. Mixins ensured that generated code would be conveniently managed without developer interaction and without losing important Java features such as code assist, debugging, source visibility, profiling, performance, and so on. The approach had not been attempted before, but it worked out nicely, and today other code generators also emit mixins (for example, Apache Magma).

One unique benefit of Spring Roo's convention-over-configuration model is the absence of any runtime component. It operates only at development time, just like Maven or Eclipse. This makes Roo completely free of lock-in or runtime expense, such as memory or CPU time. Many people use Roo to start a project and then stop using it, while others keep using it indefinitely for the same project. Since 2008, there have been tens of thousands of projects built using Spring Roo. It brings you the proven productivity benefits of convention over configuration, but with the substantial advantages of Java.

Spring Roo in Action is an insightful and comprehensive treatment of Spring Roo. Ken Rimple and Srini Penchikala have worked closely with the Roo community and engineering team for over two years, with countless emails, tickets, and forum posts that dig deep into the Roo internals. They have carefully tracked Roo's development and inspired multiple improvements. The result is a detailed book that is extensively researched, up-to-date, authoritative, and pragmatic. I hope that you enjoy *Spring Roo in Action* and the significant productivity enhancements it will bring to your application development journey.

BEN ALEX
PROJECT FOUNDER
SPRING ROO, SPRING SECURITY
AND SPRING UAA
Twitter @benalexau

preface

In the summer of 2009, I learned from Ben Alex about a new technology called Spring Roo. This project, based on a command-line shell, promised to bring the agility of other rapid development frameworks, such as Grails and Ruby on Rails, to the native Java and Spring platform. Using a shell instead of writing code seemed like a loss of control, but after downloading and experimenting with the tool, I started to realize the potential of this project. As you'll see in the book, the biggest challenge faced by Spring developers—beyond writing business logic—is how to build an application architecture and configure various application features (for example, installing JMS, email, Spring MVC, JPA, NoSQL databases, and other frameworks). Roo appeared to crack that problem and provide an elegant solution.

With Spring Roo, you issue simple commands, such as `jpa setup`, `web mvc setup`, `entity jpa`, `field`, `service`, and `repository`. Configuration tasks that normally take hours or days are performed instantly. I could see that this was going to be a useful tool for the everyday Spring developer. Since my Chariot training colleague and long-time friend Gordon Dickens was also interested in Roo, we decided to approach Manning about writing a book. Unlike so many other times in my life, I was able to position myself at just the right time to make the pitch. Manning accepted, and you are reading the result.

In the beginning of 2011, Srini Penchikala, InfoQ author and editor who had been using Roo on various projects, accepted the coauthor slot. Srini was a huge help, having penned chapters on Spring Integration, cloud computing, email and JMS, and Spring Security. During the spring and summer of 2011 we wrote the majority of these chapters. We then saw a new push for Roo 1.2, around the same time that I was working on the add-on chapters, which was exactly what was being refactored by the Roo team at the time. So this book has undergone at least three major revisions since the time we started writing it.

Our pain is your gain, and that includes all of our hard work with code that was written the night before, identifying bugs for the Roo team to fix, and working with the fantastic community of readers we have in Manning's MEAP program, aligned as well with completing the manuscript around the time of the Roo 1.2.1 release.

Our hope is that you glean from this book a sense of how Roo development operates, regardless of which version of Roo you'll be using. We also hope to spur on more developers to start using Roo as a key tool in their arsenal. The Roo community could really use some good add-ons, and though this book goes into some detail, we hope people take up the cause and contribute.

The book has been a long time in development and production, but I think the timing is good. Roo has matured, becoming viable for a wide range of projects, having added native support for many enterprise abstractions such as services and repositories, and boasting at least three active web frameworks built into the product—Spring MVC, GWT, and JSF.

—KEN RIMPLE

acknowledgments

There are many people we want to thank for their help in making this book, starting with the Manning team: Michael Stephens, who first discussed the project with us; Christina Rudloff; the inimitable Marjan Bace; marketing genius Candace Gillhoolley; and our wonderful editors, in order of appearance: Emily Macel, Sara Onstine, and Sebastian Stirling. They were absolutely invaluable in providing advice and critiques, and in revving us up when we were out of juice.

We wish to thank our production team of Mary Piergies; maestro Troy Mott and his band of merry editors: Ben Berg, Tara McGoldrick, and Bob Herbstman; our talented proofreaders: Katie Tennant and Alyson Brener; and others behind the scenes whom we are not able to name.

The reader community also deserves a huge amount of credit. Author Online forum members MikB, carcarx, Javier Beneito Barquero, Mike Oliver, Gary White, nancom, delgad9, mexxik, netname, Henry G. Brown, varevadal, Terry Jeske, and Jeff Hall, among others, helped us find bugs, from the stupid to the super-complex, and gave us honest feedback when we needed it most. Keep 'em coming, and we'll keep updating our errata and samples.

The following reviewers read the manuscript at various stages of its development and we thank them for their invaluable input: Jeroen Nouws, Deepak Vohra, Richard Freedman, Patrick Steger, Bill LaPrise, Kyle DeaMarais, Joel Schneider, Jeremy Anderson, Rizwan Lodhi, Craig Walls, Santosh Shanbhag, Shekhar Gulati, Al Scherer, John J. Ryan III, Kevin Griffin, Doug Warren, and Audrey Troutt.

Finally, we'd like to thank the Roo development team for being there and fixing bugs almost before we thought them up: Dr. Ben Alex, Stefan Schmidt, Alan Stewart, and Andrew Swan. Thank you for accepting our JIRA reports and working up fixes so we could stay on track. Special thanks to Ben for agreeing to write the foreword to our book, and to Alan and Andrew for a final technical proofread of the manuscript just before it went into production.

KEN RIMPLE

I would like to thank my wife, four children, and extended family, who deserve a big break after the almost two years I spent writing this book. I dedicate the book to my wife, Kris, because without seeing her complete more than nine books while raising our boys, I never thought I could finish this project. She can now finally stop saying, "Give the guy room, he's writing a book, you know."

Thanks to my college professor, Frank D. Quattrone, who got me started in obsessing over my writing as a literary magazine editor. And I absolutely must thank my mother, who always told me that I could do anything.

I would also like to acknowledge my employer, Chariot Solutions, for their support of the book by giving me a forum for training courses (http://chariotsolutions.com/education) and podcasts (http://techcast.chariotsolutions.com), and allowing me to participate in other endeavors, such as the Emerging Technologies for the Enterprise conference (http://phillyemergingtech.com) that also inform my writing.

A huge expression of gratitude to Srini Penchikala, who came in at the right time and helped me get this project done. His contributions in areas such as Spring Integration, JMS, email, cloud computing, and much more make this book extremely comprehensive.

I would be remiss if I didn't thank Gordon Dickens for his research and writing contributions during the beginning of this book project. He and I are close friends, and without our crazy plan, hatched one day after the interview with Ben Alex, I might not have reached out to Manning.

Finally, I'd like to single out one contributor who must have a special mention: Mete Senocak contributed key early suggestions, edits, and frank advice. He also convinced me to roast, grind, and brew my own coffee, and now I am an intolerable coffee snob. You're a good man, Mete, and I'm sure we'll see each other in a coffee support group soon.

SRINI PENCHIKALA

First of all, I would like to thank Michael Stephens and Christina Rudloff, who were my first contacts at Manning, for giving me the opportunity to be part of this book writing project. It's been a rewarding experience to contribute to the book as well as learn from others about authorship.

I also want to thank Ken Rimple for his guidance and mentoring in my transition from writing articles to writing a book.

Special thanks to our MEAP readers who provided excellent feedback and suggestions in improving the content as well as the sample application discussed in the book.

I would like to also thank my wife Kavitha and my seven year-old daughter Srihasa for their continued support and patience during the writing of this book.

about this book

Welcome to *Spring Roo in Action*! If you're reading this book, you're looking for ways to improve your Spring development productivity.

When we started writing this book, nobody had even considered a book on Roo. The tool had been out in the public sphere for only a few months, and, after all, writing a book on any emerging technology is a crazy thing to do. But crazy things are usually tried by crazy people, and once we got started there was no turning back.

This book is your guide to juicing your Spring development productivity, using a tiny, 8-megabyte project known as Spring Roo. We start by laying the groundwork for why such a tool is important, and how Roo fills the gap between the developer productivity of Spring and the configuration morass you can get into while writing enterprise applications. The writers of this book are Spring developers, trainers, mentors, and hobbyists. We develop, train, mentor, and tinker with Spring every day, so when we saw what Roo brought to the table we realized the power it represented to the everyday developer.

Craig Walls's *Spring in Action*, also published by Manning, is an excellent companion book for the new Spring developer, and is a good reference to keep nearby when you want additional information about a topic in our book.

Other good references on these topics are *Spring Integration in Action* and *ActiveMQ in Action*, also from Manning Publications.

Learning by experimenting

It's our hope that you can read this book and get a taste of how to build a Roo application, even without running a single sample. That said, the concepts are relatively easy to grasp—using Roo's TAB completion you can test the various commands and generate a working project with the features you're interested in. Then you can use your editor to review the code and test it. Soon you'll find it easy to try out new frameworks, because the feedback loop is so short.

Above all, Roo enables experimentation. Combine it with Git for version control, and you can create a branch for your new idea, try it out, and merge it back in if you like it. Of course, because branches are cheap, you can remove the branch and forget it ever happened. We encourage you to create a lot of throw-away projects with Roo.

Roadmap

Chapter 1 is a quick introduction to the Roo tool, and we get started creating applications right out of the gate. We begin by making the case for Roo and RAD on Java—how Spring makes things better, but how Roo really knocks it out of the park. We create a sample project, the Roo Pizza Shop, as a way to get you to kick the tires early, and you'll see how little you need to do to build a full-featured database-backed web application.

Chapter 2 covers the basics of using the Roo shell, and we walk through configuring a Task Manager project, installing persistence, creating an entity, and scaffolding a web application. We then dig into the code behind the application, inter-type declarations (ITDs), the various ways to structure your projects, and using an IDE such as SpringSource Tool Suite. We then discuss how to use refactoring to push-in or pull-out code, and how to remove Roo entirely if you need to.

Chapter 3 is an introduction to database persistence in Roo. We detail the options for setting up persistence using JPA, setting up a JPA entity, using the Bean Validation framework to provide annotation-driven validations, how to use finders to write simple JPA queries, and how to create repositories using the repository command and the Spring Data API.

Chapter 4 continues the discussion of database persistence and covers relationship mappings, how to write your own JPA persistence methods, reverse engineering database tables from an existing database, adding a Spring service layer with the service command, and using MongoDB, a NoSQL database supported by Roo 1.2.

Chapter 5 introduces Spring MVC, which is the base of Roo's primary web framework. We show you how to install the web framework and how to use scaffolding to automatically generate a simple CRUD application with only two commands. We also discuss accessing other Spring beans, and how to scaffold in a multimodule project.

Chapter 6 digs deeply into the scaffolding engine and Roo's tag libraries. We show you how you can customize the scaffolded web views, and how to modify the way fields are displayed. We outline how to display reference data in drop-down lists, customize date fields, deal with localization and theming, and we show you how Roo uses Apache Tiles to lay out your user interfaces.

Chapter 7 switches gears to more advanced web frameworks. We start by showing you how to use Spring MVC and Dojo to provide Ajax support for your forms. We then show you how to install two other web frameworks, Google Web Toolkit and Java-Server Faces. We end by listing a few other web frameworks and the support that Roo had for them at the time we wrote the book.

Chapter 8 covers Spring Security, including how to install it, configure it against both a database data store and LDAP, set up a login page, test security, and add event logging.

Chapter 9 is our testing chapter. We cover unit testing and Mockito, mocking the persistence tier, integration testing in-container against entities, repositories and services, and how to write functional, black box tests with Selenium, both using Roo's support for HTML table-based tests as well as using the JUnit API.

Chapter 10 discusses email and JMS, two external integration points that most developers have to work with at some point in their careers. We begin by outlining a course management system, and then lay down the JMS and email features required to support that system. We cover JMS installation, the JMS template, building a POJO listener, and testing the listener. Then we cover building email messages with an email sender, configuring SMTP support, building an email template, and hosting it behind a Spring service.

Chapter 11 is the introduction to Roo add-ons. We start by showing you how to search for publicly available add-ons and how to install and remove them. Because add-ons are OSGi components, we spend time detailing enough of OSGi to be dangerous, and then we dive right in and create three add-ons: a Norwegian language add-on, a Roo wrapper add-on to expose a non-OSGi JAR to the Roo system, and a "Simple" add-on to provide jQuery support.

Chapter 12 continues our add-on discussion and provides support for CoffeeScript by creating an advanced add-on. We install the Maven plug-in for CoffeeScript compilation, build and test it, and show you how to detect the availability of both adding and removing the feature from your project. We then wrap up the discussion by detailing how to publish and submit your add-on to the add-on community.

Chapter 13 shows you how to use cloud computing to host your Roo applications. We discuss some of the platforms, including CloudBees and Heroku, and then focus on using Cloud Foundry, a VMware hosting offering. We deploy the Course Manager application to the cloud and show how to fetch application statistics, as well as how to bind cloud resources to the application.

Chapter 14 details how to use Spring Integration from a Roo project. We discuss event-driven application architectures, how to add a workflow to handle course registration, and how to build and install the Roo integration add-on from source, because it's not yet released for Roo 1.2.

Things you'll need

To follow along with the book, you'll need to download and install Spring Roo, version 1.2.1, from http://springsource.org/spring-roo. We cover installation in chapter 1.

You'll also need an IDE; for the new Spring developer, we suggest using Spring-Source Tool Suite. Gordon has written an STS RefCard that can be downloaded free (note: registration required) from http://refcardz.dzone.com/refcardz/eclipse-tools-spring. This special version of Eclipse is fully configured to develop Spring-based applications, and can be configured to use your Roo shell.

If you're partial to IntelliJ IDEA, you can download version 10.5 or higher, though we recommend at least version 11. IntelliJ is an excellent alternative IDE, and provides support for many of the same features as SpringSource Tool Suite, the key omission being an integrated copy of the Spring tc Server web application server, which comes bundled with STS.

You'll also need to install Maven 3.0.3 or higher, because Roo projects are Maven projects. If you're going to write your own add-ons, you'll need to install GPG, an open source encryption provider. To make these add-ons available to the public, you'll want to install Git and/or Subversion (SVN) to deliver your add-ons to public repositories hosted by Google Code, GitHub, or other places where the Roo team can access and index your add-on.

Notes on earlier versions of Roo

Users of earlier versions of Roo will need to make some adjustments in their shell commands, and the classes will look notably different.

In earlier versions of Roo, the only persistence mechanism is via the Roo Active Record pattern. Only Roo 1.2 and later will provide the `service` and `repository` commands, which set up layered Spring application objects. This is a topic which we discuss in chapters 3 and 4. Also, earlier versions of the persistence framework configuration use a `persistence setup` command, which has changed to the newer `jpa setup` in light of support for configuring non-SQL databases.

Roo 1.2 introduces the concept of multimodule projects. Roo 1.1 and below have no such features.

The add-ons chapters are compile-time incompatible with versions of Roo earlier than 1.2.1, because the framework has undergone significant refactoring between versions 1.0, 1.1, 1.2, and 1.2.1. Expect additional changes for the better in future versions. Concept-wise, the chapters hold up—the concept behind simple and advanced add-ons is the same; but the individual beans, interfaces, and techniques will vary.

NoSQL database support is new in 1.2, and database reverse engineering is new as of Roo 1.1.

The official Roo documentation discussed upgrading a Roo project. We've found the best course of action is to perform the upgrade, but then create a brand new scratch Roo project with the features you're using, and diff the pom.xml file to make sure that you've been properly upgraded to the most recent version. Refer to the Roo documentation for details for each official release.

Code conventions

We use specially formatted code in non-proportional type to convey symbols, commands, and fragments of source code. Roo (and Spring) make it hard to fit code on single lines, due to the fact that Spring developers are long-name happy (consider one of the longer class names, ClassPathXmlApplicationContext, to see what gave us many headaches when formatting our listings).

If you see the line continuation character, it means that the command you're typing is required to fit on a single line, or that the code we've reformatted was meant to exist on a single line. For example:

```
roo> project --topLevelPackage org.foo.bar.long.project.package ➥
  --projectName thebigprojectname
```

We occasionally use the continuation character to show a long line in a generated artifact as well. This is shown for completeness. Other conventions:

- All code is listed in a `Courier` font.
- We use `Courier` to highlight various commands, such as `web mvc setup`.
- We skip long lists of Java import statements and nonessential source code fragments to illustrate key features.
- We use **bold code font** to emphasize some areas of code examples to show important points.
- We use *italic font* for emphasis and to detail new terms.
- Code annotations are used instead of comments in code samples. Where comments are used, they appear in the code sample as a numbered bullet, and may have corresponding discussion points in the manuscript below the sample.

Source code

The source code for Roo in Action is available at http://github.com/krimple/spring-roo-in-action-examples. You can also find links to the source code repository and a post-publication errata list on the Manning page for this book, http://manning.com/SpringRooinAction.

As the Roo project progresses rapidly, we've constantly been reworking our examples and upgrading them before publication of the book. If you find a problem with the samples, please log a bug with the project by creating a GitHub account and clicking on the Issues tab. All samples are tested with Roo 1.2.1.

We'll also be taking contributions of example code to share with our readers—contact us via GitHub with pull requests to the user-contrib directory and we'll review them. Assume that your samples will be available for use by the public Roo user community, and that the code should be freely contributed without additional restrictive source licenses. Any contributions are welcomed by the reader community, so feel free to lend your expertise.

Author Online

The purchase of *Spring Roo in Action* includes free access to a private forum run by Manning Publications where you can make comments about the book, ask technical questions, and receive help from the authors and other users. You can access and subscribe to the forum at www.manning.com/SpringRooinAction. This page provides information on how to get on the forum after you're registered, what kind of help is available, and the rules of conduct in the forum.

Manning's commitment to our readers is to provide a venue where a meaningful dialogue among individual readers and between readers and authors can take place. It's not a commitment to any specific amount of participation on the part of the authors, whose contribution to the book's forum remains voluntary (and unpaid). We suggest you try asking the authors some challenging questions, lest their interest stray!

The Author Online forum and the archives of previous discussions will be accessible from the publisher's website as long as the book is in print.

about the authors

KEN RIMPLE is a trainer, mentor, software developer, and musician who lives in the Philadelphia area. He has had an obsession with creativity in music and computers his whole life. His first real computer was a Commodore 64. At the same time he began his lifelong love affair with the drums. Today he's a jazz drummer who plays whenever he can.

Ken has been active in emerging technologies since he entered the IT sector in 1989, at the dawn of the client/server movement. He's worked on technologies from fat clients to databases to servers, ranging from WebLogic to Tomcat. He is currently immersed in Spring technologies, including Roo and Grails.

Ken runs Chariot's education services (http://chariotsolutions.com/education) where he teaches Spring-related VMWare courses, including Maven and Hibernate, among others. He also hosts the Chariot TechCast (http://techcast.chariotsolutions .com) podcast, and blogs at http://rimple.com.

SRINI PENCHIKALA works as a security architect at a financial services organization in Austin, Texas. He has over 16 years of experience in software architecture, security, and risk management. Srini's areas of interest are Agile Security and Lean Enterprise Architectures. He has presented at conferences like JavaOne, SEI Architecture Technology Conference (SATURN), IT Architect Conference (ITARC), No Fluff Just Stuff, NoSQL Now, and the Project World Conference. Srini has published several articles on risk management, security architecture, and agile security methodologies on websites like InfoQ, The ServerSide, OReilly Network (ONJava), DevX Java, java.net, and JavaWorld. He is also an editor at InfoQ (http://www.infoq.com/author/Srini-Penchikala).

Srini blogs on Java, software security, lean organizations, and leadership topics at http://srinip2007.blogspot.com/ and on twitter (@srinip).

about the cover illustration

The figure on the cover of *Spring Roo in Action* is captioned "A man from Sinj, Dalmatia, Croatia." The illustration is taken from a reproduction of an album of Croatian traditional costumes from the mid-nineteenth century by Nikola Arsenovic, published by the Ethnographic Museum in Split, Croatia, in 2003. The illustrations were obtained from a helpful librarian at the Ethnographic Museum in Split, itself situated in the Roman core of the medieval center of the town: the ruins of Emperor Diocletian's retirement palace from around AD 304. The book includes finely colored illustrations of figures from different regions of Croatia, accompanied by descriptions of the costumes and of everyday life.

Sinj is a small town in Dalmatia, about 25 miles north of Split. The figure on the cover wears black woolen trousers and a white linen shirt, over which he dons a black vest and black jacket, richly trimmed with the blue and red embroidery typical for this region. A red turban and colorful socks complete the costume. The man is also holding a pipe and has a short sword tucked under his belt.

Dress codes and lifestyles have changed over the last 200 years, and the diversity by region, so rich at the time, has faded away. It's now hard to tell apart the inhabitants of different continents, let alone of different hamlets or towns separated by only a few miles. Perhaps we have traded cultural diversity for a more varied personal life—certainly for a more varied and fast-paced technological life.

Manning celebrates the inventiveness and initiative of the computer business with book covers based on the rich diversity of regional life of two centuries ago, brought back to life by illustrations from old books and collections like this one.

Part 1

Starting Spring apps rapidly with Roo

Spring Roo is an excellent framework for the rapid development of Spring-based Java applications. With a simple command-line shell, it can create and manage Spring applications, adding and configuring components in all of the application architecture layers from SQL to URL, so to say.

We start exploring Roo with chapter 1, "What is Spring Roo?" explaining how Roo works and how it helps with creating the various configuration files required for a typical Spring application. You'll also learn how to install and launch the Roo shell. We'll look at a simple application by running one of the sample scripts provided in the Roo installation package.

Chapter 2, "Getting started with Roo," will show you how to create applications from scratch with the Roo shell. You'll also learn the details of Roo project layout and architecture. We discuss one of the new concepts Roo introduces, called *AspectJ ITDs*, that plays an important role in the overall Roo architecture. As developers, you need tools to take advantage of new technologies and frameworks. Roo comes with integration in the form of the SpringSource Tool Suite (STS) IDE tool, which is also discussed in this chapter. We wrap up the chapter with a discussion on refactoring Roo code and leaving Roo behind if, for some reason, you want to remove Roo from your project.

What is Spring Roo?

This chapter covers

- The challenges of Enterprise Java
- The Spring Framework
- Roo simplifies it all
- A sample Roo project

You're about to be introduced to a powerful new tool that makes your life as a Java application developer less stressful and more productive. That tool is Spring Roo. With a simple command-line shell, Roo can create and manage Spring-based applications, adding and configuring features such as the Java Persistence API (JPA), the Java Message Service (JMS), email, and Spring Security. Roo generates Spring MVC web applications. These allow you to manage and edit your database data, configure tests using frameworks such as JUnit and Selenium, and choose from a variety of ORM APIs and databases. At the same time, Roo reduces the amount of code written by you and rolls out efficient, customizable generated code.

In this chapter, we discuss the challenges of working with Enterprise Java applications, create a sample application with the Roo shell, and take a quick tour of Roo's features. We then review the Roo sample script file and discuss the architectural models available to you when crafting your application.

By the end of this chapter, you'll see how Roo helps you get rid of much of the tedium Java EE application development demands. You'll see that you can gain much of the productivity available in dynamic-language, convention-over-configuration platforms such as Ruby on Rails and Grails. This all comes without sacrificing the benefits of Java compile-time type safety, compiled code, and debuggability.

Let's begin our journey by discussing one of the major reasons why Java-based development projects sputter: the complexity of configuring an application architecture.

1.1 Configuration is a burden

Putting together a Java-based application can be a difficult task these days. Where do you start? There are many things to consider: build scripts, dependency management, architectural patterns, framework selections, database mapping strategies, and much more.

In traditional Enterprise Java development efforts, architects pull together a hodgepodge of open source technologies and standards-driven platforms such as JDBC, the Servlet and JavaServer Pages (JSP) APIs, and Enterprise JavaBeans (EJB) using a build tool such as Ant or Maven. If they're more advanced, they'll use an application framework such as Struts and EJB, Seam, or Spring. Many starting templates, IDE shortcuts, and architectural and/or design patterns can be used to make development more efficient, but most of the work involves a lot of coding, physical build configuration, and design work.

Contrast this with your friends programming in dynamic language platforms, such as Ruby on Rails or Grails, who take about 15 minutes to get a basic application shell up and running. That shell usually includes a web application, database data and validation, and some basic business and navigation logic. Unlike a lot of Java application prototypes, theirs is usually the beginning of the final project, whereas Java developers have to try and throw away a fair number of APIs and platforms manually until they get to a point where they're comfortable assigning a team to the project. The bottom line is that it just takes a long time to write a Java-based application.

1.1.1 Spring reduces the pain

The Spring Framework, a development platform that uses interface-driven development, dependency injection, aspect-oriented programming, and a number of helper APIs and services, significantly reduces the complexity of your Enterprise Java code. If you haven't heard of Spring by now, we strongly suggest you put this book down and read up on the framework before you dig deeply into Roo. Craig Walls' excellent *Spring in Action* is a great companion to this book.

Spring operates on the principle of making your development less about busy work and more about writing business logic. Spring application developers define interface-driven beans that are then implemented as Plain Old Java Objects (POJOs) and mounted in a *Spring container* using XML, annotations, or Java-based configuration directives.

Here's an example business interface:

```
package org.rooinaction.coursemanager.services;

...

public interface CourseManager {
  void addCourse(Course c);
  List<Course> getAllCourses();
}
```

Spring developers then create an implementation class:

```
package org.rooinaction.coursemanager.services;

...

public class CourseManagerDefaultImpl {
    public void addCourse(Course c) {
        // some logic here
    }

    public List<Course> getAllCourses() {
        // retrieve logic here
    }
}
```

One way you can use this bean is to *autowire* it as shown next:

```
package org.rooinaction.coursemanager.web;

...

public class CourseInputComponent {

  @Autowired
  private CourseManager courseManager;

  public void createACourse(String name) {
    Course c = new Course();
    c.setName(name);
    courseManager.addCourse(c);
  }
}
```

We're leaving out the configuration here, but the basic idea is a simple one: let Spring find and mount your component, deal with it at the interface level, and just write a POJO both to expose and use your component.

You can use any Java API you can think of inside a Spring application, but you're still required to add dependent JAR files and configuration to simplify the programming tasks later.

1.1.2 Shifting from code to configuration

Even Spring can't save you from all of the tedium involved in building an application. There are many decisions that you need to make, as shown in figure 1.1.

Figure 1.1   The number of choices when working in an Enterprise Java application is mind-numbing!

Spring makes those tasks easier and shifts some of them to configuration, rather than coding, such as these:

- Configuring a web framework such as Spring MVC, JavaServer Faces, GWT, or Flex
- Configuring a persistence tier
- Building web components such as forms, menus, templates, localization, and themes
- Exposing data for Ajax or web service calls
- Reverse engineering a database model from an existing database
- Handling messages from a message queue
- Sending email
- Integrating a new API or framework

Since Spring is so configurable, it almost provides you with too many choices of how to implement your solution. It's an extremely flexible platform for development, but it can be difficult to make a good decision on how to move forward. The more choices developers are faced with when attempting to make a decision, the more difficult that decision becomes. Some developers may just begin to select a configuration option at random, or start experimenting with several, comparing the results. All of this takes time and can really hold up a project.

1.1.3   *Spring makes development less painful*

Spring can wrap or enable access to other APIs, even though you're still working with those APIs and platforms to some degree. A crucial tenet of Spring is providing *template* beans for complex APIs in order to help simplify them.

For example, the *Spring JDBC API* component, `JdbcTemplate`, provides method calls to query, insert, update, and delete data, which can be as short as a single line. Rather than writing long `try... catch... finally...` blocks and worrying about whether you should close a connection when faced with an exception, Spring does the setup and tear-down work for you.

Here's the Spring JDBC template method to fetch a single value from a SQL statement:

```
int numSales = jdbcTemplate.queryForString(
               "select sum(price) from sales_order");
```

Simple, isn't it? The JDBC template does all of that boilerplate work for you and throws a translated Spring runtime exception if the query fails so that you don't have to write tedious `try ... catch` statements in your application.

Spring eliminates the layers of exception hierarchies such as your application data-layer exception, service-layer exception, and web-layer exception. Sound familiar? If not, it's likely because you've been working with Spring, which pioneered using run-time exceptions over declarative ones.

Another way Spring helps is by providing *factory beans* to easily configure enterprise APIs. Those of you who've configured Hibernate applications by hand will appreciate Spring's ability to set up Hibernate this way:

```
<bean class="org.s.o.jpa.LocalContainerEntityManagerFactoryBean"
      id="entityManagerFactory">
  <property name="dataSource" ref="dataSource"/>
</bean>
```

> **BOOK CONVENTION: WHAT'S WITH THE `org.s.o.jpa` IN THE CLASS NAME?** Spring (and Roo) code is a challenge to show in book format because the names of fully qualified classes often run quite long. We may abbreviate those names because we know that most developers can use an IDE or even Google to look up the packages of well-known classes such as the one above. By the way, it's `LocalContainerEntityManagerFactoryBean`, which is located in the `org.springframework.orm.jpa` package.

You can use this `entityManagerFactory` bean to fetch a JPA entity manager, which is the API used to interact with a JPA-supported database:

```
@PersistenceContext
private EntityManager em;

...
public List<Customer> fetchCustomers() {
  List<Customer> results =
    em.createQuery("select c from Customer c")
        .getResultList();
  return results;
}
```

Note that you use a Java EE annotation here; `@PersistenceContext` communicates with the entity manager factory and requests that it fetch or create an entity manager for use by the developer. Spring can use Java EE annotations to expose and consume resources.

1.1.4 *Batteries still required*

From the programmer's perspective, things are better under Spring. But even Spring applications require hands-on configuration activities.

Somebody still has to configure JPA for the project, come up with a persistence strategy, and show the other developers how to use it. Let's see how much work you would still have to do by hand in a Spring-based application:

- Include dependent JAR files in the project for the JPA API, as well as a number of ORM vendor JAR files.
- Install a JDBC data source, and include the JAR files for the data source and the database driver.
- Configure a transaction management strategy in Spring to associate with the database data source and JPA.
- Configure META-INF/persistence.xml with settings relating JPA to the database using Hibernate configuration settings.
- Configure a Spring `LocalContainerEntityManagerFactoryBean` to install a JPA container, and configure the transaction management to honor the JPA entity manager.

That's a significant amount of work. To actually *use* the JPA API in your project, you'd have to do the following:

- Create an `entity` class that represents the table, annotating it with JPA annotations.
- Create a `repository` class, and inject it with an `EntityManager` instance from the configuration above.
- Write methods to retrieve, save, update, delete, and search for entities.
- Develop a Spring `Service` class to provide transactional services that coordinate access to one or more calls to the repository.

You can see why it takes an average Java, or even Spring, development project a fair amount of time to set up a framework such as JPA. Because the Enterprise Java universe is a decentralized, highly compartmentalized set of libraries, it has to be wrestled with just to get a basic application in place.

Spring itself helps tremendously, but the standard Java application programmer has been steadily losing little bits of work to those *other guys*—the developers using rapid application development frameworks and writing code in oddly named languages like Ruby, Groovy, or Python.

1.1.5 *Those other guys—RAD frameworks*

Rapid application development frameworks, such as Ruby on Rails or Grails, narrow choices and implement programming patterns in a simple yet predictable way. They also focus on removing repetitious configuration and coding from your application. As a result, they are wildly popular.

You've probably seen the "Twitter in 15 minutes" or "Writing a blogging engine in 1 hour" talks. You've probably met the Java developer who says, "I'm never coming back to Java. I just did my first Rails application in 30 days and it was a joy to program."

Now, we're not here to bash any frameworks or approaches. But since we're discussing Roo, which is a framework written in Java, for Java developers, it's worth discussing some of the differences.

Most of these platforms use runtime type checking and are based on interpreted languages. The languages lack a compilation step, and problems usually occur at runtime, putting more of a burden on testing.

It's a big switch for a developer to begin thinking in a dynamic programming language, and because many parts of these platforms are convention-based, it can be difficult for new programmers to seamlessly drop into a project without a lot of time spent learning the approaches given on that project.

1.1.6 *Java needs RAD*

In our opinion, Spring is certainly the biggest leap forward for Java developers in the past five years. Coupled with tools like Maven, which helps manage project configuration and dependencies, and strong ORM frameworks like Hibernate or JPA, it can really improve code quality and developer productivity.

Various teams have attempted to use Maven templates to build starting applications,[1] and even the SpringSource Tool Suite includes a Maven archetype-based application starter.

Though useful, these tools only provide a starting point. They're only as good as the template maintainer's diligence provides. Once you create your project from the template, there generally is no easy way to upgrade it. Plus, you still end up spending time manually configuring Spring for additional features needed by your application.

And unlike RAD tools such as Rails or Grails, where adding a new feature is as simple as installing a plug-in and following the conventions to use it, this is all done by hand in Spring. This is a key reason people are moving to these rapid application development platforms.

What Spring and Java need is the ability to make it easier to configure and add features to a project, and to remove or hide any generated or mechanical code so you can easily focus on your actual business logic.

Wouldn't it be great if you could match RAD agility and still use Spring's highly productive APIs? What if you had a tool that was the equivalent of a seasoned architect, available on demand, who could take over the job of implementing your infrastructure and project architecture? What if this tool could deal with the mundane tasks of managing your application dependencies, wiring up services like JPA, email,

---

[1] See Matt Raible's project, AppFuse, at http://www.appfuse.org.

JMS, and a database persistence layer? What if you had a virtual "Spring Design Patterns" expert available at your beck and call?

1.2 *Enter Spring Roo*

Into the often tedious landscape of Java and Spring programming enters Spring Roo—a tool that acts like a really smart Spring and Java EE expert, or pair programmer, consistently nudging you in the right direction.

Roo configures and manages the infrastructure of a Spring project, hides repetitive code, manages your build process, and generally helps you focus on solving your business problems.

In short, Roo gives Java developers the same productivity that other RAD platforms have. And in some ways, it gives them more options.

Roo makes life easier for the average Spring programmer by managing the busy work and implementing the code with sound architectural patterns. Here are some examples of things Roo makes easier:

- When you ask Roo to set up your persistence tier, it responds by adding JPA, Hibernate, validations, transaction management, and a pooled data source.
- When you ask Roo to install the MVC web framework, it implements Spring MVC and pre-creates a web framework complete with layout templates, localization, themes, menu navigation, and client-side validation.
- When you need to send or receive JMS messages, a single command in Roo sets up your JMS listener or templates, and you can immediately get to work coding your sending or receiving bean.

The Roo tool provides an add-on system that enables developers to add new features, such as web application frameworks, databases, enterprise APIs, and more. You can write your own add-ons and use them for your own projects, or even contribute them to the public directory.

Roo projects are extremely flexible. If you don't like a feature provided by Roo, customize it or remove it. Roo will do as much or as little as you want.

From a developer's perspective, Roo pulls the tedious code out of your classes and into files that it manages for you. For example, your JPA entities will contain only the code that defines the fields, validation rules, and specific logic you require. Behind the scenes, Roo will implement the setters, getters, persistence management, and even `toString()` methods in hidden files. You can choose to write these elements yourself, but the advantage of doing so is eliminated for the majority of your code.

Have we whetted your appetite? Then let's get going! We'll start by installing the Roo shell.

1.2.1 *Installing the Roo shell*

To show you just how powerful Roo is, you'll create and review one of the sample applications provided by the Roo team—the Pizza Shop. But first you have to install the Roo shell.

To install the Roo shell, first visit the SpringSource project site at http://springsource.org/spring-roo and download the latest released version. Unpack it to a directory on your machine.

> **WHAT VERSION OF ROO DOES THIS BOOK COVER?** The book focuses on Spring Roo version 1.2.1. All version 1.2 releases should be compatible with the code samples within the book, but if not, please visit the author forum at http://manning.com/rimple and let us know your issue in the reader forum.

Make sure you have at least the Java Development Kit (this book was written using JDK 1.6, but Roo 1.2.1 supports development and deployment on Java 1.7) and are running Maven 3.0.3 or higher. You can verify that both are properly installed by typing

```
java -fullversion
```

and

```
mvn -v
```

For Windows users, set your operating system path to include the unpacked Roo distribution's bin folder.

On Unix and Mac systems, you can just make a symbolic link to the file *roo_directory*/bin/roo.sh as /usr/bin/roo, breaking it and replacing it with one from a new distribution whenever you upgrade:

```
ln -s /opt/spring-roo-1.2.1/bin/roo.sh /usr/bin/roo
```

1.2.2 Launching the shell

After installing the Spring Roo path into your environment, open an operating system command line in an empty directory. Launch Roo using the roo command. Roo will respond with a banner and a roo> prompt:

```
$ roo
     ____  ____  ____
    / __ \/ __ \/ __ \
   / /_/ / / / / / / /
  / _, _/ /_/ / /_/ /
 /_/ |_|\____/\____/    1.2.1


Welcome to Spring Roo. For assistance press TAB or type
"hint" then hit ENTER.
roo>
```

Congratulations! You've installed and configured Roo. You may quit the shell with the quit command.

The Roo shell does the heavy lifting of configuring and maintaining your project. Once launched, you interact with the shell by entering configuration commands, and Roo responds by modifying or creating the necessary files in your project.

THE SHELL IN AN IDE   In addition to launching the shell as a standalone, command-line tool, SpringSource Tool Suite and IntelliJ users can launch a Roo shell within their IDEs. The advantage is that an IDE will instantly see changes made by the Roo shell. We discuss this in chapter 2.

In the next chapter, we discuss how to create your own project from scratch. But for now, we'll use the Roo `script` command, which executes a script provided to it by the user. Let's use this command to set up a sample application.

1.3   Roo by example—the Pizza Shop

To illustrate how much Roo can help you boost your productivity on the Spring platform, let's take a quick dive into Spring Roo by running one of the sample scripts, `pizzashop.roo`, provided by the Roo project team. This file is located in the Roo installation folder called `samples`, along with a number of other example scripts.

Other Roo scripts

To experiment with a more complex model, create additional empty directories and experiment with the following prebuilt scripts:

- `bikeshop.roo` —This is a sample website for a bicycle shop that uses the JSF web framework.

- `clinic.roo`—The Pet Clinic is a simple Spring sample application that shows off a somewhat complex set of relationships.

- `embedding.roo`—This shows examples of embedding various media objects from Twitter, YouTube, UStream, Google Video, and others.

- `expenses.roo`—This is an expense tracking system, using Google Web Toolkit and Google App Engine.

- `multimodule.roo`—This shows off Roo's support for multimodule Maven projects.

- `vote.roo`—This is a simple voting system, using Spring MVC and Spring Security.

- `wedding.roo`—This sets up a wedding planner system, and includes Selenium web tests, email support, and security.

You can find these scripts in the /samples folder of the Roo software installation directory. Anything placed in this directory is available for execution using the `script` command.

1.3.1   The pizzashop.roo sample

The `pizzashop.roo` sample is a simple demonstration application that simulates a basic pizza shop. It allows the user to define bases, toppings, pizzas, and orders.

Let's run the script to create the application. Create an empty directory somewhere called `pizzashop`, and open your OS command-line shell in that directory. Fire up the Roo shell with the `roo` command:

```
$ roo script pizzashop.roo
[lots of activity and output]
Script required 33.005 seconds to execute
$
```

> **RUNNING A SCRIPT FROM THE COMMAND LINE** If you want to run a Roo script file, you can just use `roo script` *scriptfile* and Roo will execute the script.

You'll see Roo go to work, executing commands and building your project. If you're watching the directory from a file manager, you'll see it quickly expand into a full-fledged project structure.

What just happened? Everything! Roo just built a fully configured Spring application with the following features:

- A JPA container, using EclipseLink as the backing object-relational mapping (ORM) API
- Four JPA entities, which are classes that map to tables in databases, namely `Pizza.java`, `Base.java`, `Topping.java`, and `PizzaOrder.java`
- Four JPA repositories that persist data to the database (commonly known as data access objects—DAOs—outside of the JPA world)
- A Spring MVC web application to input and display data, interacting with the four JPA entities via the repositories

Now that we've let Roo do its magic, let's build the application, launch it, and kick the tires on your new application.

1.3.2 *Running the Pizza Shop with Maven*

Believe it or not, you're ready to run the application. Roo configures a complete Maven-based build, even preconfiguring both the Tomcat and Jetty web servers for you to experiment with. Let's use the Jetty web server to launch the application:

```
$ mvn jetty:run
```

Maven replies by building the application, and then runs the Jetty web server on port 8080.

> **IF TOMCAT IS YOUR PREFERENCE...** You can run Tomcat just by changing the command above to `mvn tomcat:run`. Roo configures both Jetty and Tomcat web servers for your testing. You can also deploy a Roo application on any application server that accepts a WAR deployment. Just use the `mvn package` command to generate your WAR, which will be located in the `target` folder.

Open your browser to http://localhost:8080/pizzashop and view the home page as shown in figure 1.2.

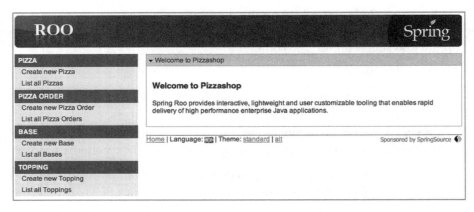

Figure 1.2   The Pizza Shop home page

This looks like a typical CRUD-based application, but looks can be deceiving. This application is a fully configured Spring MVC web application, complete with the latest version of Spring (3.0.6 at the time of writing), JPA 2.0 persistence, the EclipseLink JPA Provider, an in-memory Hypersonic database instance, entities, controllers, views, a service and persistence tier, and even a JSON-based web service interface.[2]

1.3.3   Creating toppings—forms

Let's create a new topping by clicking on the Create New Topping menu item on the left-hand menu system. Click on the Name: field. You'll see a prompt to enter the name because it's a required field. Refer to figure 1.3. (We've omitted the full-page view on these images to focus on the important elements. All pages show a full menu, title bar, and footer.)

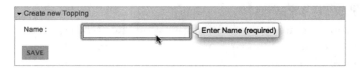

Figure 1.3   Required field checks appear visually

Try clicking on SAVE without entering a topping. Spring should have turned the input field yellow and marked it with a triangle warning, as depicted in figure 1.4.

Figure 1.4   Warnings for missed fields displayed in yellow

---

[2]   CRUD—create, read, update, delete—just the basics of managing application entities

Roo performs client-side validation against your entities. We discuss this in detail in chapter 3. Enter a few choices, perhaps Brie, Sauce, Mushrooms, and Swiss Chard (Swiss Chard?). Each time you save a choice, you'll see something like figure 1.5, a confirmation of the saved results as a separate page.

Figure 1.5 The save/edit confirmation page

Clicking the edit icon (the page with the pencil) will take you to a page similar to the creation form, except that it's working with an already persisted entity.

Finally, if you click the List all Toppings menu item, you'll see a list of the toppings you've already entered, as shown in figure 1.6.

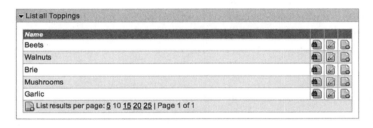

Figure 1.6 The listing page, complete with pagination

As you see in figure 1.6, Roo provides paging support. It also enables viewing, editing, and removing of entities using icons on each row, as well as creating a new one using the new page icon to the left of the list results paging control at the bottom.

1.3.4 Creating a pizza form—dependencies

Let's look at a slightly more complicated form—the pizza form. Each pizza is comprised of a base and one or more toppings. You need to be able to create your pizza and choose your toppings and base from the ones entered before.

Click on the Create new Pizza link. You'll see the form in figure 1.7.

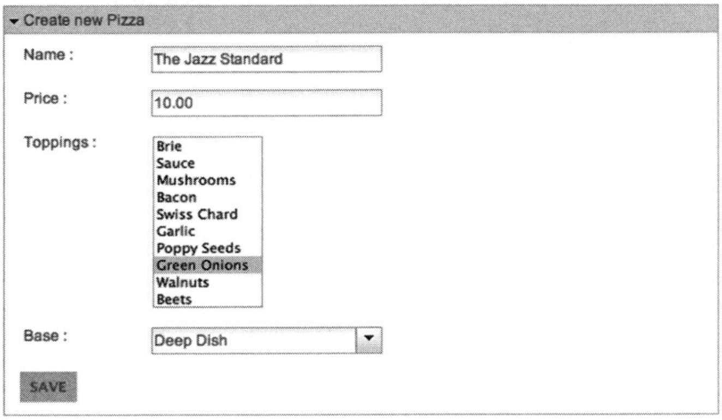

Figure 1.7 Creating a new pizza

Roo automatically creates the multiselect list for Toppings, and a single-item select list for the Base. The shell has the ability to watch your entities, detect relationships, and automatically update your web forms and controllers with widgets to pick from your related entities.

Try clicking through the application. Start with bases and toppings; create your perfect pizza components. Create some pizzas based on those bases and toppings, and finally, experiment with placing an order. You'll see the Roo client-side validations for invalid data, drop-down lists of related data, and if you take enough time to enter a lot of data, paging support. And all of this within 49 lines of Roo script code—not a single user-defined line of code.

1.3.5   *JSON-based web services with the Pizza Shop*

Spring Roo even configures your controllers to support JSON-based web service calls. If you're on a Unix/Mac machine, and have installed the Unix curl command-line tool, the script even documents several curl commands you can use to test the web service side of this application. For example, to create a Thin Crust base, you'd issue a POST call to the pizzashop/bases URL, passing it JSON data, as shown next:

```
curl -i -X POST -H "Content-Type: application/json" ➭
    -H "Accept: application/json" -d '{name: "Thin Crust"}' ➭
    http://localhost:8080/pizzashop/bases
```

> **BOOK CONVENTION: THE LINE ARROWS FOR LONG LINES**   Just as Roo creates long class and package names, Roo and operating system example commands are equally sprawling. Whenever you see the line arrow icon don't hit Return; just keep typing. This is in contrast to the Unix OS line continuation character, \, which can be typed.

Note the data sent in JSON format to create a new pizza base named Thin Crust; it was JSON data. Curl will respond with the result of the web service call, which is an HTTP 201 response code:

```
HTTP/1.1 201 Created
...
```

If you open the web application and review the listing of pizza bases, you'll now see the Thin Crust base appear.

To fetch a list of pizza bases, you'd just issue a GET call to the pizzashop/bases URL:

```
curl -i -H "Accept: application/json" ➭
    http://localhost:8080/pizzashop/bases
```

Roo happily responds with the JSON data:

```
HTTP/1.1 200 OK
...
[{"id":1,"name":"Deep Dish","version":1},
 {"id":2, "name":"Whole Wheat","version":1},
 {"id":3,"name":"Thin Crust","version":1}]
```

There! Easy RESTful web service integration.

1.3.6 *Wrapping up the walk-through*

Practice creating a few toppings, bases, pizzas, and orders. Remove something and see how Roo asks for a confirmation. Get used to the user interface. You get these features for free, all by asking Roo to configure Spring MVC and scaffolding your entities.

> **ROO AND WEB FRAMEWORKS**   Roo installs the web framework Spring MVC if you request it. But there are a number of web frameworks available to Roo directly, including Spring Web Flow (as part of Spring MVC), Google Web Toolkit, JavaServer Faces (in Roo 1.2), and Vaadin. These are all enabled by various Roo add-ons, some of which are installed with Roo itself.
>
> You aren't required to use Roo's preconfigured frameworks. You can integrate with any other framework you want to, including Struts, Stripes, Flex, or a pure JavaScript application. But if you wish to install your web framework into a number of Roo-managed applications, you may wish to write your own Roo add-on and share it with your developers or the world.

You can terminate the application at this point. Go to your command window and shut down Jetty by hitting [CTRL]-[C].

> **I RESTARTED THE WEB APPLICATION. WHERE'S MY DATA?**   If you run the application server again, you may find that the data you entered before is missing. This is because Roo's default behavior is to re-create the database on startup. We discuss how to customize this behavior in chapter 3.

Not bad for just a few lines of Roo script code. Let's take a few minutes and review the script that created your application.

1.3.7 *The Pizza Shop script*

The Pizza Shop script file, samples/pizzashop.roo in the Roo installation directory, is approximately 48 lines of scripting text, including comments, but the script does a lot of configuration. Let's walk through some of the commands in this script and touch on what they do.

CREATING THE PROJECT

First, the script creates a Roo project, defining the Java package structure that Roo will use to store objects that it generates:

```
roo> project --topLevelPackage com.springsource.pizzashop
```

At this point in time, Roo just defines the project as a JAR file—nothing yet tells it that you need a web application configuration. Roo is flexible and won't configure more than it needs to.

DATABASE SETUP

Next, the script configures the database:

```
roo> jpa setup --provider ECLIPSELINK --database H2_IN_MEMORY
```

This command does quite a bit of work, setting up your JPA database persistence tier. We describe the work Roo does in depth in chapter 3.

CREATING JPA ENTITIES

The script then sets up the four JPA entity classes—Base, Topping, Pizza, and Pizza-Order. The entity jpa and field commands comprise the content of most of this script. Here's an excerpt that installs three entities—Base, Topping, and Pizza—and begins to add fields to each of them. Notice the options, such as --sizeMin and --notNull. We talk about those in chapter 3, as well as the field reference and field set commands, which establish relationships between entities:

```
roo> entity jpa --class ~.domain.Base --activeRecord false ➥
      --testAutomatically
roo> field string --fieldName name --sizeMin 2 --notNull

roo> entity jpa --class ~.domain.Topping --activeRecord false ➥
      --testAutomatically
roo> field string --fieldName name --sizeMin 2 --notNull

roo> entity jpa --class ~.domain.Pizza --activeRecord false ➥
      --testAutomatically
roo> field string --fieldName name --notNull --sizeMin 2
roo> field number --fieldName price --type java.math.BigDecimal
roo> field set --fieldName toppings --type ~.domain.Topping
roo> field reference --fieldName base --type ~.domain.Base
```

SETTING UP REPOSITORIES

The next script section creates Spring JPA repositories using the Spring Data JPA API. These are the objects that talk to the database in the service-based Spring architecture we discussed earlier:

```
repository jpa --interface ~.repository.ToppingRepository ➥
      --entity ~.domain.Topping
repository jpa --interface ~.repository.BaseRepository ➥
      --entity ~.domain.Base
```

CONFIGURING SERVICES

Roo can also expose transactional services using Spring Beans. These services are configured to manipulate the entity passed to them, and will delegate calls to the repository methods to find, create, update, and delete data:

```
service --interface ~.service.ToppingService --entity ~.domain.Topping
service --interface ~.service.BaseService --entity ~.domain.Base
```

CONFIGURING JSON

The rest of the script concerns the web interface. Roo can optionally expose JSON to the web tier if needed. These commands provide JSON support for the web services we reviewed earlier:

```
json all --deepSerialize
web mvc json setup
web mvc json all
```

SPRING MVC

And finally, the script generates the web application. This code literally installs Spring MVC, configures the website layout, builds controllers for each entity automatically, and places the controllers in the web subpackage of the root package:

```
web mvc setup
web mvc all --package ~.web
```

> **THE TILDE (~) AND `topLevelPackage`** Take special notice of the `--topLevel-Package` attribute of the `project` command. This setting allows you to use the previously mentioned ~. (tilde-period) shortcut in future commands as a base package to build your other components from. Roo also configures the project to detect new Spring components from this package downward.

With only a few lines of Roo commands, you've already generated a complete Spring MVC web application. This script configures a number of technologies, including

- The Spring Framework
- The EclipseLink ORM implementation
- The Java Persistence API, version 2.0
- Java EE Bean Validations (JSR-303)
- Spring MVC
- JSON data translation with the Flexjson library
- Apache Tiles
- Logging via the slf4j framework and log4j

> **ROO—NOT JUST FOR WEB APPS** Although the Pizza Shop is a web-based, data-driven application, you may be building a message-driven system, perhaps using JMS or the Spring Integration API. Spring Roo will help you configure and manage the bulk of your project, regardless of whether it's a web application or a standalone program, saving valuable time you would otherwise spend wiring together your infrastructure.

Now that you've created your application, kicked the tires, and explored the script, let's dig deeper into the project's application architecture.

1.4   *Roo application architecture models*

Every application should be designed with a particular architectural pattern in mind so that developers know where to place their components. The application architecture should consider good design concepts such as loose coupling, separation of concerns, transaction management, reuse, and extension. A typical Spring web application can be broken down into at least three layers:

- *User interface*—Spring MVC, JSF, Wicket, Struts, or some other web framework.
- *Services*—Business components that expose services for the *user interface* layer. Usually where transactions are defined.

- *Persistence*—Components that access various data sources using APIs such as JDBC, object-relational mapping APIs such as Hibernate or JPA, or even messaging beans that access message queues via JMS.

When defined in layers, developers are able to switch each layer's implementation. It becomes straightforward to switch persistence strategies or user interface implementations. Spring, being a component-driven development framework, fits well with layered architectures. Developers are encouraged to build beans using interface-driven development techniques, defining business method signatures in the interface, and implementing them in a realizing bean. Spring uses the interface as the contract to the client, so that the implementation can be swapped later.

Defining interfaces also helps developers test their components in isolation, using unit testing tools such as JUnit.

1.4.1   *The web layer*

Spring Roo provides a Spring MVC–based web application layer. It uses annotation-driven controllers, and can integrate with traditional Spring business services or with Active Record–based entities, as you'll see later.

Spring MVC is an MVC platform, and as such contains all of the views as well. These views are written in a variant of JavaServer Pages that is fully XML-compliant, and all JSP files are well formed. These files are known as *JSPX files*, and are written and saved with the .jspx extension.

Roo also deploys several major Spring MVC features, which we discuss in chapter 5:

- *Layout support*—Roo installs the Apache Tiles framework to lay out your web applications, and separates the web pages into a header, menu, content, and footer.
- *Theming*—Spring themes provide a way to present the website in several ways. Roo installs theming support automatically.
- *Localization*—Roo installs Spring MVC's localization support so that you can support multiple languages, allowing you to translate elements of your website so that various native language speakers can use your application.

Roo uses a set of generated tag libraries to handle operations such as displaying result lists, providing smart form elements such as drop-down pick lists, date and time pickers, and rich text editing. As you'll see in chapters 6 and 7, you can customize the website entirely, and add support for dynamic Ajax calls or other rich components yourself.

Roo is also smart. It can generate, or *scaffold*, web application controllers, views, and logic automatically to manage your data objects. As you're about to see, it can adapt to two major forms of application architecture: services-and-repositories and Active Record.

1.4.2 *Service-and-repository layering in Roo*

Roo can provide all of the traditional features of a typical web-based layered application. Figure 1.8 shows a fairly typical component architecture for a Spring MVC–based project.

This application diagram is constructed of several well-defined components:

- *Views*—Components that display information or provide ways to edit data. Commonly Java Server Pages or JSF Facelets.
- *Controllers* —Accept incoming HTTP web requests and return responses, generally using views to present the data.
- *Web service layer*—Some applications expose web services, using a convention such as SOAP or REST. These are analogous to web controllers and views and exist in the same layer as those in this diagram.
- *Services*—Provide an abstraction of business functionality, and are usually coarse-grained, performing a task that may interact with a number of objects in the repository layer. Transactional boundaries are usually defined in the service layer.
- *Repositories*—At the bottom of the stack is the repository or data access layer (DAO) which communicates to the databases via JDBC, mapping tools such as iBatis/MyBatis or, more commonly, object-relational mapping (ORM) tools such as Hibernate or JPA. Messaging integration code using APIs such as JMS may also be defined at this level.
- *Models/Entity classes*—These components represent data that is transferred from the data access layer or service layer upward to the user interface components. These may either be simple Java Beans—data transfer objects—or "live" objects such as JPA entities, which can be manipulated and then updated directly.

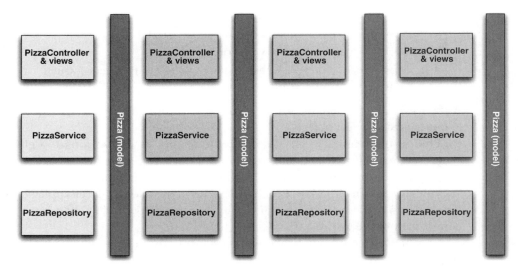

Figure 1.8 Pizza Shop as a layered architecture

Roo can operate in this traditional layered mode, using Roo entities, controllers, services, and repositories. You can even roll your own Spring Beans to represent each of these component types, and wire them together using Spring's @Autowired annotation, or even drop down to using XML or even JavaConfig to configure them. Roo *is* a Spring-based platform.

Roo is an animal with a different stripe. Not only is Roo a Spring-based application platform, but it also enables a more lightweight, rapid application development approach to Spring development that may provide for even more rapid productivity.

1.4.3 *Roo's Active Record architecture*

Roo was created to allow developers of Spring applications to become even more productive, and attempt to match the rapidity of development frameworks such as Ruby on Rails or Grails, while not leaving the Java platform. Though developers can still introduce services and repositories, by default Roo takes the approach of slimming down the required components, as shown in figure 1.9.

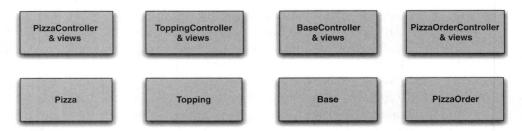

Figure 1.9   Roo's Active Record architecture

The required components are

- *Views*—Spring MVC views
- *RESTful controllers*—Spring MVC controllers
- *Entities*—Turbocharged Active Record–based entity objects, which know how to load, update, and persist themselves

At first glance, this may seem like a loss of structure. Where are the services? What about database access objects?

One of the reasons applications in enterprise Java take so long to deliver is the sheer number of artifacts required. There's a constant push-and-pull between "getting the application out the door" and "architecting it so someone else just might understand it later." Many non-Java frameworks have been able to deliver applications more quickly, with considerable maintainability, because they implement a more domain-centric view of the world. Take a look at figure 1.10.

The Active Record pattern *turbocharges* the persistence model by providing smart "Roo entities"—beans wired using AspectJ ITDs (special class-like files that weave in additional functionality)—to provide service-and-repository features within a single

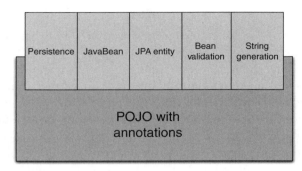

Figure 1.10 Roo's "turbocharged" entity

class. This might seem counter-intuitive to a typical service-and-repository Spring developer. But consider that this pattern, the *Active Record*, has been used by frameworks such as Ruby on Rails and Grails with great success.

In Roo, you can define your persistence objects as Spring Roo entities, and Roo automatically wires up the code to properly validate and persist the entities for you. You'll see the advantages of this in the next three chapters, but for now, consider that you're able to use this feature to reduce the amount of code you type. Who needs to write boilerplate methods to load and persist data if a tool can do it for you?

1.4.4 Which pattern is better?

You may be asking why Roo exposes two models. Actually, the original Roo platform envisioned that Active Record would take over, just as it has for those Ruby on Rails and Grails application tools.

But a large subset of Spring developers desire service-and-repository layers in their applications. Also, in most applications, there are cross-domain problems to solve—what if you want to expose a data manipulation command that spans toppings and bases? Do you place the methods in the `Base` or the `Topping` entity? In those cases, developers would at least build a service, and call both entity manipulations behind the service.

What you use is up to you. You may find less code overall for the Active Record pattern, and if you have a large number of model objects that you're manipulating, the extra work of building repositories and services for each one may be a bit tedious, especially when you aren't doing anything special in those objects. But if you truly have cross-entity transactions and you have significant business logic, you may wish to roll out services, and if you don't want to see your persistence logic held within your entities, you can ask Roo to create repositories.

Roo is flexible about application architecture, and, in fact, it can dynamically re-fit your project using the shell. Often, you'll be adding fields to your entities, or adding annotations, and the Roo shell will generate code and keep up with you.

We discuss Active Record and layered service-and-repository patterns in chapters 3 and 4.

Now let's review what you've learned about Spring Roo.

1.5   *Summary*

In this chapter we discussed the various challenges involved in writing Java applications. There are so many frameworks to choose from! Luckily, we've decided to discuss Spring, a powerful and flexible application development platform that can host a wide variety of applications and make configuring and accessing other frameworks better than doing so by hand. Then we discussed how Spring itself can even become a chore to configure as you begin to add configuration elements for your web application, persistence APIs, messaging, email, and other services.

We introduced Spring Roo, and using a built-in sample script, configured the Pizza Shop Spring-based web application in a handful of lines of configuration code. We used the built-in `pizzashop.roo` demonstration script to build a simple application, complete with validation, persistence, and a Spring MVC web framework, using only a page of Roo commands. By running the application, you saw just how much Spring Roo can help greatly simplify the configuration and setup process.

You saw how Roo even exposes JSON-based RESTful web services against the object you've created. That can certainly come in handy when wiring your application to nonweb applications or rich browser clients.

Coming up in chapter 2, we'll dive into the structure of a Spring Roo project, discuss the key Roo components, and outline a typical project layout and configuration files. We'll define a sample project, the Task Manager application, and we'll dig deeper into the Roo shell.

1.6   *Resources*

BOOKS

Walls, Craig. *Spring in Action, Third Edition* (Manning Publications, 2011)

Wheeler, Willie, et al. *Spring in Practice, Early Access Edition* (Manning Publications, 2008)

WEB

The "Spring Framework Reference Guide" and other Spring project documentation is available at www.springsource.org/documentation.

Visit and get familiar with the information on the Spring Roo project home page, available at www.springsource.org/spring-roo. You'll find a link to forums, documentation, the JIRA bug tracking system, the GitHub repository, and a whole lot more.

Getting started with Roo

This chapter covers

- Creating projects with the Roo shell
- Roo project layout and architecture
- SpringSource Tool Suite integration
- Refactoring Roo code and leaving Roo behind

You saw in chapter 1 that Spring Roo, with only a few commands, can really make you more productive as a Spring developer. And by now you're probably itching to get started on your own Roo-based application. You've come to the right place.

In this chapter, we use the Roo shell to create and manipulate an application. We look "under the hood," exploring the physical layout of a typical Spring Roo project. You'll learn where key artifacts are located and define some of the key configuration files and directory structures. We also discuss the architectural patterns used by Roo.

Roo encourages experimentation, so let's get started by firing up the shell and building a basic Roo application.

2.1   *Working with the Roo shell*

As we mentioned in chapter 1, Roo is controlled through a command-line shell. Let's use the shell to create a simple training task management application, and introduce some of the major topics we cover in the book along the way.

Using your operating system shell, create an empty directory, taskmanager. Switch to the directory and fire up the Roo shell, using the roo command. You'll be presented with the Roo command-line prompt:

```
roo>
```

> **BOOK CONVENTION: DON'T TYPE THE roo> PROMPT**   To help you figure out where to type your commands, we sometimes show the roo> prompt to the left of what you need to type. We do the same thing if you're at the operating system prompt. We use the $ symbol to show that we're on an OS prompt line, rather than executing commands in the Roo shell.

The Roo shell supports code completion, a help command, and hints. Try it now: hit your TAB key and see how Roo automatically prompts you with a list of commands you can type.[1]

2.1.1   *Give me a hint!*

Let's try the hint command to ask Roo what the next logical steps are for managing your application. When you're finished experimenting with tab completion and hint, type quit to exit the Roo shell. You can ask Roo to guide you through the project configuration process by typing the hint command:

```
roo> hint
Welcome to Roo! We hope you enjoy your stay!

Before you can use many features of Roo,
you need to start a new project.

To do this, type 'project' (without the quotes) and then hit TAB.

Enter a --topLevelPackage like 'com.mycompany.projectname' (no quotes).
When you've finished completing your --topLevelPackage, press ENTER.
Your new project will then be created in the current working directory.

Note that Roo frequently allows the use of TAB, so press TAB regularly.
Once your project is created, type 'hint' and ENTER
for the next suggestion.

You're also welcome to visit http://forum.springframework.org
for Roo help.
```

Roo provides the hint command as a way of guiding beginners in configuring a project. As you progress through the configuration process, you'll see the hints change—from creating the project, to configuring the database, to creating entities, and more. Let's do the first activity suggested above. Let's create an application.

---

[1]   If launched from the SpringSource Tool Suite, Roo uses CTRL-SPACE (or CMD-SPACE on Mac).

2.1.2 Common Roo commands

Before we go any further, we need to show you how to get a list of all commands in your Roo shell.

Make sure you're on an empty Roo command prompt, and hit the [TAB] key. You'll see the valid commands for your project at this stage:

```
roo> [TAB]
!                   */              /*              //
;                   addon           backup          class
controller          date            dependency      development
dod                 download        email           enum
exit                field           flash           focus
help                hint            interface       jms
jpa                 json            logging         metadata
mongo               osgi            perform         persistence
pgp                 poll            process         properties
proxy               quit            reference       script
service             system          test            version
web
roo>
```

The actual list will depend on the version of Roo, what stage of development you're in, and what add-ons you've configured (see chapters 11 and 12 for information on creating and using Roo add-ons). Let's review a few of the key commands:

- jpa setup—The jpa setup command installs database persistence using JPA and whatever object-relational mapping (ORM) API that backs it, including Hibernate, OpenJPA, EclipseLink, and DataNucleus. We cover the jpa setup command, as well as some other commands (among them, field) to create and manipulate JPA entities, in chapters 3 and 4. Prior to Roo 1.2, this command was named persistence setup.

- web—The web command list includes a number of commands, including web mvc install, which installs Spring MVC language files and views, web mvc embed, which can install a number of Web 2.0 objects such as videos, Twitter feeds, photos, streams, and a number of other features. The web gwt command configures the Google Web Toolkit web user interface. Finally, web flow configures Spring Web Flow, a directed navigation web technology that rides on top of Spring MVC.

- jms *and* email—These commands install the JMS using ActiveMQ, and an email sender, respectively. These two commands, which configure JMS messaging and email, are covered in detail in chapter 10.

- test—This command configures JUnit tests both inside and outside of the Spring container. dod will configure data-on-demand objects, which are used by the integration tests to generate fake test data. We cover testing the persistence tier in chapters 3 and 4 and devote a full chapter to unit and web testing in chapter 9.

- security *(not shown)*—This command installs Spring Security, which we discuss in chapter 8. The reason it's not shown is because we haven't configured Spring MVC yet, so the Roo shell is hiding the command.
- repository—This command builds Roo JPA repositories using the Spring Data JPA API. We talk about how these work in chapter 3.
- service—This command exposes a Spring service for a given entity. If the entity is backed with ActiveRecord, it will write calls to the CRUD methods on the entity. Otherwise, it will detect the repository and call methods on the repository instead. We discuss Roo services in chapter 4.

There are several other commands that perform housekeeping for you, including backup, monitoring, and scripting.

2.1.3   *Creating an application*

To create an application, type the project command, and, as instructed in the previous hint, hit the [TAB] key to trigger code completion. You should see the following:

```
roo> project --topLevelPackage
```

Roo wants you to specify the root package name for your Java artifacts. Roo will configure various frameworks to scan for any annotation-driven components (JPA entities, Spring beans, repositories, and controllers, for example) using this top-level package. Let's use org.rooinaction.taskmanager. Go ahead and type the package name, type a space, and then type a double-hyphen (--). This signifies that you're about to enter another option. Your command line should look like this:

```
roo> project --topLevelPackage org.rooinaction.taskmanager --
```

Now, hit the [TAB] key again. Roo will prompt you with a series of allowable options:

```
project --topLevelPackage org.rooinaction.taskmanager --java
project --topLevelPackage org.rooinaction.taskmanager --packaging
project --topLevelPackage org.rooinaction.taskmanager --parent
project --topLevelPackage org.rooinaction.taskmanager --projectName
```

You want the –projectName option, so start typing the beginning of the option name, pro, and hit [TAB] again. Then type taskmanager. Hit [ENTER], and watch Roo build your project:

```
roo> project --topLevelPackage org.rooinaction.taskmanager ⇥
    --projectName taskmanager
Created ROOT/pom.xml Created SRC_MAIN_RESOURCES Created SRC_MAIN_RESOURCES/
    log4j.properties Created SPRING_CONFIG_ROOT Created SPRING_CONFIG_ROOT/
    applicationContext.xml ...
roo>
```

In the preceding output, the uppercased names represent file paths; SRC_MAIN_RESOURCES equates to src/main/resources. If you've worked on any Maven-based projects in the past, you'll recognize the path structures, and especially the Maven project object model file, pom.xml. The Maven build system is used to make it easy for other developers to *on-board* themselves onto your project, regardless of IDE or operating system.

Table 2.1 outlines the key Maven folders, Roo Shell uppercase labels, and purpose for each one.

Table 2.1 Roo directories

Directory	Roo shell label	Purpose
src/main/java	SRC_MAIN_JAVA	Holds Java source code. Generally, this source code starts in the package named in the `project` command's `--topLevelPackage` argument.
src/test/java	SRC_TEST_JAVA	Holds Java test source code. The tests are generally stored within the same packages as the classes under test.
src/main/resources	SRC_MAIN_RESOURCES	Holds all application-level configuration data such as database properties, Spring configuration files, and the project's persistence configuration.
src/test/resources	SRC_TEST_RESOURCES	Holds any test-specific Spring configuration files, test property files, or anything else needed during testing to support the test classes.
src/main/webapp	SRC_MAIN_WEBAPP	Holds web application code if your project is configured with Spring MVC. This includes Spring MVC configuration, views in JSPX format, style sheets, JavaScript files, and other web tier assets.

As you'll see in section 2.2, Roo configured the Spring application context file, applicationContext.xml, in the resource directory META-INF/spring. You'll also notice the log4j.properties file installed in the root resource directory.

2.1.4 Adjusting the logging level

Now let's adjust your project configuration, specifically the logging level of your application. First, you'll ask Roo to tell you about the logging command. Type the command help logging:

```
roo> help logging
Keyword:                      logging setup
Description:                   Configure logging in your project
 Keyword:                     ** default **
 Keyword:                     level
   Help:                      The log level to configure
   Mandatory:                 true
   Default if specified:      '__NULL__'
   Default if unspecified:    '__NULL__'
...
```

As you can see, the Roo shell contains a help system, which can fetch information about the various commands that can be executed from the command line. The logging system can be configured by executing the `logging setup` command. Here's a simple example:

```
roo> logging setup --level WARN
```

Roo responds with the following:

```
Updated SRC_MAIN_RESOURCES/log4j.properties
```

The uppercased name refers to the path src/main/resources, where the log4j.properties file resides. Roo changed the logging level in the beginning of this file:

```
#Updated at Sun Oct 02 11:44:17 EDT 2011
#Sun Oct 02 11:44:17 EDT 2011
log4j.appender.stdout=org.apache.log4j.ConsoleAppenderlog4j.rootLogger=WARN,
    stdout
```

If you want to be more specific, you can change a particular component's logging level. Use the tab key to see what options are available to you. Let's say you want to increase the logging for your project files (the nonframework ones) to the level of TRACE. You could use the `--level` attribute of TRACE; then, using tab completion again, type `--package`. Roo provides several important options here:

```
roo> logging setup --level TRACE --package[TAB]

ALL_SPRING    AOP    PERSISTENCE    PROJECT    ROOT    SECURITY
TRANSACTIONS WEB
roo> logging setup --level TRACE --package PROJECT
Updated SRC_MAIN_RESOURCES/log4j.properties
```

Now Roo defines another log configuration entry, just for your project top-level package:

```
log4j.logger.org.rooinaction.taskmanager=TRACE
```

Use the logging system to your advantage

Spring errs on the side of detail when outputting log messages in trace or debug mode. Although that's a lot of potentially useful information, it can prove extremely difficult to dig through the noise to find the one thing you're interested in.

You can edit the src/main/resources/log4j.properties file yourself and narrow logging to the specific Spring class you want to observe. For example, if you set ALL_SPRING to DEBUG, and want to back off to just the JPA container class, simply change that entry from

```
log4j.logger.org.springframework=DEBUG
```

to something more targeted, such as this (package replaced with . . . for book formatting):

```
log4j.logger.org...orm.jpa.LocalContainerEntityManagerFactoryBean=DEBUG
```

Add as many of these to your log4j.properties file as needed while troubleshooting or debugging.

2.1.5 *Adding persistence and running the application*

With that step finished, let's ask for more hints:

```
roo> hint

Roo requires the installation of a persistence configuration,
for example, JPA or MongoDB.

For JPA, type 'jpa setup' and then hit TAB three times.
We suggest you type 'H' then TAB to complete "HIBERNATE".
After the --provider, press TAB twice for database choices.
For testing purposes, type (or TAB) HYPERSONIC_IN_MEMORY.
If you press TAB again, you'll see there are no more options.
As such, you're ready to press ENTER to execute the command.

Once JPA is installed, type 'hint' and ENTER for the next suggestion.

Similarly, for MongoDB persistence, type 'mongo setup' and ENTER.
```

According to the hint command, Roo requires that you configure your database. Let's do that and also create your `Task` entity. Type in these commands, each time waiting until the configuration operations complete before continuing:

```
jpa setup --database DERBY_EMBEDDED --provider ECLIPSELINK
entity jpa --class ~.model.Task --testAutomatically
field string --fieldName description --notNull --sizeMax 40
field boolean --fieldName completed --value false
web mvc setup
web mvc all --package ~.web
```

Believe it or not, you now have a complete working application. Build it now:

```
roo> quit
$ mvn jetty:run
```

Now, try it out by pointing your browser to http://localhost:8080/taskmanager. Create some tasks and complete them. See? You're pretty RAD yourself, and in only five commands. Figure 2.1 shows the listing page of your task manager.

Convinced about the productivity you can get with Spring Roo? Wait, there's more...

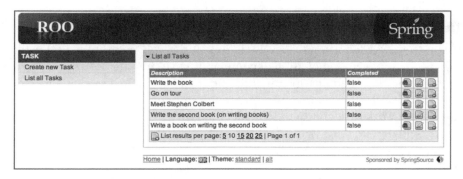

Figure 2.1   The task manager application—five lines of Roo; awesome!

2.1.6 *Backup, the Roo log, and scripting*

Before a major change, you may want to back up your application. The `backup` command does this for you. Just type `backup` at the Roo shell command prompt:

```
roo> backup
Created ROOT/taskmanager_2011-10-02_12:06:23.zip
Backup completed in 9 ms
```

Although you could argue that version control is a much better plan (especially using Git or Mercurial, where the developer keeps a copy of the entire repository on their hard drive) that's a pretty handy command for quick and dirty prototyping.

Psst... If you're using Git

A Roo add-on exists for managing your application in Git. In the Roo shell, type (on one line) this:

```
roo> pgp automatic trust ➡
roo> addon install bundle ➡
   --bundleSymbolicName org.springframework.roo.addon.git
```

You'll then get commands to manage your project from Git, including

- `git setup`—This command configures your project as a Git project, adding a handy .gitignore file.

- `git commit all`—This command commits changes to your Git repository for all changes.

- `git config`—This command configures features such as automatic commits, the repository you'll use to push your code, and other settings.

- `git push`—This command pushes your code to the Git repository.

Once you install this add-on, it's available for all Roo projects. We discuss add-ons in detail in chapters 11 and 12.

Now let's see how Roo tracks changes it has made to your project.

2.1.7 *The Roo shell log file*

If you were to look around in your file explorer, you might also find a file named log.roo. This file is a log of all shell commands typed into the Roo shell. At the start of each session, Roo date-stamps the time the shell is launched so that you can find out when a particular command was requested. A snippet from the log file for the application you're working with would look like this:

```
// Spring Roo 1.2.1.RELEASE [rev 6eae723] log ➡
   opened at 2011-12-28 04:50:352
hint
project --topLevelPackage org.rooinaction.taskmanager ➡
      --projectName taskmanager
```

```
help logging
logging setup --level WARN
logging setup --level TRACE --package PROJECT
quit
```

What if you wanted to run that script to create a new project with the same configuration? Just create another directory, copy the file into that directory (name it something other than log.roo, so it doesn't get overwritten), and edit the file to taste. Now, just fire up the Roo shell. You can execute the `script` command to create your application:

```
$ mkdir ../doppleganger
$ cp log.roo ../doppleganger/runme.roo
$ cd ../doppleganger/
$ roo
     ____  ____  ____
    / __ \/ __ \/ __ \
   / /_/ / / / / / / /
  / _, _/ /_/ / /_/ /
 /_/ |_|\____/\____/    1.2.1.RELEASE [rev 6eae723]


Welcome to Spring Roo. For assistance press TAB or type
"hint" then hit ENTER.
roo> script --file runme.roo
hint
...
help
...
project --topLevelPackage org.rooinaction.taskmanager ➥
        --projectName taskmanager
...
```

That was pretty easy. You can imagine how easy it would be to define starter project frameworks with just a handful of Roo commands. Talk about rapid productivity on the Spring platform!

2.1.8 *A final word on scripting*

Remember, Roo stores those commands you've entered in log files, and you can distribute scripts to other developers to reproduce your application template from scratch. Of course, those scripts won't write any business logic, or style a web page, but they at least can get things started for you.

The two ways of invoking scripting are using the `script` command inside of the Roo shell, and from the operating system, invoking the `script` command on the command line.

From within the Roo shell, you call the `script` command, passing it the file to execute:

```
roo> script --file ../roo-scripts/setup-roo-domains.roo
```

You can use this technique when doing rapid prototyping; perhaps somebody has created a set of domain object models, and you want to try using them from various front ends such as Spring MVC, JSF, or GWT.

The other way, as you saw in chapter 1, is to invoke the script as you load the Roo shell:

```
$ roo script pizzashop.roo
```

Either way, the Roo shell commands can be stored and shared across multiple projects. You can even use setup scripts to configure developers' Roo add-on environments and other settings.

Now let's take a look at some of the rules for developing Roo-based applications.

2.2   *How Roo manages your projects*

Now we'll review the project structure for the `taskmanager` project, discussing the files generated by Roo. We'll also switch the architecture from the default Active Record model to a service-and-repository model and see what additional files have been created.

But before we begin discussing specific project structure, we should cover some basic tenets of how you should manipulate files in the Roo system. Here are some basic rules:

- *Don't touch the AspectJ (.aj) files*—These files, generated by Roo, are meant to be managed by Roo itself, and may be upgraded when you install newer versions of Roo. Opening the shell causes Roo to adjust, create, or remove these files automatically. We discuss the ways you can extract methods from the aspects and customize them, write your own aspects, and even remove Roo entirely from your application.

- *Do manipulate standard artifacts*—Any files you'd normally create yourself, such as the Maven pom.xml file, Spring application context files, log4j configuration files, persistence files, JSPX web files, or other artifacts can be manipulated by the developer. Roo may add methods or settings to these files, so don't delete anything you think may be used by the Roo system, such as the transaction management or JPA persistence setup.

- *Take care manipulating scaffolded objects*—Scaffolding is the act of dynamically generating code for a particular object, such as the web pages and controller that expose a JPA persistent entity. If Roo scaffolds a given object, such as a controller or view, please take care to learn how Roo manipulates the object so you don't break the bidirectional synchronization between the Roo shell and the source code. Examples include scaffolded controllers and views.

- *Create your own objects and annotate them with Roo annotations*—You can create your own Java classes in your favorite editor and annotate them with Roo annotations. The Roo shell will then generate the same Roo-managed files, such as AspectJ ITDs or even JSPX web pages, being created on behalf of the user as those created by Roo commands themselves.

  For Java classes, make sure they live within the top-level package defined when the project is created. You can use any annotation, as long as you know what it does. For example, annotating a Java class with `@RooToString` and

@RooJavaBean will add the _Roo_ToString.aj and _Roo_JavaBean.aj aspects to that class. This can be quite handy and save you a lot of time when you are *heads down* in your IDE.

As we move through the book, we'll note the artifacts you can modify or should leave alone. Once you get the feel for what you can change, you'll be able to move quickly and easily throughout your Roo-managed application without fear of breaking it with simple modifications.

2.2.1 The taskmanager project layout

The application you just created, taskmanager, is a fairly typical Spring Roo project, created using Roo's default Active Record–based entities.

Let's review each of the major directories under src/main/java/org/rooinaction/taskmanager. First, look at your entity directory, model:

```
model/
    Task.java
    Task_Roo_Configurable.aj

    Task_Roo_JavaBean.aj
    Task_Roo_Jpa_ActiveRecord.aj
    Task_Roo_Jpa_Entity.aj
    Task_Roo_ToString.aj
```

Your task model uses two ITDs to manage access to the database: Task_Roo_Entity.aj and Task_Roo_Jpa_ActiveRecord.aj. The way you define your task also causes Roo to generate the @Configurable annotation, which is contained in Task_Roo_Configurable.aj (we'll discuss the other database ITDs and approaches in chapter 3). The Task entity also contains a @RooJavaBean annotation, which generates Task_Roo_JavaBean.aj, and the @RooToString annotation (Task_Roo_ToString.aj).

Next, you'll view the web controller package, web:

```
web/
   ApplicationConversionServiceFactoryBean.java
   ApplicationConversionServiceFactoryBean_Roo_ConversionService.aj
   TaskController.java
   TaskController_Roo_Controller.aj
```

You see the TaskController.java class, which is annotated with the standard Spring MVC @Controller annotation, and @RooWebScaffold, which generates the TaskController_Roo_Controller.aj aspect. This aspect contains all of the required Spring MVC controller methods to handle creation, listing, editing, and removing tasks.

Roo also generates views for each of the main create, read, update, and list actions of the controller in src/main/webapp/WEB-INF/views:

```
$ ls -1 src/main/webapp/WEB-INF/views/tasks
create.jspx
list.jspx
```

```
show.jspx
update.jspx
views.xml
```

You also see the `ApplicationConversionServiceFactoryBean.java` class, which is mounted as a Spring bean on startup and converts entity instances to Strings for the default display of drop-down option lists.

We discuss web applications in detail in chapter 5, and how to customize the fields, views, and other elements in chapter 6.

Let's convert this application to a traditional Spring service-and-repository application and see Roo adjust your source listing.

2.2.2   *Adding a service and repository*

Want to build a traditional layered application instead? You're actually almost there. Just open up the Roo shell in the `taskmanager` project and type these two commands:

```
roo> repository jpa --interface ~.repository.TaskRepository ➥
            --entity ~.model.Task

roo> service --interface ~.service.TaskService --entity ~.model.Task
```

Roo automatically creates the service and repository beans, and their respective ITDs:

```
service/
    TaskService.java
    TaskServiceImpl.java
    TaskServiceImpl_Roo_Service.aj
    TaskService_Roo_Service.aj

repository/
    TaskRepository.java
    TaskRepository_Roo_Jpa_Repository.aj
```

But Roo did more than that. It adjusted several files:

- It injected the task service into the `TaskController_RooController.aj` class and delegated all code originally written against the `Task` entity's Active Record methods to the service.
- It injected the `TaskRepository` into the `TaskService_Roo_Service.aj` file, delegating all service calls to the repository.
- It also updated all generated entity test files to test the entity via the service and repository instances.

Oh, speaking of tests, we didn't review the test file directory for entities, org/rooinaction/taskmanager/model, located in src/test/java.

2.2.3   *The tests and data on demand*

Looking at the project files before and after the service-and-repository layer should convince you that you can rapidly refit projects to different APIs with Spring Roo, at a much more rapid rate than it would take to do the same tasks by hand. Roo generates these files in src/test/java under the org/rooinaction/taskmanager directory:

```
model/
    TaskDataOnDemand.java
    TaskDataOnDemand_Roo_Configurable.aj
    TaskDataOnDemand_Roo_DataOnDemand.aj
    TaskIntegrationTest.java
    TaskIntegrationTest_Roo_Configurable.aj
    TaskIntegrationTest_Roo_IntegrationTest.aj
```

The src/test/java directory shadows the main Java directory. It contains two major components within the ~.model[2] package, the TaskIntegrationTest and a helper class to generate test data, TaskDataOnDemand. If you run the Maven command mvn test, it will execute the JUnit test, using the TaskDataOnDemand class to generate instances of valid tasks.

2.2.4 *The web layer*

The web layer is where Roo configures your web application. The files are located in src/main/webapp. Let's look at the directories generated in table 2.2.

As you can see, Roo generates an organized Spring MVC web application, another task that takes a lot of time to do by hand. But we're not done. We need to look at the key configuration files Roo uses to manage your application.

Table 2.2 Web application directories for Spring Roo projects

Directory	Purpose
src/main/webapp	The root directory of the web application. Any home page named index.jsp will be served from here by default as the home page of the application.
|– WEB-INF	The root configuration directory of the web application. As with all web applications, this directory is not visible for browsing. The web.xml web application descriptor file, generated by Roo, lives here and manages the Spring Web application context.
|– classes	Contains all compiled Java class files, with the AspectJ ITDs woven into them.
|– i18n	Contains localized property files for the application framework and user-defined form elements.
|– layouts	Contains the Apache Tiles layouts.
|– spring	Contains the Spring Web MVC configuration files.
|– tags	Contains Roo's generated JSPX tags, which aid in building menus, scaffolding, and configuring form fields and display elements.
|– views	Contains all application view files and Apache Tiles view definitions.
|– images	Contains all predefined Roo image files such as icons for country flags, add, update, delete, and list buttons, and so on.
|– styles	Contains all CSS style files.

---

[2] Remember, ~.model is shorthand for org.rooinaction.taskmanager.model, a helpful shorthand both for Roo itself and for conversations about the project structure.

2.2.5   *Spring configuration files*

Spring Roo manages a number of APIs for you when it creates your applications. They're managed by mounting them as APIs and services from within the Spring Framework. Knowing where these files live and what they do is key to the success of any Spring-based project, including one generated by Spring Roo.

Spring configuration files are generally stored in two locations in a Roo project—the business-tier application context directory, META-INF/spring in src/main/resources and the web-tier application context in WEB-INF/spring, located in the src/main/webapp directory. They serve two similar but distinct purposes:

- *Business-tier Spring configuration (META-INF/spring/applicationResources*.xml)*—This location is where Spring Roo will store Spring context files. As Roo adds features, such as JMS, email, or Spring Security, it may add files to this directory.

    When Roo creates an initial project, this directory contains a single Spring context file, applicationContext.xml. If you add, for example, Spring Security, it will add an additional context file, applicationContext-security.xml. Roo configures Spring to look for any files *starting with* applicationContext and *ending in* xml in this directory, so you may add your own Spring configuration files as needed here.

- *Web-tier Spring configuration (WEB-INF/spring)*—If you configure your application as a web application, Roo will generate the Spring MVC context files in this location to manage the web artifacts such as controllers, views, URL handling, Apache Tiles configuration, and a number of other features. The main file here is webmvc-config.xml.

Other configuration files you should be aware of include

- *log4j.properties (in src/main/resources)*—The Apache log4j logging framework settings file.
- *META-INF/persistence.xml (in src/main/resources)*—The JPA deployment descriptor, which is configured when you configure your database settings. See chapter 3 for more details.
- *META-INF/spring/database.properties (in src/main/resources)*—The JDBC connection settings for establishing access to a database in Roo, if you're using a standard JDBC data source. We discuss this file in chapter 3.
- *WEB-INF/web.xml (in src/main/webapp)*—The standard web application deployment descriptor. Review this file to see how the Spring MVC and Spring Security frameworks are mounted using filters and servlets. We cover Spring MVC in detail beginning in chapter 5, and Spring Security in chapter 8.

Spring Roo configured all of these files for you, without any work on your part, beyond stating preferences in the shell commands. Better still, if a feature is upgraded, such as a newer version of Spring, a newer version of Roo may upgrade generated files, or change the version property in the Maven pom.xml file. But Spring

Roo won't remove your Java code from artifacts you create, so you can go about developing your application logic without worrying about losing your code.

2.2.6　About AspectJ ITDs

When you issue a Roo entity command, Roo builds not only the entity class, but a series of AspectJ inter-type declaration files, abbreviated ITDs. For example, when creating the Active Record–driven `Task` entity and field commands,

```
entity jpa --class ~.model.Task --testAutomatically
field string --fieldName description --sizeMax 40 --notNull
field boolean --fieldName completed --value false
```

Roo responds by generating the Roo entity as shown next.

Listing 2.1　The `Task` entity—`Task.java`

```
package org.rooinaction.taskmanager.model;

import javax.validation.constraints.NotNull;
import javax.validation.constraints.Size;
import org.springframework.beans.factory.annotation.Value;
import org.springframework.roo.addon.jpa.activerecord.➥
    RooJpaActiveRecord;
import org.springframework.roo.addon.javabean.RooJavaBean;
import org.springframework.roo.addon.json.RooJson;
import org.springframework.roo.addon.tostring.RooToString;

@RooJavaBean
@RooToString
@RooJpaActiveRecord
public class Task {

  @NotNull
  @Size(max = 40)
  private String description;

  @Value("false")
  private boolean completed;
}
```

❶ Getters/Setters

❷ toString()

❸ ID/Version

❹ Validation rule

This class, which is seen as a JPA entity, is managed by Roo via the `@RooJpaActive-Record` annotation ❸. It's defined as a JavaBean due to the `@RooJavaBean` annotation, ❶ and it sports a handy generated `toString()` method due to the `@RooToString` ❷ annotation. It contains two fields, `description` ❷, which is required and must not exceed 40 characters, and an optional Boolean `completed` ❷ field. You were able to quickly surmise this because all of the boilerplate code has been extracted elsewhere, and you're only looking at the code that makes this class unique.

2.2.7　What ITDs did you just generate?

The files Roo created when you defined your entity mix behavior into the entity class at *compile* time, and are generated by the Roo shell in response to the annotations that Roo added to the class definition. The key ITD files are as follows:

- `Task_Roo_Javabean.aj` *(via @RooJavaBean)*—This aspect contains the getters and setters for all member variables defined in `Task.java`.
- `Task_Roo_Configurable.aj` *(via @RooJpaActiveRecord)*—This adds the `@Configurable` annotation to the `Task` class.
- `Task_Roo_Jpa_Entity.aj` *(via @RooJpaActiveRecord)*—This defines the primary key, key generation, and version management strategies for the entity.
- `Task_Roo_Jpa_ActiveRecord.aj`—This contains all JPA methods to find, persist, update, list, and remove `Task` entity instances.
- `Task_Roo_ToString.aj`—This defines the `toString()` method based on all of the fields mapped by this entity. Generated via the `@RooToString` annotation.

To see how these ITDs work, we'll take a look at one from the `Task` class.

2.2.8 *Exploring an ITD*

We've mentioned ITDs and other likely unfamiliar terms a lot so far. You're probably wondering what these ITDs look like. Let's take a look. The following listing shows the definition of an ITD, `Task_Roo_JavaBean.aj`.

> **Listing 2.2   The JavaBean ITD for the `Task` entity**

```
// WARNING: DO NOT EDIT THIS FILE. THIS FILE IS MANAGED BY SPRING ROO.
// You may push code into the target .java compilation unit if you wish
to edit any member(s).

package org.rooinaction.taskmanager.model;

import java.lang.Boolean;
import java.lang.String;

privileged aspect Task_Roo_JavaBean {

    public String Task.getDescription() {
        return this.description;
    }

    public void Task.setDescription(String description) {
        this.description = description;
    }

    public Boolean Task.getCompleted() {
        return this.completed;
    }

    public void Task.setCompleted(Boolean completed) {
        this.completed = completed;
    }

}
```

ITDs are not Java classes per se; they're defined by the keywords `privileged aspect` rather than `class`. But they contain Java source code. You'll notice that each method or variable is prefixed with the name of the class into which they are being woven—for example, `Task.getDescription()`.

Roo uses the Maven aspectj-maven-plugin tool to compile these ITDs during the compile phase of your build process. When the compiler sees a definition starting with the class name of a Java class, it weaves the code into that type; hence the name inter-type declaration. The aspect type `Task_Roo_JavaBean` mixes code into the Java type `Task.java`.

In this way, the byte code for all of the methods, variables, and annotations defined in these ITDs are folded into the class file of your original Java object.

What do all of these ITDs do for your `Task` entity? Anything repetitive or boiler-plate. They handle your dirty work.

2.2.9   *Yeah, they handle your dirty work*

We all know the standard line of movie Mafia Dons when they want to get rid of a trou-blemaker: "Take care of my dirty work..." How much dirty work do you have to do on a daily basis? Chances are, to write and test the code that manages a `Task` object, quite a lot. But you're using Spring Roo; it generated all of that code behind the scenes so that you don't have to.

When you issued the `entity` command to build your `Task`, the Roo shell emitted the entity class. Then it went on to generate all of the aspects defined in the annota-tions `@RooJpaActiveRecord`, `@RooJavaBean`, and `@RooToString`, as shown in figure 2.2.

You may even find more AspectJ ITD files than the preceding ones, as Roo evolves to add additional features to the entities you create. Roo expects you to mostly ignore these generated files and focus on writing your business logic. But if you open up the ITDs in a text editor, you'll see it's the *dirty work* you're used to coding yourself.

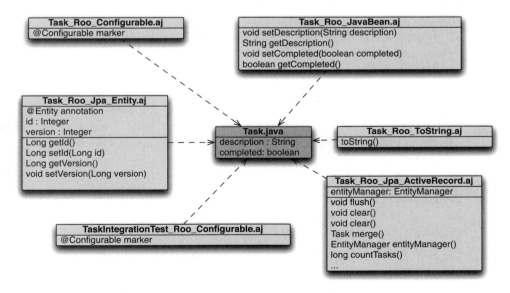

Figure 2.2   The `Task.java` Roo entity and all related ITDs. See the tiny class, `Task.java`?

As you saw, all of these files are created by the Roo shell, which takes direction from special annotations contained within the source file, Task.java. At compile time, the Maven aspectj compiler plug-in weaves them into the actual Task class file. Any Roo ITD can be mixed into the class definition so that it appears exactly as if you wrote that code in Task.java yourself.

Roo will create the TaskIntegrationTest, TaskDataOnDemand, and the related ITDs only if you specify the --testAutomatically flag on the entity command, or use the test integration command after the entity is created. The generated test class and ITD actually spins up the Spring container and runs integration tests against the entity, helping you identify problems with the database design and mapping process early in the project lifecycle. You can execute the Roo-generated tests within an IDE or by executing the Maven command mvn test. We begin working with Roo's testing framework in chapter 3, and devote an entire chapter to testing, chapter 9.

> **JPA, ORM, ACTIVE RECORD, ENTITY! WHAT ARE THEY TALKING ABOUT?**   If these terms confuse you, don't worry. We'll demystify them a bit in chapters 3 and 4. For now, just remember that the Roo shell can generate database persistence code in special Java classes that are annotated with @RooJpaActive-Record, and a few other annotations.

2.2.10 *Multimodule projects*

Roo can even build a multimodule project comprised of multiple Maven projects called *modules*. These modules are created to separate your application into horizontal tiers, such as web and business layers, or vertical slices, such as functional business layers. A single Roo project can potentially contain several web applications, JAR projects that provide business or infrastructure logic, or other components.

To create a multimodule project, you begin by defining the outer project using the --packaging tag, setting the value to POM:

```
roo> project --topLevelPackage org.rooinaction.taskmanager ➥
    --packaging POM --projectName taskmanager
```

Roo uses Maven's pom project type as an aggregator; it allows you to add subprojects below but doesn't actually create a new deliverable artifact. For example, to create a JAR-based project to hold Spring beans, you'd issue a module command:

```
roo> module create --moduleName infrastructure ➥
    --topLevelPackage ~ --packaging JAR
```

Note the special --topLevelPackage syntax to refer to the outer project's package—the ~ symbol used when referring to top-level packages when defining other Roo objects. This symbol can be post-fixed with your module's specific subpackage. This allows you to define your services within your outer project, separated in their own jar:

```
--topLevelPackage ~.infrastructure
```

When you create a module, the roo> prompt will switch to that module, focusing to it, prefixing the module name before the word roo:

```
infrastructure roo>
```

Whatever commands you issue affect the current module. You can switch to another module using the `module focus` command. For example, to switch to another module use the following:

```
infrastructure roo> module focus --moduleName taskmanager-data
infrastructure roo>
```

You can also move to the top-level Maven project by focusing on ~ (available via tab completion, as for all module names):

```
taskmanager-data roo> module focus --moduleName ~
roo>
```

You can define a web-based application module as well:

```
roo> module create --moduleName taskmanager-web ⇥
    --topLevelPackage ~.web --packaging WAR
... much fanfare ...
taskmanager-web>
```

Mind the currently focused module when working on Roo projects. Working with modules adds an additional level of complexity to your project, so when beginning just focus on nonmodular web applications. You'll do much better adding modules later, when you can appreciate the component models you're building and how they relate each other.

Now that you've configured your project files using the Roo shell, let's look at how you can open these Roo projects in your favorite Java IDE.

2.3 *I want my IDE!*

Most developers find it easier to work within an IDE for many reasons, including the immediate visual feedback. It would be inconvenient if you had to flip back and forth between the command line and an IDE when building applications. Currently, two IDEs are able to work with Roo applications: SpringSource Tool Suite and IntelliJ IDEA. Let's take a look at the support for Roo projects in both applications.

2.3.1 *SpringSource Tool Suite*

SpringSource has a version of the Eclipse IDE known as the SpringSource Tool Suite, which we'll call STS. Geared toward developing Spring-based applications, STS is chock full of features supporting the Spring Framework, such as

- *Spring context editing support*—STS provides automatic code fill-in features and namespace support for Spring context files. The editor can visualize these files graphically as well.
- *Code completion*—Not only does STS provide the fairly typical [CTRL]-SPACE code completion features from Eclipse, it does so when completing information in Spring XML context files.
- *Maven*—Built-in support for Maven using the m2e Eclipse Maven plug-in.
- *API-based editors*—Editing support for Spring WebFlow, Spring Integration, Spring Batch, and other features is provided. Open one of these files in the editor and see the tabs along the bottom, which provide graphical editing features.

- *Spring template project support*—Kick off any Spring project quickly using some Maven archetype-based starter projects.
- *RAD*—Full support for SpringSource's rapid application development platforms, Grails and Roo.

We could go on and on about STS. But this isn't a sales call, so let's discuss the features specific to Roo:

- *The Roo command shell* —STS can open a Roo command shell on any Roo project.
- *AspectJ ITD support*— Part of STS's support for AspectJ, it will let you show or hide the generated ITDs and provides navigational access to the code written in those ITDs when editing source code or debugging your application.
- *Refactoring support*—STS supports refactoring of code written in Roo ITDs; you can *push-in* refactor methods out of ITDs and into Java code for customization purposes.

Loading your project into STS can be done with the Eclipse's import function.

To `import` the project from within STS, select File > Import... > Maven > Existing Maven Projects. Then navigate to the directory where the project was created.

2.3.2   *The Roo context menu*

Roo projects are automatically detected upon being opened, and display two small letter indicators in their project icons, an *M* to denote that they're managed Maven projects, and an *S* to show that they're Spring projects. Roo projects have a special nature to them, and STS adds special right-click menu options within the Spring Tools section as seen in figure 2.3.

There are a number of features directly available to you in a Roo project, over and above the typical Spring application:

- *The Roo Shell*—You can open the Roo shell on the current project within STS.
- *The Roo Command Wizard*—You can browse all commands, which is essentially the same as running help *command* on each one and presenting it in a graphical user interface.
- *Remove Roo Project Nature*—You can remove Roo features from STS; this will disable access to the Roo shell. This is useful if you've decided that you've

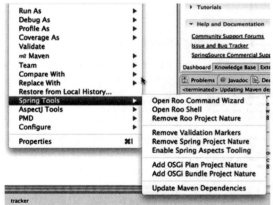

Figure 2.3   The right-click menu is enabled when a Roo project is imported into the STS workspace.

taken your application as far as you want to with Roo, and want to treat it like a regular Spring project.

- *Enable Spring Aspects Tooling*—This enables weaving of the ITD code within Roo. You can turn on this feature and then use [CTRL]-[SPACE] to use methods from these ITDs in your Java source code.
- *The Refactor menu (not shown)*—A menu item in the Refactor ... menu, Push-In, is meant to be used to push code out of an ITD (.aj file) and back into a Java file for customization and editing.

Let's take a look in detail at the Roo shell support provided by STS.

2.3.3 The Roo shell

The Roo shell is opened automatically when opening a Roo-based project in STS, as shown in figure 2.4.

THE ROO COMMAND-LINE SHELL IN STS In STS, the Roo shell has one functional difference from the command-line version. Instead of pressing [TAB] to complete commands, you use the standard Eclipse code completion [CTRL]-[SPACE] keystroke.

2.3.4 Showing and hiding Roo ITDs

Initially, STS will hide the Roo ITDs (*.aj) files. This provides you with a concise view of the objects that you work with day to day. But to see the generated code, you need to bring up the Filters dialog. This can be done from two places:

- From the Package Explorer, click on the drop-down triangle and select the Filters ... menu item.
- From the Project Explorer, click on the drop-down triangle and select the Customize View ... menu item.

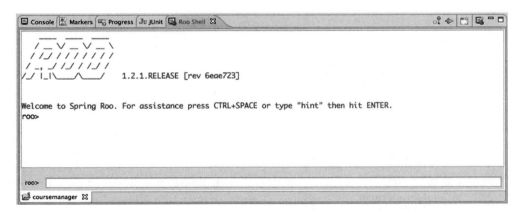

Figure 2.4 Roo shell view

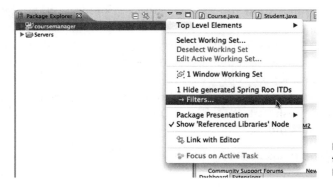

Figure 2.5   The drop-down triangle menu, shown in the Project Explorer view

Figure 2.5 shows the way to select the Customize View menu from the Project Explorer view.

Once you select the Filters... menu, you'll be presented with a Filter dialog, where you can toggle the Hide Generated Spring Roo ITDs option off and on. If you've done this before, it appears as a selectable shortcut. This feature will toggle display of the generated AspectJ ITD files. Figure 2.6 shows the filter dialog.

Figure 2.7 shows the resulting project pane, which will look quite different when displaying the generated ITDs.

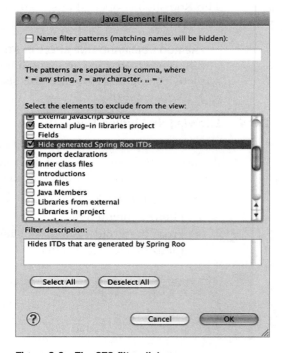

Figure 2.6   The STS filter dialog

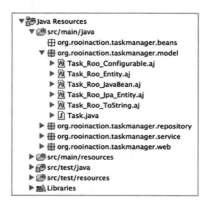

Figure 2.7   The project pane with ITDs

You can see all of the ITDs generated for each artifact. Viewing the aspects isn't just a convenience; as you get more used to Roo, you may find yourself customizing the behavior of a given Roo entity or controller to handle an atypical problem. That is where push-in refactoring comes in, which is the ability to push code out of the ITDs and into the Java classes themselves.

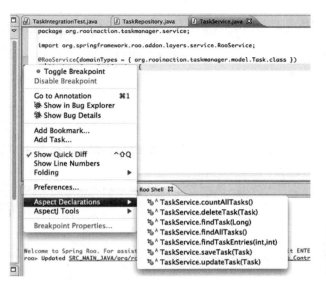

Figure 2.8 The Aspect Declarations menu in action; note the weaved data access ITD methods for this service

Now take a look at another STS feature—the ability to navigate to the woven ITD methods right from the Java source editor. If you see a special icon to the left of your editor pane, that means that the class has been woven with ITD methods. You can right-click on that icon and select from several menu options, including the Aspect Declarations pane shown in figure 2.8.

In short, support for Roo in STS is first-rate, and it's improving with each release. Being a free option, STS is a good choice for developers who are beginning to experiment with Spring Roo, and who want to work with frameworks such as Spring and AspectJ.

2.3.5 *IntelliJ IDEA and other IDEs*

Of the two other popular Java IDEs (NetBeans and IntelliJ IDEA), NetBeans doesn't support AspectID ITD files, so it won't launch the AspectJ weaver. It won't make methods in the ITDs available in code fill-in features, and will only show the AspectJ files as pure text files. Any code that references ITD methods directly, such as integration tests, will fail to compile.

On the other hand, IntelliJ 11.0 and above provides full support for Roo as well, including a command-line utility, code completion, and syntax highlighting for the Roo aspects as shown in figure 2.9.

IntelliJ IDEA also has built-in support for Spring Beans, Hibernate, JSPs, JavaScript, and Maven. This makes it another excellent choice for developing Roo-based applications. You can choose to run the Roo shell in the IDE, or you can keep the shell running in the background in an operating system window. Which method you choose is up to you. You will want to turn on the Maven auto-import feature so that you get configuration changes as soon as Roo reconfigures your project.

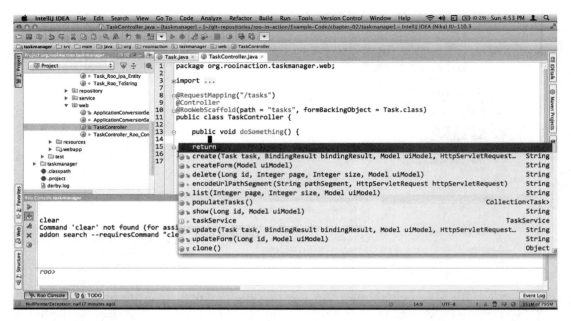

Figure 2.9   IntelliJ code completion and command-line console

In short, basic IDE support for Roo is available from SpringSource Tool Suite and Jet-Brains IntelliJ. Unfortunately, AspectJ support, the key enabling technology for Spring Roo, is dormant in the NetBeans IDE to date. Until a solution arrives that allows developers to edit code built on AspectJ ITDs on that platform, developers who use Net-Beans will have to use command-line Maven or another IDE to work with Spring Roo.

2.4   Refactoring, Roo ITDs, and leaving Roo

Now we'll discuss how you can work with your ITDs. There are three techniques you need to learn to make the most out of the Roo development platform: push-in refactoring, pull-out refactoring, and removing Roo from your project.

Each of these techniques is supported from the SpringSource Tool Suite. IntelliJ also allows you to perform these operations, but we will focus on STS in this discussion.

We'll begin by discussing push-in refactoring.

2.4.1   Push-in refactoring

Push-in refactoring is used to customize and replace the default behavior of Roo's aspects. The technique moves a method or attribute from a Roo project to the Java source file. From there, the developer can modify the method code directly. Push-in refactoring is used for many purposes. Here are a few:

- Sorting the data to be retrieved to feed a list from the Roo JPA ITD
- Adding custom server-side validations to your Spring MVC controllers

- Customizing the way your entity is created, setting code-based defaults or pre-populating data from a web service

To perform push-in refactoring using the SpringSource Tool Suite, make sure STS is showing the Roo-generated ITDs (see section 2.3.4). Switch to the Package Explorer view using Window...> Show View...> Package Explorer.

You'll implement a new business requirement for your task manager. Every time you mark a task complete, you'll prepend the task text with (completed) so that it is obvious you've done your work.

ABOUT OUR APPROACH   Because of the fact that JPA doesn't guarantee the order of setters called when persisting an entity, you can't implement this customization using the entity setter method, setCompleted(). Instead, you'll implement this in the service tier as you're updating your task, and manually set the data on the way to the repository, thus skipping any strange JPA implementation logic issues.

Open up the Java source folder org.rooinaction.taskmanager.service, and expand the TaskServiceImpl_Roo_Service.aj aspect. Expand the ITD to show the member methods. Right-click on the updateTask(Task) : void method, as shown in figure 2.10.

You'll then see the Push In Intertype Declaration dialog, as shown in figure 2.11. If you selected the method correctly, only the Task.setCompleted method will be pushed in. If, on the other hand, you clicked on the ITD itself and not a method or member variable, the entire ITD will be pushed in. This dialog is a chance to review your pending changes.

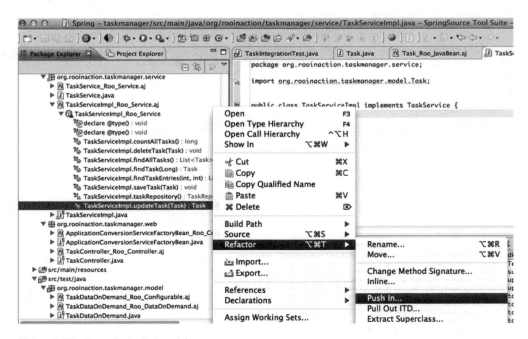

Figure 2.10   The refactoring push-in menu

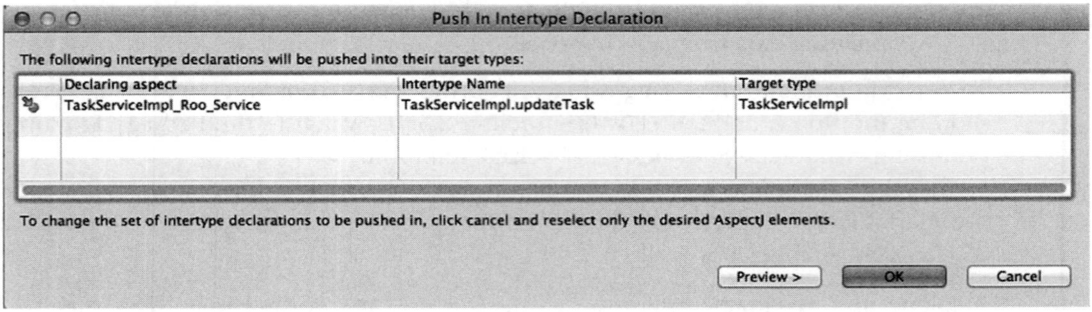

Figure 2.11   Refactoring in STS using the push-in dialog

You can preview your changes by clicking the Preview > button, as shown in figure 2.11. Click OK to perform the operation, as shown in figure 2.12.

Once the refactoring is complete, you'll see the method vanish from the ITD, and appear in `TaskServiceImpl.java`. This will only happen if your Roo shell is running. If nothing happens, fire up the shell. Now you can customize it to prepend your message to the task text:

```java
public Task updateTask(Task task) {
  if (Boolean.TRUE.equals(task.getCompleted())) {
    task.setDescription("(completed) " + task.getDescription());
  }
  return taskRepository.save(task);
}
```

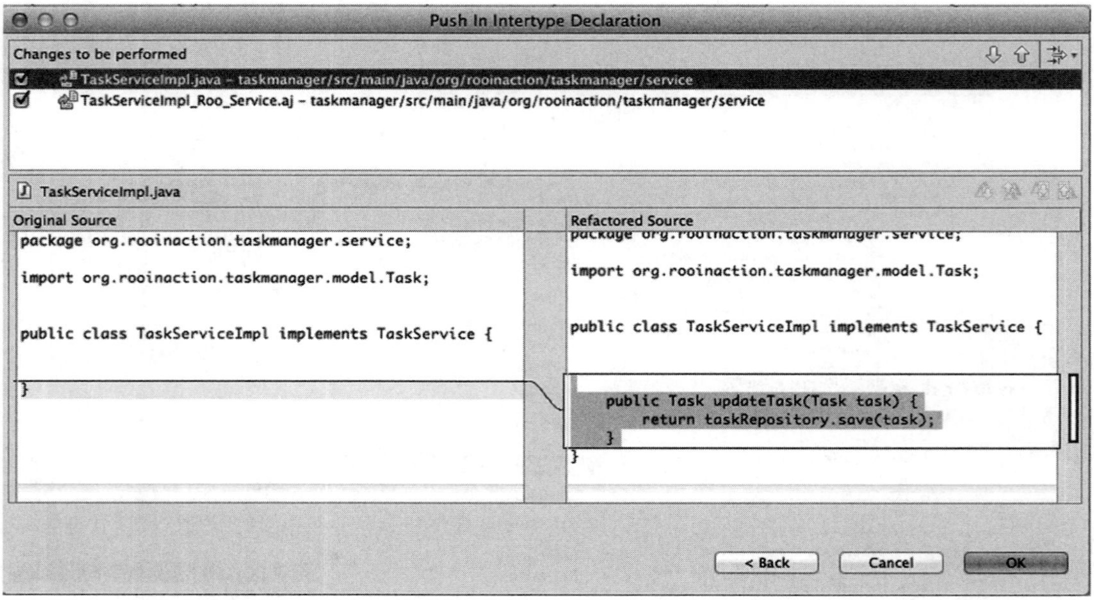

Figure 2.12   Previewing the push-in

And there you have it. You've just extracted the default implementation of `update-Task` from the `TaskServiceImpl_Roo_Service.aj` ITD and pushed it in to the `Task-ServiceImpl.java` service implementation.

2.4.2 Verify refactoring

Let's run the application now, this time on tc Server within STS. To do so, just drag the project from the Package or Project Explorer bar to the VMWare Fabric tc Server Developer Edition server, either v2.5 or 2.6. This is located in the Servers view. You can then right-click on the server and select Start. Once the server is started, you can right-click on the application name in the server pane, and select Open Home Page.

If you execute your `taskmanager` web application again and complete a few tasks, you'll see the completed message appear when you click on the checkbox and update your task.

> **WHAT IF I DON'T USE STS?**   If you don't download STS, you're missing out on a productive IDE. Although Eclipse can be clunky at times, STS installs several plug-ins that make developing Roo applications a snap, including AspectJ refactoring techniques, the Spring MVC namespace editor, and Maven editing support.
>
> But if you don't use STS, you can just cut and paste the code from your AspectJ ITDs, and use your editor's search/replace feature to remove the *Classname.* prefix from the elements. Fire up the Roo shell and allow it to remove the methods from the ITD. Roo can then remove the ITD completely if you remove the annotation that created it, such as `@RooWebScaffold`.

2.4.3 Pulling code out to ITDs

You can actually create your own ITDs and pull code out of your class file into them. This works as long as the code you're pulling out isn't supposed to exist because of the presence of another Roo annotation. You can't push in your JavaBean setters and getters and then pull them out to another aspect without removing the original `@Roo-JavaBean` annotation, for example.

To create your own ITD, you just use the File> New> Aspect menu item in STS. The ITDs you generate need to be marked as `privileged aspect` ITDs—you can just swap the `public` keyword with `privileged`. Once the ITD is created, you can use the Package Explorer to select a method of a Java class, then use the right-click menu to select Refactor> Pull Out ITD. Figure 2.13 shows the pull-out dialog.

Once finished, the method will be extracted into the AspectJ ITD you selected.

2.4.4 Leaving Roo behind

As much fun as you might have with Spring Roo, there may come a time when you want to remove it from your project. Perhaps you aren't comfortable with supporting an AspectJ-based application platform, or you're using Roo to prototype your project, but then will switch over to a traditional Spring application architecture.

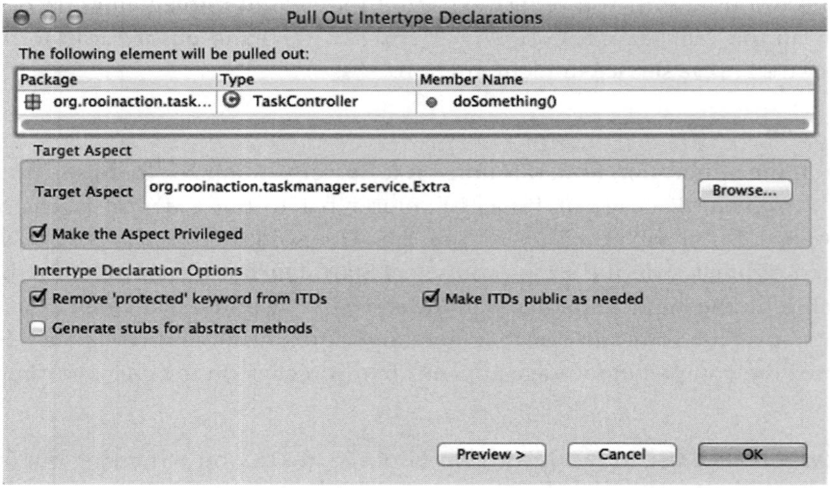

Figure 2.13   Pulling out Java code to an ITD

Leaving Roo, because it's a compile-time platform, is as simple as several steps:

1   Right-click on the project in the STS Package Explorer and select Refactor > Push-In.

2   Accept the settings to remove all ITDs.

3   Edit the Maven pom.xml file and remove the aspectj-maven-plugin from the configuration.

As outlined in the Roo installation guide, you can leave the Roo annotations in the source code. That way, if you decide to re-install Roo and continue coding, you don't have to redefine the annotations. You may remove the Roo annotations if you wish. If you do so, you can actually remove all of the Roo configuration, including AspectJ support, from the Maven pom.xml file by removing the `aspectj-maven-plugin` plug-in configuration entry from the `build/plugins` stanza.

> **DON'T FORGET TO SWITCH YOUR TRANSACTION CONFIGURATION IF YOU REMOVE ASPECTJ**   If you remove AspectJ from your Maven build, you'll also want to switch to the standard Spring proxy mode of providing transaction support by removing the italicized `mode="aspectj"` entry from the `application-Context.xml` fragment below:

```
<t:annotation-driven mode="aspectj"
    transaction-manager="transactionManager"/>
```

Other configuration settings are no longer relevant either, such as the AspectJ Maven Plugin, and skipping the scan of AspectJ ITDs, because they'll no longer exist in the project. Remove what you wish, unless you think at some point you may want to resume using Roo on your project.

Now let's review what you've learned about working with the Roo shell, aspects, and the Eclipse IDE.

2.5 Summary

In this chapter, you've seen how you can work with the Roo shell to manipulate projects. We introduced some of the Roo configuration commands, and explained how they create artifacts or configure project settings.

We reviewed how Roo organizes project structure, including where it stores various configuration files. If you're already a Maven or Spring developer, much of this looks familiar, since Roo follows common architectural patterns. We also discussed the tiers in a typical application, and how Roo provides a more entity-driven model of developing a data-driven application, using either the Active Record pattern or the service/repository pattern.

You also worked with the SpringSource Tool Suite to import a project, and enabled the Roo shell. You experimented with pushing in code from an ITD, and pulling code out to your own ITDs. We also discussed how to leave Roo if the time comes.

The next three chapters should be read together. Chapter 3, "Database persistence with entities," discusses how Roo manages database applications using the JPA API and JPA Entities. Chapter 4, "Relationships, JPA, and advanced persistence," explains how to create and manage relationships, add a service layer, and call JPA API code directly. We also discuss the MongoDB NoSQL database. Finally, chapter 5 explains how Roo helps you develop web-based applications, and how you can use those entities you learned about in the prior chapters.

2.6 Resources

BOOKS

Laddad, Ramnivas. *AspectJ in Action, Second Edition* (Manning Publications, 2009)

WEB

For more internals on Roo from the founder of the Roo project, Dr. Ben Alex, see http://mng.bz/s8Rc. Although out of date, this is a great read to see what they were thinking when they originally architected Roo.

Ken's interview with Ben Alex provides an audio history of the project. See Episode #45 of the Chariot TechCast podcast, "SpringSource's Ben Alex on Roo, a Java-based agile framework," located at http://techcast.chariotsolutions.com.

Part 2

Databases and entities

In part 1, you learned how Roo aids in rapid Java application development. Most real-world enterprise software applications use some type of database to store and retrieve business data to display on user interface screens. Data persistence and data access are the main topics of part 2.

In chapter 3, "Database persistence with entities," we'll explore database persistence using the Java Persistence API (JPA), and you'll learn how to set up JPA in a Roo application. You'll also learn how you can create entities and add fields to those entities, and you'll write a JUnit test to test the Roo entity you created. Validation is another important aspect of keeping data in the database clean. We'll discuss how to enable data validation using the Bean Validation Framework to configure automatic data validation in your entities. Then, we'll discuss search finders. We'll finish chapter 3 by discussing how to create repositories in Roo, including the features of Spring Data JPA.

Entities stored in the database typically have relationships with other entities. Chapter 4, "Relationships, JPA, and advanced persistence," provides guidance on how to define and manage entity relationships using JPA. We'll also look at reverse engineering JPA entities and adding a service layer, which is a new feature added in a recent release of Roo. Not all types of data are good candidates to store in a relational database. This is where NoSQL databases come into the picture; these nonrelational databases have been getting a lot of attention lately. You'll learn how to persist data into a NoSQL database like MongoDB.

Database persistence with entities 3

This chapter covers

- Your business objects and persistence
- Working with entities
- What about validation?
- Searching with finders

In the last chapter, we discussed Spring Roo from a developer's perspective. We discussed the various component types, and how the Roo shell creates and maintains objects in your projects, hiding tedious, repetitive code behind AspectJ-driven .aj files.

In this chapter, you'll learn how to store and load data from relational databases. You'll start by defining object-relational mapping (ORM) APIs and the standard Java Persistence API, and then learn how to configure persistence in a project using the *Roo shell*. Next, you'll define Roo entities, which are an enhanced version of the standard JPA Entity class. You'll create entity components in the shell, and we'll show you how to load, persist, and remove them, using Roo's JUnit-based integration test framework.

Next, you'll use the Bean Validation Framework to configure automatic data validation in your entities. We'll discuss both built-in and custom validations, and how to provide validation messages. We'll discuss finders—methods that allow for searching for properties within a Roo entity. We'll wrap up by discussing JPA Repositories.

3.1   Your business objects and persistence

No matter how cool your application architecture is, it often boils down to loading data from a database, editing it, and then saving it back again with changes from the user or external system. The challenge is to get the data to flow between your object-driven Java application server and the relationally mapped database server.

3.1.1   The Java Persistence API

The Java Persistence API, or JPA for short, was created to provide a standard programming interface for object-oriented database mapping. Hibernate, EclipseLink, OpenJPA, and other frameworks implement the JPA 2.0 specification, which allows developers to write code to a single API regardless of the implementing vendor. JPA defines the following components:

- *The JPA entity*—A Java class that's mapped to a database table, using either annotations or XML.
- *The persistence context*—A storage area assigned to an individual session or thread, this is the workspace that keeps track of changes to relational data.
- *Persistence annotations*—The `javax.persistence.*` annotations define mapping instructions such as tables, relationships, primary key generation techniques, and query mapping.
- The `EntityManager` *API*—Provides access to a *persistence context*.
- *The JPA configuration file*—JPA-compliant ORMs are configured using the special file, META-INF/persistence.xml.

JPA was originally developed as part of the Java EE 1.5 specification, as a replacement for the more vendor-specific and heavyweight Enterprise JavaBeans. Spring provides a factory to configure the JPA API, whether or not the Spring application is running as a standalone application or within a Java EE application server like WebSphere or JBoss.

> **MORE ON THE JAVA PERSISTENCE API**   Although a full review of JPA is beyond the scope of this book, Spring Roo uses JPA 2.0, which is documented as part of the Java community process. The specification, JSR-317, is available at http://mng.bz/FU7w. There are a number of books available on the subject of JPA 2.0.

Now let's use the Roo shell to set up JPA. Then you can get started coding against relational databases, Roo-style.

3.1.2 Setting up JPA in Roo

Configuring JPA in a traditional Spring project involves setting up various configuration elements and programming directly to the JPA API. Spring Roo configures all of these features for you using the `jpa setup` command. This command will configure a JDBC `DataSource`, Spring transaction management features, the JPA 2.0 API, JPA entities, inter-type declarations, and validations via the Bean Validation Framework. You don't even have to manually wire up a configuration at all!

In this chapter, you'll begin to configure your application, the Course Manager, which manages a set of courses for a fictitious training company. If you're following along, you can start by creating your own project with the `project` command, naming the project `coursemanager`.

Let's use the `jpa setup` command to set up your database. We'll assume you don't have a database engine installed on your machine; for simplicity, let's use the Hypersonic SQL standalone database. Here's the proper Roo shell command. We'll assume you've already set up the project itself with the name of `coursemanager` and a base package of `org.rooinaction.coursemanager`:

```
roo> jpa setup --database HYPERSONIC_PERSISTENT ➡
     --provider HIBERNATE
```

> **SAVE SOME TYPING**   Remember, in the shell, you can type the first two or three characters of this command—for example, `jp [TAB]`—and Roo will complete the command for you. This goes for your options and values as well. You can type `-- [TAB]` to see what options are available, and when when an option such as `database` is selected, you can hit `[TAB]` to get the available options.

As we described in the quick-start in chapter 2, the `jpa setup` command performs a number of configuration steps. Roo will

- Include the dependent JAR files in your Maven pom.xml configuration file for the selected JDBC driver, the JPA API, and a number of Hibernate JARs (and their dependencies)
- Configure a JDBC data source, Spring transaction manager, and a Spring JPA configuration in META-INF/spring/applicationContext.xml
- Configure META-INF/persistence.xml with settings relating JPA to the database using Hibernate configuration settings
- Install the JSR-303 Bean Validation Framework, which provides annotation-based validations

Let's look at the `jpa setup` command in a little more depth. Listed in table 3.1 are the key parameters.

Using `[TAB]` completion, you'll be prompted for the appropriate parameters. The most useful options of course are `--provider` and `--database`. Of particular note, when running Spring Roo on an application server such as WebSphere, WebLogic, or JBoss, you can take direct advantage of a JNDI data source; just put the proper data source name in the `--jndiDataSource` option.

Table 3.1   JPA setup command parameters

Option (prefixed with --)	Required	Options/Notes
`provider`	Yes	The JPA provider to configure. Includes `HIBERNATE`, `ECLIPSELINK`, `OPENJPA`, and `DATANUCLEUS` (required for use with Google App Engine).
`database`	Yes	The database to configure. `DB2`, `DERBY`, `ORACLE`, `SYBASE`, `MSSQL`, `HYPERSONIC_PERSISTENT`, and many more. *Please note:* Oracle and some other proprietary database drivers aren't provided by the Maven public repository. You'll have to manually install the Oracle driver by downloading it, installing it into Maven manually, and adjusting the pom.xml file to reference the appropriate `groupId`, `artifactId`, and `version` of the installed JAR.
`applicationId`	No	For Google App Engine (`DATANUCLEUS`) provider, the Google application ID.
`hostName`, `databaseName`, `userName`, `password`	No	Values to override that are set in src/main/resources/database.properties.
`jndiDataSource`	No	If using JNDI, the data source to reference in your Java EE application server. For JDBC data sources this isn't required.
`persistenceUnit`, `transactionManager`	No	Advanced usage. You can use several data sources, each linked to individual transaction managers. For each one, a separate JPA environment is set up. The `--persistenceUnit` parameter names the JPA environment, and the `--transactionManager` specifies which Spring transaction manager to use. We don't cover this configuration in the book.

Rerun `jpa setup` to change your database configuration

You can run the `jpa setup` command over and over again. Each time it will replace the configuration entry and reconfigure JPA to support whatever settings you'd like to change. This makes the ORM implementation changeable without affecting your code, and lets you mix and match combinations of the various persistence providers and JDBC drivers to find the best fit for your application. Note that this will rewrite your database.properties file, so be prepared to reenter your connection information.

One way this makes your life easier as a developer is that you can quickly get going using `HIBERNATE` against a `HYPERSONIC_PERSISTENT` database to provide a simple relational database. Later, you can modify your persistence provider by running again and selecting another JPA vendor such as `ECLIPSELINK` or `OPENJPA`. Later, when setting up your desired environment's database, you may switch to `ORACLE`, `MYSQL`, or any other database supported by your ORM provider.

When using Google's cloud database, you would use `DATANUCLEUS` to support running Roo on Google App Engine.

Your database properties are configured and stored in `database.properties`, located in src/main/resources/META-INF/spring. Colons (:) may be escaped in the file with a preceding backslash (\). To view, change, or set properties, either edit the file yourself, or use the Roo `properties` shell commands. To view properties, issue the `properties list` command:

```
roo> properties list --name database.properties ➥
    --path SPRING_CONFIG_ROOT
databasedriverClassName = org.hsqldb.jdbcDriver
databasepassword =
database.url = jdbc:hsqldb:file:coursemanager;shutdown=true
database.username = sa
```

To add a property, use `properties set`:

```
roo> properties set --name database.properties ➥
    --path SPRING_CONFIG_ROOT --key password --value f00b@r
Updated SRC_MAIN_RESOURCES/META-INF/spring/database.properties
```

To remove a property, use `properties remove`:

```
roo> properties remove --name database.properties ➥
    --path SPRING_CONFIG_ROOT --key password
Updated SRC_MAIN_RESOURCES/META-INF/spring/database.properties
```

The `properties` shell command can manipulate any properties file, and takes a symbolic `--path` attribute for the various paths in a Roo application. Explore it with tab completion to view various files in your application.

3.1.3 *Schema management settings*

Another file Roo creates for you is the standard JPA configuration file, META-INF/persistence.xml. JPA uses this file to configure the `persistence unit`, or JPA configuration, to use when accessing the database. In the current example, this file passes along configuration parameters to your selected ORM API, Hibernate. You can use this file to send configuration information to the ORM layer, controlling settings such as schema generation.

When using Hibernate, the `hibernate.hbm2ddl.auto` property controls whether the tables are re-created on startup. It can be found within a `<properties>` tag:

```
<property name="hibernate.hbm2ddl.auto" value="create"/>
```

The settings available include `create`, `create-drop`, `update`, `validate`, and `none`. Here's a list of the settings:

- `create`—This creates the database tables on startup. Drops them first if they already exist.
- `create-drop`—This creates the database tables on startup. On shutdown, Hibernate will attempt to drop the tables.
- `update`—Only adds new fields and tables to the schema; doesn't remove existing columns or tables if removed from the Hibernate table definitions.

- validate–Uses the discovered table definitions to validate the database model. If any table or field is incorrectly named, typed, or configured, throws an exception and reports the problem. This is good if you're using Hibernate against a preconfigured database.
- none—Does no validation or modification of the database on startup. Can speed startup against a known database but often developers choose validate to spot changes in the database that may cause problems against the defined schema.

The default setting, create, drops and re-creates tables on startup. Change this value to update to allow restarting your application and preserving existing data, since Hibernate won't delete the data from the tables for you automatically. Note that this option won't delete columns you remove from your mappings; it will only add or alter existing columns.

Other persistence APIs have differing options. For example, when configuring EclipseLink, Roo defines this property to determine whether to drop or create tables:

```
<property name="eclipselink.ddl-generation" ➥
    value="drop-and-create-tables"/>
```

As you switch JPA drivers, Roo will define the appropriate DDL generation configuration syntax for you automatically.

Now you're ready to start creating some entities and writing some code. You'll start by defining the courses for your Course Manager application.

3.2   *Working with entities*

The Course Manager application primarily focuses on delivering courses to students. In this section, you'll define the Course class as a persistent entity and configure it with the appropriate fields. We'll then discuss how to use and test the Course in a Roo application.

3.2.1   *Creating your first entity*

Let's define the Course entity, which will hold your course definitions. If you were doing this by hand, you would have to annotate a class with @Entity and define primary key attributes such as @Id and perhaps a @GeneratedValue annotation to handle key generation. Also, you'd have to define field settings, table names, and other settings via the javax.persistence annotations.

But here's some good news! The Roo shell has a command for that, jpa entity. You can open up the Roo shell and execute this:

```
roo> entity jpa --class ~.model.Course --testAutomatically
Created SRC_MAIN_JAVA/o.r.c/model
Created SRC_MAIN_JAVA/o.r.c/model/Course.java
Created SRC_TEST_JAVA/o.r.c/model
Created SRC_TEST_JAVA/o.r.c/model/CourseDataOnDemand.java
Created SRC_TEST_JAVA/o.r.c/model/CourseIntegrationTest.java
```

```
Created SRC_MAIN_JAVA/o.r.c/model/Course_Roo_Configurable.aj
Created SRC_MAIN_JAVA/o.r.c/model/Course_Roo_ToString.aj
Created SRC_MAIN_JAVA/o.r.c/model/Course_Roo_Jpa_Entity.aj
Created SRC_MAIN_JAVA/o.r.c/model/Course_Roo_Jpa_ActiveRecord.aj
...
~.model.Course roo>
```

Roo just created your `Course` entity, a suite of AspectJ ITDs to manage it, and a set of files for testing purposes. This includes the integration test and a strangely named series of files labeled DataOnDemand—we'll get to those later. For now, we'll focus on adding fields to the generated `Course` entity. Here it is:

```
package org.rooinaction.coursemanager.model;

import o.s.roo.addon.javabean.RooJavaBean;
import o.s.roo.addon.jpa.activerecord.RooJpaActiveRecord;
import o.s.roo.addon.tostring.RooToString;

@RooJavaBean
@RooToString
@RooJpaActiveRecord
public class Course {
}
```

Rather short, isn't it? We've abbreviated `org.springframework` to `o.s.` in the imports to save space. We'll cover the Roo annotations and what they mean shortly, but for now, you need to define the fields in order for this class to be useful to anybody.

> **WHAT'S WITH THE EXTRA STUFF IN THE ROO> PROMPT?** See how the Roo shell prompt moves from `roo>` to `~.model.Course roo>` when you create the `Course` entity? That's because the shell keeps the context of the last entity it's been working on, known as the *focus*. Any modifications you make, such as adding additional fields, will take place with that entity by default. You can set the focus on a particular entity by using the `focus` command, or use the `--class` option when creating a field element.

Even though you don't know how Roo does it, you probably figured out from the annotations that Roo provides several automatic services for this entity: something about JavaBean support, a `toString()` method, the JPA code, and an equals method. Each of these resides in a separate ITD:

```
Course_Roo_Configurable.aj
Course_Roo_Jpa_ActiveRecord.aj
Course_Roo_Jpa_Entity.aj
Course_Roo_ToString.aj
```

We'll talk about all of those things in a little bit. But for now, let's go ahead and add some fields to this entity.

3.2.2   *Adding fields to the Course*

To add database fields to the `Course` entity, you use the `field` shell command. This command adds the appropriate variables to your `Course.java` class, and also maintains the various generated methods in your `Course` ITD files.

Let's add five fields to the `Course`:

```
field string --fieldName name
field number --fieldName listPrice --type java.math.BigDecimal
field string --fieldName description
field number --fieldName maximumCapacity --type java.lang.Integer
field date --fieldName runDate --type java.util.Date ➥
  --persistenceType JPA_DATE --dateFormat SHORT
```

With these five commands, you've just added five fields to the `Course` class: name, description, listPrice, maximumCapacity, and runDate. Let's take a bird's-eye view of the `Course.java` entity Roo just updated.

Listing 3.1   The `Course` entity

```
package org.rooinaction.coursemanager.model;

...

@RooJavaBean                                          Feature
@RooToString                                          annotations
@RooJpaActiveRecord
@RooEquals
public class Course {

  private String name;

  private BigDecimal listPrice;                       JPA fields

  private String description;

  private Integer maximumCapacity;

  @Temporal(TemporalType.DATE)                  ◁─── Date formatting
  @DateTimeFormat(style = "S-")
  private Date runDate;
}
```

Let's walk through each of the key features of the Roo entity defined in the listing. For each feature, we'll show the code snippet that corresponds to the feature itself.

JAVABEAN SUPPORT

All Roo entities are automatically Java beans. For example, the fields you've defined via your command are implemented as private member variables:

```
private String name;

private BigDecimal listPrice;

private String description;

private Integer maximumCapacity;
...
```

Though you see no getters or setters, Roo has generated them, in the `Course_Roo_JavaBean.aj` file:

```
privileged aspect Course_Roo_JavaBean {

    public String Course.getName() {
        return this.name;
    }

    public void Course.setName(String name) {
        this.name = name;
    }

    public String Course.getDescription() {
        return this.description;
    }

    public void Course.setDescription(String description) {
        this.description = description;
    }
...
}
```

Roo built this file when it detected at least one private member variable in your class definition, which was annotated with `@RooJavaBean`.

DATE CONVERSION

Roo can handle date conversion issues. For example, the `runDate` field uses two annotations, `@Temporal` and `@DateTimeFormat`:

```
@Temporal(TemporalType.DATE)
@DateTimeFormat(style = "S-")
private Date runDate;
```

The `@Temporal` annotation tells JPA that this is a date field. Roo did this for you when you defined the field with `field date`. Roo also added the `TemporalType.DATE` parameter when you used the field option `--persistenceType JPA_DATE`. Finally, the `@DateTimeFormat` annotation was generated based on the `--dateFormat SHORT` option, which will help Spring MVC and other user interfaces parse and format the date. We'll discuss this in more detail in chapter 6.

DATABASE CODE

Roo also detected the `@RooJpaActiveRecord` annotation, added as part of the standard `jpa entity` command:

```
@RooJpaActiveRecord
public class Course {
  ...
}
```

In response, Roo generated three files:

- `Course_Roo_Configurable.aj`, which provides basic Spring bean support when creating new instances of the `Course` automatically

- `Course_Roo_Jpa_ActiveRecord.aj`, which provides helpful JPA-based methods such as `findAll()`, `countCourses()`, and `persist()`
- `Course_Roo_Jpa_Entity.aj`, which provides an automatically defined JPA primary key, `id`, and a `version` field to detect changes made to stale data

You'll see later in the chapter how Roo can also generate true JPA repositories, in a more traditional tiered approach to application software development. In that case, a different combination of ITDs are generated.

STRING REPRESENTATIONS OF ENTITIES

A common task in programming involves printing the string representation of data within a given object. Roo provides this feature using the `@RooToString` annotation:

`@RooToString`

This annotation tells the Roo shell to generate a `toString()` method in the `Course_Roo_toString.aj` ITD. This a typical informational method, useful for logging or diagnostic information. Here's the one generated for the `Course` entity:

```
privileged aspect Course_Roo_ToString {

  public String Course.toString() {
    return ReflectionToStringBuilder.toString(
          this, ToStringStyle.SHORT_PREFIX_STYLE);
  }

}
```

Roo 1.2 uses the Apache commons-lang3 library to generate the string using reflection. If you don't like this strategy, you can push-in the `toString()` method and/or remove the annotation, and write your own.

PUTTING IT ALL TOGETHER

Let's take a bird's-eye view of the ITDs as they relate to the `Course` entity. Figure 3.1 shows how the generated ITD files relate to the `Course` class.

Roo provides you convention-over-configuration, but without doing it dynamically. All of these files are viewable, and with Roo's support for push-in refactoring, you can migrate any generated method to the `Course` Java source file itself and override the implementation.

This approach gives the developer visibility of the key details, such as the course fields themselves, and relegates the boilerplate code to the ITDs; an elegant, but accessible approach.

> **BROWSE SOURCE IN ECLIPSE/SPRINGSOURCE TOOL SUITE** If using STS/Eclipse, use CTRL-SHIFT-T (CMD-SHIFT-T on Mac) to bring up the class browser and type in the `Course` class name. You can enter fragments of your class name to look up the entries (even using the capital letters only) to locate a class. And you can use this shortcut (or CTRL/CMD clicking on a class name) to browse the open source frameworks (JPA, Bean Validation, Spring) the entity is based on.

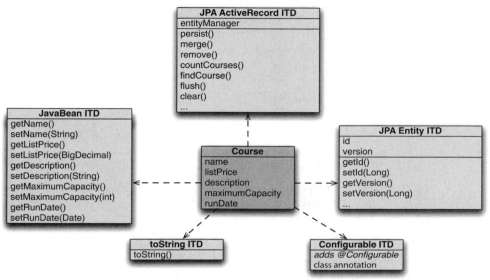

Figure 3.1 Course ITDs

3.2.3 Adding the course type enum

Let's add one more field: an enumerated data type, `courseType`. You'll support seminars, courses for college credit, and continuing education seminars:

```
enum type --class ~.model.CourseTypeEnum
Created SRC_MAIN_JAVA/➥
    org/rooinaction/coursemanager/model/CourseTypeEnum.java

~.modelCourseTypeEnum roo>
```

When you create the `CourseTypeEnum` field, you'll see Roo change the shell's focused type to `~.model.CourseTypeEnum`, so that your next command, `enum constant`, operates on that type.

Now, let's add the fields:

```
enum constant --name SEMINAR
enum constant --name CREDIT
enum constant --name CONTINUING_EDUCATION
```

Browse to the class, which looks like

```
package org.rooinaction.coursemanager.model;

public enum CourseTypeEnum {
    SEMINAR, CREDIT, CONTINUING_EDUCATION
}
```

> **DO I NEED TO USE ROO TO CREATE SIMPLE CLASSES LIKE ENUMS?** No, but for setting up model objects it's a way to script the creation process. You can just build your Java classes normally, even adding Roo annotations, and the Roo shell will keep up, manipulating ITDs as needed.

Now you'll add the field to your entity, using that enum type. First, you'll switch the focus back to your Course,

```
focus --class ~.model.Course
```

and then you'll add the field:

```
field enum --fieldName courseType --type ~.model.CourseTypeEnum ➡
    --enumType STRING
```

Roo adds the following field definition to Course:

```
@Enumerated(EnumType.STRING)
private CourseTypeEnum courseType;
```

> **DO IT BY HAND!**   You can also skip the Roo commands and add this property by hand. Roo will update the Course_Roo_JavaBean.aj ITD to add the appropriate getters and setters.

Now you can use CourseTypeEnum to define values for your courseType field. While not always practical, this is handy for values that don't often expand, such as Boolean selections and static discrete values (active/inactive, normal, warning, error). In coming chapters you'll see how to establish relationships between Course and other tables, and how to use the user interface to expose lists of values to select from.

> **ISN'T ALL OF THIS CODE SLOW?**   No. Remember, all of these ITD files are woven into the class at *compile* time using the Maven AspectJ compiler. As such, the code is compiled into the Course directly. Roo projects have the same runtime dependencies as normal JPA projects, with no Roo runtime libraries.

So far, so good. Now let's actually write some code to use our Course. As you've seen above, the @RooJpaActiveRecord annotation generated all of the JPA code we need. In fact, technically it is already built into the class itself.

3.2.4   *Exercising the Course entity*

In chapter 5, we'll explore how Spring Roo can help you quickly build web applications to interact with your newly created JPA Course entity. But rather than make you wait, and in the spirit of testing early and often, let's use the power of Roo's *Active Record persistence API* to interact with your model.

   Let's write some code in the automatically generated JUnit test class, Course-IntegrationTest.java, to exercise the API. The Roo shell created this class when you specified --testAutomatically on the entity jpa command. Here's the class definition:

```
package org.rooinaction.coursemanager.model;

import org.junit.Test;
import org.springframework.roo.addon.test.RooIntegrationTest;

@RooIntegrationTest(entity = Course.class)
```

```
public class CourseIntegrationTest {

  @Test
  public void testMarkerMethod() {
  }
}
```

Looks pretty empty, doesn't it? Actually, it's backed by an AspectJ ITD, Course-IntegrationTest_Roo_IntegrationTest.aj, which *is* chock-full of tests against the methods in the entity ITDs, thanks to the Roo shell and the @RooIntegrationTest annotation.

Here's a small fragment of generated test ITD code for one of the methods, testPersist():

```
@Test
public void CourseIntegrationTest.testCountCourses() {
   Assert.assertNotNull(
      "Data on demand for 'Course' failed to initialize correctly",
      dod.getRandomCourse());

  long count =
    org.rooinaction.coursemanager.model.Course.countCourses();

  org.junit.Assert.assertTrue(
     "Counter for 'Course' incorrectly reported there were no entries",
     count > 0);
}
```

This method woven into CourseIntegrationTest, checks to see that the test data is initialized, calls the Course entity ITD method countCourses(), and then checks to make sure that courses are returned.

We'll get to how this all works in a moment. First, you should probably run the tests:

- *Maven users*—Issue an mvn test OS shell command from the root of the Roo project, or issue the Roo shell command, perform tests.
- *STS/Eclipse*—Right-click on the CourseIntegrationTest class, select Run As... and then select JUnit Test. The more adventurous among you may want to use Debug As... instead and set breakpoints, tracing through the code. We encourage this!

You'll see a number of tests execute (and hopefully pass). To review the test output, Maven users can browse the project's target/surefire-reports directory and review files for each test, ending in .txt, and STS users can review the JUnit Runner output in STS, illustrated in figure 3.2 in the STS JUnit test results view.

We'll discuss the Roo integration test framework in greater detail in chapter 9. For now, you'll use it to form a base for running your own integration tests, so that you can exercise your newly created Course entity.

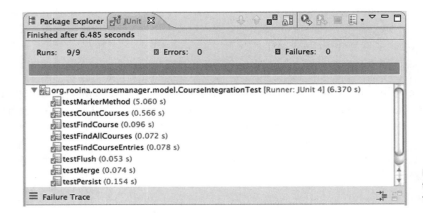

Figure 3.2   Tests from the Roo entity test framework

Roo shell and the `perform` command

Not only can you run your tests without leaving the shell with `perform tests`, but Roo provides some other very useful `perform` commands:

- `perform package`—This packages up your application. In this stage, being only a JAR file, the application will merely be a JAR of all classes and resources, but when deploying to the web, this command will create a WAR file. The packaged JAR will live in the target directory.
- `perform assembly`—If you've configured the Maven assembly plug-in (to distribute a ZIP file for example), this command will perform that action.
- `perform clean`—This will clean the project by removing the target directory.
- `perform command`—Executes a specific Maven lifecycle command or plug-in goal (for example, `perform command --mavenCommand pmd:pmd` will run the PMD code metrics report).

Roo 1.2 also includes the handy ! command to execute any operating system command. For example,

```
roo> ! ls target
```

on Unix-like systems will execute the `ls` command to list files in the target directory.

3.2.5   *Exploring the Course entity API*

You might be thinking that this is all smoke and mirrors. You may also be concerned that the code isn't optimally written. To allay your fears, we'll dig a bit deeper and review the JPA code that Roo generates.

For example, the `testPersist(Course)` and `testFindCourse(Long id)` methods in the `CourseIntegrationTest` ITD exercise the methods `persist(Course)` and `findCourse(Long id)`. But if you look inside `Course.java` you don't see anything but your attributes. You need to find and review the generated code. As we mentioned before, this code is hidden within AspectJ ITD files.

Let's review a JPA entity method. Look at `Course_Roo_Jpa_ActiveRecord.aj`, located in the `org.rooinaction.coursemanager.model` package of the src/main/java directory. Review the `Course.persist()` method, which should be similar to the following code:

```
@Transactional
public void Course.persist() {
  if (this.entityManager == null) this.entityManager = entityManager();
  this.entityManager.persist(this);
}
```

This is a simple method that calls the `persist()` JPA method. JPA developers will note that the `entityManager` is held as a member variable, which is defined in the ITD. This means each instance of a `Course` can persist itself. Although this method looks simple, the key benefit of Roo's entity ITD code is that you're not directly writing JPA code yourself.

> **THE ACTIVE RECORD PATTERN** By default, Roo uses a design pattern for entities called *Active Record*. This pattern was defined by Martin Fowler in the book, *Patterns of Enterprise Application Architecture* (see http://mng.bz/7pG8). In this pattern the entities are treated as first-class objects that contain their own data, and know how to load and persist themselves. You'll see later how they can even implement their own validation rules.

If Spring Roo needs to modify the code for persisting the data in a future version, your calling code doesn't have to change. And although this is code you'd normally have to write yourself, why should you? It is purely mechanical. Another method `findCourse(Long id)`, looks like this:

```
public static Course Course.findCourse(Long id) {
  if (id == null) return null;
  return entityManager().find(Course.class, id);
}
```

This static method fetches a `Course` by the primary key value. Roo works a little harder here; JPA stipulates that if the row isn't found, it returns `null`, but Roo also returns `null` if the primary key passed in is `null` as well.

> **WHAT IS THIS STATIC ENTITYMANAGER() METHOD?** This method constructs an empty `Course` and then returns the Spring-injected `entityManager` instance. If you write static helper methods for your entities, you can just use the `entityManager()` method to fetch a valid entity manager to use for persistence.
>
> How was Roo able to inject a JPA entity manager into a brand-new, developer-created `Course` instance? The secret is that Roo entities are annotated with the `@Configurable` annotation, woven into the definition by the `Roo_Jpa_ActiveRecord.aj` ITD. The `@Configurable` annotation, coupled with Spring's `<context:component-scan />` configuration element, triggers Spring's dependency injection when an instance is instantiated by a constructor, rather than by Spring itself.

How many times do you think you've written methods like that by hand? Roo automatically defines it for you, assuming you'll likely need to use it in the future. And it does it the same way for all Roo entities, by default.

3.2.6 *Roo's Active Record entity methods*

Let's review the complete list of Active Record–driven JPA entity methods (as of Roo 1.2) provided in your sample `Course_Roo_Entity.aj` ITD in table 3.2.

Table 3.2 Some Spring Roo entity methods (example uses `Course` as the entity)

Method	Usage	Comments
`countCourses()`	Counts the number of rows in the table that backs the `Course` entity.	Issues a `select count(o) from Course o` query and returns the result.
`findAllCourses()`	Queries the entire table and returns as a list.	Be careful not to use this method against tables with many rows.
`findCourse(Long id)`	Returns a single `Course` by primary key `id`.	If not found, returns `null`.
`findCourseEntries (int firstResult, int maxResults)`	Returns a range of courses, starting with the row position (not primary key value) of `firstResult`, for `maxResults` rows.	If no rows found, returns an empty list. Used to paginate results in Roo web applications by default.
`flush()`	Forces the persistence provider to issue any SQL statements to update data changed within the persistence context. Note, this includes *any* entities, not just `Course`.	May throw validation exceptions if any modified entities have not yet been flushed.
`clear()`	Resets the persistence context and clears any cached entity rows.	Useful for testing purposes. Also useful in conditions where you want to cancel any potential changes that may have been made in the cache before it is flushed.
`merge()`	Updates the data in the persistence context using data provided in the entity.	The merge operation loads data from the database matching the primary key of the detached entity. It then replaces any data in the loaded entity with data from the detached class. Keep in mind that it overwrites data from the data in the database that may have changed since the detached instance was loaded.
`persist()`	Marks an entity as ready to persist in the persistence context.	May throw validation exceptions if the data scheduled is persisted at the time of this call (see section 3.3).
`remove()`	Marks a course for removal in the persistence context.	May cause errors if data constraints are violated. This may not happen when calling this method, as JPA may remove at flush time.
`entityManager()`	Provides access to the JPA entity manager.	You may use this API to provide your own JPA methods in the `Course.java` source code file.

The Roo product developers may add more methods in the future. You'll get them automatically when you upgrade to the newest version of Roo by running the new Roo shell against your existing project.

Other ITDs provide additional generated code. For example, the `Course_Roo _Jpa_Entity.aj` ITD contains the definition of the primary key and version fields, as well as their getters and setters. You should review all Roo ITDs and become familiar with their APIs, since you can use them directly in code that accesses these classes.

REPOSITORIES AND SERVICES—TRADITIONAL SPRING DEVELOPMENT IN ROO? If you're not enamored of the Active Record pattern, you don't have to work this way. More advanced users can take advantage of Roo 1.2's repository and service features. We'll discuss using Spring-based JPA repositories in section 3.5, and transactional Spring services in chapter 4.

Now let's write some code against the entity API, using Roo's support for JUnit testing.

3.2.7 Using the entity API

Writing code against the Roo entity API is a cinch. Beyond the automatically generated calls you'll see when you wire up a Roo web application in chapter 5, you can get started coding right away using JUnit.

Conceptually, working with Roo entities is a straightforward process. For example, to get a list of all `Course` objects in a method, you'd simply have to write

```
List<Course> courses = Course.findAllCourses();
```

To load a `Course` by ID, modify the class capacity, and update it, you could do this:

```
Course course = Course.findCourse(1L);
course.setMaximumCapacity(500);
course.merge();
```

To create a new `Course`, you only need to construct it, set the fields, and call `persist()`:

```
Course course = new Course();
course.setName("Stand-up Comedy");
course.setMaximumCapacity(8);
course.setDescription("It'll make you laugh...");
c.setCourseType(CourseTypeEnum.CONTINUING_EDUCATION);
c.persist();
```

To delete the `Course` you've built, you just call the `remove()` method:

```
c.remove();
```

By now, you should see where we're going. Roo provides a useful API for the CRUD-based work you usually end up doing in most data-driven applications.

3.2.8 Writing a JUnit Roo entity test

Let's try adding a course and retrieving it from the database using your pregenerated JUnit test. Add the following method to the `CourseIntegrationTest.java` class as shown here (use your IDE's Fix Imports feature to discover the `org.junit.Assert` static import as well as the `org.springframework.transaction.annotation` `.Transactional` annotation):

Listing 3.2   Adding and fetching a `Course`

```
@Test
@Transactional
public void addAndFetchCourse() {
    Course c = new Course();
    c.setCourseType(CourseTypeEnum.CONTINUING_EDUCATION);
    c.setName("Stand-up Comedy");
     c.setDescription(
       "You'll laugh, you'll cry, it will become a part of you.");
    c.setMaximumCapacity(10);
    c.persist();

    c.flush();
     c.clear();

    Assert.assertNotNull(c.getId());

    Course c2 = Course.findCourse(c.getId());
     Assert.assertNotNull(c2);
    Assert.assertEquals(c.getName(), c2.getName());
    Assert.assertEquals(c2.getDescription(), c.getDescription());
    Assert.assertEquals(
      c.getMaximumCapacity(), c2.getMaximumCapacity());
    Assert.assertEquals(c.getCourseType(), c2.getCourseType());
}
```

- Save Course
- ❶ Flush/ Clear JPA
- Verify PK
- Load Course

In the preceding sample, you create a new `Course`, set the fields to valid values, and persist it to the database. You flush and clear your persistence context ❶, which executes the SQL `INSERT` statement to persist the data to the database and clears the cached entity. This detaches the `Course` instance, `c`, but at the same time fills in the primary key value in the `id` field.

Finally, you query for the same data using the `Course.findCourse(Long id)` method, and make sure that it was saved appropriately using assertions to check the field values. Not too shabby for just a few lines of code.

Roo marks the test class as `@Transactional` (which you can find in the Test ITD), so that the unit tests automatically roll back any changes. You can test this code again and again without worrying about adding duplicate data rows. This is a Spring Framework test best practice, automatically implemented by Roo.

Now that you've seen some of the power of Roo for creating entities, and some of the code generated by the tool, let's discuss how to add validation logic to your entity using the Bean Validation Framework.

3.3   *Validating Courses with Bean Validation*

Validation is a difficult topic for any application architecture. You may ask yourself a bevy of questions, such as these:

- Where do I perform validation—at the web layer, in the middle tier, or in my database?
- How do I validate? Should I use a validation rules engine, scripted code, data-driven rules, or annotations?
- How will my errors be returned? Should I localize the messages?

There are many APIs available to implement validation rules. Spring MVC has it's own validation API, but it's MVC-based, and doesn't necessarily suit itself to embedding rules within the entities. You want to do this, as it helps you to encapsulate the behavior of validation within the entity tier. A more object-driven approach is needed. Enter the Bean Validation API.

The Bean Validation API is a recent standard. Created by the Java EE Expert Group, it was developed to address the lack of a standard validation API on the Java EE platform. This API uses Java annotations to define specific rules, which are attached to attributes of a Java bean. Some validations are built in to the framework, such as `@Not-Null`, `@Null`, `@Min`, `@Max`, `@Past`, `@Future`, `@Pattern`, and `@Size`. You can also define your own classes for validation purposes, and register custom validation methods using `@AssertTrue` or `@AssertFalse`.

3.3.1 Validating Courses

Spring Roo supports automatic validation of Roo entities, if annotated with Bean Validation annotations. Roo entities are automatically validated when a `persist` or `merge` method call is executed. Any errors will result in the throw of a `Constraint-ViolationException`, which contains all `ConstraintViolation` instances for errors encountered during the validation process.

Let's redefine the `Course` entity fields. With the Roo shell already fired up, open up a source code editor and delete all of the field definitions in the `Course` entity. Then add them back in, this time with Bean Validations:

```
field string --fieldName name --sizeMin 1 --sizeMax 60 ➥
    --column course_name
field string --fieldName description --notNull --sizeMax 1000
field number --fieldName listPrice --type java.math.BigDecimal ➥
    --decimalMin 0.0 --decimalMax 99999.99 ➥
    --digitsFraction 2 --digitsInteger 5 --notNull
field number --fieldName maximumCapacity --type java.lang.Integer➥
    --min 1 --max 9999➥
    --notNull --column max_capacity
field date --fieldName runDate --type java.util.Date ➥
    --dateTimeFormatPattern MM/dd/yyyy
field enum --fieldName courseType --type ~.model.CourseTypeEnum ➥
    --enumType STRING --notNull
```

You've just added back in your fields, but this time you set some constraints, as outlined in table 3.3.

Table 3.3 Course entity constraints

Field	Constraint	Annotation	Notes
name	--notNull --sizeMin 1 --sizeMax 60	@NotNull @Size(min = 1, max = 60)	Sets the minimum and maximum characters of text.
description	--notNull --sizeMax 1000	@NotNull @Size(max = 1000)	Must contain a value, and cannot exceed 1000 characters. Note: an empty or all-spaces string is still a value.
listPrice	--notNull --decimalMin 0.0 --decimalMax 9999.99 --digitsFraction 2 --digitsInteger 5	@NotNull @DecimalMin("0.0") @DecimalMax("99999.99") @Digits(integer = 5, fraction = 2)	Use --decimalMin and --decimalMax annotations to define validation constraints, and --digitsInteger and --digitsFraction to provide JPA column data settings.
maximumCapacity	--notNull --min 1 --max 9999	@NotNull @Min(1L) @Max(9999L)	Note this is a numeric range, whereas sizeMin/sizeMax are text-based.
courseType	--notNull	@NotNull	Must contain a value. Values are defined by the enum and can only be set as Enum values.

And now the entity contains Bean Validation annotations, as shown next.

Listing 3.3 Course entity fields—with Bean Validation annotations

```
@Column(name = "course_name")
@Size(min = 1, max = 60)
private String name;

@NotNull
@Size(max = 1000)
private String description;

@NotNull
@DecimalMin("0.0")
@DecimalMax("99999.99")
@Digits(integer = 5, fraction = 2)
private BigDecimal listPrice;

@NotNull
@Column(name = "max_capacity")
@Min(1L)
```

```
@Max(9999L)
private Integer maximumCapacity;

@Temporal(TemporalType.TIMESTAMP)
@DateTimeFormat(pattern = "MM/dd/yyyy")
private Date runDate;

@NotNull
@Enumerated(EnumType.STRING)
private CourseTypeEnum courseType;
```

Each option in the Roo shell turns into a similar annotation in the Java source code. From the @NotNull annotation to force an entered value, to @Min and @Max for the numeric range in maximumCapacity, to @Size to define a String length range for name and description, the Roo command options are merely ways to get Roo to generate the appropriate Bean Validation annotations. If you forget to set them during creation, you can edit the source file and add them later.

3.3.2 *Testing Course validations*

To test failure cases, you can write some tests in your CourseIntegrationTest class. First, you'll build a simple test to prove that you're running validations. You'll just create a test that defines a Course, and not set any field values, which should trigger the @NotNull validations:

```
@Test(expected = ConstraintViolationException.class)
public void testInvalidCourse() {
    Course c = new Course();
    c.persist();
}
```

If you're following along, use STS and choose to automatically fix/optimize imports with CTRL-SHIFT-O. When resolving the exception class, choose the one from the javax.validation package over the Hibernate one.

The test should throw a ConstraintViolationException, which will contain a series of ConstraintViolation instances, one for each error. In the preceding test, the fact that the test threw this exception causes the test to pass.

For a more detailed look at the errors returned by Bean Validation, look at the more detailed test in the following listing.

Listing 3.4 Testing Course violations

```
@Test
public void testSpecificException() {
    Course c = new Course();
    c.setCourseType(CourseTypeEnum.CONTINUING_EDUCATION);
    c.setMaximumCapacity(10);
    c.setRunDate(new Date());
    c.setName(null);
     c.setDescription(null);                              ❶ Invalid
    try {                                                    values
        c.persist();
```

```
    } catch (ConstraintViolationException cve) {              Should
       Assert.assertEquals(2,                                 have two
          cve.getConstraintViolations().size());
       Iterator<ConstraintViolation<?>> it =                  ❷ Review
          cve.getConstraintViolations().iterator();              violations
       while (it.hasNext()) {
          ConstraintViolation<?> constraintViolation = it.next();
          ConstraintDescriptor<?> descriptor =
             constraintViolation.getConstraintDescriptor();
          Annotation annotation = descriptor.getAnnotation();
          if (!(annotation.annotationType()
                .getName().equals(                             ❸ Is
                   "javax.validation.constraints.NotNull"))) {    @NotNull?
             Assert.fail(
                "invalid error raised.  Should be 'not null'");
          }
       }
       return;
    } catch (Exception e) {
       Assert.fail("Unexpected exception thrown " + e.getMessage());
       return;
    }

    Assert.fail("Exception not thrown.");
}
```

In the example, you trigger the validation exception by passing nulls to the name and description fields ❶ and attempting to persist the data. The Bean Validation throws a ConstraintViolationException, and the framework loads each violation into that exception as an implementation of the ConstraintViolation interface, held in the constraintViolations property.

You create an iterator ❷ and fetch each ConstraintViolation, which contains a constraintDescriptor member detailing the error. You then test the annotation property of the descriptor, checking the annotation type name. If the name of the annotation isn't the class name of your annotation type, in this case javax .validation.NotNull ❸, then the test fails.

A list of the available attributes of the ConstraintViolation is defined in table 3.4.

Table 3.4   ConstraintViolation attributes

Field	Usage
invalidValue	The value entered which caused the validation error. For @NotNull validations, this field will be null.
message	The interpolated message (after substituting parameter values).
messageTemplate	The non-interpolated message (equal to the value specified in the annotation itself).

Table 3.4   ConstraintViolation attributes *(continued)*

Field	Usage
rootBean	The top-level bean that triggered violation errors. In the case of a hierarchy of JPA entities, such as a department and all employees within, this will be the top-level class, Department.
leafBean	The bean that caused the violation, or contained the property that caused the violation.
propertyPath	The path of properties leading to the value, from the rootBean.
constraintDescriptor	A class representing details about the annotation that caused the violation.

As you'll see in chapter 5, Roo can configure and generate a web application that includes CRUD operations for your entities automatically. It generates automatic error handling for form elements, populating the page with messages when these Bean Validation errors occur. Further, Roo generates client-side validations based on these annotations, which will appear whenever a user attempts to enter an invalid value.

3.3.3   *Bean Validation annotations*

There are a number of validation annotations available in the javax.validation package. In addition, Hibernate Validator, the reference implementation, includes several of its own in the org.hibernate.constraints package.

The validations in table 3.5 are built into the Bean Validation API.

Table 3.5   Built-in Bean Validation annotations

Annotation (javax.validation)	Datatypes supported	Description
@AssertTrue, @AssertFalse	boolean and Boolean	Item must evaluate to true/True or false/False.
@DecimalMin and @DecimalMax	BigDecimal, BigInteger, String, byte, short, int, long, and wrappers	Define a lower and upper boundary for the range of a number. Support datatypes such as BigDecimal, BigInteger, String, byte, short, int, long, and the wrapper types.
@Digits	BigDecimal, BigInteger, String, byte, short, int, long, and wrappers	Defines the integer and fractional digits of a given fixed-point decimal or scalar number.
@Future, @Past	java.util.Date or java.util.Calendar	Ensure the date is either later than or before the current system date at the time of validation.
@NotNull	Any type	Ensures the element is not null.
@Null	Any type	Ensures the element is null.

Table 3.5   Built-in Bean Validation annotations *(continued)*

Annotation (javax.validation)	Datatypes supported	Description
@Pattern	String	Validates against a regular expression pattern.
@Size	String, Map, Collection, Array	Validates against a minimum/maximum size. For String, compares string length. For Array, Map, and Collections, validates against number of elements.

Some of these validations may not make sense on the surface—why would you want to define a @Null validation if it makes the field unsettable? That's because in the specification, the Bean Validation Framework supports the concept of validation groups. In the current release of Roo, the only validation group supported is Default, so unless Roo entities begin to support validations with multiple groups, this particular validation won't really be easily used.

So far we've looked at implementing validations, and we've seen how Spring Roo automatically executes validation checks before saving an entity. Now let's take a look at how you can create your own validator annotations.

3.3.4   *Using the @AssertTrue annotation*

The Bean Validation API provides an @AssertTrue annotation that can make expressing one-off rules like the one above quite easy. Instead of that three-step process we discussed earlier, you can just build a Boolean method and annotate it with the @AssertTrue annotation. If the method returns true, the entity is valid. If not, it fails validation.

Here's the same validation logic, expressed with an @AssertTrue annotated method within the Course entity:

```
public class Course {
  ...

  @NotNull
  @DecimalMin("0.0")
  @DecimalMax("99999.00")
  @Digits(integer = 5, fraction = 2)
  private BigDecimal listPrice;

  ...

  @AssertTrue(message =
    "Price is invalid. No fractional values allowed.")
  public boolean isPriceValid() {
    if (listPrice == null) return true;
    BigDecimal remainder = listPrice.remainder(new BigDecimal("1.0"));
    return remainder.compareTo(new BigDecimal("0")) == 0;
              .compareTo(new BigDecimal("0.0")) == 0;
  }
  ...
}
```

Believe it or not, that's it. You can also interrogate any field in the entity. This is the easiest way to build multifield and one-off validations. But there are several rules you must adhere to:

- The method must have no arguments and return a Boolean value. It can have any visibility level, including `private`.
- The method must have a standard JavaBeans name compatible with a Boolean getter. Specifically, the method name must start with `get` or `is`, as in `get-Validity()` or `isValid()`.
- The `@AssertTrue` annotation must provide an error message (which can be localized, as you'll see in chapter 5).

TIP If you define this validation you may have to modify any automatically generated DataOnDemand tests to provide a valid value for your price. Push in the `setPrice` method in the `CourseDataOnDemand_Roo_DataOnDemand.aj` file and set a valid, nonfractional price. The rest of the samples assume this has been done.

You can test this method with the same test suite; it has the same effect. Run your `CourseIntegrationTest` suite to make sure you're validating appropriately. As you can see, this mechanism is much easier to deal with than defining your own Bean Validation annotations and validators. But it may cause other tests to fail, because the Roo test framework can't introspect the valid values of any method marked with `@AssertTrue`.[1]

> ### Other validation options
>
> There are still other ways to trigger validation in any Spring project. For example, you could either implement your own custom bean validators, or use Spring's programmatic `Validator` framework.
>
> To write your own bean validators in JSR-303 style, you define an annotation to represent your validation rule, attach it to a class that extends `javax.validation.ConstraintValidator`, and implement the `isValid()` and `initialize()` methods.
>
> We'll briefly discuss the Spring MVC validation framework in chapter 5.

3.3.5 Bean Validation in review

As you've just seen, if you need to validate your beans before persisting them, you can use the Bean Validation Framework. Try to stick to a few simple rules:

---

[1] To fix this, push-in refactor the `getNewTransientCourse(int index)` method of `CourseDataOnDemand _RooDataOnDemand.aj`, and return a valid value for the fields you're using for the assertion.

- *Validation by composition*—When building validation for a particular bean, go ahead and stack validators on a field. If you'd like to compose your own grouped validation, just build a validation annotation that's comprised of the validators you need. You can get a lot done by using a combination of `@NotNull`, `@Size`, and `@Pattern`, for example.

- *Be sparing in your processing power*—Just because you can call a stored procedure behind a service to validate an entry in that list, doesn't mean that you should. Realize that if you're saving a collection of objects, this validation will be called on *each* item within the list, thus causing many calls to the same procedure.

- *Use `@AssertTrue` for multicolumn checks*—A quick way to get your complex, logic-based validation to work is to build a Boolean test method within your entity, annotating it with `@AssertTrue`. Within this method you have access to other fields in the entity.

- *Use your own custom validations sparingly*—When you have a cross-cutting validation rule, such as a business-driven primary key, complex part number, or other complex validation, you can build your own validators and annotations. Use this technique sparingly because these are more complex to build, and spread out your validation away from the entities themselves.

MORE VALIDATION OPTIONS   If you are familiar with Spring MVC's programmatic validation routines, you can use those in a Roo web application as well. See how to build and apply Spring validators in the "Spring Framework Reference," sections 5.2, "Validation using Spring's Validation Interface," and 5.7.4.2, "Configuring a Validator for use by Spring MVC" at http://mng.bz/B9G3.

Now that you've seen how to define well-validated entities with the Bean Validation framework, let's switch gears a bit and discuss how to enable users of your entities to locate entities that they've created, using the `finder` Roo shell command.

3.4   *Searching with finders*

Searching for data in a database-centric application generally involves writing a lot of queries: fetching a list of items, pulling back a single item by a particular key, joining data together from various tables. In pre-ORM days, people wrote a lot of SQL to do this task. But JPA aims to simplify the query process by providing the JPA-QL (JPA Query Language) API.

This API treats the database as an object graph, but still allows you to express queries in a SQL-like language. Here's an example query, which fetches all `Courses` within a range of priorities:

```
Query q = entityManager.createQuery(
            "SELECT course FROM Course AS course " +
            "WHERE course.maximumCapacity BETWEEN :min AND :max",
            Course.class);
q.setParameter("min", 2);
q.setParameter("max", 3);
List<Course> results = q.getResultList();
```

There are some key differences in the way regular SQL and JPA-QL operate:

- SQL references *tables*, but JPA-QL references *entities*. Use the name of the entity in the query and the mapped table will be substituted at query time.

- JPA-QL can dig deep into related entity graphs. For example, query patterns such as `course.catalog.name = "Fall Catalog"` are completely acceptable. For collections, developers can define `JOIN` statements to query between associations. JPA-QL will actually write out the proper SQL joins or queries to pull the data from the related tables.

- Since JPA-QL runs on top of JPA, it manages all connection information for the developer through the persistence context. Developers need not concern themselves with setting up and tearing down connections.

Now you can write your own JPA-QL queries and place them in methods on an entity or service bean object. Let's look at how easy it is to have Roo write them for you.

3.4.1 A sample Roo finder

Roo finders provide methods to search your entities, which are attached to the entities automatically like the JPA methods defined in the beginning of this chapter. You create them with the Roo shell using the `finder` command. There are generally two steps involved in generating a finder: First, you get a list of all of the methods that Roo can generate for your entity. Next, you tell Roo to generate a finder with a specific name and, using that name, the Roo shell will write an ITD and weave it into the entity for you.

CREATING A FINDER

Let's take a look at an example that implements the search we just discussed, one that searches the `name` field in your `Course` object. First you'll ask Roo for a list of finders that you can generate:

```
roo> focus ~.model.Course
~.model.Course roo> finder list --filter name
findCoursesByNameEquals(String name)
findCoursesByNameIsNotNull()
findCoursesByNameIsNull()
findCoursesByNameLike(String name)
findCoursesByNameNotEquals(String name)
 ~.model.Course roo>
```

This is simply a mechanical list of all finders Roo can generate for you, filtering on the fields that contain the search term name. Let's use `finder add` to create a method that uses the SQL LIKE keyword, comparing the value passed to the `name` field, `findCoursesByNameLike`:

```
~.model.Course roo> finder add --finderName findCoursesByNameLike
Updated SRC_MAIN_JAVA/org/rooina/coursemanager/model/Course.java
Created SRC_MAIN_JAVA/[...]/Course_Roo_Finder.aj
```

Spring Roo adds a parameter to the @RooJpaActiveRecord annotation, finders, that tells the Roo shell to generate a finder:

```
@RooJpaActiveRecord(finders = { "findCoursesByNameLike" })
```

The shell then generates the finder and places it in Course_Roo_Finder.aj, where it's immediately mixed into the Course object, as Course.findCoursesByNameLike.

REVIEWING THE FINDER CODE

Let's take a look at the code that the Roo finder add method set up.

Listing 3.5   The Course_Roo_Finder.aj ITD

```
package org.rooinaction.coursemanager.model;

import java.lang.String;
import javax.persistence.EntityManager;
import javax.persistence.TypedQuery;
import org.rooinaction.coursemanager.model.Course;

privileged aspect Course_Roo_Finder {
  public static TypedQuery<Course>
                 Course.findCoursesByNameLike(String name) {
    if (name == null || name.length() == 0)
       throw new IllegalArgumentException(
                  "The name argument is required");
    name = name.replace('*', '%');
    if (name.charAt(0) != '%') {
      name = "%" + name;
    }
    if (name.charAt(name.length() -1) != '%') {
        name = name + "%";
    }
    EntityManager em = Course.entityManager();
    TypedQuery<Course> q = em.createQuery(
         "SELECT Course FROM Course AS course
          WHERE LOWER(course.name) LIKE LOWER(:name)", Course.class);
    q.setParameter("name", name);
    return q;
  }
}
```

The finder rejects null or empty parameters, allows using * or % at the end of the search string, and prefixes % to the beginning. This makes the like command search anywhere in the name field. Instead of writing the JPA-QL queries yourself, Roo can generate them for you, saving you a significant amount of activity. But what about multifield queries?

TESTING THE FINDER

Here's the test that exercises the finder, which we've added to CourseIntegration-Tests:

```
@Test
public void testFindByNameFinder() {
```

```
Course c = new Course();
c.setName("Basket Weaving");
c.setCourseType(CourseTypeEnum.SEMINAR);
c.setDescription("Weaving baskets is an essential skill.");
c.setMaximumCapacity(100);
c.setRunDate(new Date());
c.setListPrice(new BigDecimal("100"));
c.persist();

c.flush();
c.entityManager().clear();

List<Course> courses =
    c.findCoursesByNameLike("Bas").getResultList();

Assert.assertEquals(1, courses.size());

}
```

Most of that test method involved test setup, but in the end it resulted in a one-line call to your pregenerated finder. Note the fact that after you call the finder, you chain a call to the `QuerygetResultList()` method; the finder doesn't know whether you want a single result or a list, so it lets you choose.

3.4.2 *Multifield finder queries*

Roo makes it easy to build multifield queries. The `finder` command includes the `--depth` option, which lets you ask for combinations of finders for several fields at the same time. Keep in mind that the output begins to get a bit voluminous after a depth of two, or with entities that have a large number of attributes. You can use the `--filter` method to list the attributes you wish to see, separated by commas, to limit the output. Let's see the finders Roo can generate for a combination of both the `courseType` and `runDate` fields:

```
~.model.Course roo> finder list --depth 2 --filter courseType,runDate
```

```
findCoursesByCourseTypeAndRunDate(CourseTypeEnum courseType, Date runDate)
findCoursesByCourseTypeAndRunDateBetween(CourseTypeEnum courseType,
    Date minRunDate, Date maxRunDate)
findCoursesByCourseTypeAndRunDateEquals(...)
findCoursesByCourseTypeAndRunDateGreaterThan(...)
findCoursesByCourseTypeAndRunDateGreaterThanEquals(...)
...
```

The one you're interested in is `findCoursesByCourseTypeAndRunDateBetween`, which finds any course of a particular `CourseTypeEnum` within an offer date range. To install that finder, issue the following command:

```
~.model.Course roo> finder add --finderName ➥
    findCoursesByCourseTypeAndRunDateBetween
Updated SRC_MAIN_JAVA/org/rooina/coursemanager/model/Course.java
Updated SRC_MAIN_JAVA/[...]/model/Course_Roo_Finder.aj
```

This command results in the following additional finder method in `Course_Roo_Finder.aj`:

```
public static TypedQuery<Course> Course.➥
      findCoursesByCourseTypeAndRunDateBetween(
          CourseTypeEnum courseType,
          Date minRunDate,
          Date maxRunDate) {
  if (courseType == null)
    throw new IllegalArgumentException("courseType is required");
  if (minRunDate == null)
    throw new IllegalArgumentException("minRunDate is required");
  if (maxRunDate == null)
    throw new IllegalArgumentException("maxRunDate is required");
  EntityManager em = Course.entityManager();
  TypedQuery<Course> q = em.createQuery(
     "SELECT Course FROM Course AS course
      WHERE course.courseType = :courseType AND
            course.runDate BETWEEN :minRunDate AND :maxRunDate",
            Course.class);
  q.setParameter("courseType", courseType);
  q.setParameter("minRunDate", minRunDate);
  q.setParameter("maxRunDate", maxRunDate);
  return q;
}
```

Now finding all courses of a particular type, within a particular date range, is as simple as calling the static `Course` method `findCoursesByCourseTypeAndRunDateBetween`, passing three parameters, the `CourseType` enum value, and a minimum and maximum date to establish the search range.

3.4.3   *More complex finders*

Finders can make simple queries relatively easy to build. The `finder list` command is simply there to make your job easier by showing you potential combinations. But if you happen to understand the pattern, you can issue finder commands to build queries like those in table 3.6.

You can even tie three or four fields together, if you know the pattern. In this way, you can save yourself from having to write boilerplate JPA query code. Since finders are added to the entity along with the persistence code and validation rules, they help you to contain your complex data query logic within the entities themselves.

Table 3.6   Sample finder query patterns

Pattern	Query result
ByRunDateGreaterThan (Date)	course.runDate > :runDate
ByDescriptionLike	LOWER(course.description) like LOWER(:description)
ByDescriptionIsNotNull	course.description IS NOT NULL
ByDescriptionIsNullAndCourseTypeEquals	course.description IS NULL and course.courseType = :courseType

The finder feature is currently limited to defining finders on fields within the same entity. But using the finder to generate the bulk of your code, you can always use *push-in refactoring* to bring the code into the entity itself, and then modify it to suit your needs. You could also use more advanced features of JPA, such as querying by example, which are beyond the scope of this book.

3.5　*Leaving Active Record—JPA repositories*

What if you don't like the approach of encapsulating your JPA code within each entity? Perhaps you have a more complex model, one where the boundaries for queries and transactions is a bit more blurred, and some of the code fits best manipulating or querying more than one entity at a time? If this is your situation, or if you prefer a layered approach that separates the data logic from your entity classes, you can tell Roo to build JPA repositories for you.

Roo repositories are built using the relatively new Spring Data API. Spring Data provides support for dynamically generated proxy classes for a given entity, and those classes handle all of the methods you're used to coding by hand (or using in the Active Record entities).

It is quite easy to generate a repository. Let's build a repository to back the Course entity:

```
repository jpa --interface ~.db.CourseRepository ➥
    --entity ~.model.Course
```

This command generates a repository class:

```
package org.rooinaction.coursemanager.db;

import org.rooinaction.rooinaction.coursemanager.model.Course;
import org.springframework.roo.addon.layers.repository➥
        .jpa.RooJpaRepository;

@RooJpaRepository(domainType = Course.class)
public interface CourseRepository {
}
```

There are no methods defined in this interface; it exists merely as a holding place for the @RooJpaRepository annotation. The interface *is* backed by an ITD. In this case, the file is named CourseRepository_Roo_Repository.aj:

```
package org.rooinaction.rooinaction.coursemanager.db;

import java.lang.Long;
import org.rooinaction.rooinaction.coursemanager.model.Course;
import org.springframework.data.jpa.repository.JpaRepository;
import org.springframework.data.jpa.repository.JpaSpecificationExecutor;
import org.springframework.stereotype.Repository;

privileged aspect CourseRepository_Roo_Jpa_Repository {

    declare parents: CourseRepository ➥
      extends JpaRepository<Course, Long>;
```

```
declare parents: CourseRepository ➟
    extends JpaSpecificationExecutor<Course>;

declare @type: CourseRepository: @Repository;

}
```

These two files may be a bit baffling to you if you're used to coding your own repositories. Roo uses the typical Spring pattern of annotating the repository with @Repository, which marks it as a Spring bean and provides exception translation, but it also extends it with two additional interfaces—JpaRepository and JpaSpecificationExecutor. Let's take a look at each one, starting with JpaRepository.

3.5.1 The JpaRepository API

Look at the methods implemented by the JpaRepository class:

```
java.util.List<T> findAll();
java.util.List<T> findAll(org.springframework.data.domain.Sort sort);
java.util.List<T> save(java.lang.Iterable<? extends T> iterable);
void flush();
T saveAndFlush(T t);
void deleteInBatch(java.lang.Iterable<T> tIterable);
```

These are all methods to search, save, and remove data from the entity. Note that the <T> designation is a Java generic type. Since the CourseRepository is defined as implementing JpaRepository<Course, Long>, all of the generic <T> methods will take Course entities as arguments, and expect a Long-based primary key.

Let's test this API using a JUnit test. Add the following test to your CourseIntegrationTest class:

```
@Test
@Transactional
public void addAndFetchCourseViaRepo() {
  Course c = new Course();
  c.setCourseType(CourseTypeEnum.CONTINUING_EDUCATION);
  c.setName("Stand-up Comedy");
  c.setDescription(
    "You'll laugh, you'll cry, it will become a part of you.");
  c.setMaximumCapacity(10);

  courseRepository.saveAndFlush(c);
  c.clear();

  Assert.assertNotNull(c.getId());

  Course c2 = courseRepository.findOne(c.getId());
  Assert.assertNotNull(c2);
  Assert.assertEquals(c.getName(), c2.getName());
  Assert.assertEquals(c2.getDescription(), c.getDescription());
  Assert.assertEquals(
    c.getMaximumCapacity(), c2.getMaximumCapacity());
  Assert.assertEquals(c.getCourseType(), c2.getCourseType());
}
```

So now you can use a Roo repository to implement your JPA code. The methods save-AndFlush() and getOne(Long) are provided dynamically at runtime via the Spring Data API.

3.5.2 Queries with JpaSpecificationImplementor

But wait, there are more features to explore here. What does the second interface, JpaSpecificationImplementor, provide?

```
T findOne(Specification<T> tSpecification);
List<T> findAll(Specification<T> tSpecification
Page<T> findAll(Specification<T> tSpecification, Pageable pageable);
List<T> findAll(Specification<T> tSpecification, Sort sort);
long count(Specification<T> tSpecification);
```

This interface provides access to the Spring Data features for providing criteria-based query and paging support. The methods accept a Specification class, which is used to define the search criteria to pass to the repository to find, sort, and page through a list of entities, or fetch a single entity. For example, to provide a predicate that expects a non-null run date:

```
public class CourseSpecifications {

  public static Specification<Course> hasRunDate() {

    return new Specification<Course>() {
      @Override
      public Predicate toPredicate(
        Root<Course> root,                                    Exposes
         CriteriaQuery<?> query,                              field types
         CriteriaBuilder cb) {
        return cb.isNotNull(                                  Literate API
          root.get("runDate"));
      }
    };
  }
}
```

The toPredicate() method takes a Root<Course>, which provides access to the types in the JPA entity, a JPA CriteriaQuery, which is built by Spring and passed into the method automatically at runtime to be executed, and a CriteriaBuilder, which allows you to add predicates to the query using English language–like calls, such as cb.isNotNull above.

To use the specification, you just need to call the static CourseSpecifications .hasRunDate() method, and pass it to the appropriate finder:

```
List<Course> courses = courseRepository.findAll(
                    CourseSpecifications.hasRunDate());
```

This approach is similar to writing criteria-based JPA queries, but is in marked contrast to Roo finders, which are attached normally to Active Record entities annotated with @RooJpaActiveRecord.

3.5.3   *Annotation-driven queries with @Query*

One of the most powerful features of the Spring Data JPA API is providing annotation-driven queries. Since Spring Data builds the implementation class at runtime, you can define methods in your interface that Roo can use to implement custom queries and even updates.

Let's look at an example method. You can define a query method in your Course-Repository interface to find all student registrations for a given student and date range (we define the Registration entity in chapter 4, but this code shows you more complex queries):

```
@Query("select distinct r from Registration as r " +
    "where r.student.id = :studentId " +
    "and r.offering.offerDate between :start and :end")

@Transactional(readOnly = true)
List<Registration> findStudentRegistrationForOfferingsInDateRange(
        @Param("studentId") long studentId,
        @Param("start") Date start,
        @Param("end") Date end);
```

Roo implements the code for this method at runtime, based on the Spring Data @Query annotation. All parameters in the example above are defined using the @Param annotation, and the type returned is defined as the return type of the method, List<Registration>. Note that you've also passed the @Transactional annotation, and marked the query as a read-only transaction.

You can perform updates using the @Query method as well, as long as you mark the method as @Modifying:

```
@Query("update Registration r set attended = :attended " +
        "where r.student.id = :studentId")
@Modifying
@Transactional
void updateAttendance(
        @Param("studentId") long studentId,
        @Param("attended") boolean attended);
```

In this example, you've marked your interface method with @Modifying to signify that you're expecting a data manipulation statement, not just a simple SELECT statement. You also define your method with @Transactional, so that it's wrapped with a read/write transaction.

Spring Roo builds the implementation classes automatically, based on a Spring configuration file in META-INF/spring named applicationContext-jpa.xml. This file contains the Spring Data XML configuration element, <repositories/>, which scans for and mounts interface-driven repositories:

```
<repositories base-package="org.rooinaction.coursemanager" />
```

The package defined in this Spring XML configuration element is your root project package. You can now add repositories in whatever subpackage makes sense. You don't have to use Roo to generate your Spring Data classes either, so if you're already a Spring Data or JPA expert, just code away!

For more about the Spring Data JPA API, visit the project website at http:// mng.bz/63xp.

3.5.4 *Repository wrap-up*

As you've seen, you can use repositories in a more traditional Spring layered application instead of applying the Active Record pattern. Roo even rewrites your automated entity integration tests automatically, when it detects that you've added a repository for a given entity. You can always fall back to the typical interface-and-implementation JPA repository where necessary.

As an added bonus, you can skip the Active Record generation for Roo entities by issuing the `--activeRecord false` attribute when defining an entity:

```
roo> entity jpa --class ~.model.Course --activeRecord false
```

> **IF YOU'VE BEEN USING ACTIVE RECORD AND WANT TO MIGRATE...** Just edit your entity, and replace @RooJpaActiveRecord with @RooJpaEntity. Fire up the Roo shell and watch it remove all of those Active Record ITDs. Follow up by creating a JPA repository and you're all set. If you take advantage of Roo's web interface scaffolding, Roo will even reroute calls in the controller to the repository after you create one.

In the next chapter, we'll show you how to use Roo's service support to automatically provide a wrapper service around your repositories.

3.6 *Code samples*

The examples we used around the Active Record Course object are contained in the github samples repository under the directory /chapter-03-jpa/coursemanager. This includes the Course ITD, the Course finder, the integration tests for Course, and the finder. We also include the repository samples under /chapter-03-jpa/coursemanager-repository.

All of these examples work against the Hypersonic SQL database by default, but feel free to re-execute the jpa setup command and switch to your favorite database.

Now let's review the topics we covered in this chapter.

3.7 *Summary*

In this chapter, we discussed the two major ways that Roo provides access to database entities—the Active Record pattern and via repositories. You've seen that Roo provides a rich database API called Spring Data, which is distributed as part of the Spring JPA container beginning in Roo 1.2. With this container, you saw that you can define queries using annotations and Java interfaces. You can also extend other interfaces, such as JpaRepository, which provide automatically generated CRUD methods.

Just think of all the things Roo does for you as a Spring developer:

- Roo generates entities automatically using a simple `entity` command.
- Roo also uses AspectJ ITD files to wrap entities with JPA persistence code, adding methods to entities such as `persist`, `findCourse`, `merge`, and `flush`.
- Roo gives you the ability to use your own JPA code, or to harness the power of the Spring Data JPA API, to manage your persistence layer.
- Roo has a comprehensive system testing facility, enabled by the Spring JUnit Test Runner. You can either execute the standard Spring JUnit Test Runner, or allow Roo to scaffold tests automatically by using the `@RooIntegrationTest` annotation.
- Roo supports JSR-303, the Bean Validation Framework API, and executes validation processing whenever an entity is persisted or updated.
- Roo supports adding *finders* to your entities, which provide results for various searches enabled as simple Java methods.

In the next chapter, we'll take a look at how to relate entities to each other. You'll also see some of the more advanced features of the JPA persistence framework and how you can make them work in Roo.

3.8   *Resources*

The online reference for the Spring Data JPA project: http://mng.bz/Q9X4

The Spring Data JPA project home page, which includes references to blog entries by Oliver Geirke, Gordon Dickens, and others: http://mng.bz/63xp

Relationships, JPA, and advanced persistence

4

This chapter covers

- Object relations
- Defining entity relationships
- Reverse engineering JPA entities
- Adding a service layer
- Using JPA directly
- NoSQL databases with MongoDB

In chapter 3, we discussed how to install Roo's JPA-based persistence engine, create entities, and manipulate them using Roo's domain-driven entity ITD methods such as persist(), find(), and merge(). You saw how to validate entities using the Bean Validation API and how to generate search queries using the finder facility. You also saw how to build Spring-based repositories so that developers who want a separation of application layers can still provide a data layer for their applications.

In this chapter, you'll learn how to relate entities to each other, building JPA relationships via the Roo shell. You'll use the `field reference` and `field set` commands, which establish JPA relationships via various annotations, collections, and references. You'll explore several mapping strategies, including one-to-many, many-to-many, many-to-one, and inheritance hierarchies. You'll see how to use the reverse engineering facility to automatically create entities from an existing database. You'll then see how to build Spring-based services to expose the repositories and to create a traditional, layered, service-based architecture.

Let's begin by reviewing how JPA manages relationships between database entities.

4.1   *Object relations: it's all relative*

Courses can't just live in the world all by themselves; they need students, rooms, teachers, offerings, and registrations. In a relational database, you relate data from one table to another table via special columns called *primary* and *foreign keys*. But in the object-oriented world, you relate entities via references to each other through object references, composition, and aggregation. That's where object-relational mapping (ORM) comes in—it defines a mapping strategy to relate these Java objects to relational tables.

JPA defines relationships using field and collection annotations, such as `@OneTo-Many`, `@ManyToOne`, and `@OneToOne`. To make the process of mapping easier for the developer, Spring Roo provides variants of the `field` shell command that define references between entities. These commands can map either a single object reference or a collection of elements of a particular type.

JPA supports the major relationship types and their variants as shown in table 4.1.

Let's use the Roo shell commands to create and relate other entities to your `Course`. You'll use several relationship types and let the Roo shell configure the JPA annotations for you. We'll begin by reviewing the Course Manager database requirements.

Table 4.1   JPA relationship categories

Type	Definition
One-to-many	Relates a row in a parent table to zero or more rows in a child table. The relationship can either be defined as bidirectional or unidirectional.
One-to-one	A single row in one table is related to a single row in another table. Often database tables are partitioned into multiple smaller tables for performance or security reasons, and if that's warranted, the one-to-one relationship can manage this for you.
Many-to-many	Rows from each table are related to rows in another table. For example, tracking the authors for a series of books, where books can be authored by more than one author, and an author can write any number of books.
Many-to-one	A reference from a child entity back to its parent.
Inheritance hierarchies	JPA supports object-based inheritance and provides several physical models to map this onto a database.

4.2 A sample Course Manager database

In your Course Manager application there are more than just courses. You need to track training programs, tags to describe your courses, students, instructors, and course offerings. Let's review some of the requirements. You need to be able to perform the following activities:

- Assign courses to a particular training program
- Tag courses with various labels or keywords
- Schedule courses in your training locations
- Assign a trainer to a course offering
- Register students to attend a specific course offering

To better understand where you're going, let's take a look at a proposed database diagram of a superset of entities you'll be manipulating throughout the book, illustrated in figure 4.1.

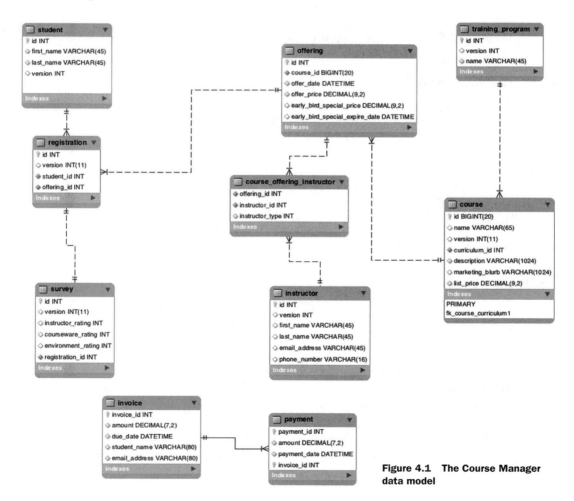

Figure 4.1   The Course Manager data model

Most of these relationships are connected in some way to a Course entity—the training program it's related to, the offerings of the courses themselves, registrations of students in the courses, and the instructors. Although you may not implement all of these entities in the book, this gives you a model to practice with when creating your own sample applications.

> **ALL THE JPA THAT'S PRINT TO FIT...**   We don't have enough space to teach all of the JPA in this chapter, but we focus on some of the major relationship types that you'll use on a regular basis. We refer you to a number of books at the end of this chapter to help you continue your JPA learning journey.

Let's dive right in and create some entities and relationships. You'll start by adding a TrainingProgram entity so that you can group courses together.

4.3   *Course Manager relationships*

Your Course Management application is comprised of a number of JPA entities, related together via a combination of relationship types, such as one-to-many, many-to-one, and many-to-many. You'll use this model to put Roo's entity command through its paces.

4.3.1   *One to many: training programs to courses*

The training company wants to offer collections of courses, which they call training programs. To support this requirement, you need to add another entity, TrainingProgram, and relate it to your Course entity. Let's begin by defining the TrainingProgram:

```
roo> entity jpa --class ~.model.TrainingProgram --testAutomatically
[entity created]
~.model.TrainingProgram roo> field string --fieldName name
[field created]
```

The resulting TrainingProgram entity:

```
package org.rooinaction.coursemanager.model;

...

@RooJavaBean
@RooToString
@RooJpaActiveRecord
public class TrainingProgram {
private String name;
}
```

Next let's create the relationship between TrainingProgram and the Course entity. You'll make a bidirectional, one-to-many relationship, meaning that you can navigate from training programs to courses, and from courses to their training program. This is a two-step process.

First you establish the one-to-many side of the relationship, using the field set command. This command creates a Course-typed Java set in the TrainingProgram entity:

```
~.model.TrainingProgram roo> field set --fieldName courses ⇒
    --type ~.model.Course ⇒
    --cardinality ONE_TO_MANY --mappedBy trainingProgram
```

Here's the resultant set in the `TrainingProgram` entity:

```
@OneToMany(cascade = CascadeType.ALL, mappedBy = "trainingProgram")
private Set<Course> courses = new HashSet<Course>();
```

The `@OneToMany` annotation tells JPA that a relationship is established between `Course` and `TrainingProgram`, so that when queries are issued, JPA can write the proper SQL statements. You've used the `mappedBy` attribute, which describes the *name* of the *attribute* in the `Course` object that represents the related `TrainingProgram`. This is done so that JPA manages the relationship at the *many* end, which you'll configure next.

In order to complete this relationship, you need to define the reverse side: the many-to-one relationship between the `Course` and the `TrainingProgram`, which you'll do by defining a `trainingProgram` attribute using Roo's `field reference` command:

```
~.model.TrainingProgram roo> focus --class ~.model.Course
~.model.Course> field reference --fieldName trainingProgram ⇒
    --type ~.model.TrainingProgram ⇒
    --cardinality MANY_TO_ONE
```

Now the relationship has been established. Here's the attribute definition in the `Course` entity:

```
@ManyToOne
private TrainingProgram trainingProgram;
```

You've now established the following rules:

- Training programs contain sets of courses in a collection named `courses`.
- Courses reference their training program in the reference variable `training-Program`.
- Any change to the training program, including adding a course, cascade. Removing a training program will remove its courses.
- If you use a JPA query to load a training program, JPA will fetch courses for you when you call the `getCourses()` method from the `TrainingProgram_Roo _Javabean.aj` ITD.

Figure 4.2 illustrates what you've done in Java.

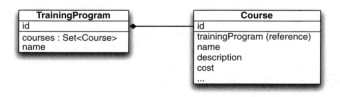

Figure 4.2 How Java sees your relationship—using a reference and a set

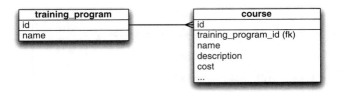

Figure 4.3   Database relationship, established via the `training_program_id` foreign key

From the Java perspective, a `TrainingProgram` holds a `Set` of `Course` objects. The `Course` object holds a reference to a `TrainingProgram`. But, in the database, you relate these objects using primary and foreign keys, as in figure 4.3.

> **REMEMBER: STAY FOCUSED!**   If you restart Roo, or want to switch to adding fields to another entity, you can use the `focus` Roo shell command to switch the entity you're working on. Forgetting to switch back to the `Course` entity when adding the reference to `TrainingProgram` will add the reference to the `TrainingProgram` entity. You won't receive a warning because Roo doesn't know you made a modeling mistake!
>
> Alternatively, use the `--class` parameter to apply the field or reference to another entity and ignore the currently focused class.

Let's test this relationship straight away. You'll add the code in listing 4.1 to the `TrainingProgramIntegrationTest` class, which Roo added when you defined your `TrainingProgram` with the `--testAutomatically` option of Roo's `entity jpa` command.

Listing 4.1   Testing the `TrainingProgram`-to-`Course` relationship

```
@Test
public void addProgramAndCourse() {
  CourseDataOnDemand courseDod = new CourseDataOnDemand();
   Course course = courseDod.getNewTransientCourse(0);
   course.setListPrice(new BigDecimal("100"));

  TrainingProgram trainingProgram = new TrainingProgram();
  course.setTrainingProgram(trainingProgram);
   trainingProgram.getCourses().add(course);

  trainingProgram.persist();

  trainingProgram.flush();
  trainingProgram.clear();

  TrainingProgram t2 =
     TrainingProgram.findTrainingProgram(trainingProgram.getId());

  Assert.assertNotNull(t2.getId());
  Assert.assertEquals(trainingProgram.getName(), t2.getName());
  Assert.assertEquals(1, t2.getCourses().size());
}
```

Test data generator

Generate ❶ entity

❷ Many-to-one

One-to- ❸ many

Save and ❹ prep

❺

Verify persistence

In this test you assert that you can store and retrieve a one-to-many relationship between a training program and a related course. You create an instance of `Course-`

DataOnDemand, which is used to create an unsaved `transient` instance of an entity ❶, saving you the work of creating a course by hand.

Next you create an instance of your `TrainingProgram` ❷, and set the reference to your `Course` instance.

You still need to add the course to the collection, so ask the `TrainingProgram` for the set of `Course` instances with `getCourses()` and add your `Course` to the collection ❸. Now, both sides of the relationship are satisfied, from both Java and JPA perspectives.

Next you make sure the data is persisted, and the JPA context is cleared for the verification process ❹. You'll call `save()` on the training program so that it persists to the database, and so that the foreign key can be properly populated. At this time, JPA needs to create the course that you've added to the training program too, so that will generate an insert.

Calling `flush()` will force JPA to execute your SQL statements, and `clear()` will reset the context, so any future requests will have to come from the database and not the JPA session cache.

Finally you attempt to reload the training program from scratch and verify that the name that you loaded matches the name that you created, and that you have one course attached to the training program ❺.

4.3.2 *More on database keys*

Databases relate these same entities using a primary and foreign key. To see this in action in Hibernate, you can add the following entry to your `log4j.properties` file:

```
log4j.logger.org.hibernate.tool.hbm2ddl=debug
```

Now run your JUnit tests again, using `mvn test`.

The log setting above causes the actual DDL to be emitted in the STS console, and in log output files in target/surefire-reports, such as CourseIntegrationTest-output.txt. Here's sample output from a configuration using the MySQL database, which includes both primary and foreign key definitions:

```
create table course (id bigint not null auto_increment, ...
    training_program bigint, primary key (id)) ENGINE=InnoDB
create table training_program (id bigint not null auto_increment,
 name varchar(255), ...
 primary key (id)) ENGINE=InnoDB
alter table course add index FKAF42E01B903B83EE (training_program),
 add constraint FKAF42E01B903B83EE
 foreign key (training_program) references training_program (id)
```

As you can see, you can focus on configuring and manipulating Java objects, and let the persistence layer figure out how to generate the appropriate SQL statements, both to create and manipulate your database tables.

Here are some tips when dealing with Roo's relationship mapping commands:

- Though Roo generates some baseline sanity tests against your entities, always exercise your entities and relationships before you start coding services and user interface code. JPA relationship mappings are sometimes hard to understand, and may not behave the way you think they will. Just because the built-in test *goes green* doesn't mean it does what you want it to.

- If you're defining a bidirectional one-to-many mapping as you did in the preceding example, make sure to use the `--mappedBy` attribute so that JPA keeps the relationship defined with two physical tables. See the tip below for more details.
- Don't forget to switch focus when adding relationships. You may be adding the inverse relationship to the same class if not. You can also use the `--class` attribute on the `field set` or `field reference` commands to define the relationship on a particular class directly.

TWO TABLES OR THREE?   If you forget to specify the `--mappedBy` setting in the one-to-many mapping, you might find that you'll end up with three tables in this relationship: `training_program`, `course`, and `training_program_course`, with the extra table containing both the `course_id` and `training_program_id`.

This is an alternate form of mapping for a one-to-many relationship that allows for switching later to a many-to-many relationship without major restructuring of your data. But it's not a typical database table design. So, when defining one-to-many relationships, be sure to use the `--mappedBy` option unless you expect this behavior.

For more information about the details of JPA 2.0 mappings, consult the books we refer to at the end of this chapter.

Now you've seen how to define a basic, bidirectional one-to-many relationship in Roo. Let's explore some other mapping options, starting with a many-to-many relationship.

4.3.3   *Many-to-many relationship: courses to tags*

The administrators also want to tag courses with a set of keywords, assigning predefined labels such as `developmental skills`, `advanced`, `beginner`, and `expert`. The end users would then be able to search by these tags to find courses of interest.

You'll hold your predefined keywords in a `Tag` entity. Because tags can be used by many courses, and courses can be assigned a number of tags, the association is logically defined as a many-to-many relationship.

You have two options for how to define your relationship in JPA:

- Using three entities. You can define an intersecting entity that associates `Tag` entities to `Course` entities using two `@OneToMany` relationships.
- Using two entities, and a `@ManyToMany` relationship.

Although the three-entity solution allows you to define attributes in the intersecting entity, you'll use the simpler many-to-many relationship instead. Regardless of how you map the entities, the relational database will require three tables, as shown in figure 4.4.

Let's create this relationship as a bidirectional, many-to-many relationship, so you can easily fetch the courses for a given tag, or the tags assigned to a particular course.

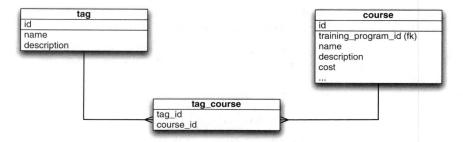

Figure 4.4   How databases resolve a many-to-many relationship

You'll begin by defining the Tag entity:

```
entity jpa --class ~.model.Tag --testAutomatically
field string --fieldName tag --sizeMin 1 --sizeMax 25 --notNull
field string --fieldName description --sizeMax 250 --notNull
```

Roo responds by creating the Tag entity and adding the fields, as shown in the following listing.

Listing 4.2   The Tag entity

```
package org.rooinaction.coursemanager.model;

...

@RooJavaBean
@RooToString
@RooJpaActiveRecord
public class Tag {

    @NotNull
    @Size(min = 1, max = 25)
    private String tag;

    @NotNull
    @Size(max = 250)
    private String description;
}
```

Next you need to relate the Tag to your Course entity. Assume your Roo shell focus is still on the Tag entity:

```
field set --fieldName courses --type ~.model.Course➥
  --cardinality MANY_TO_MANY
```

> **CAN I TELL THE FIELD COMMAND TO WORK ON A SPECIFIC ENTITY?**   Yes, you can.
> Just use the --class argument to specify the target entity.

The preceding command defines a Java Set collection, named courses, on the Tag entity:

```
@ManyToMany(cascade = CascadeType.ALL)
private Set<Course> courses = new HashSet<Course>();
```

To test your association, let's add a method to the `TagIntegrationTest` JUnit test, shown in the next listing, that creates several courses and assigns a tag.

Listing 4.3   Testing the `Tag-to-Course` association

```
@Test                                                          ❶ Create
public void associateTagsAndCourses() {                          the DODs
  CourseDataOnDemand courseDod = new CourseDataOnDemand();
   Course c1 = courseDod.getNewTransientCourse(0);

  Course c2 = courseDod.getNewTransientCourse(1);             ❷ Get two
                                                                 Courses
  TagDataOnDemand tagDod = new TagDataOnDemand();
  Tag tag = tagDod.getNewTransientTag(0);

  tag.getCourses().add(c1);                                   ❸ Add
   tag.getCourses().add(c2);                                      members

  tag.persist();
  tag.flush();
  tag.clear();

  Assert.assertEquals(2,
    tag.findTag(tag.getId()).getCourses().size());

}
```

The test is remarkably similar to the preceding tests, except that you use a little more of your `DataOnDemand` testing framework. First you create your `CourseDataOnDemand` object ❶, which allows you to get access to a number of `Course` entities, prefilled with legal data values. You use the `getNewTransientCourse(int index)` method ❷ to generate two `Course` instances, c1 and c2. The `getRandomCourse()` method you saw earlier may return the same `Course` twice, so you can't use it here.

You also generate a single random `Tag` object, which is the focus of your test. You then add the course to both tags using your convenience method, `Tag.addCourse()` ❸.

Finally, you save the tag instance, which cascades into saving the courses. To test, you flush and clear the entity manager and then reload the `Tag` from the database, verifying that it is attached to two courses.

> **GET TO KNOW THE DATAONDEMAND CLASSES**   These classes are pretty handy for generating test entities. In fact, if you look at the `Course_Roo _IntegrationTest.aj` ITD you'll see that it uses the `CourseDataOnDemand` class extensively. Both the test *and* the `CourseDataOnDemand` class have backing AspectJ files.

All of this is great, but what about the reverse relationship? What if your users need to fetch the tags assigned to a given course? In that case, you need to define the collection in `Course` that will contain the associated `tags`.

4.3.4   *The inverse many-to-many: courses have tags*

To define your `Course` to `Tag` mapping, you'll create another `@ManyToMany` relationship. But this time you'll add the `--mappedBy` option so that you can define this as the *inverse* relationship. An inverse relationship provides a way to navigate between entities, but doesn't automatically persist changes by itself:

```
focus --class ~.model.Course
field set --fieldName tags --type ~.model.Tag➠
   --cardinality MANY_TO_MANY ➠
   --mappedBy courses
```

The inverse relationship, defined on the `Course` entity, looks like this:

```
@ManyToMany(cascade = CascadeType.ALL, mappedBy = "courses")
private Set<Tag> tags = new HashSet<Tag>();
```

As you can see, the `mappedBy` attribute defines the name of the `set` within the `Tag` entity and establishes that `Course` is *not* in charge of persisting the `Tag`s. In a bidirectional many-to-many relationship, one side must be the primary, and the other side must be the inverse side. The inverse side is indicated here as `Course`, because it defines the `mappedBy` attribute.

Now that the relationship is bidirectional, you need to modify both sides to make Java *and* JPA happy. The JUnit test method, added to `CourseIntegationTest`, is shown next.

Listing 4.4   Testing tag persistence from `Courses`

```
@Test
@Transactional
public void testPersistTagsInCourses() {
    CourseDataOnDemand courseDod = new CourseDataOnDemand();
    Course course = courseDod.getNewTransientCourse(0);
    course.setListPrice(new BigDecimal("100"));
    TagDataOnDemand tagDod = new TagDataOnDemand();
    Tag t1 = tagDod.getNewTransientTag(0);
    Tag t2 = tagDod.getNewTransientTag(1);

    course.getTags().add(t1);                          ⬅──❶ For Java
     course.getTags().add(t2);

    t1.getCourses().add(course);                       ⬅──❷ For JPA and Java
     t2.getCourses().add(course);

    t1.persist();
    t2.persist();
    t2.flush();
    t2.clear();

    Assert.assertEquals(2,
        Course.findCourse(
            course.getId()).getTags().size());
}
```

You'll notice that you add the tags to the tags collection on course ❶, and also ask each tag for its courses collection, adding the course to that collection as well ❷. This satisfies both sides of the relationship. As before, you then flush and clear the persistence context via the course, and try to load the course again to verify that it contains a reference to two tags.

It turns out that this code wouldn't work if you only updated the tags collection in course. Try it out by commenting out the two lines that add the course to the tags. The assertion would fail, because the Course entity isn't the active side of the relationship.

Because the active side is the Tag entity, when you add a course to t1 and t2, JPA will see this change and generate SQL INSERT statements for the new course entity. JPA can't watch both sides of the relationship; otherwise it might actually insert the same rows twice. You need to know which side is active; updating the inverse side may not actually trigger JPA persistence, but updating the active end will always do so.

> **DID WE PICK THE RIGHT OWNER?**   In the example, Tag is the owning side of the relationship, which means that any changes to Tagcourses entries get automatically flushed to the database. You picked this side by making the other side define the mappedBy annotation attribute.
>
> For most bidirectional one-to-many relationships, the appropriate active end is the *many* side, as the foreign key lives in the child. For many-to-many relationships, the choice is arbitrary and something you need to decide on a case-by-case basis.

Next you'll deal with registering students for your courses, which will help you learn about inheritance hierarchies and JPA.

4.3.5   *Putting the people in courses...*

Now you've come to a very important part: actually registering students and tracking instructors. Courses would be useless unless you provide both instructors and students. You will define your students and teachers by using JPA *entity inheritance.* This feature allows you to define common fields in a base class, while placing fields specific to an entity in the refined subclass.

To implement entity inheritance in your model, you'll define an abstract Person entity, with typical fields such as firstName and lastName, and then define separate entities for Instructors and Students, which will extend the Person entity.

While you could use the Roo shell to define your fields, in this example you'll just enter the field definitions in the editor. You can use the STS Organize Imports feature ([CTRL/CMD]-SHIFT-O) to automatically find your annotations. This technique is used during rapid prototyping and enables developers to make changes to a data design quickly.

OTHER RELATIONSHIP TYPES Although Roo's persistence engine supports any JPA construct you can create, the web scaffolding we discuss in chapter 5 doesn't support every potential construct. Nor may the automatic integration testing system. Features such as embedded components aren't properly supported yet. When defining a complex data model, generate your integration tests and prototype a user interface using the scaffolding to see what Roo can support out of the box.

You have several additional entities to create—students, instructors, and course registrations. Let's start this process by defining the people who are taking and teaching courses.

4.3.6 *People teach and attend courses—inheritance*

All of the relationships we've discussed so far are either "has-a" (one-to-many, many-to-many) or "belongs-to" (many-to-one) relationships. Sometimes an instance of one entity is a more specific instance of another (referred to by the moniker *is-a"*). JPA supports defining these hierarchical relationships. These are exposed in Roo using the familiar entity and field commands.

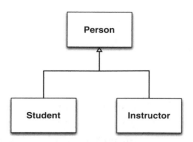

Figure 4.5 The Person hierarchy

You have two types of people that you track in your system—students and instructors. Both have some common elements, so you can define an inheritance hierarchy to collect the common elements in a parent entity.

You'll define this hierarchy using three entities, as shown in figure 4.5. You'll use Person to hold common elements: address information and a name, for example. For Students, you need to track dietary preferences and emergency contact information. You'll also need to track your Instructors' tax ids, and whether they are still active trainers within your organization. You'll define these attributes in the Student and Instructor entities, which you'll inherit from Person.

From the Java side, this is a straightforward inheritance design. Student and Instructor entities can simply extend the Person entity. But JPA needs additional information to map this hierarchy to a database. JPA gives you three distinct ways to map an inheritance relationship: as a single table, a table for each child class, and tables for all classes. Table 4.2 outlines the mapping options, which you can specify with the Roo entity attribute, --inheritanceType.

One important issue with Roo and the hierarchical relationships is that it doesn't completely support all settings in the entity shell command. For example, Roo doesn't have a command to let you configure the discriminator for the SINGLE_TABLE model, so you'll just have to edit the classes and add the proper annotations yourself.

Table 4.2   Inheritance models available from `--inheritanceType`

`inheritanceType`	Description
SINGLE_TABLE	Puts all data from the parent and child classes into a single table. Each row is identified with a *discriminator* that defines which entity to create when fetching the row from the database. You'll need to tell JPA how to locate the rows, using a combination of `@DiscriminatorColumn`, `@Discriminator-Formula`, and `@DiscriminatorValue` annotations. Consult your provider's JPA reference manual for an example. Note that each field must be nullable in the child classes, so that the SQL statement can insert the row without those columns.
TABLE_PER_CLASS	Also known as "Table per concrete class," this strategy only creates the tables of the child classes in the relationship. All parent entity data is defined in each physical child table. Parent classes can be abstract or concrete. Fields can be nullable or required in the child tables. JPA simply inserts rows into the appropriate table based on the mappings for the class of the child entity.
JOINED	This is the fully database normalized version of the hierarchy. The JPA provider will create the parent and child tables for the relationship, and use SQL joins to fetch the data for a given entity.

For this relationship, you'll choose the `TABLE_PER_CLASS` option, since you're not going to query across the different subtasks on a regular basis. You don't want to incur either the overhead of the joins in the `JOINED` relationship, or the nullability requirement on child entity columns in the `SINGLE_TABLE` arrangement.

First, let's define the `Person` entity. You'll use the Roo entity command:

```
entity jpa --class ~.model.Person --abstract➥
   --inheritanceType TABLE_PER_CLASS
```

This command is slightly different than the ones before it. You make the person *abstract* because you don't want anyone to create a generic one. You also select the `TABLE_PER_CLASS` *inheritance type*.

You'll just add the fields and annotations to this class directly, rather than running the Roo shell commands. The completed `Person` entity is shown in the following listing. Keep your Roo shell running so that it can adjust your ITDs once you save the changes to `Person`.

Listing 4.5   The completed Person entity

```
package org.rooinaction.coursemanager.model;

...

@RooJavaBean
@RooToString
@RooJpaActiveRecord(inheritanceType = "TABLE_PER_CLASS")     ◁─❶ Inheritance strategy
 public abstract class Person {

    @Size(min = 1, max = 30)
    private String firstName;
```

```
    @Size(min = 1, max = 30)
    private String middleNameOrInitial;

    @NotNull
    @Size(min = 1, max = 30)
    private String lastName;

    @NotNull
    @Size(min = 1, max = 60)
    private String addressLine1;

    @Size(min = 1, max = 60)
    private String addressLine2;

    @NotNull
    @Size(min = 1, max = 40)
    private String city;

    @NotNull
    @Size(min = 2, max = 2)
    private String stateCode;

    @NotNull
    @Size(min = 1, max = 10)
    private String postalCode;

    @NotNull
    @Size(max = 80)
    private java.lang.String emailAddress;
}
```

You used the `@RooJpaActiveRecord` annotation ❶ to define both the fact that Roo manages the entity and that you're using the TABLE_PER_CLASS strategy.

Now you'll define each of your subclasses. First you'll create your Student:

```
entity jpa --class ~.model.Student --extends ~.model.Person➥
    --testAutomatically
```

You'll fill it in with the appropriate field definitions in the IDE:

```
package org.rooinaction.coursemanager.model;

...

@RooJavaBean
@RooToString
@RooJpaActiveRecord
public class Student extends Person {

    @NotNull
    @Size(min = 1, max = 30)
    private String emergencyContactName;

    @NotNull
    @Size(min = 1, max = 80)
    private String emergencyContactInfo;

    @Size(max = 30)
    private String dietaryRestrictions;

}
```

The difference between this and any other entity is minimal; the extends is the only part of the code that changes. But because of Java inheritance, Student now includes fields from Person. In JPA, all of these fields are combined into a new table in the database named student.

Let's do the same for the Instructor:

```
entity jpa --class ~.model.Instructor --extends ~.model.Person➥
    --testAutomatically
```

Here's the Instructor class. You've added the fields by hand:

```
package org.rooinaction.coursemanager.model;

...

@RooJavaBean
@RooToString
@RooJpaActiveRecord
public class Instructor extends Person {

    @NotNull
    @Size(min = 9, max = 9)
    private String taxNumber;

    @NotNull
    private boolean active;
}
```

> **JUST EDIT THE JAVA FILES!**   If you already know what you want, and are in an IDE, the quickest way to develop is to just plop the fields into the class. If your Roo shell is running it will immediately update the ITDs.

Nothing different again, except the fact that it extends Person.

4.3.7 *Testing your inheritance hierarchy*

Because you defined both Student and Instructor using the --testAutomatically flag, you just have to run the integration tests to verify their behavior. From Spring-Source Tool Suite, just open up the InstructorIntegrationTest entity and run the tests. Repeat this for the StudentIntegrationTest class. If you want to run all tests for the project at once, either use the Roo perform tests command or Maven's mvn test command.

All tests should pass, unless you're using Hypersonic SQL, Derby, Sybase, or a SQL Server database engine. If you'd like to write more complex tests, ones that use the Student with other entities, feel free to do so.

MY TESTS DIDN'T PASS...
So, you're one of the unlucky ones...

Roo uses JPA annotations to define the primary key of each entity, holding them in the Jpa_Entity.aj ITD. From your Course entity:

```
@Id
@GeneratedValue(strategy = GenerationType.AUTO)
```

```
@Column(name = "id")
private Long Course.id;
```

On database engines that use an IDENTITY data type, such as MySQL, you can't use the AUTO key generation strategy.

When using Hibernate as the persistence engine, your integration tests will fail when running on these databases, due to a database mapping failure on startup (see http://mng.bz/PpLH for details).

CORRECTING THE MAPPING

To fix this problem, you can manually copy the id field and the getId() and setId() methods from the Roo_Jpa_Entity.aj file, paste them into the Person.java class, and change the key generation strategy. You can use another generation strategy, such as TABLE or SEQUENCE (with databases that support it). The additional code you'll add to your Java entity class when selecting the TABLE strategy looks like this:

```
@Id
@GeneratedValue(strategy = GenerationType.TABLE)
@Column(name = "id")
private Long id;

public Long getId() {
    return id;
}

public void setId(Long id) {
    this.id = id;
}
```

The TABLE strategy defines a table that keeps track of the next highest value for a given entity's primary key. The SEQUENCE strategy uses a high performance internal number sequence, which the database will increment automatically when creating the primary key. On databases that support sequences, you'll get far higher performance by selecting the SEQUENCE strategy.

> **STS USERS: USE PUSH-IN REFACTORING** If you're using STS, open up the Package Explorer, make sure you're showing your Roo Generated ITDs, and click on id(), getId() and setId(Long id), and right-click on one of the methods. There you can select Refactor ... Push-In Refactor and Roo will move the elements for you.

You can make the change above and rerun the Roo shell. Roo will detect the implementation of the primary key and remove it from the Person_Roo_Entity.aj file. Roo will also remove the getter and setter from the Person_Roo_JavaBean.aj file automatically.

> **FOR MORE INFORMATION ON JPA INHERITANCE** More information on JPA inheritance models can be found in a number of books on JPA. Remember that Spring Roo currently uses JPA 2.0, so you have the full range of features provided in that release.

4.3.8   *JPA providers and your database schema*

Let's take a look at the database tables that Roo generated for the Student and Instructor entities. You configured your database for MySQL using the persistence setup command and then used the mysql client tool to describe your tables. First let's look at the student table:

```
mysql> desc student;
+------------------------+-------------+------+-----+------------+
| Field                  | Type        | Null | Key |
+------------------------+-------------+------+-----+------------+
| id                     | bigint(20)  | NO   | PRI |
| address_line1          | varchar(60) | NO   |     |
| address_line2          | varchar(60) | YES  |     |
| city                   | varchar(40) | NO   |     |
| first_name             | varchar(30) | YES  |     |
| last_name              | varchar(30) | NO   |     |
| middle_name_or_initial | varchar(30) | YES  |     |
| postal_code            | varchar(10) | NO   |     |
| state_code             | varchar(2)  | NO   |     |
| version                | int(11)     | YES  |     |
| dietary_restrictions   | varchar(30) | YES  |     |
| emergency_contact_info | varchar(80) | NO   |     |
| emergency_contact_name | varchar(30) | NO   |     |
+------------------------+-------------+------+-----+
```

All of the fields from the Person entity appear, as well as fields specific to the Student such as dietary_restrictions, emergency_contact_info, and emergency_contact _name. You can see in this example that Roo changes camel-cased variables to underscored table field names when generating the DDL.

Interestingly, if you choose EclipseLink as your JPA provider, you get a slightly different schema:

```
mysql> desc student;
+----------------------+--------------+------+-----+
| Field                | Type         | Null | Key |
+----------------------+--------------+------+-----+
| id                   | bigint(20)   | NO   | PRI |
| LASTNAME             | varchar(255) | YES  |     |
| MIDDLENAMEORINITIAL  | varchar(255) | YES  |     |
| EMERGENCYCONTACTINFO | varchar(255) | YES  |     |
| STATECODE            | varchar(255) | YES  |     |
| ADDRESSLINE2         | varchar(255) | YES  |     |
| ADDRESSLINE1         | varchar(255) | YES  |     |
| DIETARYRESTRICTIONS  | varchar(255) | YES  |     |
| CITY                 | varchar(255) | YES  |     |
| version              | int(11)      | YES  |     |
| POSTALCODE           | varchar(255) | YES  |     |
| EMERGENCYCONTACTNAME | varchar(255) | YES  |     |
| FIRSTNAME            | varchar(255) | YES  |     |
+----------------------+--------------+------+-----+
```

Note that your datatypes are all completely different—the Hibernate provider honored your @Size attributes and @NotNull directives, but EclipseLink did not.

EclipseLink also uppercased all fields except the primary key id and version columns. Roo defines a @Column annotation for the id and version attributes, each of which defines the field name in lowercase.

You should *always* take a good look at your database table mappings and learn to use your JPA provider effectively. Since you don't specify the @Column annotation for your fields, EclipseLink's defaults kick in, which are different than Hibernate's defaults.

Although Hibernate honors the schema settings in your Bean Validation annotations, all JPA providers pay attention to the @Column mapping. The Bean Validation API isn't a part of JPA itself; rather, it's part of Java EE 6. To be 100% portable, you'd need to define your fields with both sets of annotations, even though this leads to duplication and potentially errors between these settings. For example, the emergencyContactName field should be defined as follows:

```
@NotNull
@Size(min = 1, max = 30)
@Column(length = 30, name = "emergency_contact_name", nullable = false)
private String emergencyContactName;
```

This will cause the proper mapping for the field in all JPA systems, regardless of whether they support Bean Validation. Also, when you build your Spring MVC web interface, the bean validations will be used to generate client-side web browser validation logic, as you'll see in chapter 5.

Now the EclipseLink mapping looks like this:

```
mysql> desc student;
+-----------------------+--------------+------+-----+
| Field                 | Type         | Null | Key |
+-----------------------+--------------+------+-----+
...
| emergency_contact_name | varchar(30)  | NO   |     |
...
+-----------------------+--------------+------+-----+
```

Let's wrap up by reviewing the instructor table:

```
mysql> desc instructor;
+-----------------------+--------------+------+-----+
| Field                 | Type         | Null | Key |
+-----------------------+--------------+------+-----+
| id                    | bigint(20)   | NO   | PRI |
| address_line1         | varchar(60)  | NO   |     |
| address_line2         | varchar(60)  | YES  |     |
| city                  | varchar(40)  | NO   |     |
| first_name            | varchar(30)  | YES  |     |
| last_name             | varchar(30)  | NO   |     |
| middle_name_or_initial | varchar(30) | YES  |     |
| postal_code           | varchar(10)  | NO   |     |
| state_code            | varchar(2)   | NO   |     |
| version               | int(11)      | YES  |     |
| active                | bit(1)       | NO   |     |
| tax_number            | varchar(9)   | NO   |     |
+-----------------------+--------------+------+-----+
```

Again, you see the `tax_number` and `active` fields from the `Instructor` entity and the common fields from the `Person` entity.

4.3.9   *The rest of your schema*

You have a few more entities to define. We'll show their JPA entity definitions for completeness. By now you should be able to use the Roo shell to create the empty entity definition and just type in the fields themselves.

COURSE OFFERINGS

Course offerings define each run of a course. Students and instructors are assigned in this entity:

```
@RooJavaBean
@RooToString
@RooJpaActiveRecord
public class Offering {

    @Temporal(TemporalType.DATE)
    @NotNull
    private Date offerDate;

    @NotNull
    @Size(min = 1, max = 80)
    private String locationName;

    @ManyToOne(cascade = CascadeType.ALL)
    private Course course;

    @ManyToOne(cascade = CascadeType.ALL)
    private Instructor instructor;
}
```

REGISTRATIONS

Whenever a student registers for a course, you enter a row in the `registration` table via the `Registration` entity:

```
@RooJavaBean
@RooToString
@RooJpaActiveRecord
public class Registration {

    @ManyToOne
    private Student student;

    @ManyToOne
    private Course course;

    private boolean paymentMade;

    private boolean attended;

}
```

This schema gives you a good combination of data to experiment with. In chapter 5, you'll learn to use Roo's user interface features to build a web-based frontend to this database.

Spring Roo makes it easy to work with JPA relationships and hierarchies. A full reference of JPA relationship definitions goes beyond the scope of this book; but exploring the Roo shell field commands alongside this book and a good JPA reference will give you everything you need to start building your persistence model. Remember to write integration tests to confirm your assumptions about related data. This will help you when you begin to build your web application layer in the next chapter.

What if you're given a separate database schema, and you need to reverse engineer it into your current entity model? Roo has this covered using the database reverse engineering add-on.

4.4   Reverse engineering your database

Using the `database reverse engineer` Roo shell command, you can scan an existing database and have Roo generate entities automatically. As your database evolves, Roo can keep the database and your entity model in sync.

Suppose you have to interface into a payments system via two SQL tables, `invoice` and `payment`. If these tables exist in your current schema, you can have Roo generate entities for them automatically using the `database reverse engineer` command:

```
database reverse engineer --schema coursemgrch04 ➥
    --includeTables "invoice payment" ➥
    --package ~.model --testAutomatically
```

The preceding command takes several parameters, as shown in table 4.3.

As with other entities, you can generate automated tests with `--testAutomatically`.

Table 4.3   Important options for `database reverse engineer`

Command	Use	Notes
`--schema`	Provides the name of a database schema to use	This operates on the configured database connection in `database.properties`.
`--includeTables`	The list of tables to include when reverse engineering	By default, all tables are included, except those listed by the `--excludeTables` option. This option can list multiple tables, separated by spaces, in quotes. Example: `--includeTables "invoice payment"`
`--excludeTables`	The list of tables to exclude when reverse engineering	By default, no tables are excluded. Use this when you wish to exclude a certain table or set of tables. Takes the same syntax as `--includeTables` above.
`--package`	The target Java package that will contain the reverse engineered entities	You can use the `~.` wildcard to refer to the base package name. Example: `--package ~.model.reveng`

The first time you run this command against your database, you'll receive an error message about a missing driver. You'll need to install a piece of software known as an add-on, which will provide the JDBC driver for your database. The Roo shell uses this JDBC driver to perform the database reverse engineering process.

> **WHAT IF MY DATABASE DOESN'T HAVE AN ADD-ON?**   The Roo team provides add-on drivers that support a number of databases, including (at the time of this writing) JTDS (for Sybase and Microsoft SQL Server), PostgreSQL, Firebird, MySQL, AS400JDBC, Derby, and H2. But if you're not using one of those databases, you can follow a series of steps to OSGi-ify a JDBC driver for use by the reverse engineering process. See chapter 11, section 6 for details on creating an OSGi wrapper add-on.

For example, when you run this command against a project that points to a MySQL database, you get this (cleaned up for print) message:

```
Located add-on that may offer this JDBC driver
1 found, sorted by rank; T = trusted developer; R = Roo 1.1 compatible
ID T R DESCRIPTION ---------------------------------------------
01 Y Y 5.1.13.0001 #jdbcdriver driverclass:com.mysql.jdbc.Driver...

[HINT] use 'addon info id --searchResultId ..' to see details about a
       search result
[HINT] use 'addon install id --searchResultId ..' to install a specific
       search result, or
[HINT] use 'addon install bundle --bundleSymbolicName TAB'
       to install a specific add-on version
JDBC driver not available for 'com.mysql.jdbc.Driver'
```

Roo is telling you that the Roo add-on #01 is actually a JDBC Driver for MySQL. You can install this add-on into the Roo shell so that it can communicate with MySQL. The command to install the driver is

```
addon install id --searchResultId 01
```

Roo installs the driver as shown here:

```
roo>
...
Downloaded 0% of ....o.s.roo.wrapping.mysql-connector-java-5.1...jar
Downloaded 100% of....o.s.roo.wrapping.mysql-connector-java-5.1...jar
Downloaded 0 kB of lookup
Downloaded 11 kB of lookup
Target resource(s):
-------------------
    Spring Roo - Wrapping - mysql-connector-java (5.1.13.0001)

Deploying...done.

Successfully installed add-on: Spring Roo - Wrapping -
    mysql-connector-java [version: 5.1.13.0001]
[Hint] Please consider rating this add-on with the following command:
[Hint] addon feedback bundle --bundleSymbolicName
    org.springframework.roo.wrapping.mysql-connector-java
    --rating ... --comment "..."
```

MORE ABOUT ADD-ONS Add-ons provide additional functionality to the Roo shell. We devote two chapters to writing add-ons in this book.

Now rerun the `database reverse engineer` command. If you're successful, Roo will generate JPA entities automatically, as well as define a set of tests.

You can now run your suite of tests again, using the Maven `mvn test` command. If Roo can properly test the entities, you can then write further tests to assert whether your mappings are properly defined.

> ### Reverse engineering tips
>
> The Roo reverse engineering features heavily rely on the quality of the database schema. If your schema has nontraditional database keys, mappings, or data types, expect that you might run into trouble.
>
> Roo defines your database schema data in a file under src/main/resources, dbre.xml. This is an XML file that is managed by the `database reverse engineer` command. You may also decide to *push-in* your generated JPA fields, which are contained within an `EntityName_Roo_DbManaged.aj` file.
>
> To detach a Roo entity from the reverse engineering system, you need to perform the following steps:
>
> - Copy the field definitions from the `Entity_Roo_DbManaged.aj` file into your entity Java class, or use the push-in refactoring feature in STS.
> - Remove the `@RooDbManaged` annotation.
> - Rerun the Roo shell, which should delete the unused ITD.

So far, we've looked at how to create your own entities and database elements, and how to relate them to each other using one-to-many, many-to-one, many-to-many, and inheritance mapping strategies. You also saw how to reverse engineer them from an existing schema. Roo makes coding applications using this persistence model rather easy—just create or look up entities using their ITD `findbyId`, `merge`, `persist`, and `remove` methods, or define a finder.

You could code this logic directly in a web-based controller, for simple applications. And Roo actually will do this automatically, using the web scaffolding feature we discuss in chapter 5. But you can also take advantage of your Spring platform and define business methods so that you can expose services to your web and other client tiers in a more organized fashion. Now let's use that technique to define a service layer in your Roo application.

4.5 Adding a service layer

If you recall from chapter 3, Roo can provide repositories to back your objects, rather than using the Active Record approach we've been focusing on. You were able to create repositories, based on the Spring Data API, that you could then inject into other Spring components.

You can define services in your application in two ways:

- Using the `service create` command, which fronts one or more entities and/ or their repositories with a Spring service bean automatically
- Writing the service yourself, using the `@Service` annotation

Both approaches give you a traditional Spring bean for wiring to components such as controllers and web service interfaces.

4.5.1   *Building services with service create*

Your services can either directly interact with your Active Record models or use a repository. Roo will automatically detect the correct approach and write the service code appropriately.

Defining a service to expose the `Course` entity is quite simple:

```
service --entity ~.model.Course --interface ~.service.CourseService
```

Roo builds several files:

- `CourseService.java`—The interface that defines your service. This component will contain an annotation, `@RooService`, which defines the entities exposed by your service:
  ```
  @RooService(domainTypes = { ➥
      org.rooinaction.coursemanager.model.Course.class })
  public interface CourseService {
  }
  ```

- `CourseService_Roo_Service.aj`—Contains the method signatures for the methods you'd normally find in your Active Record API:
  ```
  privileged aspect CourseService_Roo_Service {
      public abstract long CourseService.countAllCourses();
      public abstract void CourseService.deleteCourse(Course course);
      public abstract Course CourseService.findCourse(Long id);
  ...
  }
  ```

- `CourseServiceImpl.java`—This class implements the interface. Any user-defined business methods can be defined here, provided you expose the method definition in the `CourseService.java` interface:
  ```
  public class CourseServiceImpl implements CourseService {
  }
  ```

- `CourseServiceImpl_Roo_Service.aj`—The heavy lifting is done here. In this aspect, which we omit for brevity, the `CourseServiceImpl` is weaved with the `@Service` annotation, marking it as a Spring Bean, and the `@Transactional` annotation, marking all methods transactional by default; also the code for managing persistence is woven into the class. For repository-based entities, methods delegate to an injected `Repository` bean:
  ```
  public void CourseServiceImpl.deleteCourse(Course course) {
    courseRepository.delete(course);
  }
  ```

For Active Record–based entities, the entity itself is used:

```
public void CourseServiceImpl.deleteCourse(Course course) {
  instructor.remove();
}
```

If you want to write your own service methods, Roo has already provided the interface *and* a stub implementation class, so you can place your signature in `CourseService` and the implementation code in `CourseServiceImpl`. Your service methods will just come along for the ride. They can use the `@Transactional` annotation, but keep in mind the implementation ITD weaves `@Transactional` into all methods automatically, so you'll generally only need to use `@Transactional(readOnly = true)` to speed up queries.

Again, Roo saves you a lot of time and coding effort. Although you could do these operations by hand using `@Service`, with the Spring Data–based repository APIs and the handy Service builder command, you can put your data and service layers together in a jiffy.

4.6 *Using JPA directly*

You may find that you want more control over your persistence code, or want to access JPA or provider-specific features yourself. Since Roo is a Spring JPA application development platform, there's no reason why you can't use JPA code yourself.

If you've reviewed the entity ITD files, such as `Course_Roo_Entity.aj`, you've seen that Roo uses an entity manager object to do its work. You can also access the entity manager and make calls yourself. There are two basic approaches you can use to gain access to the entity manager:

- Ask an entity for the entity manager with the `entityManager()` method.
- Tell Spring to inject an entity manager into your repository.

You've already seen the first way in your `Registration.java` custom query method; you used `Registration.entityManager()` to tell Roo to give you a preconfigured instance. That's great if you're in the middle of coding against the Roo APIs in your own service, and just need to make a single call to JPA that isn't provided by the ITD.

But if you wanted to move your query into a formal Spring Repository, and separate it from the Roo entity itself, you need to

1. Create an interface to define the repository with the finder method signature.
2. Implement the interface and move the finder implementation method into it.
3. Inject an entity manager using the Java EE `@PersistenceContext` annotation.
4. Use this injected persistence context to access the database.
5. Use the `@Autowired` annotation in your controller or service class to inject the repository.

The next listing shows this technique, defining both the `CourseQueryRepository` interface and an implementing class, `CourseQueryRepositoryJPA`.

Listing 4.6   The course query repository

```
public interface CourseQueryRepository {
    TypedQuery<Registration> findRegistrationsByStudent(
        Long studentId, Date startDate, Date endDate);
}

...

@Repository
public class CourseQueryRepositoryJPA {                         ❶ Spring
                                                                   repository
    @PersistenceContext                      ⟵─── Standard Java EE    bean
    private EntityManager em;

    @Transactional
    public TypedQuery<Registration> findRegistrationsByStudent(
        Long studentId, Date startDate, Date endDate) {

        TypedQuery<Registration> q = em.createQuery(
            "SELECT DISTINCT r " +
            "FROM Registration AS r " +
            "WHERE r.student.id = :studentId " +
            "AND r.offering IN (SELECT o from Offering o " +
            "  WHERE o.runDate between :start and :end)",
            Registration.class);
        q.setParameter("studentId", studentId);
        q.setParameter("start", startDate);
        q.setParameter("end", endDate);
        return q;
    }
}
```

The finder method is largely the same as it would be in the finder itself. The difference is that you're starting to use some of the more familiar Spring Framework conventions. First you define a business interface, `CourseQueryRepository`, to define your exposed Spring bean method, `findRegistrationsByStudent()`. You annotate the implementation class with the `@Repository` annotation ❶ which, in addition to mounting it as a Spring bean, provides translation of all persistence exceptions to Spring's `DataAccess-Exception` exception hierarchy. You mark the method as `@Transactional`, in case the method is called by any external services.

You can now use the `CourseQueryRepository` bean by autowiring it into your controllers. Simply use the following syntax to inject it:

```
private CourseQueryRepository repository;
@Autowired
public void setCourseQueryRepository(CourseQueryRepository repository) {
    this.repository = repository;
}
```

Remember—Roo applications are Spring applications, and therefore you can do anything you're used to doing in Spring. You don't even need to use Roo's entities, controllers, or services. You can treat Roo like a big army knife; use it as you see fit.

A word of warning, though: Roo may not support the automatic generation of web-based applications based on handwritten services and repositories. The scaffolding feature in chapter 5 will only work against the Roo-generated ITDs.

Finally, we should point out that you can even use Roo with JDBC. Just configure your Spring application with the appropriate JDBC driver and data source, and then start using the Spring JdbcTemplate API, or MyBatis (a common SQL-mapping API), or even a non-SQL database platform. You may not get all of the baked-in features of Roo, such as automatic website generation, but perhaps future add-ons will support these APIs.

> **BE CAREFUL WHEN MIXING JDBC AND JPA**   Because JPA caches data in the persistence context, it may decide to write the data to the database periodically during a *flush* operation. If you query that data using SQL before it's been written, you may not find the data you're looking for. Always be careful about using SQL and JPA together. At a bare minimum, consider executing the `flush()` method on the entity or entity manager before executing SQL queries.

We discuss more complex tests, such as integration tests against services and repositories, in chapter 9.

4.7   NoSQL databases with MongoDB

Added in Roo 1.2 is support for NoSQL databases using the NoSQL Spring Data APIs. NoSQL databases[1] attempt to address a number of challenges inherent in using a relational database, such as these:

- *Normalization kills query performance*—Because relational data is normalized, or factored in to the least duplicated form, it can become hard to query across a number of entities. Consider the performance issues with querying an overly normalized database that leads to a crazy 10 table joins.
- *Rigid database structure*—Relational databases require structure to perform properly. Each column must be defined with a specific type, and the database engine optimizes indexing and performance around this structure.
- *Difficulty querying large volumes of data quickly*—Although some database vendors have rolled out text searching capabilities, and other developers are using tools such as Lucene to index their data, databases themselves can't quickly search through large volumes of loosely structured text without scanning vast amounts of data. This makes them less than ideal for searching through content stored in XML or JSON format.

---

[1]   The term *NoSQL* was coined by Carlo Strozzi in 1998 as a name for his nonrelational, RDB derivative database. This project is ongoing, and can be visited at http://www.strozzi.it.

For these and other reasons, the NoSQL movement was born. A number of types of NoSQL databases have been developed, but they generally fall into several types, as outlined in table 4.4.

Table 4.4 Several NoSQL database variants

Type	Description	Examples
Document store	Each entry in a document store is a single document. Stored in a format such as JSON, XML, or even binary JSON (BSON), these databases are geared toward quickly searching content within the document stores and storing internally structured data.	MongoDB, CouchDB, SimpleDB
Graph	Data is related in a node-to-node graph structure, and can be quickly navigated across these nonfixed relationships. Great for storing associations of data elements where the network of data can be reorganized quickly. A favorite of some semantic web developers.	Neo4J
Column store	Places focus primarily on the column, rather than collected rows of data. Powers huge websites such as Facebook, Twitter, Digg, and others. Google pioneered column-based storage with BigTable when indexing the internet through linear means proved too difficult.[a]	Cassandra, HBase, BigTable
Key/Value store	If the world is a hashmap, this is your database. The objects can be structured in any way possible, such as primitive values or serialized objects, and are fetched by unique keys.	Redis, MemcacheDB

a. Facebook created Cassandra, a column store NoSQL database, and open sourced an implementation. See http://mng.bz/5321.

We won't get into the religious debates about which NoSQL variant or engine to choose in this book. But as Roo supports at least one (at the time of publication) NoSQL database, we *will* show you how to use it as a database store.

4.7.1 Persistence with MongoDB

As discussed earlier, document store NoSQL databases treat each element as a searchable document. Roo supports accessing these databases using the Spring Data MongoDB API (http://mng.bz/rLm9), which is part of the larger Spring Data project. To use this data store, you'll need to install a MongoDB engine, configure it, and then use a variant of the `entity` command to create your Mongo-based entities.

Native MongoDB data is stored in a JSON data format, and can be accessed using a number of APIs. The Mongo default client uses JavaScript. Here's a sample code snippet from this client that creates and then retrieves a document from the data store:

```
> db.people.save( {
... "name" : "Ken",
... "age" : 42,
... "city" : "Philadelphia"
... })
> db.people.find({ "name" : "Ken"})
{ "_id" : ObjectId("4e7df1f0a3c4b6fc99496731"),
  "name" : "Ken", "age" : 42, "city" : "Philadelphia" }
```

The first block of code creates a new element in the newly defined db.people object. The data held within it is defined as a JSON string. Later, in the second statement, we use a fragment of that string, { "name" : "Ken" }, to find all of the people with the name of Ken. We didn't have to predefine the object, or field definitions, or even the database. MongoDB just took our data and stored it.

4.7.2 Setting up MongoDB

Let's get started and set up MongoDB. Like other servers, you'll install the database engine and client by downloading it and configuring it as a standalone service.

To install MongoDB, visit the project website at http://mongodb.org and download the server for your operating system. We've used the OS X utility, brew,[2] to install it on our machines with a minimum of fuss. You'll also have to configure an empty database directory, /data/db by default. We recommend reading and using the "Getting Started" guide and the basic tutorial to get a sense of how to start up the server, mongod, and how to access the client, mongo. After you've created several documents and experimented with the client, you should be ready to build your first MongoDB-based application.

Our tutorial assumes that you've configured a working MongoDB database and that your mongod daemon process is running when you work with MongoDB and Roo.

4.7.3 MongoDB and Roo

Obviously, Java programmers need a bit more structure than that. First of all, they deal mostly with classes in the real world, so one way of approaching a MongoDB implementation would be to serialize and deserialize JSON using a Java POJO.

That's where Roo's support for the Spring Data MongoDB API comes in. Instead of using a relational data store and the @Entity pattern, Roo uses a new annotation, @RooMongoEntity, which is configured when using the entity mongo shell command. To build your course with Mongo support, you'd first set up your MongoDB database layer:

```
roo> mongo setup
```

This configures support for MongoDB, assuming that the engine is running on the same machine, on the default port. It also assumes that security is not enabled. You can use parameters to adjust your MongoDB settings, or edit them later in database .properties.

---

[2] brew installs MongoDB. That's it. Really.

USING CLOUD FOUNDRY?   If you're using Cloud Foundry, use the --cloud-Foundry true option to configure support for the Cloud Foundry MongoDB instance.

After your configuration is updated, you'll see a new configuration file, application-Context-mongo.xml, which contains the Spring Data Mongo API configuration elements. Now you're ready to create MongoDB-based entities.

4.7.4   A MongoDB Course entity

Let's build a Course object using MongoDB. You'll start by defining the entity with the new entity mongo shell command:

```
entity mongo --class ~.model.Course --testAutomatically
```

Roo responds by building your MongoDB entity:

```
package org.rooinaction.coursemanager.model;

import org.springframework.roo.addon.javabean.RooJavaBean;
import org.springframework.roo.addon.layers.
    repository.mongo.RooMongoEntity;
import org.springframework.roo.addon.tostring.RooToString;

@RooJavaBean
@RooToString
@RooMongoEntity
public class Course {

}
```

Comparing this entity with the others, the major difference is the @RooMongoEntity annotation. Beyond this, you can treat it the same way as your other entities. Let's add some fields and a relationship to a simplified Offer object. First, the Course fields:

```
private String name;
private String description;
private BigDecimal listPrice;
private Integer maximumCapacity;
private CourseTypeEnum courseType;
private Set<Offering> offerings =
    new HashSet<Offering>();
```

Next, you'll define your Offering POJO, for embedding within your Course:

```
package org.rooinaction.coursemanager.model;
@RooJavaBean
@RooToString
public class Offering {
    private Date offerDate;
}
```

Note, this is just a simple Java POJO which you'll embed into your database.

4.7.5 Generating a Course MongoDB repository

To enable access to your Roo MongoDB entity, you need to build a repository. You can do this via the `repository mongo` command:

```
roo> repository mongo --entity ~.model.Course ⇥
       --interface ~.repositories.CourseRepository
```

This command will build a `CourseRepository` interface and build an ITD, `CourseRepository_Roo_Mongo_Repository.aj`, to back it. The repository definition:

```
@RooRepositoryMongo(domainType = Course.class)
public interface CourseRepository {

    List<org.rooinaction.coursemanager.model.Course> findAll();
}
```

The other methods, such as `find(BigInteger)`, `save(Course)`, and `update(Course)` are provided by the ITD, which uses Spring Data MongoDB calls to perform the persistence activities. These calls are enabled by the annotation `@RooRepositoryMongo`. They're similar in feature to the JPA repository CRUD methods. But they act on a NoSQL database, so the method signatures aren't an exact match. You should thoroughly research MongoDB before writing an application that uses it for persistence.

You can then execute code against the repository, as in this test, which uses a method, `createCourseWithOffering()`, to create the `Course` and a single offering:

```
@Autowired
private CourseRepository courseRepository;

...

@Test
public void testPersistCourseUsingRepository() {
  Course course = createCourseWithOffering();
  courseRepository.save(course);
  Assert.assertTrue(courseRepository.count() > 0);
  Course course2 = courseRepository.findOne(course.getId());
  Assert.assertEquals( course.getId(), course2.getId());
  Assert.assertEquals(1, course.getOfferings().size());
}
```

4.7.6 Creating a service for your MongoDB repository

Creating a service is the same procedure, whether you are using a JPA or MongoDB repository. Simply issue the `service` command:

```
roo> service --interface ~.service.CourseService ⇥
       --entity ~.model.Course
```

If you aimed your tests against the service, your methods would look similar to the SQL-based service wrapper methods. Roo tries to normalize the method names a bit. Here's the same test, but focused on a service instead:

```
@Autowired
private CourseService courseService;
```

```
@Test
public void testPersistCourseWithOffering() {
  Course course = createCourseWithOffering();
  courseAndOfferingService.saveCourse(course);
  Assert.assertTrue (courseAndOfferingService.countAllCourses() > 0);
  Course course2 = courseAndOfferingService.findCourse(course.getId());
  Assert.assertEquals( course.getId(), course2.getId());
  Assert.assertEquals(1, course.getOfferings().size());
}
```

The major differences between NoSQL and regular database services are

- NoSQL databases *don't* participate in transactions. The @Transactional annotation is ignored for methods called by Spring Data NoSQL stores.
- Tests don't clean up after themselves. You'll need to use JUnit annotations such as @Before and @After to remove or reset data.
- Relationships will behave differently and may need special supporting code. The example above just nests an Offering POJO within each Course, and doesn't attempt to create a true two-way relationship similar to JPA.

This feature is quite new, and may change in the future. But SpringSource is committed to the Spring Data API and to supporting both SQL and non-SQL data stores. For more information, please refer to the Spring Data project and the various subprojects for databases of interest.

4.8   Summary

In this chapter, we discussed how Spring Roo enables quick creation of JPA relationships and hierarchies. We showed how to work with transactions, and to create a traditional layered, service-based architecture that you'll usually find in other web-based applications using services and repositories.

We also discussed the support in Roo 1.2 for MongoDB, via the new Spring Data API. Spring Data will prove to be a huge asset to Spring Roo projects, as you saw in this chapter, and also enhance standard JPA, as you saw in the previous chapter.

Coming up in chapter 5, we'll begin to discuss web-based application development using Spring Roo. You'll configure your project as a web-based application, and learn how to leverage Roo to generate and manage your web user interfaces.

4.9   Resources

BOOKS

Keith, Mike, and Merrick Schincariol. *Pro JPA 2: Mastering the Java Persistence API* (Apress, 2009)

Yang, Daoqi, Ph D. *Java Persistence with JPA* (Outskirts Press, 2010)

WEB

A great, open source reference site for the JPA 2 standard and all of the myriad implementations is the JPA Wikibook—http://mng.bz/1a1v.

The Spring Data MongoDB API—http://mng.bz/rLm9. Pay close attention to the various GIT repositories that contain examples for the various features of the API.

Part 3

Web development

With the back-end data persistence out of the way, we'll switch gears in part 3 to focus on the user interface layer of your application.

Chapter 5, "Rapid web applications with Roo," covers Roo support for the Spring MVC framework and how you can develop controllers and view components of the application. You'll also learn how to web scaffold the entities to create web pages as well as RESTful controllers that take care of the CRUD requirements of entities.

In chapter 6, "Advanced web applications," you'll build on the web application created in the previous chapter and customize it by modifying view layouts. You'll also get a high-level overview of the theming concept, and we'll wrap up the chapter with a discussion on localization.

There are several other web technologies, such as the Dojo Toolkit, GWT, JSF, and AJax. Chapter 7, "RIA and other web frameworks," shows you how to integrate with these web APIs and frameworks in a Roo application.

Application security is a critical part of any software application. This is the focus of chapter 8, "Configuring security," where you'll learn how to implement security aspects such as authentication, access control, and restricting the URLs in an application. We'll also look at how to enable security event logging so you can log all security events that occur when your application is running.

Rapid web applications with Roo

This chapter covers
- Converting your application into a web application
- Developing controllers and views
- The web scaffolding engine
- Customizing your application

If you're like us and have written a lot of web application code, you probably expect to spend a significant amount of time to configure a web application. Because you want to get started, you may just want to dive right in, install Spring MVC by hand, and write some code against these entities.

Stop! Don't touch that keyboard yet! We'll show you how to save even more time by letting Roo configure and generate your web application for you.

In this chapter we use a simple Roo shell command, `web mvc controller`, to install Spring's MVC web framework, and generate a sample controller and view. Then we use `web mvc scaffold` to generate full web pages complete with create, read, update, delete, and searching capability. We review the scaffolding in depth so that you understand how it functions, and to prepare you for customizing the user interface in chapter 6.

You'll see that Roo provides a comprehensive Spring MVC solution at a fraction of the time it would take you to configure your own, and that it installs and configures key usability features, such as layout management and internationalization.

Let's get started by reviewing Spring's MVC framework.

5.1 The Spring MVC web framework

Spring MVC is an annotation-driven model-view-controller web framework that runs within the Spring container. The key components used by Spring MVC are as follows:

- *The dispatcher servlet*—Spring MVC controls all incoming requests by routing them through a *dispatcher servlet* that determines the appropriate action to perform based on the URL pattern, parameters, HTTP headers, and a number of other factors. This servlet controls the lifecycle of the HTTP request; it selects and processes the appropriate *controller*, captures the resulting *model*, and renders the correct *view*.

- *Controller*—Spring relies on user-defined MVC controllers to process the HTTP request. These controllers are POJOs that contain Spring's MVC annotations, such as @Controller, @RequestMapping, @PathVariable, and a number of others. Spring MVC controllers are just specialized Spring beans; they can use the @Autowired annotation to access other beans.

- *Model*—Generally, controllers execute calls to other Spring beans, and then gather results that need to be rendered to the end user. These results are loaded into a *model* object, a simple map-based class that can be injected into a Spring MVC controller method. The *dispatcher servlet* then passes along this model for rendering by the correct view.

- *View*—A view is the output of a Spring MVC operation, a representation of the results of a given request. Views can access any object provided in the model, and can be written using a number of rendering technologies, such as JSP, Velocity, FreeMarker, or even using PDF or Excel. Spring Roo is configured to use XML-compliant JSPs, which are commonly referred to as *JSPX views*.

  Roo's JSPX views are configured to use Apache Tiles, which is a layout engine that separates boilerplate code such as headers, footers, and other panels from the code specific to the view being rendered.

Figure 5.1 illustrates the interplay between the dispatcher servlet, controllers, models, and views.

> **WHAT ABOUT OTHER WEB FRAMEWORKS?** Spring MVC is the predominant web application framework for Spring, since it's an API within the Spring Framework, supports direct injection of Spring beans, and has full access to the application lifecycle.
>
> In the next chapter we look at other web frameworks supported by Roo, including Google Web Toolkit and JSF.

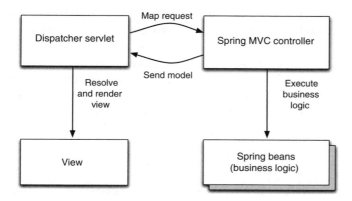

Figure 5.1   Spring MVC key components

It takes a significant amount of time and expertise to completely configure a web-based Spring application by hand. But as you've seen, Roo helps you by handling your dirty work, and for a web project architect there's plenty of that to go around. Roo takes care of configuring Spring MVC for you so you can focus on coding your web applications. Let's dive in and convert your project to a web application.

5.2   Roo Spring MVC quick-start

Remember the pizza shop example from chapter 1? The MVC setup was only two lines of Roo commands. In this section, you'll see how to direct Roo to generate and configure an entire web application structure, even the Tomcat and Jetty web servers, in just one command. We'll review components that Roo creates, such as the controller and view, and explain how to pass model information to the view for rendering. Let's go!

5.2.1   The web application and first controller

When Roo built your Course Manager application, it just configured it as a `jar` project. JAR projects are useful for things like command-line utilities, but they can't be deployed directly to a web application container such as Tomcat or Jetty. To get Roo to change the project type to a web application and output a `war` artifact, you need to execute the Spring MVC setup command:

```
roo> web mvc setup
```

Roo responds with a ton of output. Here's a bit of it:

```
Created SRC_MAIN_JAVA/.../web
...
Managed ROOT/pom.xml ➡
[Added dependency org.springframework:spring-web:${spring.version}]
Managed ROOT/pom.xml ➡
[Added dependency org.springframework:spring-webmvc:${spring.version}]
...
Managed ROOT/pom.xml
...
Managed SRC_MAIN_WEBAPP/WEB-INF/i18n/application.properties
Managed SRC_MAIN_WEBAPP/WEB-INF/views/menu.jspx
```

As usual, Roo just did your dirty work for you. It upgraded your project to a fully functional web application, installed Spring MVC, and configured a user interface that now includes a number of features: a menu system, header, footer, localization, and a bunch of custom JSP tags to make it easy to build pages and forms.

Roo installs Spring MVC artifacts in the src/main/webapp directory. This directory can contain raw HTML, JavaScript, CSS files, and other static resources. Table 5.1 shows key subdirectories of this root directory and their purpose.

Table 5.1   Key directories in src/main/webapp

File/Directory	Description
WEB-INF	The web descriptor directory—holds web.xml and other subdirectories.
WEB-INF/spring	Contains webmvc-config.xml, which defines the Spring MVC configuration.
WEB-INF/i18n	Contains all localized properties files. These files define the values of messages, labels, form elements, and page titles.
WEB-INF/layouts	Spring Roo uses Apache Tiles, a layout engine, to render views. The overall Tiles page layouts are defined in this directory.
WEB-INF/tags	Spring Roo custom JSPX tag libraries, used by views to render pages, forms, fields, and other elements.
WEB-INF/views	Contains the view files, which are comprised of JSPX pages and Apache Tiles view composition files.

If you had to configure all of the installed features yourself, you'd probably spend the better part of a couple of days researching and experimenting, perhaps with some cut-and-paste operations from other projects and examples on blogs and forum posts. Instead, Roo gives you a good starting place: a fully configured MVC project.

5.2.2   *Creating your first controller*

Ultimately you just want Roo to create a controller for you, so to do this you issue the web mvc controller command:

```
roo> web mvc controller --class ~.web.TestDriveController
```

You receive output similar to this:

```
Created SRC_MAIN_JAVA/org/rooinaction/coursemanager/web/➥
    TestDriveController.java
Updated SRC_MAIN_WEBAPP/WEB-INF/i18n/application.properties
Created SRC_MAIN_WEBAPP/WEB-INF/views/menu.jspx
Updated SRC_MAIN_WEBAPP/WEB-INF/i18n/application.properties
Created SRC_MAIN_WEBAPP/WEB-INF/views/testdrive
Created SRC_MAIN_WEBAPP/WEB-INF/views/testdrive/views.xml
Created SRC_MAIN_WEBAPP/WEB-INF/views/testdrive/index.jspx
Created SRC_MAIN_WEBAPP/WEB-INF/tags/menu/menu.tagx
Created SRC_MAIN_WEBAPP/WEB-INF/tags/menu/item.tagx
Created SRC_MAIN_WEBAPP/WEB-INF/tags/menu/category.tagx
Updated SRC_MAIN_WEBAPP/WEB-INF/views/menu.jspx
```

Roo builds the `TestDriveController` class and view artifacts, and even configures an entry on the menu system as well. Let's take a look at the generated `TestDrive-Controller`, shown in the following listing.

Listing 5.1   TestDriveController.java

```
package ...web;

...

@RequestMapping("/testdrive/**")
@Controller
public class TestDriveController {

  @RequestMapping(method = RequestMethod.POST,           POST
              value = "{id}")                            /testdrive/id
  public void post(@PathVariable Long id, ModelMap modelMap,
              HttpServletRequest request,
              HttpServletResponse response) {
  }
                                                         GET
  @RequestMapping                                        testdrive/*
  public String index() {
      return "testdrive/index";
  }
}
```

This controller uses the `@RequestMapping` annotation, which tells Spring MVC to map any requests with the given pattern to methods within this controller. The classlevel mapping, /testdrive/**, makes sure anything with a URL that begins with /testdrive is handled by this controller. Each method then provides its own request mapping, defining a unique URL subpattern, based on portions of the path, request attributes, request types (POST, GET), and other options.

Two methods are mapped:

- POST *on/testdrive/{id} via the* `post` *method*—The `post` method defines a further `@RequestMapping` with two further refinements: that the method responds to an HTTP POST call, and that the path includes a value after /testdrive/ which is mapped to the variable id. Note the curly-brace matcher syntax. A POST call to /testdrive/234 would be received by this method, and the id variable automatically converted to a `Long` variable.

- GET *on/testdrive/* via the* `index()` *method*—Because the `index()` method doesn't further refine the path, and the default method of `@RequestMapping` is GET, a simple GET to any path starting with /testdrive will call this method. This method actually functions, returning a view with the path of demo/index, which Spring's dispatcher servlet then resolves to a file named WEB-INF/views/testdrive/index.jspx, and renders the JSP file.

Controllers wouldn't be useful without a way to display the data that they place in their models. Let's take a look at the next component of your web application, the view.

Spring MVC and convention-driven programming

To better understand what's going on here, you need to know the underlying conventions. Spring MVC is a convention-driven API, which means that it processes methods based on the presence or absence of annotations, parameters, and return types in controller method definitions. Here are a few key concepts to keep in mind as you begin to look at some of these methods.

- If you define an `HttpServletRequest`, `HttpServletResponse`, `HttpSession`, `ModelMap` (map of values to render in the view), an `Errors` object, or a number of other components, they'll be injected automatically.

- If the method returns a String (as in the `index()` method above) it will be treated as a *view name*, and Spring MVC will attempt to resolve it based on the Roo-configured path for all views, /WEB-INF/views.

- As you saw earlier, `index` and `post` are all annotated with `@RequestMapping`, and although the `post` method currently does nothing, it can respond to POST requests to /testdrive. The index method responds to /testdrive/id, where *id* is a number. You'll see why this is important when we discuss Roo scaffolding in section 5.3.

5.2.3 *Views, tags, and templates*

One of the more complex parts of Spring Roo is the way it configures and manages MVC views. Roo uses an XML-compliant version of Java Server Pages, known as JSPX. These files must be XML-parseable, so that the Roo shell can manipulate them. As you'll see later, Roo can generate and maintain forms and form fields in your views automatically.

Roo uses the Apache Tiles templating framework to provide layout and a consistent look and feel from view to view, and to provide support for a menuing system, headers, and footers for each page. In addition, Roo makes heavy use of its own JSPX custom tags to simplify the view code.

When you installed `TestDriveController`, Spring Roo generated the testdrive directory in WEB-INF/views. In this directory are two files, index.jspx and views.xml. Ignore the views.xml file for now. The view for your controller's `index()` method is index.jspx, shown next.

Listing 5.2 The testdrive/index.jspx view

```
<?xml version="1.0" encoding="UTF-8" standalone="no"?>
<div xmlns:jsp="http://java.sun.com/JSP/Page"
  xmlns:util="urn:jsptagdir:/WEB-INF/tags/util"                    ⟵─── Install taglibs

  xmlns:spring="http://www.springframework.org/tags"
  version="2.0">

  <jsp:directive.page contentType="text/html;charset=UTF-8"/>
```

```
<jsp:output omit-xml-declaration="yes"/>                    ◁──── No <? XML ?>

    <spring:message code="label_testdrive_index" htmlEscape="false"
                          var="title"/>
    <util:panel id="title"
            title="${title}">
        <spring:message code="application_name"
              htmlEscape="false" var="app_name"/>
        <h3>
            <spring:message arguments="${app_name}"
              code="welcome_titlepane"/>
        </h3>
    </util:panel>
</div>
```

Store in ${title} ─┐→ (points to spring:message code="label_testdrive_index")

Container element ──┘← (points to util:panel)

Fetch app name ─┐→ (points to spring:message code="application_name")

Print message ──┘← (points to spring:message arguments)

This is a pretty compact view file, for several reasons. First Roo installs several tag libraries—the Spring MVC `spring:` tag library, JSTL tags, and the Roo-specific `util:` tag library. Next, because Roo uses Apache Tiles, the bulk of the page structure is hidden within a template. You're viewing only a fragment of the page, known as the *tile*, that represents the display area for your controller. The other tiles are combined with it to render the title, header, footer, and menu structure that you saw back in chapters 1 and 2.

The `page:page` tag wraps the page content in a bordered box, complete with a title bar.[1] The content is a simple message. However, how it's computed requires a bit of explanation.

LABELS AND THE MESSAGE TAG

This view makes heavy use of the `<spring:message />` tag, which fetches properties from two files, application.properties and messages.properties, located in the webapp directory WEB-INF/i18n. This tag can be used in two ways—first to fetch messages from localized properties files and store them in page variables, such as in this fragment, which stores the value of the property `application_name` in the local page variable `app_name`:

```
<spring:message code="application_name" var="app_name"/>
```

It can also be used to render output, such as in this fragment, which renders the message `welcome_titlepane`, using the fetched variable above as an argument:

```
<spring:message arguments="${app_name}" code="welcome_titlepane"/>
```

The `application_name` message referred to by the first example is located in the web application's WEB-INF/i18n directory, in a file named application.properties:

```
application_name=coursemanager-chapter-05
```

─────────────────────

[1] This is actually a Dojo rich JavaScript component, as are the fields that provide client-side validation and drop-down date fields. You can use Dojo to build your own view with your own hand-selected components. For now, keep in mind that Roo uses rich web interface components like this to give your web application a dynamic look and feel.

You may change your application's friendly name by editing that file. The `welcome_titlepane` message is located in another file in that directory—messages `.properties`:

```
#welcome page
welcome_titlepane=Welcome to {0}
```

The two files serve slightly different purposes:

- *messages.properties*—This provides the Roo web framework scaffolding page element labels, such as `button_save`, which defines the label for all Save buttons, and `field_invalid_integer`, which defines the error message to display when a field doesn't contain a valid integer value. Generally you don't need to add anything to this file that's application-specific.
- *application.properties*—This provides your application-specific and navigational framework label values, such as the label to use for each field, or for each element in the menu structure. The `application_name` in this file shows the name of your application in the title bar, and elements such as `label_testdrive _index` describe the labels to use for menu items that trigger controller invocations—in this case the `TestDriveController.index()` method. This file is heavily used by the scaffolding engine that we discuss later in this chapter.

CUSTOMIZING TEXT IN PROPERTIES FILES   You may customize the text of generated labels in application.properties. Roo will not overwrite your entries, and will not touch the ones created even by itself—once an entry is created in this file, it's available for customization by you from that point forward.

When you're defining your own labels for nonscaffolded controllers, generally you'll want to place them in the application.properties file in src/main/resources/META-INF/spring. You'll also have to register the filename (without extension) in the `p:basenames` property of the `ReloadableResourceBundleMessageSource` in src/main/webapp/WEB-INF/webmvc-config.xml.

After that, you can use the `<spring:message code="your code" />` tag to display your message. You could place messages in application.properties, as well, but since Roo adjusts that file each time it scaffolds, you could have a harder time organizing your properties.

5.2.4   *Launching the web application*

Now that you've created your controller and view, what do they do? Let's find out by firing up the server. Issue the following Maven command in your Roo project directory:

```
mvn package tomcat:run
```

The `package` keyword builds your Roo application, as you've seen in earlier chapters. The `tomcat:run` command launches Apache Tomcat on port 8080, and automatically loads your application to a web URI based on the name of your project, in this case /coursemanager.

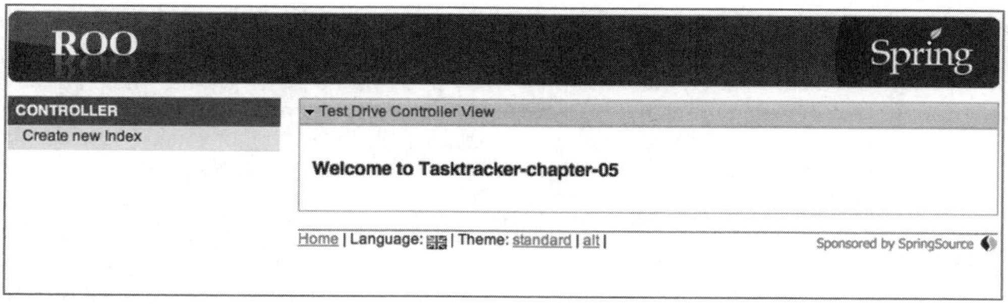

Figure 5.2   The default view page—terribly exciting!

PICK YOUR FAVORITE WEB CONTAINER   Roo installs both the Apache Tomcat and Jetty web container plug-ins. Choose between Tomcat and Jetty by issuing `tomcat:run` or `jetty:run`. See below for details on Jetty.

Browse to http://localhost:8080/coursemanager to view your web application's default page. Figure 5.2 shows the terribly exciting view.

Running on a different port

Tomcat runs by default on port 8080. You can customize what port the Tomcat web server runs on by modifying the plug-in settings within the pom.xml file. For example, replace the existing plug-in definition with something like this:

```
<plugin>
  <groupId>org.codehaus.mojo</groupId>
  <artifactId>tomcat-maven-plugin</artifactId>
  ...
  <configuration>
    <port>9090</port>
  </configuration>
</plugin>
```

Review other options for the Tomcat plug-in by visiting the plug-in's website at http://mng.bz/lgJ5.

If you're a SpringSource Tool Suite user, you can drag the project to a configured server in the Servers pane and install it in Tomcat or SpringSource tc Server automatically. If you leave your web server running, STS will automatically redeploy the application when it recompiles the project.

You can also run Jetty as your web server. In fact, some developers really dig Jetty because it's so easily customizable, and it's quite polite: it even tells you your web application name if you hit the root of the server by mistake! To kick off your application with Jetty, just use

```
mvn jetty:run
```

Customizing the Jetty plug-in

Here's a nice customization for you—Jetty has a setting, scanIntervalSeconds, that will scan for changes to the Maven project, and reload the web application automatically. You can edit the Maven pom.xml file in the root of your project, and change the jetty-maven-plugin to take advantage of this feature:

```
<groupId>org.mortbay.jetty</groupId>
<artifactId>jetty-maven-plugin</artifactId>
<version>7.4.2.v20110526</version>
  <configuration>
    <scanIntervalSeconds>5</scanIntervalSeconds>
  </configuration>
</plugin>
```

Now every time you perform an mvn package command, Jetty will automatically reload. There are a ton of other configuration features in jetty-maven-plugin; it's worth spending an hour reviewing the documentation, at http://mng.bz/1MM6.

5.2.5 *Customizing your view*

Of course, Roo isn't psychic. It can't automatically figure out what you want the TestDriveController to do. It expects you to actually *code something* in that index() method before it returns the view name. So, let's start small. What if you wanted to render the current time? You'd have to place the current date and time in the Model, so that you can render it in the view.

To do this, you just add a parameter to the index method, Model map, and then use the addAttribute method of the model to inject the currentDate attribute to the view. Let's change the index() method in the TestController class to something like this:

```
@RequestMapping
public String index(Model map) {
  map.addAttribute("currentDate", new java.util.Date());
  return "testdrive/index";
}
```

When Spring MVC sees the ModelMap class, it injects it into the method automatically.

In the testdrive/index.jspx view file, you can now reference ${currentDate} and omit the String value of the current date. The lines between <util:panel> and </util:panel> can be changed to

```
<h3>
  <spring:message arguments="${app_name}" code="welcome_titlepane"/>
</h3>
<p>
  It is now ${currentDate} - you should be doing something productive.
</p>
```

You've changed Java code, so restart the server. Figure 5.3 shows the newly customized example, complete with dynamic evaluation from the controller.

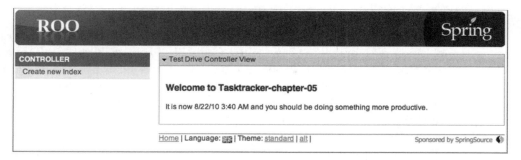

Figure 5.3 index.jspx rendering the time

How does Spring MVC resolve the right view?

When the method returns `testdrive/index`, Spring MVC delegates to the Tiles view resolving mechanism, passing it a template named `testdrive/index`. Look in the WEB-INF/views directory for the testdrive subdirectory, and review views.xml:

```
<definition extends="default" name="testdrive/index">
   <put-attribute name="body"
       value="/WEB-INF/views/testdrive/index.jspx"/>
</definition>
```

Roo configures a definition for a tile named `testdrive/index`. It uses the `default` layout, and the `body` tile resolves to testdrive/index.jspx.

5.2.6   Customize that message!

Simply done, eh? But to be a better web developer (cue the music) you should probably follow the Spring Roo conventions and externalize this message. Add your message to the end of the #welcome page section of WEB-INF/i18n/messages.properties, keeping the original `welcome_titlepane` message:

```
#welcome page
welcome_titlepane=Welcome to {0}
testdrive_date_message=It is now {0} ➥
  and you should be doing something productive.
```

To use this message in the view, replace the `${currentDate}` paragraph fragment with this snippet:

```
<p>
  <spring:message arguments="${currentDate}"
    code="testdrive_date_message" />
</p>
```

Spring replaces the value of `{0}` in the message with the model attribute, `currentDate`, and uses some built-in formatting rules to render it properly. More complex objects, including things like a list of query results, can be placed in the model map, which is generally how Spring MVC deals with data that needs to be rendered in a view.

You'll learn more about messages and locales in chapter 6.

5.3 *Web scaffolding for entities*

Ken remembers someone once lamenting about the trials and tribulations of web application development. They wanted to do all of this really cool stuff, integrating with other systems, doing complex graphical work, and meaty programming. But they said, "It's ridiculous. What do we always do, day in and day out? Suck data out of a database, show it to the user, and let them change it. Period." Yep, that's right. You spend 90% of your time fetching, displaying, modifying, creating, and deleting that pesky data!

Why is manipulating database data so much work? Most of your Spring coding traditionally involves wiring up data access objects, services, controllers, and views to present and modify data. Shouldn't it be easier to do this? And less manual? That's where Spring Roo can really help.

In this section we'll delve into the world of scaffolded Roo controllers. You'll see how to generate a scaffolded course controller, and we'll review each of the generated controller methods and views for the list, create, update, and delete operations. We'll also look at how Roo integrates finders into these controllers.

5.3.1 *Creating the course scaffold*

Fully functional Spring Roo controllers that can handle create, read, update, and delete operations can be generated automatically by using the web mvc scaffold command. To generate a Roo scaffolded controller and views for a Course entity, just enter the following command in the Roo shell:

```
roo> web mvc scaffold --class ~.web.CourseController ➥
    --backingType ~.model.Course
```

The options, --class and --entity, specify the name of the new controller and the entity to use, respectively. Again, Roo responds by performing a number of actions. Assuming you've already set up the MVC framework with the first web mvc controller command, the output will look like this:

```
Created SRC_MAIN_JAVA/org/rooinaction/coursemanager/➥
  web/CourseController.java
Created SRC_MAIN_JAVA/org/rooinaction/coursemanager/web/➥
  CourseController_Roo_Controller.aj
Created SRC_MAIN_WEBAPP/WEB-INF/views/courses
Created SRC_MAIN_WEBAPP/WEB-INF/views/courses/list.jspx
Created SRC_MAIN_WEBAPP/WEB-INF/views/courses/views.xml
Created SRC_MAIN_WEBAPP/WEB-INF/views/courses/show.jspx
Managed SRC_MAIN_WEBAPP/WEB-INF/views/courses/views.xml
Created SRC_MAIN_WEBAPP/WEB-INF/views/courses/create.jspx
Managed SRC_MAIN_WEBAPP/WEB-INF/i18n/application.properties
Managed SRC_MAIN_WEBAPP/WEB-INF/views/menu.jspx
Managed SRC_MAIN_WEBAPP/WEB-INF/views/courses/views.xml
Created SRC_MAIN_WEBAPP/WEB-INF/views/courses/update.jspx
Managed SRC_MAIN_WEBAPP/WEB-INF/views/courses/views.xml
Managed SRC_MAIN_WEBAPP/WEB-INF/i18n/application.properties
Managed SRC_MAIN_WEBAPP/WEB-INF/views/menu.jspx
```

Again, that's a lot of processing. Of course, this time Spring Roo generates a few key files, including

- The controller, `CourseController.java`
- The AspectJ ITD, `CourseController_Roo_Controller.aj`
- Menu items to list and create courses in the shared file, `menu.jspx`
- Views to manage listing, creating, reading, updating, and deleting courses contained in WEB-INF/views/courses

We'll focus on a number of these components, but first let's start by identifying the views contained within WEB-INF/views/courses in table 5.2.

Table 5.2   Key scaffolded views

File/Directory	Use
list.jspx	A view that displays a list of entities in a tabular format.
show.jspx	A view that displays a single entity row in a form-based view.
create.jspx	A view that generates an editable form that can create a new entity.
update.jspx	A view that generates an editable form that can edit an existing entity.
views.xml	The Apache Tiles configuration for all views in this directory. This file defines the Tiles layout to use, which is defined in /WEB-INF/layouts/layouts.xml.

These view files are generated and configured using the Roo JSPX tag libraries, which are installed in WEB-INF/tags. You've already seen the `util:panel` tag in listing 5.2; but various page wrapper tags, such as `page:create`, `page:update`, and `page:list`, will wrap the various view pages to provide the proper forms and container elements. All fields available in the entity are generated as fields in these various view files.

Just as it did with entities, Roo creates the `CourseController.java` class, but also generates an AspectJ ITD, `CourseController_Roo_Controller.aj`. This aspect contains all scaffolded logic to manage creating, reading, updating, and deleting `Course` entities.

Roo also edits WEB-INF/i18n/application.properties with labels for all fields and the entity name itself for form rendering purposes, and adds menu items to `menu.jspx`, which was created when Roo generated the web application.

Just as the `Course.java` Roo entity itself seems a bit simple and empty, so does the actual Java controller. But that's because the magic is in the generated ITD file. Let's review the generated `Controller` class, `CourseController.java`, in the following listing.

Listing 5.3   The `CourseController.java` Roo scaffold controller

```
package org.rooina.coursemanager.web;
import org.rooina.coursemanager.model.Course;
import org.springframework.roo.addon.web.mvc.controller➥
    .scaffold.RooWebScaffold;
```

```
import org.springframework.stereotype.Controller;
import org.springframework.web.bind.annotation.RequestMapping;

@RooWebScaffold(path = "courses",
                formBackingObject = Course.class)
@RequestMapping("/courses")
@Controller
public class CourseController {
}
```

Establish scaffold

Maps /courses

Spring bean annotation

This controller class manages all operations against the Course entity. The code to implement the controller actions is stored within the AspectJ ITD. Roo generates and maintains the JSPX pages based on the @RooWebScaffold annotation.

> **CODE GENERATION? ICK, I'VE SEEN THIS BEFORE!**   Yeah, we've seen this before as well. It's very difficult to write a good system and then keep it up to date by forward- and reverse-engineering changes to the software. We think that Roo is a different animal because it makes a distinction between *user-editable arti-facts* and generated *ITDs*. If Roo generates a normal file, such as a class like CourseController, or a localization file like application.properties, it won't overwrite it later. But if Roo creates a Roo-managed intermediate file, such as the Course_Roo_Controller.aj AspectJ ITD, it'll manage it entirely via the Roo shell.
>
> The gray area in all of this is the view technology. Since Roo generated the views as user-editable elements, any changes made by a developer must generally be honored. In fact, if you change your templates around, modify the HTML code, or otherwise modify the boilerplate code, Roo will allow this to happen. But if you change fields within forms, special considerations must be made, which we'll review in chapter 6, section 1, "Customizing Roo CRUD views."

Now, let's take a look at the various views and controllers generated by your web mvc scaffold operation. We'll review the files based on the operations they provide. First, let's take a look at the GET operation.

5.3.2   *Fetching courses*

The GET operations your scaffolded controller supports are both a list of all of the Course objects and the display of a single Course. Both operations are supported by different generated controller methods and views. We'll look at both in turn, starting with the listing operation.

LISTING COURSES

The list operation is called by performing HTTP GET operations on http://localhost :8080/coursemanager/courses. First, review the next listing to see the list method Roo generates in the CourseController_Roo_Controller.aj file.

Listing 5.4 The list method in `CourseController_Roo_Controller.aj`

```
                  @RequestMapping(method = RequestMethod.GET)          ◄─── Map to GET
                  public String CourseController.list(
Paging              @RequestParam(value = "page", required = false) Integer page,
params              @RequestParam(value = "size", required = false) Integer size,

                    Model uiModel) {                                   ◄─── Inject model

Calculate         if (page != null || size != null) {
page size
                      int sizeNo = size == null ? 10 : size.intValue();
                      final int firstResult = page == null ? 0 : (page.intValue() - 1)
                                  * sizeNo;
                      uiModel.addAttribute("courses",                    | Limit
                        Course.findCourseEntries(                      ◄─┘ results
                            page == null ? 0 : (page.intValue() - 1) * sizeNo, sizeNo));
                      float nrOfPages = (float) Course.countCourses() / sizeNo;
                      uiModel.addAttribute("maxPages",
                            (int) ((nrOfPages > (int) nrOfPages || nrOfPages == 0.0) ?
                                    nrOfPages + 1 : nrOfPages));        ◄─┐ Set max
                  } else {                                               | page #
Simple                uiModel.addAttribute("courses", Course.findAllCourses());
fetch all         }
                  return "courses/list";                               ◄─── Render list view
                  }
```

This method is mapped to /courses. When you ask to GET tasks based on this URL, the controller fetches all of the tasks and places them in ${courses} to render in the view. The controller supports paging results if the page and size parameters are passed as parameters to the URL; otherwise it fetches all rows. The controller also tells the view how many pages of rows were available, if paging was enabled.

> **ROO BUILDS RESTFUL CONTROLLERS**   Roo URLs are all based on the REST web URL philosophy, which treats URLs as nouns (resources) and HTTP verbs such as GET, POST, PUT, and DELETE as actions. Getting the /courses resource returns all courses, whereas getting the /courses/1 resource returns the course with the primary key of 1. You'll see the syntax {id} in many mapped URLs; this refers to the primary key in the path.
>
>   These verbs are also used by other actions, such as creating (POST of /courses), updating (PUT of /courses/1 with updated field values), and deleting (DELETE of /courses/1).[2]

The list method returns the value courses/list, which resolves to the JSPX view file list.jspx in the WEB-INF/views/courses directory. Let's review the contents of list.jspx. If you're familiar with Spring MVC and the form taglib, you'll be pleasantly surprised by the use of tag libraries, which shorten the amount of code in the next listing.

---

[2] For more information about REST, start with the excellent Wikipedia article at http://mng.bz/1PMN.

Listing 5.5   Displaying courses with list.jspx

```
<?xml version="1.0" encoding="UTF-8" standalone="no"?>
<div xmlns:jsp="http://java.sun.com/JSP/Page"
   xmlns:page="urn:jsptagdir:/WEB-INF/tags/form"
   xmlns:table="urn:jsptagdir:/WEB-INF/tags/form/fields" version="2.0">
 <jsp:directive.page contentType="text/html;charset=UTF-8"/>
 <jsp:output omit-xml-declaration="yes"/>

 <page:list
   id="pl_org_rooinaction_coursemanager_model_Course"           ◁─┐  Wrap page/add
   items="${courses}"                                                title bar
   z="96XNQVUu9T1imC4uiLwuHR/mKek=">

   <table:table data="${courses}"                                ◁─┐  Define
     id="l_org_rooinaction_coursemanager_model_Course"              result table
     path="/courses"
     z="qVCdFgjW5phyYDfJQjmF1RSutAU=">

     <table:column
       id="c_org_rooinaction_coursemanager_model_Course_name"
       property="name"
       z="+Od93IeY6yNEhIqYKMtNvd3VFhI="/>
     <table:column
       id="c_org_rooinaction_coursemanager_model_Course_description"
       property="description"
       z="xzNe6X4uX1G8fjujNE/WAf2Sllc="/>
     <table:column
       id="c_org_rooinaction_..._model_Course_maximumCapacity"
       property="maximumCapacity"
       z="k+14ZPOEtltYpPYoniqaCy+lxNI="/>
     <table:column
       id="c_org_rooinaction_coursemanager_model_Course_courseType"
       property="courseType"
       z="v6SsRm1w+xYp8X4Uj1zzOsOOQ3Q="/>
     <table:column
       id="c_org_rooinaction_c..._model_Course_trainingProgram"
       property="trainingProgram"
       z="/tgEAE0TzwtEI8UwkYG5h9Q7nyM="/>
     <table:column
       id="c_org_rooinaction_coursemanager_model_Course_tags"
       property="tags"
       z="LGrxj3NPcOmRo83ddIG8NpSCWgo="/>

   </table:table>

 </page:list>
</div>
```

The first thing you might notice is that you're not defining a full JSP page. In fact, the file looks a lot more like an XML document than an HTML page. That's because the combination of using Apache Tiles to render page fragments and the heavy use of JSP tag libraries reduces the view to a tighter, more compact version of the usual view. That is, except things like those strangely long id and z fields. More about those later.

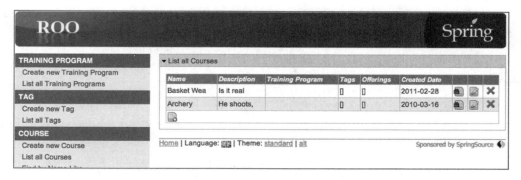

Figure 5.4   The course list view

Roo composes this tile fragment using the JSP tag `page:list`. This tag sets up the container for the next tag, `table:table`, which renders an HTML table of results. The results, coming from `${courses}` in the controller, are rendered using `table:column` elements. All of these tags are available for review and editing in webapp/web-inf/tags.

The resulting output of the course listing view should be similar in appearance to figure 5.4.

As you can see, the results are paginated, with alternating grey and white bars for the rows. The list is wrapped with a box that's entitled List all Courses, and if you click on the List all Courses drop-down arrow, it collapses the entire view. Icons are shown for various actions, which all result in further calls to methods in the course controller's ITD. These icons are

- ▪ —Adds a new course. Displays a form that you can use to enter the data for the new course.
- ▪ ✖ —Deletes a course. Prompts the user before deletion.
- ▪ —Displays the course in a single-object view page. Useful for showing larger fields such as comments.
- ▪ —Updates/edits a course. Displays a form, populated with data values, that persists updates to the given course.

Clicking on any of these icons navigates to the other actions.

You should spend some time getting familiar with the custom tag libraries, such as `list.tagx`, `table.tagx`, and `column.tagx`. We'll continue to customize the user interface as we go through the `CourseController` example.

Now let's see how you can review an individual course.

SHOWING A SINGLE COURSE

If a user clicks on the icon for a given course in the web application, the browser navigates to another URL, passing the primary key as part of the path. If the key value selected is 42, the URL generated is /courses/42. The method mapped to this URL pattern is called `show`. Let's take a look at it:

```
@RequestMapping(value = "/                                          /courses/{id}
        {id}", method = RequestMethod.GET)
public String CourseController.show(@PathVariable("id") Long id,     Capture
                                    Model uiModel) {                 path
    uiModel.addAttribute("course", Course.findCourse(id));
    uiModel.addAttribute("itemId", id);                             Selected key
    return "courses/show";
}
```

Fetch into "course" → `uiModel.addAttribute("course", Course.findCourse(id));`

/courses/{id} ← `@RequestMapping(value = "/{id}", ...)`

Capture path ← `public String CourseController.show(...)`

Selected key ← `uiModel.addAttribute("itemId", id);`

There's a bit of interplay going on between this view and the list view in listing 5.5. The list view's `table:table` tag generates a table of results, each of which contains a link to edit an individual `Course`.

The `show` method, mapped to the `/tasks/{id}` URL pattern, takes the course primary key from the incoming URL path directly after courses/ and places it in the `show` method as the parameter `id`. Then it retrieves a course using the `Course.find-Course(id)` entity method, storing the result in the `Model` as `course`, which will be referenced by the JSP view below.

The `show` method returns the value `courses/show`, which resolves to the view file in the WEB-INF/views/tasks directory named show.jspx. The following listing reviews this file.

Listing 5.6   Showing a single course with show.jspx

```
<?xml version="1.0" encoding="UTF-8" standalone="no"?>
<div xmlns:field="urn:jsptagdir:/WEB-INF/tags/form/fields"
    xmlns:jsp="http://java.sun.com/JSP/Page"
    xmlns:page="urn:jsptagdir:/WEB-INF/tags/form" version="2.0">
    <jsp:directive.page contentType="text/html;charset=UTF-8"/>
    <jsp:output omit-xml-declaration="yes"/>
    <page:show id="ps_org_rooinaction_..._model_Course"            Uses show tag
            object="${course}"
            path="/courses"                                        Renders
            z="Qrf8vecfH2gWwxWHG3q4QtjF0Zg=">                      view-only
        <field:display field="name"                                field
                id="s_org_rooinaction_..._model_Course_name"
                object="${course}"
                z="k6vilxSyD8vQwd4un1clBGrNjXI="/>
        ...
    </page:show>
</div>
```

Uses show tag ← `<page:show id="ps_org_rooinaction_..._model_Course"`

Renders view-only field ← `<field:display field="name"`

The page looks similar to the list view above, but you'll notice that the page is now surrounded by a `page:show` tag, and that each field is no longer rendered by `table:column`, but by a `field:display` tag. This form is rendered as a read-only view of a single `Course`. Roo automatically shows this view if you click on the 🗄 icon for a given row in the list view, or once you create or update a row using the Create New Course menu item or click the 🖊 icon.

Of course, it would be rather difficult to list or show tasks without actually creating one. Let's see how to create a `Course`, using the HTTP `POST` operation.

5.3.3 Creating a new course

Spring MVC follows a very specific pattern for form-based processing, illustrated in figure 5.5.

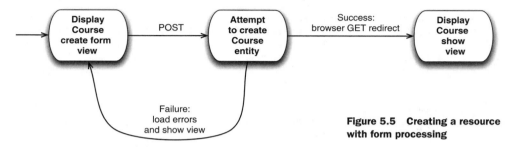

Figure 5.5 Creating a resource with form processing

As you see above, creating new entities requires first the display of a form that can edit the data. To create a new empty Course and edit it with the form, users would select the Create New Course menu item, which requests /courses?form. This URL maps to the createForm controller method in the Course_Roo_Controller.aj ITD:

```
@RequestMapping(params = "form", method = RequestMethod.GET)
public String CourseController.createForm(Model uiModel) {
    uiModel.addAttribute("course", new Course());
    return "courses/create";
}
```

The params = "form" code in the @RequestMapping annotation is what makes Roo map this form using /courses?form. In this method, Roo calls the new Course() constructor to create a single Course entity instance. This instance is then added to the model map as *course* and the JSPX Tiles view rendered is courses/create, which renders the view fragment located in WEB-INF/views/course/create.jspx, as shown next.

Listing 5.7 Creating a new course with create.jspx

```
<?xml version="1.0" encoding="UTF-8" standalone="no"?>
<div xmlns:c="http://java.sun.com/jsp/jstl/core"
  xmlns:field="urn:jsptagdir:/WEB-INF/tags/form/fields"
  xmlns:form="urn:jsptagdir:/WEB-INF/tags/form"
  xmlns:jsp="http://java.sun.com/JSP/Page"
  xmlns:spring="http://www.springframework.org/tags" version="2.0">
 <jsp:directive.page contentType="text/html;charset=UTF-8"/>
 <jsp:output omit-xml-declaration="yes"/>

 <form:create id="fc_org_rooina_coursemanager_model_Course"        ◁┐ Map
   modelAttribute="course" path="/courses"                            POST/courses
   render="${empty dependencies}"
   z="1dbo16WMREluRULwzHVH0bkl1Rs=">

  <field:textarea field="name"                                      ◁┐ Editable
    id="c_org_rooinaction_coursemanager_model_Course_name"             TextArea
    required="true"
    z="yGVxN/bavsqgDzN24/udCm+MpYw="/>
```

```
<field:textarea field="description"
  id="c_org_rooinaction_coursemanager_model_Course_description"
  required="true"
  z="dulpIS46tuOqeAFu0bbOlchgsLE="/>                          ◁─┘ Editable
                                                                    input
                                                                    field
<field:input field="maximumCapacity"
  id="c_org_rooinaction_coursemanager_model_Course_maximumCapacity"
  max="9999" min="1" required="true"
  validationMessageCode="field_invalid_integer"
  z="bw8OLox9ujpvV3FDaCqbKFOkycs="/>                          ◁─┘ Single
                                                                    select
<field:select field="courseType"                                    box
  id="c_org_rooinaction_coursemanager_model_Course_courseType"
  items="${coursetypeenums}"
  path="coursetypeenums"
  required="true"
  z="9Wjhb/YldSfBx/NGqUHcOL81498="/>
<field:select field="trainingProgram"
  id="c_org_rooinaction_coursemanager_model_Course_trainingProgram"
  itemValue="id"
  items="${trainingprograms}"
  path="/trainingprograms"
  z="PIDOSj5EPAbkyLOBrO7UHh7MVcE="/>                          ◁─┘ Multiselect
<field:select field="tags"                                          box
  id="c_org_rooinaction_coursemanager_model_Course_tags"
  itemValue="id"
  items="${tags}"
  multiple="true"
  path="/tags"
  z="OjMaU8+t56vaoiVt+RZTpV7kZ9U="/>
<field:simple field="offerings"
  id="c_org_rooinaction_coursemanager_model_Course_offerings"
  messageCode="entity_reference_not_managed"
  messageCodeAttribute="Offering"
  z="2RF1uqlkibELoOAa2snrwO7TTJA="/>
                                                             ◁─┘ Manages
</form:create>                                                      relationship
                                                                    links
<form:dependency dependencies="${dependencies}"
  id="d_org_rooinaction_coursemanager_model_Course"
  render="${not empty dependencies}"
  z="wjqVoEysCSIfkBbzWw9vmQjMvhg="/>
</div>
```

This is a fully functional HTML form page. The HTML form tag is generated by the `<form:create>` tag, which establishes that the form will be submitted using the POST method to the URI /courses.

Users with JavaScript-capable browsers will see the automatic rich field generation, including date pop-ups for date fields, and automatic rule validation. Try clicking in a field, and entering invalid data. Experiment with skipping required fields. You should get feedback from the web page immediately upon leaving the field.

There are several field types used in the form above. Table 5.3 lists the field types available in the Roo tag library.

Table 5.3 Roo form field types

Tag name	Supported datatypes	Notes
checkbox	boolean	Used to set a Boolean field value.
datetime	java.util.Date, java.util.Calendar	Several validation options available, including regular expressions, future, past, and required.
editor	String	A rich text editor, used for fields that need to incorporate HTML elements. Includes tool bar. Not used by default in scaffolding.
input	String	Standard HTML input text box. The default for any field not selected by another strategy, and for String fields less than 30 characters in length.
reference	Not used directly	The dependency and select tags call this tag to render an HTML fragment which can create a new entity reference; for example, if a course depends on a curriculum, the select tag may defer to a reference tag to render the create link when the curriculum is unassigned.
select	Set, Enums	Supports relationship and enumerated type assignments. Using multiple=true allows for multiple select values; false allows for single-ended relationship element selections. Falls back to rendering reference fields if no collection rows found. This shows a create link to build a new instance of the referenced type.
simple	Reference to entity	Since one-to-many collections are managed from the *many* end, on the *one* end you simply display the fact that this side does not manage the relationship.
textarea	String, javax.persistence.Lob	Used for String or large object fields if they exceed 30 characters.

What is the `form:dependency` tag?

The `<form:dependency>` tag will render any dependent collections (defined in the entity using the JPA `@ManyToOne` annotation, for example) when there's no corresponding `@OneToMany` annotation in the parent relationship. An example exists in the Roo sample `petclinic.roo`: in the `VisitController_Roo_Controller.aj` ITD:

```
List dependencies = new ArrayList();
if (Pet.countPets() == 0) {
    dependencies.add(new String[]{"pet", "pets"});
}
uiModel.addAttribute("dependencies", dependencies);
```

This fragment sets up a `<field:reference>` tag for the `Pet` entity within the `Visit` form.

Next, let's review the `CourseController.create` method, which processes submitted data from this form. This is the heart of the forms processing in figure 5.5:

```
@RequestMapping(method = RequestMethod.POST)
public String CourseController.create(@Valid Course course,
                        BindingResult result, Model uiModel,
                        HttpServletRequest request) {
    if (result.hasErrors()) {
        uiModel.addAttribute("course", course);
        return "courses/create";
    }
    uiModel.asMap().clear();
    course.persist();
    return "redirect:/courses/" +
            encodeUrlPathSegment(course.getId().toString(), request);
}
```

The request accepts all POST requests to /courses, and then validates the data using the `@Valid` annotation. The result of the validation is placed in the `BindingResult` attribute, `result`, and is interrogated. If no errors are returned in the result object, you're redirected to the single-task view, *show*. However, if errors do exist, you're redirected back to the create page (and the errors are automatically displayed).

After performing the POST operation, the MVC framework is asked to *redirect after posting* to the `list` view by issuing a browser HTTP response code 302 MOVED. This forces the browser to browse to a new location. Redirecting after POST makes it impossible for the user to bookmark the actual POST operation, since the URL rewritten is now a GET of the /courses URL instead of the /courses/{id} URL using a POST.

HOW CAN I CUSTOMIZE MY FORM FIELD VALUE DEFAULTS?   That's actually pretty easy. Push-in the `CourseController.createForm` method to your `Course-Controller.java` and modify the code.

   You can then create the course any way you wish and set values that make sense to you. If you're manually moving the `createForm` method, be sure to run the Roo shell to have it remove the ITD-generated one.

The combination of the `createForm` action, the `create.jspx` form, and the `create` action comprise the complete `Course` creation page and controller logic. Course modification is just as easy, and follows a parallel set of files and behaviors. Let's see how we can perform updates to existing courses in an almost identical way.

5.3.4   *Updating courses with PUT*

Just as the create course process is performed using a combination of the `createForm` method, `create.jspx`, and `create` method, the update course process is performed using an `updateForm` method, an `update.jspx` page, and an `update` action, as you see in figure 5.6.

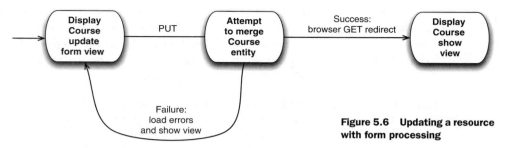

Figure 5.6 Updating a resource with form processing

First, let's take a look at the updateForm method, which responds to a GET request for the URL /courses/{id}?form (where {id} is the actual course primary key field):

```
@RequestMapping(value = "/{id}", params="form"
                method = RequestMethod.GET)
public String CourseController.updateForm(
                @PathVariable("id") Long id, Model uiModel) {
    uiModel.addAttribute("course", Course.findCourse(id));
    return "courses/update";
}
```

This method is remarkably similar to the create method in section 5.3.3. However, the major difference is that it maps to a GET method that passes a Course ID via the URL path just after /courses. The updateForm method uses this id field to call the Course.findCourses(id) method, which fetches the entity row. The method then adds the course to the model map, and redirects to the edit form.

Let's take a look at this form view, courses/update.jspx, in the following listing.

Listing 5.8 Updating a course with update.jspx

```
<?xml version="1.0" encoding="UTF-8" standalone="no"?>
<div xmlns:field="urn:jsptagdir:/WEB-INF/tags/form/fields"
  xmlns:form="urn:jsptagdir:/WEB-INF/tags/form" ...>

  <jsp:directive.page contentType="text/html;charset=UTF-8"/>
  <jsp:output omit-xml-declaration="yes"/>                              ⊲┐ Render
                                                                          │ PUT
                                                                          │ form
  <form:update id="fu_org_rooinaction_coursemanager_model_Course"     ⊲┘
        modelAttribute="course" path="/courses"                       ⊲
                                                                          ┐ PUT to /courses
        z="W+tY688qI4UrvLOmD4oC8et5MVM=">

      <field:textarea field="name"                                       ⊲┐ Field
          id="c_org_rooinaction_coursemanager_model_Course_name"          │ definitions
          required="true"
          z="yGVxN/bavsqgDzN24/udCm+MpYw="/>

      ...

  </form:update>
</div>
```

So far, this should look very familiar. This is a mirror image of the create form pattern above. The major differences are that you're submitting your form data to the same URL using the HTTP PUT method and that you've embedded hidden form data including the existing primary key field value (known as *id*), and a version field, which can be used to detect modifications by others after you've fetched your data.

> **WAIT, BROWSERS ONLY ISSUE GET AND POST OPERATIONS!** You've seen for things like the update and remove operations that the tags look like they're issuing PUT and DELETE operations. However, in general, web browsers can only operate on several operations: GET, OPTIONS, POST, and HEAD being the main ones. PUT and DELETE are operations defined by the HTTP RFC. However, you'll notice you're mapping all of your operations to the other operations, such as RequestMethod.DELETE. How does Roo identify these?
>
> The reason this works is because Roo uses a HiddenHttpMethodFilter. This method looks for an HTTP request parameter named _method, which is set to the desired HTTP method such as GET, POST, PUT, and DELETE. Spring MVC then converts these GET and POST requests internally to PUT and DELETE requests based on that field.
>
> Spring Roo builds RESTful URLs using this technique, and if you install the proper Spring configuration elements, you can also support RESTful calls to manipulate your entities using Spring's REST support and JSON or XML automatically. You'll see an example of this in the next chapter.

Below you see the update method in the ITD, which will save your changes to the course object, or redirect you back to editing the form in the case of an error:

```
@RequestMapping(method = RequestMethod.PUT)
public String CourseController.update(
      @Valid Course course, BindingResult bindingResult,
      Model uiModel, HttpServletRequest httpServletRequest) {
   if (bindingResult.hasErrors()) {
     uiModel.addAttribute("course", course);
     return "courses/update";
   }
   uiModel.asMap().clear();
   course.merge();
   return "redirect:/courses/"
           + encodeUrlPathSegment(course.getId().toString(),
                 httpServletRequest);
}
```

Just like the create() method in section 5.3.3, you're accepting Course data, validating it, and then either persisting with merge() and showing the single course view, or redirecting to the entry page to display errors. This is the kind of boilerplate code Roo excels at generating, saving you the time to build, wire up, and debug the methods and views.

We are almost finished looking at the basic data manipulation operations. Finally, we should review the delete course action, so you can remove Courses you're no longer interested in.

5.3.5 Removing a course with DELETE

Let's say you're ready to remove a course. Roo has this operation covered too. You can click on the ✖ icon to trigger the delete operation. The HTTP DELETE operation is mapped to a method on the CourseController ITD named delete:

```
@RequestMapping(value = "/{id}", method = RequestMethod.DELETE)
public String CourseController.delete(
        @PathVariable("id") Long id,
        @RequestParam(value = "page", required = false) Integer page,
        @RequestParam(value = "size", required = false) Integer size,
        Model uiModel) {
    Course.findCourse(id).remove();
    uiModel.asMap().clear();
    uiModel.addAttribute("page",
            (page == null) ? "1" : page.toString());
    uiModel.addAttribute("size",
            (size == null) ? "10" : size.toString());
    return "redirect:/courses";

}
```

The Course.findCourse(id).remove() statement from the Course ITD performs the delete operation. First, the course id passed to the delete method is used to look up the course using findCourse, and then the remove method removes the found course.

The rest of the code within the delete method handles any paging settings, such as the number of rows per page and the number of the current page passed to the original list view, which is where the DELETE operation is generally being called from.

The DELETE operation then redirects the browser to the list operation again, by navigating to /courses.

5.3.6 Scaffolding and finders

You can expose the finders we discussed in chapter 3 to your web pages. Let's assume a finder is defined on the Course entity to search using the SQL LIKE keyword, which we defined in chapter 3. The syntax for that command would have been

```
~.model.Course roo> finder add --finderName findCoursesByNameLike
```

To expose the finders to your scaffolded controller, you have two choices:

- Use the web mvc finder add command:

  ```
  roo> web mvc finder add --formBackingType ~.model.Course ⇨
      --class ~.web.CourseController
  ```

- Just annotate the CourseController with the @RooWebFinder annotation (which has the same effect as using the web mvc finder add command).

Once you do one of the above, Roo wakes up and generates the web-tier methods and artifacts:

```
Updated SRC_MAIN_JAVA/org/rooinaction/.../web/CourseController.java
Updated SRC_MAIN_WEBAPP/WEB-INF/views/courses/views.xml
Updated SRC_MAIN_WEBAPP/WEB-INF/i18n/application.properties
```

```
Created SRC_MAIN_JAVA/org/rooinaction/coursemanager/web/➥
  CourseController_Roo_Controller_Finder.aj
Created SRC_MAIN_WEBAPP/WEB-INF/views/courses/➥
  findCoursesByNameLike.jspx
Updated SRC_MAIN_WEBAPP/WEB-INF/views/menu.jspx
```

The shell adds a new ITD, CourseController_Roo_Controller_Finder.aj, with two
new controller ITD methods. It also generates input and result views to handle the
search and adds the search page to the menu. First the new ITD method that renders the search form, findCoursesByNameLikeForm in CourseController_Roo
_Controller_Finder.aj:

```
@RequestMapping(params = {"find=ByNameLike", "form"},➥
                method = RequestMethod.GET)
public String CourseController.findCoursesByNameLikeForm(➥
                        Model uiModel) {
  return "tasks/findCoursesByNameLike";
}
```

This method is requested when the URI /courses?find=ByNameLike&form
method is requested with a GET, which is the link provided in the menu file,
menu.jspx. This method renders the input form, which gives you a text input field
and a submit button. Here's the key portion of the search page:

```
<form:find finderName="ByNameLike"
    id="ff_org_rooinaction_coursemanager_model_Course"
    path="/courses"
    z="bwOQxLqK/eMbWXGmvLpgh8c4Oq8=">

    <field:input disableFormBinding="true" field="name"
      id="f_org_rooinaction_coursemanager_model_Course_name"
      max="60" min="1" required="true"
      z="yXP0sm876zw9NEZ3jEiqqxawWqw=" />

</form:find>
```

As you can see, a special Roo form tag, <form:find>, is used to submit a search form.
Though it appears that the form submits to the /courses path, the <form:find> tag
actually sends along a hidden field, find, whose value is set to ByNameLike, which is
the name of the finder method and is sent via the attribute above named finderName.
Roo can add additional finders by changing the value of this tag.

Once you submit the search form, the finder is executed via the other method in
the new ITD, findCoursesByNameLike:

```
@RequestMapping(params = "find=ByNameLike",➥
                method = RequestMethod.GET)
public String CourseController.findCoursesByNameLike(➥
              @RequestParam("name") String name, Model uiModel) {
    uiModel.addAttribute("courses",➥
            Course.findCoursesByNameLike(name).getResultList());
    return "courses/list";
}
```

The method calls Course.findCoursesByNameLike(String) and renders the list view
again, which now contains search results.

5.3.7 Scaffolding wrap-up

Spring Roo does a lot of work for you with the scaffolding process—creating the views and controller ITD, wiring up JSPs with custom tags, and providing RESTful URLs for every operation. In addition, Roo will keep the scaffold up to date based on changes you make during development. Although Roo does make some decisions up front, such as the use of Apache Tiles, XML-compliant views, the use of tag libraries, localization and personalization, and a number of other features, it does so to make you more productive. And Roo heavily leverages your Roo-managed JPA entities, relationships, and finders.

If you don't like the way Roo configures web applications, you can choose to roll your own web interface, but for getting basic work done, the scaffolding process can really do the trick.

Now it's time to step back a bit and think about how the web framework fits within the overall picture. Remember back in chapter 4 when we discussed building Spring beans as business logic services, annotating them with `@Service`? What about accessing those service beans rather than embedding business logic in the controllers? Let's see how Spring itself makes this quite easy.

5.4 Accessing other Spring beans

Roo controllers can write logic directly against Roo entities or in layered applications. Your controllers can access the Roo entities directly as you've seen in your scaffold above, but also may call Spring services and repositories, including those you created in chapters 3 and 4.

Although Spring Roo doesn't expect developers to write software with the level of separation that you saw in section 5.3, you may need to add Roo and Spring MVC to an existing, larger effort. Perhaps the application logic has already been written as a series of Spring beans, or you may need to expose the business logic to a number of different consumers, from web clients to integration engines and desktop applications.

5.4.1 Automatic detection in scaffolds

In scaffolded interfaces, Roo repositories and services are automatically detected and used. The rule is to use the repository automatically, unless a Roo service exposes the repository. In this way, you can easily refactor your data tier to various persistence models without modifying a single line of your scaffolded code. If you've defined a repository for your `Course` entity, Roo will respond by adjusting the scaffolding calls. Here's a fragment of the `CourseController_Roo_Controller.aj` `delete` method with a repository defined against the `Course` entity:

```
Course course = courseRepository.findOne(id);
courseRepository.delete(course);
```

Here's the same method fragment with a Roo service defined against the same Course:

```
Course course = courseService.findCourse(id);
courseService.deleteCourse(course);
```

Feel free to experiment with various persistence configurations while keeping your scaffolding in place.

5.4.2 Nonscaffolded controllers and Spring beans

You can inject Roo-generated services and repositories into your own controllers by using the @Autowired annotation. You can then directly access the service as with any injected Spring bean. Here's a simple example:

```
@RequestMapping("/coursenonscaffolded/**")
@Controller
public class CourseNonScaffoldedController {

  @Autowired
  private CourseService courseService;

  @RequestMapping
  public String index(Model uiModel) {
    long numCourses = courseService.countAllCourses();
    uiModel.addAttribute("numCourses", numCourses);
    return "coursenonscaffolded/index";
  }
}
```

In the preceding example, simply inject the CourseService instance and use it in your index method to fetch the number of courses.

5.4.3 Multimodule scaffolds

If you're using multimodule projects using the module command, you'll need to be aware of the additional syntax for referencing models from scaffolds in other projects. Roo can scaffold controllers and views against other modules in the same project. But you'll need to make sure you prefix the entity name with *module|* (that's the module name, plus a vertical pipe |).

Roo will still detect ActiveRecord models, or services and repositories, and will do exactly the same scaffolding you've seen previously.

For example, if you've created an entity in a module known as business, which is a JAR-based Roo module, you'd need to change module focus to your web module (here shown as web) and issue the scaffolding command as in the example below:

```
roo> module focus --moduleName ~.web
roo> web mvc scaffold --class ~.controller.CourseController ➥
    --entity business|~.service.CourseService
```

You can use the project top-level package prefix (~.) in each case to refer to the top-level package of the module in question.

To execute a web-based project in the Jetty or Tomcat runtimes, you'll need to do some gymnastics:

```
$ cd [top-level directory of entire project]
$ mvn install
$ cd web
$ mvn jetty:run
```

This will install the various projects into your local Maven repository and then run the web application, looking for collaborating libraries in the repository itself.

Now let's take a few moments to review what you've learned about Spring MVC and Roo.

5.5 Summary

You can see just how much power Roo packs into its Spring MVC web framework support. At the simplest level, Roo generates a template-driven website, complete with JSP tags and a predefined MVC configuration. This alone is worth considering.

But the real power lies within the scaffolding engine. For applications that require a ton of data manipulation, scaffolding can save you weeks of effort. Roo automatically scaffolds all CRUD behavior for you, even providing finder forms and views, if those are defined on your entities.

Finally, you saw that you can easily inject your Spring beans into a Roo controller using `@Autowired`, so your Roo web applications can support those business logic beans your development team has been building, and so you can keep that logic out of the controller.

In chapter 6, we'll start customizing your web applications, modifying views, controls, layout, and more. In chapter 7, we'll discuss other web frameworks that can be installed in Roo, such as GWT, JSF, and Vaadin.

5.6 Resources

You can find out more information on Spring MVC in a variety of resources. Here are a few:

BOOKS

Walls, Craig. *Spring in Action, Third Edition* (Manning Publications, 2011) covers Spring MVC in depth.

WEB

The Spring MVC Showcase sample library, located at http://mng.bz/B91V, contains a number of useful samples.

The Spring MVC reference guide contains a wealth of information: http://mng.bz/nZQX.

Advanced
web applications

In the last chapter, we discussed how to build Spring MVC web applications, apply scaffolding to automatically generate your controllers and views, and how the Roo custom tag libraries add dynamic behaviors such as client-side validation.

PUSH-IN THE SCAFFOLDS FOR FULL CONTROL   When you're ready to diverge from the standard scaffolding, you can choose to either start with a new controller and views, or use the scaffolding as a baseline. To do the latter, use your IDE (STS or IntelliJ) to push-in every method so that all of the controller code resides in the controller itself. You can then simply remove the @RooWebScaffold annotation and begin to customize your forms directly.

Once the scaffold has been pushed in, you can do anything you want. The z= view tags won't be used anymore, so you can make changes to the views in any way you see fit. Keep in mind that your views will no longer be maintained against your entity, so any new fields you add must be manually added to your view code.

156

In this chapter you'll learn how to customize your view layer. We'll start by discussing the generated scaffold CRUD views, and how to customize them by hiding, disabling, or modifying the field types attached to various form elements. We'll discuss how to provide reference data and how to customize date formats, and then dig into how Roo deals with layouts, localization, and themes.

By the end of this chapter, you'll be able to strike out on your own and customize your Roo web applications.

Let's begin by discussing Roo's generated views and how you can customize them.

6.1 *Customizing Roo CRUD views*

As you saw in the last chapter, the Roo web interface heavily relies on a number of features: Apache Tiles, tag libraries, and Spring's localization process. Let's take a closer look at some of these elements and see how you can configure them.

Before we begin, we need to lay out the rules behind some of the common field and component names. Later, we'll discuss techniques for manipulating and hiding pregenerated form elements.

6.1.1 *Element naming conventions*

Recall that most elements require an id attribute to identify them. This id is generally created, for data-based operations, using the following scheme:

```
id_[java-packages].[entity-name][.[field-name]]
```

For example, your Course entity would generally have the following id:

```
id_com_rooinaction_coursemanager_course
```

For the Course field name, you'd have

```
id_com_rooinaction_coursemanager_course_name
```

These HTML id field naming conventions are manipulated by the custom tags to pull various other values. For example, to show an entity label:

```
label_com_rooinaction_coursemanager_course=Course
```

The label for a collection of those entities:

```
label_com_rooinaction_coursemanager_course=Course_plural=Courses
```

The label for a given field within a table:

```
label_com_rooinaction_coursemanager_course_name=Name
```

These values are generated by the scaffolding process. This is done within the custom tag files themselves, which are located in the WEB-INF/tags directory.

In the HTML form views, all field id values are reduced to _fieldname_id so that they are easily scripted. For example, _name_id is the HTMLid field representing the name column.

> **What if I'm building my own views?**
>
> If you want to benefit from Roo's predefined localization structure, you need to follow these naming guidelines. Roo should automatically add labels for the component and fields for any entity you define, provided it's a Roo-managed entity (@RooJpaEntity, @RooJpaActiveRecord, etc).
>
> You can also choose to bypass these conventions, and use the custom tag attributes such as `label` to define your text in-line. But these won't be localized, so it's up to you to decide whether you want to buck the conventions for more control, or learn them and benefit from them.

You can customize the contents of these generated views. To do so, you can modify the tag attributes for the various list and form views.

6.1.2   *Scaffold's magic z attribute*

If you're modifying scaffolded forms, rather than building your own, you'll encounter the z attribute, which is assigned a generated unique ID. This seemingly random value tells Roo that the field is being managed by Roo itself. You don't want to change this value unless you decide to manage a field yourself. The valid values for z are

- A generated unique value, such as T5MViHc0PXnvBhkOlpd, meaning that this field is controlled by Roo.
- `user-managed`, which obviously means that the field is being controlled by the user. Less obviously, it tells the Roo shell to ignore this field definition, and specifically not to generate another definition for this generated, but customized, element.

HOW DO I RESET A FIELD BACK TO THE SCAFFOLDED VERSION?   When you save your view, the scaffold fixes it up and replaces the element that was removed, along with any subelements.

Beyond the ID fields and z attribute, Roo has a number of settings in the tag libraries that make it easy to customize your web views. Above all, read through the tag libraries and learn their features.

With the conventions behind us, let's see how to change the views to suit your needs.

6.1.3   *Modifying list views*

List views are composed of tags nested as shown in figure 6.1.

Roo automatically iterates through the rows in the collection, first outputting the column headers in a title row, and then listing all data in the collection. If paging is enabled, the content is paginated automatically.

In the list view, the tags you can customize include `page:list`, `table:table`, and `table:column`. Table 6.1 shows some customizations you can make. Keep in mind, you are limited in the scaffolding to showing the data returned by the controller, and may

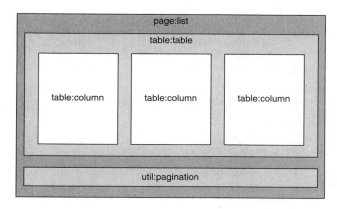

Figure 6.1 Nested tags in a typical generated list view

have to set the z parameter to "user-managed" if you make any changes to the attributes so that Roo doesn't overwrite the field values.

Table 6.1 Some key `page:list` tag attributes

Attribute	Description	Examples
label	The label to show representing the entity if no entries are found. This should be written as a singular value. Defaults to the locale key emitted, which is resolved from the localized `application.properties` file.	label="Course"
labelPlural	The label to show instead of the name of the entity, to the right of the title prefix List All from `messages.properties`. Defaults to the pluralized name of the entity.	labelPlural="Courses"
items	The collection to be iterated through in the nested table. It's listed here so that the outer tag can determine whether to show a table of results, or a message that there are no items available.	items="${courses}"

But more important customizations occur at the `table:table` and `table:column` level. Let's look at the customizations you can perform on your results table in table 6.2.

Table 6.2 `table:table` attributes

Attribute	Description	Examples
create update delete	Whether or not to show the icons for creating, updating, or deleting entries from the table. Defaults to displaying all of these features.	create="false" update="false" delete="false"

Table 6.2 `table:table` attributes *(continued)*

Attribute	Description	Examples
data	The data collection to iterate through.	data="${courses}"
path	The URL path fragment to prepend to any requests to edit or remove data.	path="/courses"
render	Whether to render the table at all. You may wish to replace the table with other form elements instead.	render="false"
typeIdFieldName	The field name for the primary key of the row—id is the default.	typeIdFieldName="course_id"

Finally, each field is emitted using the `table:column` tag. Table 6.3 shows table column attributes.

Table 6.3 `table:column` customizations

Attribute	Description	Examples
label	The label to display. Unless overridden by this property, the label defaults to the localized label for the field name in `application.properties`.	label="Times"
maxLength	Columns default to showing a maximum of 128 characters,[a] so this is the first setting you'll want to override if you want to trim the output.	maxLength="30"
render	Whether to render a column in the table output. You won't want to render all 60 fields of your massive employee record, for example. Setting render="false" for the ones you don't want will omit them from the page.	render="false"
date calendar	Tells the tag whether the value is a stored `java.util.Date`, or a long that can be converted into a `java.util.Calendar`. For scaffolded date fields, this value will be automatically set.	date="true"
dateTimePattern	The pattern to apply when formatting a field marked as a date or calendar. Scaffolded controllers create these patterns and add them to the request. You may use your own pattern instead (see section 6.2.4).	dateTimePattern="mm/dd/yy"

a. This was changed in Roo 1.2. In earlier versions, users were only shown 10 characters of each field.

You can customize any of the attributes in these fields, as long as you don't change the generated id field value, or, in the case of the column definitions, modify the name of the properties they're attached to. This way, Roo marks the customized elements as user-managed and leaves them alone.

> **WHAT IF I WANT TO REMOVE A FORM ELEMENT IN A SCAFFOLD?** Just set render ="false" on the element and it won't be rendered. Remember, if it's a key HTML form field value, you may have to add it as a hidden HTML field manually to carry it in the form.

Now let's move on to form field views. What can you customize there?

6.1.4 *Form view customizations*

There are two generated forms—the create and update variants. They're nearly identical to what you saw in the previous chapter. Figure 6.2 shows the tag nesting.

The form view tags also take a number of attributes. You can choose to replace a generated form field with another type, or customize the way the form is rendered, simply by modifying the attributes or form field tag names.

Unlike the list view, form views are generally relatively flat. That's because they're editing a single entity.

Table 6.4 shows some attributes from the form:create and form:update tags.

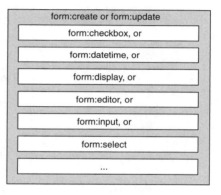

Figure 6.2 Nesting of form and field tags

Table 6.4 form:create and form:update customizations

Attribute	Create?	Update?	Description	Examples
label	Y	Y	The label for the entity being created. Will be added to the localized version of the message Create new, as in Create new Course.	label ="Training Course"
render	Y	Y	Whether to render the generated form. By default only renders if all parent dependencies are satisfied.	render ="false"
multipart	Y	Y	If a file upload field is present (see field:file), you need to set this attribute to true. Otherwise the file will not be uploaded.	multipart ="true"

There are other parameters, mostly used by the scaffolding system. But the key customizations take place in the form fields.

6.1.5 Common form field attributes

Table 6.5 has a list of fields that are common to many field types, and their relevant uses.

Table 6.5   Common form field attributes

Attribute	Description	Field Type(s)
label	The label to use to identify the field on the screen. This version is not localized, and is useful during prototyping or for applications that don't need localization.	all
labelCode	As with label above, identifies the field on the screen. The label is interpolated using the localized properties files.	all
required	Whether the field is required to submit the form. If this value is set to true, and the field is skipped, the client-side JavaScript validators won't allow the form to be submitted. This is a form of client-side validation.	input, editor, textarea, datetime, select
disabled	Whether the field can be edited. This may be useful if set based on user permissions using the Spring Security API or other data-based permission scheme.	input, editor, textarea, datetime, select
validationRegex validationMessage validationMesageCode	The regular expression defining the validation to apply for this field and the message to return when invalid. The messageCode variant looks up the message in the localized property stream, and the message variant takes a literal error message. Don't forget to apply this pattern and message to both the create and update forms if you're going to allow both creation and update editing of the field. Example: validationRegex="[A-Z,a-z]*$" validationMessage="Invalid Name"	input, textarea, editor, datetime

Armed with these tables of information, you should be able to customize your views nicely. You can always drop in additional HTML elements where needed, and update your CSS styles as well. But what else can you do?

6.2 Advanced customization

Here are a few additional helpful techniques you can use while customizing your forms and views.

6.2.1   *Changing field types*

For example, you can switch the `description` field to use the `field:editor` tag, so that users can enter HTML data. Simply replace the original `field:textarea` tag name with `field:editor`, leaving the same z value. This is also useful when Roo has chosen a `textarea` field instead of a single-line input field, or when you want to switch from a `checkbox` to a Yes/No select list. After you make this change, the Roo shell will update your page for you, switching the field tag value to `user-managed`.

> **WHAT ABOUT HIDDEN FIELDS?**   Roo doesn't have a hidden field tag. But you can just use the standard HTML input form element `<input type="hidden" name="fieldName" value="fieldValue" />` tag structure wherever you need a hidden field, and Roo will deliver the field along with the rest of the form. Use the model name and field attribute for the value, such as `${course .title}`. The field name should be the name of the member variable in the model.

Remember that if you'd like to reset scaffolded field settings for a given field, you can remove the field from the file, and Roo will replace it with a brand-new Roo-managed field.

6.2.2   *Disabling or hiding features*

Roo has two attributes attached to most scaffolded field and form elements: `render` and `disabled`.

- `render`—Set this to `false` when you don't want to generate this element. This isn't the same as making it nonvisual; it literally removes it from the view output.
- `disabled`—Set this to `true` if you want to render a given field, but not enable editing for that field. For text fields, the value will be emitted as text only, for example.

Let's say you only want to allow `Course` comments once the course has been successfully completed. Remove the comment field from the `create.jspx` form by setting the `render` property to `false`. In a more advanced configuration, add an expression on the update.jspx page to evaluate the value of `disabled` for the field you want to selectively edit, based on the existence of another field value.

> **IF ROO ISN'T UPDATING YOUR JSPX FILES ...**   Sometimes Roo can get a bit temperamental, ignoring updates to your view files, especially when you want to regenerate your fields. Just quit and reenter your Roo shell to reset the state and detect the changed views.

Let's look at another customization—modifying the appearance of date format fields.

6.2.3   *Style-based date formatting*

In the `Offering` entity, you've defined your offering date using the style-based format as the parameter to the Roo `@DateTimeFormat` annotation:

```
@Temporal(TemporalType.TIMESTAMP)@DateTimeFormat(style = "S-")
private Date offeringDate;
```

Roo uses this annotation to define a format String for the date field in the controller ITD, so that the form field can look it up and use it. The first character determines the format of the date portion of the field, and the second character determines the format of the time portion.

In addition to -, which means suppress the date or time portion of the field, @DateTimeFormat supports three formats—S, M, and L. In the US English locale, these resolve as shown in table 6.6.

Table 6.6 US English date and time style samples

Code	Date sample	Time sample
S	2010-06-15	12:15 PM
M	Jun 15, 2010	12:15:05 PM
L	June 15, 2010	12:15:05 PM EDT

During scaffolding, Roo takes this information and uses it to translate the date into a localized String using the Joda-Time library. It does this by generating an addDateTimeFormatPatterns method to the Controller ITD. For example, the Offering-Controller:

```
void OfferingController.addDateTimeFormatPatterns(Model uiModel) {
  uiModel.addAttribute(
    "offering_offerdate_date_format",
    DateTimeFormat.patternForStyle(
      "S-", LocaleContextHolder.getLocale()));
}
```

Roo will add one addAttribute() setting for each field annotated by @DateTimeFormat.

The scaffolded field will use this format automatically in the attribute dateTimePattern during the scaffolding process:

```
<field:datetime
  dateTimePattern="${offering_offerdate_date_format}"
  field="offerDate"
  ...
/>
```

You can use this technique yourself for your own nonscaffolded date fields.

6.2.4 *Pattern-based date formatting*

Another way to date formats is to use the format attribute of @DateTimeFormat:

```
@Temporal(TemporalType.DATE)
@DateTimeFormat(pattern = "MM/dd/yyyy")
private Date offerDate;
```

Roo simply adds the format as a String in the `Controller` ITD:

```
void OfferingController.addDateTimeFormatPatterns(Model uiModel) {
  ...
  uiModel.addAttribute("offering_offerdate_date_format", "MM/dd/yyyy");
  ...
}
```

You can then use the `dateTimePattern` attribute to inject the pattern:

```
<field:datetime
 dateTimePattern="${offering_offerdate_date_format}"
 field="offerDate"
 ...
/>
```

SHARING AND LOCALIZING DATE FORMATS

If you want to localize your date formats for nonscaffolded views, or want to use the same patterns across many date fields in your nonscaffolded or modified scaffold views, you can directly add the formats to a localized version of your `application` `.properties` file and use `<spring:message>` to load it into a variable at runtime.

In your application.properties file:

```
short.date.format=MM/dd/yyyy
```

In your view:

```
<spring:message var="dateFormat" value="${short.date.format}" />
  ...
<field:datetime dateTimePattern="${short.date.format}"
    ...
/>
```

Roo may also have problems converting these formats into a value supported by the date picker held in the `field:datetime` form field.

6.2.5 *Adjusting date formats in views*

The brute-force method is to apply a format pattern to the field directly, using the `dateTimeFormat` attribute on the view:

```
<table:table ...>
   <table:column dateTimeFormat="MM/dd/yyyy" ... />
   ...
</table:table>
```

Of course, this pattern won't be updated based on changes to the entity's @DateTime-Format annotation. But if you need to display a very specific date or time format for a given view, at least you have an option.

6.2.6   *Providing reference data*

Let's say you need to provide a list of values for a given field as a drop-down list, such as a course complexity level, a query from a database, or a list of values provided by a collection.

On the server side, you'll need to provide the reference data to the page in the form of request data.

- Use a Java enumerated type and annotate your type with the `@Enumerated` annotation:

```
@Enumerated(EnumType.STRING)
private CourseTypeEnum courseType;
```

Roo will provide the options by stringifying the enumeration elements. This is the easiest, but least flexible, way to provide a set of choices to a view because you can't add a new value unless you change your enumeration. Use this for extremely static choices.

- Use a query to a Roo entity and store it in `Model`. Roo does this with relationship data, so you can do it too. Just annotate a new method in the controller with the `@ModelAttribute` annotation, and return your collection. For example, to select from a list of offerings, add

```
@ModelAttribute("offerings")
public Collection<Offering> OfferingController.populateOfferings() {
   return Offering.findAllOfferings();
}
```

- Use your own finder, service, or JDBC query to populate the list. This uses the same `@ModelAttribute` annotation, but the method would delegate to the other collaborating components.

On the view itself, you can use the `field:select` tag to expose the options and allow them to be selected:

```
<field:select
   field="offering"
   items="${offerings}"
   itemlabel="offerDate" itemValue="id"

.../>
```

The `itemLabel` and `itemValue` clauses refer to properties of the collection provided in the `Offering` bean, and the provided collection is assigned with the attribute `items`.

You can even navigate to another controller to do a search, perhaps even making a modal dialog out of the selection process. Anything you can do in standard Spring is available to you here.

6.3 View layouts, theming, and localization

You may not be happy with the way Roo lays out your web application, and you probably have designs on better layouts, localization, and perhaps a set of themes. No matter: you are in complete control of that as well. In this section we'll tell you how to prepare your application for localization, how to set up different themes, and how to adjust your layouts.

6.3.1 How Roo resolves scaffold labels

Spring Roo automatically builds support for localized user interfaces. In fact, every scaffolded text element is fetched either from the database (via the entities) or via locale-aware properties files such as application.properties and messages.properties.

Here's how Roo identifies and renders various elements on the page:

- *Table names*—When Roo renders a scaffolded entry page for a given entity, it uses labels such as "Find by *entityName*" and "Create new *entityName*." This name is held in `application.properties` under the value `label_` appended with the lowercased, fully qualified class name (including package). In the example, it would be `label_org_distracted_tracker_model_course`. If you'd like to change the way your entity is described, you can modify this file.
- *Column names*—Column names are also stored within the `application.properties` file in the same way as the singular and plural entity names (the field is appended to the end of the preceding label).
- *Error messages*—Error messages are stored in `messages.properties` and can be customized to suit.

Remember, Roo won't overwrite the tag libraries or layouts it creates, but it will attempt to keep fields in sync.

Now, armed with the knowledge of how Roo resolves messages, let's dig into localization.

6.3.2 Configuring additional locales

Roo supports any valid locale in the WEB-INF/i18n directory. The icons placed in the footer.xhtml file of your standard layouts are automatically generated if you issue the web mvc language command. For example, to configure Spanish, issue

```
roo> web mvc language --code es
```

Roo responds by adding a new locale file, `messages_es.properties`, and configuring it with all standard Roo messages relating to the default layout and features. It will be your responsibility to copy your `application.properties` file to `application_es.properties` and translate the field labels and messages to the proper locale. Because all files are mounted in this directory, you don't need any additional configuration.

Roo also copies an icon for the language flag into the webapp/images directory, and updates the footer to allow you to click on that image to switch locales. You can also manually switch locales for your browser session using the `lang` query string parameter. For example, to translate the site to Spanish, you can issue

```
http://localhost:8080/coursemanager?lang=es
```

By default this setting is kept in an in-memory browser cookie. If you'd like to make it more permanent, you can switch from the default `CookieLocaleResolver` to the `SessionLocaleResolver`. You can store and reload the session for each user from a data store if you wish. You can also use the `AcceptHeaderLocaleResolver` to automatically detect the locale based on the browser's reported language.

See chapter 11 for details on how to create other language locales by writing an add-on.

Now that we've talked about the mechanics of rendering the page contents, we're ready to discuss page layout concepts. Roo uses Apache Tiles to provide a composite view: a view composed of various individual parts. In this section we'll take a look at just how Roo works with localized property files; the configuration of Apache Tiles in a Roo application; how you can define page layouts via tiles definitions; and then how to customize individual elements of the Roo layout.

6.3.3 *Tiles and Roo*

Remember that we told you, back in chapter 5, to ignore the views.xml files? Although Spring Roo view files are rather small, Roo ends up rendering complex views, complete with a menu system, header, footer, and content areas. Tiles does this work for you transparently. It's installed as a special *view resolver*, a strategy object that resolves names of views returned by controllers to physical files and other resources. Here's the TilesViewResolver, defined by Roo in WEB-INF/webmvc-config.xml:

```
<bean
  class="org.springframework.web.servlet.view.tiles2.TilesConfigurer"
        id="tilesConfigurer">
  <property name="definitions">
    <list>
      <value>/WEB-INF/layouts/layouts.xml</value>
      <!-- Scan views directory for Tiles configurations -->
      <value>/WEB-INF/views/**/views.xml</value>
    </list>
  </property>
</bean>
```

TilesViewResolver processes view names, emitted in the controller, and attempts to find *layout definitions* within configuration files specified in the `definitions` property. The main layout definitions file, `layouts.xml`, is what tells Roo about the two main layouts—default and public, as shown in the following listing.

> **Listing 6.1 Top-level tiles defined in `WEB-INF/layouts.xml`**

```
<?xml version="1.0" encoding="UTF-8"?>
<!DOCTYPE tiles-definitions PUBLIC
        "-//Apache Software Foundation//DTD Tiles Configuration 2.1//EN"
```

```
                "http://tiles.apache.org/dtds/tiles-config_2_1.dtd">
<tiles-definitions>

   <definition name="default"
      template="/WEB-INF/layouts/default.jspx">
      <put-attribute name="header"
         value="/WEB-INF/views/header.jspx" />
      <put-attribute name="menu"
         value="/WEB-INF/views/menu.jspx" />
      <put-attribute name="footer"
         value="/WEB-INF/views/footer.jspx" />
   </definition>

   <definition name="public"
       template="/WEB-INF/layouts/default.jspx">
      <put-attribute name="header"
         value="/WEB-INF/views/header.jspx" />
      <put-attribute name="footer"
         value="/WEB-INF/views/footer.jspx" />
   </definition>

</tiles-definitions>
```

In the previous example, each layout is given a physical file that defines the contents of the layout, and values to substitute for various tiles within that file, such as `header`, `footer`, and `menu`.

6.3.4 Roo's tile layouts

Hang in there, though: Tiles loves levels of indirection! That's why you can create a number of layouts, assigning them to views, rather quickly by extending or modifying layouts. There are two layouts defined in this file:

- `default`—The standard layout used by most pages in Roo. This includes a header, footer, and menu.
- `public`—The layout used by pages that don't require a menu bar. This layout gives users a larger amount of screen real estate.

Let's take a look at the default layout, as defined by WEB-INF/layouts/default.jspx, shown next.

Listing 6.2 The default layout—`default.jspx`

```
<html
   xmlns:jsp="http://java.sun.com/JSP/Page"
   xmlns:c="http://java.sun.com/jsp/jstl/core"
   xmlns:tiles="http://tiles.apache.org/tags-tiles"          ❶ Install
   xmlns:spring="http://www.springframework.org/tags"           taglibs
   xmlns:util="urn:jsptagdir:/WEB-INF/tags/util" >

   <jsp:output doctype-root-element="HTML"
       doctype-system="about:legacy-compat" />                ❷ HTML5
                                                                 compatibility
   <jsp:directive.page contentType="text/html;charset=UTF-8" />
```

```
<head>
    <meta http-equiv="Content-Type"
        content="text/html; charset=UTF-8" />

    <meta http-equiv="X-UA-Compatible" content="IE=8" />

    <util:load-scripts />

    <spring:message code="application_name" var="app_name"/>
    <title>
        <spring:message code="welcome_h3" arguments="${app_name}" />
    </title>
</head>

<body class="tundra spring">
    <div id="wrapper">

        <tiles:insertAttribute name="header" ignore="true" />
        <tiles:insertAttribute name="menu" ignore="true" />

        <div id="main">
            <tiles:insertAttribute name="body"/>
            <tiles:insertAttribute name="footer" ignore="true"/>
        </div>
    </div>
</body>
</html>
```

Header defines layout, CSS, JavaScript

IE 8 support

Load JavaScripts ❸

Menu tile

Footer tile

Header tile

Body tile

This layout defines a very comprehensive page structure, including features such as HTML5 compatibility ❷, JavaScript and CSS support, the Dojo widget library, ❸ CSS, and preinstalled tag libraries ❶. The template also includes a set of div elements, each of which defines areas that can be rendered with content at runtime.[1]

Figure 6.3 shows the layout divs, styled by Roo's generated stylesheet, in a simple block diagram.

Tiles inserts the content defined in these div elements when it sees the <tiles:insert-Attribute /> tag. For example, in the line

```
<tiles:insertAttribute name="header
" ignore="true" />
```

the actual content will be replaced by the file referenced in the attribute header, which is defined in the layouts.xml file:

```
<put-attribute name="header
" value="/WEB-INF/views/header.jspx" />
```

6.3.5   *Putting it all together*

At this point, you're probably wondering just how the heck this information is relevant to

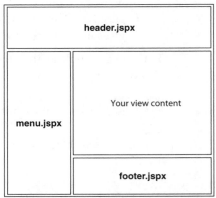

Figure 6.3   JSPX files involved in the Tiles layout process. These files are located in /web-app/WEB-INF/views.

[1] To find out more about Internet Explorer's support for various modes, see http://mng.bz/jQou.

you. Yep, you're right—Tiles is maddeningly distributed. Careful readers also will notice that the attribute for the page content itself isn't being passed to the definitions. So how in the world does it know about the page? Ah, that's because the crux of the whole matter is that views.xml file in your WEB-INF/views/testdrive directory:

```
<?xml version="1.0" encoding="UTF-8" standalone="no"?>
<!DOCTYPE tiles-definitions PUBLIC " ...
<tiles-definitions>
    <definition extends="default" name="throwaway/index">
        <put-attribute name="body"
            value="/WEB-INF/views/throwaway/index.jspx"/>
    </definition>
</tiles-definitions>
```

Hopefully this is your Tiles eureka! moment... Finally, you see that the layout named `default` will be used to render the `throwaway/index` page. The `header`, `footer`, and `menu` tiles will be loaded from files based on the settings in WEB-INF/layouts, and the `body` tile will be loaded using the index.jspx file in the `views/throwaway` directory.

6.3.6 *Customizing the tiles layout engine*

You can modify the content in any of these tiles just by changing the view files. Here are a few suggestions for quick modifications you can do:

- Add a copyright entry to the footer of every page by editing footer.jspx and adding a fragment such as `<em>© 2010 Course Management Incorporated</em>` in an appropriate place.
- Add a menu item for nonscaffolded controllers or views: just edit menu.jspx and add a `<menu:item>`, or if you want to add a menu category (boldfaced headings before groups of related menus) add a `<menu:category>` element. Read the documentation at the top of the menu.tagx, category.tagx, and item.tagx files for details.
- Change the header to incorporate your logo. Just edit and replace the logo filename in the `banner` URL within the header.jspx file. The banner dimensions are 800 pixels long by 75 pixels deep if you would like to develop a drop-in replacement.

Then again, why not completely replace the entire layout? Just modify your tiles layout and related CSS files, and go to town. Realize that there are key elements to the various tag libraries generated by Roo, so you'll have to take care and follow Roo's variable naming conventions in order for the Roo-generated components to function.

6.3.7 *Theming*

Roo also supports the concept of theming, which is closely related to layouts. Two themes are installed: `standard` and `alt`. If you look closely at the footer of each Roo page in a web browser, you'll see two clickable links for these themes. When you click on one of these, Roo uses Spring's theming support to switch a simple client-side HTTP cookie named `theme` between the values of `standard` and `alt`.

A little too complex for this book, theming boils down to special properties files, stored in WEB-INF/classes in the web application, for each theme. Roo uses a special generated tag, theme.tagx, to generate these links, and the theme resolver accepts clicks to these links, which sets the cookie value for the browser. Each time the browser renders a page, it passes the theme name in a cookie to Spring. Spring accepts it, and the CSS file pointed to in the standard.properties or alt.properties files is used to mount a different stylesheet.

The upshot for you is that you can style two different themes. Currently, the only difference between the CSS layouts is the position of the menu: standard layout puts the menu on the left, and the alternative one puts it on the right. Feel free to customize standard.css and alt.css to suit your needs.

6.4   Summary

As you can see, you have a range of options for customizing your web application. Remember to follow these basic rules:

- Change the z attribute to user-managed when changing a scaffolded component entry.
- Hide scaffolded components using the render="false" attribute.
- Follow component naming conventions when adding your own fields, and read up on the generated tags that Roo generates.
- Learn to work within the generated layout, theming, and localization engines, customizing your themes and layouts as you see fit.
- Get comfortable with JSPX files. Since Roo needs XML-parseable files to manage scaffolding and generating your pages, you'll benefit from digging in.
- The same goes for Spring's own MVC form tags, which Roo uses inside of the scaffold tags.

If you follow these simple guidelines, you can go far in transforming the generated Roo web application files to suit your needs. If that fails you, just push-in refactor your scaffolded web application controllers and rework the pages and tags to suit your needs.

In chapter 7, we'll look at Spring's support for the Dojo component library and JavaScript, delve a bit into Ajax, and look at several other advanced web frameworks supported by Roo: GWT and JSF.

6.5   Resources

BOOKS

Hogan, Brian P. *Web Design for Developers* (Pragmatic Press, 2010). Although rather general, if you get into CSS and HTML editing, this is a great reference.

WEB

Official Apache Tiles project page: http://tiles.apache.org.

Spring MVC and Tiles: http://mng.bz/Wb3O.

Tiles 2 tutorial on the project site: http://mng.bz/ejF1.

RIA and other
web frameworks

This chapter covers

- Communicating with the server with Ajax
- Event handling with Dojo
- The Google Web Toolkit (GWT) and
  JavaServer Faces (JSF) web frameworks

In the last chapter, we discussed how the Roo custom tag libraries add dynamic behaviors such as client-side validation, and how you could customize the form elements, messages, layout, and look and feel of your web pages.

In this chapter you'll learn how to work with more advanced web frameworks in Roo. You'll set up a simple Ajax interaction using the Dojo Toolkit and Spring MVC's Ajax support. Then we'll discuss some of the other web platforms available to Roo developers today via add-ons: Google Web Toolkit, Vaadin, and JSF.

7.1   JavaScript and Ajax

Roo can provide dynamic, rich application features out of the box, providing both client-side widgets such as tab folders and tree views, and server-side support for Ajax. It does this by installing two key technologies in every Spring Roo web application: Spring JavaScript and Spring MVC Ajax support.

In this section, you'll learn how Roo mounts Spring JavaScript and how the Roo tag libraries use it to create rich widgets. Then you'll wire a text field to an Ajax server-side method and invoke it using a JavaScript event.

7.1.1   Spring JavaScript

Roo includes the *Spring JavaScript* library when it generates a Spring MVC web application. This library includes the following components:

- *The Dojo Toolkit*—A JavaScript API that provides Ajax support, dozens of user interface widgets, a common event handling system, graphing, and a lot more. The Dojo scripts are mounted in the /resources/dojo, /resources/dojox, and /resources/dijit URIs within Roo web applications. All form elements and panels in Spring Roo are built using Dojo, and Dojo validation routines provide dynamic, client-side error messages to your forms.
- *Spring JavaScript API*—A set of Spring-developed utility JavaScript methods to install Dojo widgets and perform automatic client validation. Spring JavaScript APIs are located in /resources/spring/ URIs.
- *Resource handling support*—This used to be a Spring JavaScript feature, but was moved into the Spring Core in version 3.0.4. The `<mvc:resources/>` tag in the webmvc-config.xml file defines the various classpath directories to search when requesting a URL starting with /resources. Spring will cache these resources and serve them to the client automatically.

The Spring JavaScript resources JAR is automatically added when Roo installs Spring MVC support. It's installed as the Maven artifact named `spring-js-resources`. Roo mounts the scripts to provide these libraries to each page in the default.jspx layout file, by calling the `<util:load-scripts />` tag.

7.1.2   Calculating Course cost with Ajax

To add a more dynamic nature to your forms, let's create an Ajax interaction between your page and the server. As you probably know, Ajax is a label for technology that calls web services from a previously loaded page. Ajax calls can be performed synchronously or asynchronously.

The example is trivial but shows the minimum plumbing required to set up an Ajax call. You'll use the Dojo framework to wire changes to a course duration field to trigger calls to a Spring MVC method. Every time you modify the field value, the Ajax method will calculate the list price of your course.

Spring MVC has full support for Ajax on the server side, as does Dojo on the client. You'll use a specially annotated Spring MVC method to handle the server-side call, but first you need to wire up the input field to trigger a JavaScript method every time you type a digit.

7.1.3 The JavaScript event handler

We'll use Dojo event handling to wire changes in the duration field to a method that executes the Ajax call. First, add a <spring:url> tag at the top of the page, which you use to define the URL path to the Ajax call on the server side:

```
<spring:url value="/courses/calcCostByDay?days=" var="ajax_url" />
```

Next, you'll add the code inside a Dojo addOnLoad() methodaddOnLoad() script block. This block is executed after the page is fully loaded, but before the user can access it. In this block of code, you look up your duration field and connect a Dojo event handler to it, which calls your Ajax method.

Listing 7.1 Responding to duration onKeyUp event

```
<script type="text/javascript">
  dojo.addOnLoad(function() {                            ❶ Dojo
                                                            form
    var duration = dijit.byId("_duration_id");             field

    dojo.connect(duration, "onKeyUp", function() {

      var url = "${ajax_url}?days=" + duration.get("Value");   Build
                                                               Ajax
      dojo.xhrGet({                                          ❸ URL
        url : url,
        handleAs : "text",
        load : function(data, args) {                        data
          loadListPrice(data);                               contains
        },                                                  ❹ price
        error : function(error) {
          console.log("error", error);
        }
      });

    });
  });
  function loadListPrice(data) {                          ❺ Value
    var listPrice = dijit.byId("_listPrice_id");            sets
    listPrice.set("Value", data);                           field
  }
</script>
```

Wire keystroke event ❷ (points to `dojo.connect` line)

The dijit.byId() method call ❶ tells Dojo to hold a reference to the JavaScript object representation of the Dojo component for the duration field, which is a Dojo ValidationTextBox.

You then use the `dojo.connect` method ❷ to wire up an `onKeyUp` event, which fires each time the user presses and releases a key. The connect method's third parameter is an anonymous function which handles the event.

The `dojo.xhrGet` method executes a `GET` call as an Ajax method. In this example, it sends the amount typed as a URL parameter you'll construct beforehand ❸, and it expects the return as a text value. The call is handled asynchronously, and results in a call to the anonymous function specified in the `load` parameter ❹. In that method, you place the returned value in your `listPrice` text field. You do so by using the `dijit.byId` method to locate the `listPrice` field and then calling the `listPrice.set` ❺ method to modify the `Value` attribute, which is what holds the HTML form field data for the list price. If an error occurs, the function assigned to the `error` parameter is called instead.

> **JAVASCRIPT ANONYMOUS FUNCTIONS**   For the uninitiated, or those who haven't read Douglas Crockford's *Javascript, the Good Parts*, an anonymous function in JavaScript serves the same function as an anonymous inner class method in Java, or a closure or block in Groovy or Ruby. The method can be defined and used in-line. Further, you can assign an anonymous function as a property of an object, which is what you're doing in the `xhrGet()` method above in the `load` and `error` properties

Your last step is to actually implement the Ajax calculation method. That turns out to be the easiest part.

7.1.4   *Easy Ajax with Spring MVC*

To calculate the list price, you'll use the Spring MVC `@ResponseBody` annotation. This annotation tells Spring MVC to return the result of the method as the output, and not trigger traditional view resolution. Place this method in your `CourseController`:

```
@RequestMapping(method = RequestMethod.GET, value="calcCostByDay")
public @ResponseBody String calcCostByDay(@RequestParam Integer days) {
    return String.valueOf(days * 50);
}
```

In this method, mapped to the URL /courses/calcCostByDay, Spring MVC accepts a single integer, `days`, as a request parameter, calculates the list price, and then returns it as a String response. That's the entire Ajax server method—of course, the server-side developers have it easier than the web developers do in this case.

Save your controller and kick off your application with the `mvn tomcat:run` command. Try changing the duration of the class—if the list price changes, everything's working. If not, open up Firebug and check the console—chances are you have a scripting error. You can also use the `console.log` method and the JavaScript debugger to troubleshoot the page.

This code has a subtle bug. If you try to type anything other than numbers into the numDaysduration field, the listPrice field will be replaced with a large amount of HTML text.

The text returned is actually a standard HTML error page that reports an invalid mapping; because your method was coded to accept an integer parameter, it didn't find a suitable method to map to the incoming request, which, since specified as a set of characters, was not numeric.

There are a number of ways to solve this little problem. The easiest is to simply *zero out* the field if the user submits invalid data. You can change your method in the CourseController to look like this:

```
public @ResponseBody String calcCostByDay(@RequestParam String days) {
   try {
      int val = Integer.parseInt(days);
      return String.valueOf(val * 50);
   } catch (NumberFormatException e){
      return "0";
   }
}
```

JAVASCRIPT AND CONSOLE DEBUGGING   Many new JavaScript developers like using the alert function because it brings up a dialog that displays information. But unless you want to give yourself repetitive stress injuries from hitting Enter, the better way to debug is to use the excellent *FireBug* JavaScript development plug-in tool in FireFox, or one of the other provided debuggers in Chrome or Safari.

The console.log method is your logging method for JavaScript, and anything you put in there automatically ends up in the JavaScript log output in FireBug's Console pane. Be careful to remove these statements if you're going to host your application on an older browser such as Internet Explorer 6.0, or you may find error messages about not finding a console object when the page loads.

The create.jspx file can be customized the same way; the major difference is that you don't have to carry along hidden id and version fields, and you use the POST method to create a new course using the /courses URL.

So far, you've learned how to configure Dojo widgets and handle Ajax requests and responses. Now let's switch gears and take a look at two other web frameworks available to Roo developers. We'll start with Roo's support for the Google Web Toolkit.

WE'RE ONLY SCRATCHING THE SURFACE HERE   Ajax and JavaScript user interfaces are a huge topic, worthy of an entire series of chapters. We have more information available online on the book website, http://manning.com/rimple, including articles on using the Dojo framework, passing data with JSON, and more.

7.2   *Google Web Toolkit*

GWT is a highly dynamic web application framework developed by Google. It's used to build many of their applications, including GMail and Wave. GWT gives Java programmers access to Ajax-based web programming techniques, using Java and XML. Swing developers will feel right at home with the familiar Java, event-driven API, and XML. Rather than programing in JavaScript, GWT's client-side API is cross-compiled into JavaScript code, HTML, and CSS. Developers use Java, XML, and some HTML for pages and layouts, and Java for composition of client-side user interface components, event handling, and interaction with the server layer.

GWT is a powerful web application development framework, but it can be a challenge to configure. You'll use the Roo shell to install a GWT user interface in your Course Manager application, and then we'll walk through the implementation. In future MEAP (Manning Early Access Program) posts we'll outline how to customize the scaffolded interface elements.

7.2.1   *The GWT Course Manager*

Roo provides a simple, one-line installation command, `gwt setup`, that installs the GWT compiler, server-side infrastructure, and build instructions. You'll use your Course Manager Roo starter schema to build out a GWT application. You'll create a project and run the `course-manager-schema-setup.roo` script (available in the Example-Code/roo-scripts directory) to prep your application configuration. Then use the one-line command to install GWT:

```
roo> web gwt setup
```

Roo responds by building out your GWT application, installing the GWT Maven plug-in and dependencies in the pom.xml file, and generating a scaffolded GWT web application.

You'll need to decide whether you want to let Roo generate your GWT components using a scaffold, or whether you want to roll your own. Table 7.1 lists the commands you can use to set up your GWT code.

Table 7.1   Roo GWT commands

Shell command	Functionality
`web gwt scaffold`	Generates all code for a single entity.
`web gwt all`	Generate scaffolds for all entities.
`web gwt proxy` `web gwt request`	These commands can be used to create and maintain the infrastructure for remoting your entities, but allow you to write your own GWT frontend code.
`web gwt gae`	Installs or updates your GWT environment and adds or updates support for Google App Engine.

These commands may take one or more of these options:

- `--proxyPackage`—The GWT proxy classes will be located in this package.
- `--requestPackage`—The GWT request classes will be generated here.
- `--type`—The Roo entity to scaffold.

After the GWT application is generated, or you've developed your GWT code to suit, Roo is able to execute your GWT application from the Maven command line. Go ahead and execute it by running the following commands:

```
mvn gwt:run
```

GWT cross-compiles Java code into a series of small JavaScript applications, tailored for each supported browser. These applications are referred to as *permutations,* as you may see during the build phase:

```
[INFO] Compiling module org.rooina.ria.gwt.ApplicationScaffold
[INFO]    Compiling 12 permutations
[INFO]       Compiling permutation 0...
[INFO]       Process output
[INFO]          Compiling
[INFO]             Compiling permutation 1...
[INFO]          Compiling permutation 2...
....
```

After a significant amount of processing, the application will start in an embedded Maven Jetty container. GWT automatically detects your browser type and runs the GWT application generated for your environment when you hit the entry point page. Browse to that page now:

```
http://localhost:8080/course-manager-gwt
```

If you use the `gwt scaffold` or `gwt all` commands to generate your GWT frontend, the user interface will be ready to test. The frontend presented will act more like a desktop application than a typical website. Figure 7.1 illustrates this with an example of the Courses pane.

> **GWT AND ROO—AN EVOLVING RELATIONSHIP** As of the current edition of *Roo in Action,* the GWT add-on is undergoing heavy development, and these notes refer to lots of in-flight features. Please refer to the Roo forums to gain details on the current version of this framework. Also, track any Roo GWT JIRA issues at the Roo project issue tracker at http://mng.bz/rQlu.

You can also run the GWT application out of an exploded EAR by issuing

```
mvn jetty:run-exploded
```

In this mode, GWT runs as a web application only, in the same way it will run on web application servers in test or production.

7.2.2   *Supporting browser types*

GWT frontend applications are built using the GWT APIs and the GWT cross-compiler, which takes the Java and XML code and transforms it into HTML and JavaScript code. GWT has support for every major browser on the market, and even includes support for nontraditional user interfaces such as mobile phones.

Each of these permutations is a copy of the application, targeted for a supported browser type. You can control which browsers you target by modifying your GWT configuration file, ApplicationScaffold.gwt.xml, which is held within the root package in the src/main/java directory of your project.

To target a specific browser only, such as Safari, add the following configuration entry:

```
<?xml version="1.0" encoding="UTF-8"?>
<!DOCTYPE module PUBLIC ➥
  "-//Google Inc.//DTD Google Web Toolkit 2.0.1//EN"
    "http://google-web-toolkit.googlecode.com/svn/tags/2.0.1/➥
  distro-source/core/src/gwt-module.dtd">
<module rename-to="applicationScaffold">
  ...
  <set-property name="user.agent" value="safari" />
  ...
</module>
```

7.2.3   *Summary—GWT*

We've looked at Spring Roo's support for building GWT-based scaffolded user interfaces. The Roo development team worked closely with Google to implement the Model-View-Presenter pattern, and Roo uses the most up-to-date, state-of-the-art

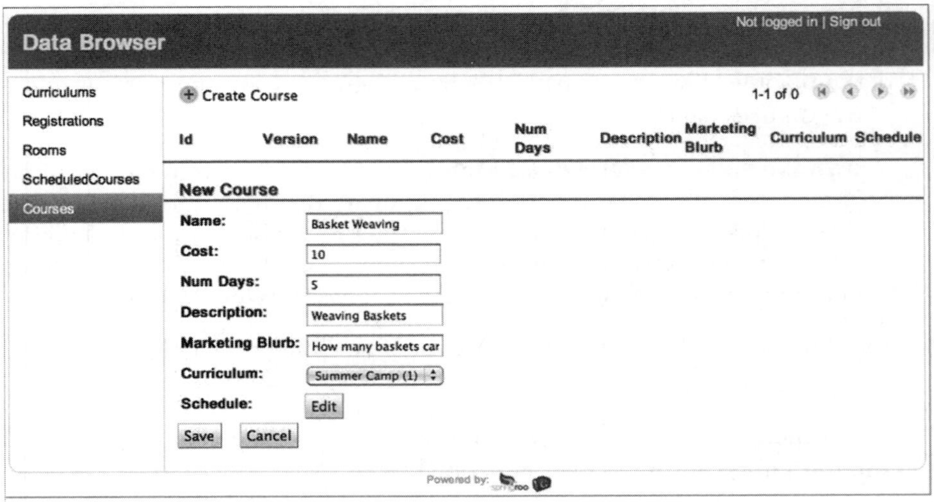

Figure 7.1   The Data Browser

version of GWT. The Roo GWT add-on lets developers see what a modern implementation of Google's RIA platform looks like.

Now let's move on to another web platform. Roo has support for the standard Java EE web framework, JavaServer Faces.

7.3 Using JavaServer Faces

Roo provides support for JavaServer Faces (JSF), the Java EE web framework, in version 1.2. It allows for selection of the Oracle Mojarra or Apache MyFaces implementations, and can use a number of predefined UI themes.

JSF is a component-based framework, similar in concept to Swing, in that each element of a page is nested inside an outer element, and the user interface is driven by views, rather than a direct controller mechanism.

JSF developers build *page beans*, which expose data and react to events on a given page. The pages themselves, known as *facelets*, are composed of containers and components.

Roo uses the `PrimeFaces` JSF widget library (http://www.primefaces.org), which provides a wide array of JSF components.

Let's take a look at how to set up JSF as an alternative web framework.

7.3.1 Installing JSF

To install JSF on an existing JAR-based project, use the `web jsf setup` command:

```
roo> web jsf setup
```

Roo responds by installing the JSF framework using the Oracle Mojarra implementation of JSF, with a JSF theme named `south-street`. Of course, you can override these choices:

```
roo> web jsf setup --theme [TAB]
 ARISTO            BLACK_TIE         BLITZER           BLUESKY
CASABLANCA         CUPERTINO         DARK_HIVE         DOT_LUV
EGGPLANT           EXCITE_BIKE       FLICK             GLASS_X
HOT_SNEAKS         HUMANITY          LE_FROG           MIDNIGHT
MINT_CHOC          OVERCAST          PEPPER_GRINDER    REDMOND
ROCKET             SMOOTHNESS        SOUTH_STREET      START
SUNNY              SWANKY_PURSE      TRONTASTIC        UI_DARKNESS
UI_LIGHTNESS       VADER

roo> web jsf setup --implementation [TAB]
APACHE_MYFACES     ORACLE_MOJARRA
```

You can change these options later if you want to experiment with the other implementation or themes.

7.3.2 *JSF installation details*

JSF is configured primarily in the web.xml Java EE descriptor file. JSF is *not* a Spring subsystem, but relies on facelets (views) and page beans to provide their implementation. This means the architecture is inverted when compared with traditional Spring MVC.

Roo installs JSF files in several directories under the src/main/webapp directory, including

- *Pages*—All JSF pages for your views are stored in here. They're defined in an XML page format named *facelets*, which have the extension .xhtml.
- *Templates*—The header, footer, menu, and container views are based on template files. These files, similar in concept to Tiles components, live here. Facelets define the templates they use for a given view.
- *WEB-INF/faces-config.xml*—This file is used in Roo to define localization rules, and defines the directory within WEB-INF where the localization files are stored.

We won't go into the depths of JSF in this book. There are plenty of resources we can point you to. But let's take a look at how Roo can scaffold JSF interfaces and dissect a scaffolded view and a page bean.

7.3.3 *Scaffolding in JSF*

As with Spring MVC, Roo offers scaffolding in JSF. You can use the web jsf scaffold command to scaffold a single entity, or web jsf all to scaffold all entities.

To scaffold all entities at once:

```
roo> web jsf all --package ~.jsf
```

To scaffold a single entity:

```
roo> web jsf scaffold --class ~.jsf.CourseBean --entity ~.model.Course
```

In either case, Roo will generate page beans and pages in the appropriate directories. Let's take a look at a typical page bean.

7.3.4 *The CourseBean page bean*

This file, backed by ITDs, is quite empty:

```
package org.rooinaction.coursemanager.pagebeans;

import org.rooinaction.coursemanager.model.Course;
import org.springframework.roo.addon.jsf.managedbean.RooJsfManagedBean;

@RooJsfManagedBean(entity = Course.class, beanName = "courseBean")
public class CourseBean {
}
```

Of course, by now you should assume the heavy lifting is provided by an ITD, and that the ITD is generated by the presence of an annotation. This annotation, @RooJsf-ManagedBean, defines the entity to scaffold (entity =) and the name of the bean in the container (courseBean).

One of the bean methods, `allCourses()`, is called when the course view is initially rendered. Here's a fragment of that method:

```
public List<Course> CourseBean.getAllCourses() {
  return allCourses;
}
```

Observant Spring developers will see that these page beans are stateful. Somehow, the `allCourses` collection was loaded before the view requested the course list.

JSF page beans can be defined as stateful objects, where each instance is closely attached to the view page code that manipulates it. In some ways, this is a simpler, more Swing-like programming model than the typical MVC approach.

Table 7.2 outlines some key methods generated by the scaffolding.

Table 7.2 Key scaffolded page bean methods

Method name	Usage
`init()`	In Roo, provides the field properties used for the fields within the view.
getters/setters for properties	Used to set or fetch the values of a single edited entity value. These methods are called to data-bind the form fields of the form view to the page bean before persisting or displaying a single entity.
`getAllCourses()`	Displays the values for the list view of the page.
`populateViewPanel()`	Creates the JSF widgets, dynamically, to define the elements of a single entity view dialog.
`populateCreatePanel()`	Creates the JSF widgets to show a single entity create dialog.
`populateEditPanel()`	Creates the JSF widgets to show a single entity editing dialog.

JSF uses these methods and a number of others to manage the JSF view. More advanced JSF users may choose to remove the dynamic widget definitions from the `populate` methods and define them in the view itself by pushing in the method and modifying the code in the bean's Java class.

Now let's take a quick look at the JSF facelet for your course page bean.

7.3.5 The Course page view

We won't go into the deep details of the page view, but keep in mind that it handles processing for the entire view. And, unlike JSP-based views, the Roo JSF facelets contain views for all CRUD operations in the same .xhtml page.

Figure 7.2 shows the page layout of the JSF user interface, and displays the `Course` list scaffolded view.

Roo uses a mechanism similar to the MVC list view, embedding all columns in each row and providing icons to delete, edit, and view each row in a form view. There's

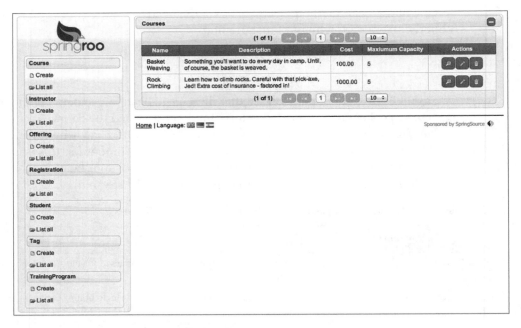

Figure 7.2   The JSF layout—course listing view

currently no create icon; you'll have to use the `Create` menu option to trigger the operation. The form views are essentially modal dialogs, as shown by the create view in figure 7.3.

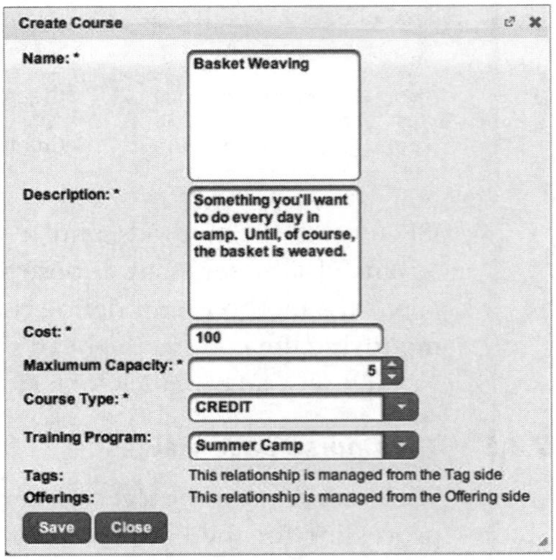

Because this is a new web framework implementation for Roo, expect a number of changes in the view configuration.

7.3.6   *The facelet itself*

Let's take a quick look into a few elements of the facelet view, WEB-INF/pages/course.xhtml.

First we'll take a look at the list view. This is provided by the table of results and is bound to the `getAllCourses()` method in the page bean as shown next.

Figure 7.3   The `Course` list view

Listing 7.2   The Course list view

```
<p:panel id="data" toggleable="true" toggleSpeed="250">          Respond to
  <h:form prependId="false">                                     form actions

    <p:dataTable id="list"                                       List view
        value="#{courseBean.allCourses}"                         table
        var="course"
        rendered="#{courseBean.dataVisible}"
        resizableColumns="false"
        paginator="true" ...
    >
    ...
    <p:columns                                                   Provides
        value="#{courseBean.columns}"                            fields
        var="column"
        columnIndexVar="colIndex">

        <f:facet name="header">
          <h:outputText
            value="#{applicationBean.getColumnName(column)}" />
        </f:facet>
        <h:outputText value="#{course[column]}" />
    </p:columns>

    <p:column styleClass="action-column">                        Action
        <f:facet name="header">                                  buttons
          <h:outputText value="Actions" />
        </f:facet>

        <p:commandButton id="viewButton"                         View
            image="ui-icon-zoomin"                               button
            update="viewDialog"
            oncomplete="viewDialog.show()"
            title="#{messages.label_view}">
          <f:setPropertyActionListener value="#{course}"
              target="#{courseBean.course}" />
        </p:commandButton>

        <p:tooltip for="viewButton"
            value="#{messages.label_view}"
            showEffect="fade" hideEffect="fade" />

        <p:commandButton id="editButton" ...>
        </p:commandButton>
        ...
    </p:column>
  </p:dataTable>
  </h:form>
</p:panel>
```

The list view is driven by the getAllCourses() method in the backing bean. The fields are provided using the Java EE @PostConstruct method init(), which you can push-in and customize to provide a custom list of fields to display.

A column is defined with the various action buttons, such as view, edit, and delete. Events are bound, such as the backing bean `viewDialog` method, which constructs the components to display a view.

The appeal of JSF is the use of a view to provide the driving force for events. Rather than relying on a controller to intercept the FORM post and determine the view to display, JSF components are driven from the view outward, with the view defining which events are bound and methods are called.

To wrap up, let's look at one of the embedded dialogs, the create dialog, which lives within the panel just after the list view definition:

```
<p:dialog id="createDialog"
    header="#{messages.label_create} Course"          ◁┐ Define
    modal="true"                                          ┘ dialog
    widgetVar="createDialog"
    dynamic="true"
    visible="#{courseBean.createDialogVisible}"
    resizable="true" maximizable="true"
    showEffect="fade"
    hideEffect="explode">                                  ┐ Update fields
                                                          ◁┘ on close
    <p:ajax event="close" update="data"
        listener="#{courseBean.handleDialogClose}" />

    <h:form id="createForm" enctype="multipart/form-data">
                                                           ┐ Generate
        <h:panelGrid id="createPanelGrid"                ◁┘ dialog
           columns="3" binding="#{courseBean.createPanelGrid}"
            styleClass="dialog" columnClasses="col1,col2,col3" />

        <p:commandButton value="#{messages.label_save}"
           action="#{courseBean.persist}"
           update="createPanelGrid growl" />

        <p:commandButton value="#{messages.label_close}"
           onclick="createDialog.hide()"
           type="button" />

    </h:form>
</p:dialog>
```

The code created for the rest of the JSF implementation is beyond the scope of this book, but you can see the patterns in the example. The dialog is defined in the backing bean, and is invoked when one of the grid action buttons is clicked.

Although support for JSF is early, the feature set is rather complete, and you have the ability to define your own custom JSF views as needed.

7.3.7 *JSF developer guidelines*

Unlike MVC, the JSF add-on takes a slightly different approach to scaffolding. You don't have the z= tags anymore. If you're adding additional tag elements to the view, be careful not to remove the form views for editing, creating, and viewing.

As with Spring MVC, you don't have to use the scaffolding; just drop your views and page beans in the appropriate places and go to work. The best way to learn is to push-in a page bean and review the interaction between it and the facelet it backs.

7.4 *Other Roo UI frameworks*

Roo provides support for several other key frameworks. They range from HTML and JavaScript-based frontends to platforms such as the Flex API. Here are some you may wish to research:

- *Spring Web Flow*—Roo provides support for building flow-based applications using Spring Web Flow. Using web flow setup from the Roo shell, you can get Roo to generate the proper installation scripts, and mount a new Web Flow script. Visit our book website (manning.com/rimple) for some examples and an article describing how to use Spring Roo with Web Flow.

- *Vaadin (http://www.vaadin.com)*—Based on GWT's component model, but implemented in a more lightweight fashion, Vaadin is a very interesting platform. The developers originally distributed a Roo add-on for Roo 1.1. Vaadin includes a set of Eclipse IDE extensions to perform drag-and-drop editing of components and user interfaces. Check out the add-on using the addon search command, which we discuss in chapter 11.

- *Flex*—Flex is a true client/server development platform when coupled with a smart application tier such as Roo. The Roo Flex add-on, which configures Spring BlazeDS remoting (a super-fast binary API), is currently being taken over by the Roo community. As of the time of this writing, it doesn't work out of the box with Roo. Check the Flex forum on SpringSource.org for details on the current state of the add-on.

  Flex users don't need to use the Flex Roo add-on to program in Flex. They can just install the powerful Spring BlazeDS library directly and use it themselves. However, once the Flex add-on is finalized, Flex developers can enjoy automatic scaffolding of entities in Flex ActionScript and manual or scaffolded user interface views.

WRITE YOUR OWN WEB FRAMEWORK INTEGRATION   You may develop your own Roo add-ons to support web frameworks such as Wicket, Stripes, and others. Refer to the source code of the Spring MVC, WebFlow, JSF, and GWT add-ons to see how it's done. We cover how to write your own Roo add-ons in detail in chapters 11 and 12.

More web and rich internet platforms will surely appear in the future, so make sure you keep up to date with the Roo add-ons by visiting the Roo forums.

7.5   *Summary*

Spring Roo has support for a number of rich internet APIs. From roll-your-own JavaScript and Ajax components and using Spring's excellent support for partial server requests, to the embedded rich web components and Ajax libraries in Spring JavaScript and Dojo, to sophisticated frameworks like GWT, Vaadin, and Flex, you have tons of options to choose from.

If you're looking to support a rich user interface but don't want the sophistication of a GWT or Flex approach, the Dojo and/or other JavaScript toolkit approaches will serve you well. But it would be wise for your team to bone up significantly on JavaScript mastery, because there are many pitfalls awaiting the Java developer who attempts to treat JavaScript as just another programming language. Crockford's *JavaScript, the Good Parts* is an essential read.

If your development team consists mostly of Java Swing developers, GWT is a great alternative to the HTML/CSS/JavaScript programming model. The downside is that the current MVP design causes a ton of code generation and can be difficult for the uninitiated programmer to approach. A more easy-to-grasp alternative is JSF, because it nests in the same way Swing components do, and has a component-driven lifecycle.

7.6   *Resources*

BOOKS

There are a number of books available on Dojo, including *Mastering Dojo: JavaScript and Ajax Tools for Great Web Experiences*, by Rawld Gill, Craig Riecke, and Alex Russell (The Pragmatic Programmers, 2008), and *Getting StartED with Dojo* by Kyle Hayes and Peter Higgins (Springer-Verlag, 2010), which also includes a very good introduction to JavaScript.

For JavaScript, Douglas Crockford's *JavaScript, the Good Parts* (O'Reilly, 2008) is essential reading. Also see *Secrets of the JavaScript Ninja* (Manning Publications, 2008) by John Resig, or the new *Third-Party JavaScript* (Manning Publications, 2012) by Benjamin A. Vinegar and Anton A. Kovalyov, both of which are in Manning Early Access status at the time of this publication.

WEB

For more information about Dojo, visit http://dojotoolkit.org.

The folks at SitePoint (http://www.sitepoint.com) support and write about Dojo.

Douglas Crockford has abundant resources, including extensive videos, at http://www.crockford.com.

Configuring security

This chapter covers

- Spring Security concepts
- Configuring security
- Generating configuration files
- Protecting URLs
- Customizing authorization credential storage
- Creating user and role management pages
- Implementing authentication to resources
- Enabling security event logging

Most applications have to provide some level of security to prevent unauthorized users or external programs from accessing the system. In traditional Java EE applications, developers would delegate security to the application server infrastructure. Although there's a standard API for Java security—the Java Authentication and Authorization Service, or JAAS—it doesn't standardize the entire process of implementing the application security. As a result, integrating security into applications ends up being a one-off affair for each application server a team encounters.

Spring developers know there's a better solution: configure the Spring Security API. Originally called ACEGI Security (and later acquired by SpringSource), the

Spring Security API is a platform-neutral, general-purpose, security API that can be hosted on any Java application server without changing the code written by a developer.

In this chapter, you'll learn about the Spring Security API and how to install it within a Spring Roo application, including the web URL security and a customized login page. You'll review the security artifacts and how to tailor security configurations to suit your needs. You'll also learn how to turn on security event logging, which logs all security-related activity, allowing you to run security analytics and receive alerts to any unauthorized access to your application.

Let's get started by installing Spring Security in the Roo application.

8.1   *Installing Spring Security*

Security commands aren't available until you install the web components of a Roo application. After you've typed in the `controller` command, the Roo framework will generate the controller classes and configuration files. Now you're ready to install and configure the security API in the Roo application.

To configure the Spring Security API in Roo, follow these three steps:

1 Issue a `security setup` command inside the Spring Roo shell, and install the framework.
2 Configure a Spring context file to define your security rules.
3 Enable special security annotations and tag libraries.

To install Spring Security in an existing Roo application, issue the command `security setup`:

```
roo> security setup
```

Security commands are contained in the `org.springframework.roo.addon.security` `.SecurityCommands` class.

Roo will automatically configure these features in your application. As you'll see, Roo installs the following security elements:

- Proper Maven dependencies for the Spring Security JARs, including `spring-security-core`, `spring-security-config`, `spring-security-web`, and `spring-security-taglibs`.
- A brand-new Spring application context file to store the security configuration, META-INF/spring/applicationContext-security.xml.
- A login page (called `login.jspx`) and a views.xml layout file. The views.xml file has the tile definitions for different views in the application.
- An updated web.xml web descriptor file, which includes the Spring Security servlet filter.
- Extra web URL protection settings in webmvc-config.xml.

Because Spring Security follows the convention-over-configuration philosophy to enable authentication and authorization in web applications, Roo's security configuration command doesn't create or modify any Java classes. It generates only the

Spring Security configuration XML file and the view components (JSPX files) of the application.

Let's take a look at some of these changes in detail, starting with the new security context file.

8.1.1 *The security context file*

The following listing details the new applicationContext-security.xml Spring Security context file.

Listing 8.1   The Spring Security context configuration file

```xml
<?xml version="1.0" encoding="UTF-8"?>

<beans:beans
    xmlns="http://www.springframework.org/schema/security"
     xmlns:beans="http://www.springframework.org/schema/beans"
    xmlns:xsi="http://www.w3.org/2001/XMLSchema-instance"
    xsi:schemaLocation="
      http://www.springframework.org/schema/beans
      http://www.springframework.org/schema/beans/
      spring-beans-3.0.xsd
      http://www.springframework.org/schema/security
      http://www.springframework.org/schema/security/
        spring-security-3.0.xsd">

    <http auto-config="true" use-expressions="true">

        <form-login
            login-processing-url="/resources/
            j_spring_security_check"
            login-page="/login"
            authentication-failure-url="/login?login_error=t"/>

          <logout
              logout-url="/resources/j_spring_security_logout"/>

        <intercept-url pattern="/choices/**"
            access="hasRole('ROLE_ADMIN')"/>
         <intercept-url pattern="/member/**"
            access="isAuthenticated()" />
        <intercept-url pattern="/resources/**" access="permitAll" />
        <intercept-url pattern="/**" access="permitAll" />
    </http>

    <authentication-manager alias="authenticationManager">

      <authentication-provider>
        <password-encoder hash="sha-256"/>
        <user-service>
            <user name="admin"
                  password="8c6976...48a918"
                  authorities="ROLE_ADMIN"/>
            <user name="student"
                  password="04f899...df8fb"
                  authorities="ROLE_STUDENT"/>
        </user-service>
```

Annotations:

- ❶ Security namespace as primary namespace
- ❷ Configure HTTP security
- ❸ Login page and failure URL
- ❹ Security logout URL
- ❺ URL patterns to secure
- ❻ Authentication source
- ❼ In-memory database for account information
- ❽ Admin user
- ❾ Regular user

```
        </authentication-provider>

    </authentication-manager>

</beans:beans>
```

The first part of the previous listing uses the Spring Security namespace (http://
www.springframework.org/schema/security) ❶ as the primary namespace, so you
don't have to use a separate prefix when defining the Spring Security XML elements.
You'll use the HTTP element ❷ to configure HTTP security, basic authentication, and
other defaults. It also supports scripting in security elements with SpEL. From an
authentication standpoint, you'll use the form-login ❸ and logout ❹ elements to
enable a login page, with a login failure URL and a security logout page, respectively,
for your web application.

When you use the form-based login approach, it's important to note that the form
submit must be encrypted to protect the user's password, and the credentials must be
sent in encrypted form rather than in plain text. The URL patterns you want to
secure are defined using the interceptor-url ❺ element. Note that this configuration element also takes care of the role-based authorization for specific web pages
(URLs). The next section in the configuration file deals with authentication details,
such as the authentication manager ❻, an in-memory database ❼, an administrator
user named admin ❽, and another user named student ❾, who will have public
access to the website.

The password encoder hash configuration in listing 8.1 uses the SHA-256 algorithm. SHA-256 is more secure than other password hashing algorithms such as MD5, so
the password hash algorithm specified here uses the industry-recommended hashing
algorithm. Note that the passwords should be hashed using salt, which makes the
hashed passwords more secure. Without salt, the hashed passwords are vulnerable to
security attacks like SQL injections, dictionary attacks, and brute-force attacks.
Though beyond the scope of this book, you should become familiar with the many
other implementation best practices in the application security space. Websites such
as OWASP's (The Open Web Application Security Project) Top Ten Project list security
vulnerabilities and provide helpful discussions of application security best practices.

Ben Alex discusses another authentication option in his blog post on a wedding
RSVP application (http://mng.bz/9z4D). He suggests you configure the authentication setup to have the password *ignored*. This is useful when you want to let users access
the web application using a single credential like a token, or as in Ben's sample application, the RSVP confirmation code. This security configuration is shown in the following listing.

Listing 8.2   Spring configuration snippet with special identification for anonymous users

```
<http auto-config="true"                                      ⟵❶ HTTP config

    use-expressions="true">                                      ⟵┐
                                                              ❷ Express security
    <form-login                                                  constraints
        login-processing-url="/resources/j_spring_security_check"
```

```
        login-page="/login"
        authentication-failure-url="/login?login_error=t"/>

    <logout
        logout-url="/resources/j_spring_security_logout"/>

    <intercept-url pattern="/choices/**"
        access="hasRole('ROLE_ADMIN')"/>
    <intercept-url pattern="/member/**"
        access="isAuthenticated()" />
    <intercept-url pattern="/resources/**" access="permitAll" />
    <intercept-url pattern="/**" access="permitAll" />
</http>

 <authentication-manager alias="authenticationManager">
    <authentication-provider>
        <!--
        <password-encoder hash="sha-256"/>
        -->
        <user-service>
            <!--
            <user name="admin" password="8c697...48a918"   ➥
                authorities="ROLE_ADMIN"/>
            <user name="user" password="04f899...9df8fb"   ➥
                authorities="ROLE_STUDENT"/>
            -->
            <user name="admin1234" password="ignored"               ❸ Password
                authorities="ROLE_ADMIN"/>                          ⟵┘  ignored
             <user name="user12345" password="ignored"   ➥
                authorities="ROLE_STUDENT"/>
        </user-service>
    </authentication-provider>
</authentication-manager>
```

When you set the password value in the previous listing to `ignored`, you make the authentication occur based only on the username. For this to work, you also need to edit the login page (src/main/webapp/WEB-INF/views/login.jspx) to change the password HTML field (`j_password`) to be a hidden field and remove the password label. Don't forget to comment out the `password-encoder` element as well; otherwise, the authentication will fail, with a message such as `Bad Credentials`.

The file applicationContext-security.xml is the heart of the Spring Security configuration. It defines the overall security configuration, which consists of two key facets that drive the security engine: the authentication and authorization settings.

AUTHENTICATION

Authentication is the act of verifying the identity of the agent requesting access to your system. In Spring Security, authentication can be tied to various physical security mechanisms, such as BASIC authentication, form-based security, certificate-based authentication (CERT), or SSH-based key pairs.

In listing 8.2, the `<http>` tag ❶ establishes that you are going to use HTTP-based authentication. It tells Spring Security to automatically configure the default settings for security, which allows for a basic form-based login, a special identification of anonymous(or non-logged-in users ❸), a logout URL, the ability to remember sign-in sessions for two weeks, and HTTP basic authentication. In addition to these settings, Roo also configures the use-expressions attribute of the http element ❷, which allows you to express your security constraints using the Spring Expression Language (SpEL).

Note that in both form-based and basic authentication the user credentials are sent unencrypted to the web server. You can use a secure HTTP (HTTPS) mechanism to address this concern by enabling the SSL certificates. But unlike basic authentication, with form-based authentication you have the flexibility to add or modify any custom security event–related auditing, as well as user attributes and level of logging for your requirements. You can set limits so the login page is SSL-encrypted, but for your website's other pages that contain only static content and no user-sensitive information, you can use HTTP. Finally, a login form allows you to present a page with a look and feel consistent with your overall application. The basic authentication option only provides a dialog, which you can't customize.

AUTHORIZATION

Authorization (also known as access control) is the process by which Spring Security checks whether or not a given *authenticated user* has access to a given *resource*. Completely decoupled from the authentication process, authorization can be defined in a number of ways: using the <intercept-url> tag to protect controllers, pages, and other web resources; using the @Secured annotation (org.springframework.security.access.annotation package) to protect various Spring bean methods or classes; or using AOP pointcut expressions to protect code by convention.

As you've learned, Spring Security has already configured both authentication and authorization. The users are defined in an in-memory data store, and two roles are defined as ROLE_ADMIN and ROLE_STUDENT. These roles are attached to the admin and user logins.

The security descriptor doesn't function on its own. You have to install Spring Security in the container. Let's take a look at how this is done.

8.1.2   *Web configuration elements*

You can install the Spring Security engine into any web container using a standard servlet filter. Here's the Roo-generated configuration, defined in src/main/webapp/WEB-INF/web.xml:

```
<filter>
    <filter-name>springSecurityFilterChain</filter-name>
    <filter-class>org.springframework.web.filter.<➥
        DelegatingFilterProxy</filter-class>
</filter>
...
<filter-mapping>
    <filter-name>springSecurityFilterChain</filter-name>
    <url-pattern>/*</url-pattern>
</filter-mapping>
```

Installing the `DelegatingFilterProxy` filter allows the web application to make requests to the Spring Security configuration when web requests are issued. As you can see with the URL pattern of `/*`, all URLs pass through the filter, which means Spring Security can protect more than just controllers.

The `security setup` command also adds a login page. Let's take a look at an excerpt of that page, `login.jspx`:

```
<c:if test="${not empty param.login_error}">
  <div class="errors">
    <p>
      <spring:message code="security_login_unsuccessful" />
      <c:out value="${SPRING_SECURITY_LAST_EXCEPTION.message}" />
      .
    </p>
  </div>
</c:if>
...
<spring:url value="/resources/j_spring_security_check" ➥
    var="form_url" />
<form name="f" action="${fn:escapeXml(form_url)}" method="POST">
...
    <input id="j_username" type='text' name='j_username' ➥
        style="width:150px"/>
...
    <input id="j_password" type='password' name='j_password'
        style="width:150px"/>
    <spring:message code="button_submit" var="submit_label" />
    <input id="proceed" type="submit" ➥
        value="${fn:escapeXml(submit_label)}" />
</form>
```

Despite a hefty amount of formatting and validation code, the sole purpose of the login page is to submit to a special Spring security URL, `j_spring_security_check`, and send two parameters, `j_username` and `j_password`. This is similar to how a traditional Java EE web security implementation works. The login form is submitted to the URL `j_spring_security_check`. If the security system recognizes the credentials of the passed user, Spring Security marks this fact and authenticates the user. Otherwise, the error is passed back to the page, and rendered in the `errors` div above the form.

This security configuration can be extended and customized by adding more JSTL scriptlets and conditions using the Expression Language (EL). For example, you can implement a feature called Remember Me so the application remembers the identity of a logged-in user between sessions (a feature supported in the Spring Security framework). Also, once you modify and customize the configuration files, Roo remembers those changes and doesn't override them the next time you run the Roo commands.

Now that you've been briefed on the configuration elements, let's discuss how to use Spring Security to configure security in a simple application.

8.2   *Securing a sample application*

Let's discuss the application security module of the Course Manager application. In this application, you'll use one of the two preinstalled roles, ROLE_ADMIN, and a new custom role called ROLE_STUDENT:

- ROLE_ADMIN—Able to create new courses, and manage all the existing courses
- ROLE_STUDENT—Able to view course details, and register for a specific course or courses

You can also define additional roles like ROLE_INSTRUCTOR and ROLE_TRADING _PARTNER, which are useful in a Course Manager application. You'll learn more details about these later in the book.

With these application security requirements in the areas of authentication and role-based authorization defined, you're ready to secure the web application.

8.2.1   *Restricting URLs*

First, you have to replace the default URL protections installed by Spring Security. You'll change the intercept-url tags to something that makes sense for your application, such as

```
<intercept-url pattern="/coursecatalog/**" access="permitAll" />
<intercept-url pattern="/coursecatalog/**" method="DELETE"
    access="hasRole('ROLE_ADMIN')" />
<intercept-url pattern="/courses/**" method="GET" access="permitAll" />
<intercept-url pattern="/courses/**" method="POST"
    access="hasRole('ROLE_ADMIN')" />
<intercept-url pattern="/courses/**" method="PUT"
    access="hasRole('ROLE_ADMIN')" />
<intercept-url pattern="/courses/**" method="DELETE"
    access="hasRole('ROLE_ADMIN')" />
<intercept-url pattern="/**" access="permitAll" />
```

These patterns create the following rules:

- Both roles may view the course catalog and course details, but only the admin can delete them.
- Any web request can access the GET method on /coursecatalog, making it effectively public.

This is a specific set of choices, but one that can be easily tweaked by modifying the tags in the previous code.

Note that the access attribute is populated with a permitAll value for some of the URL patterns. This configuration allows all users access to the URLs matching the pattern value specified in the pattern attribute of the intercept-url element. In real-world applications, you shouldn't allow access to URLs that aren't explicitly protected. If a user tries to access a URL that's not specified, you should use a denyAll value to prevent access to the pattern that the URL matches. This approach gives you better control over what URLs in the application are accessible to a specific group of users and results in a more secure web application.

Roo is based on version 3 of the Spring Security framework, which includes several built-in expressions (as of 3.0.5) for web and method-level security. The expressions you can use in the access= tag are listed in table 8.1.

Table 8.1　Common, built-in expressions in Spring Security

Expression	Description
hasRole(rolename)	Allows only principals with the *rolename* role
hasAnyRole(rolename1, rolename2, ...)	Allows principals with any role listed
permitAll	Disables Spring Security for this URL pattern and allows access to all
denyAll	Refuses entry to the given URL for any user
isAnonymous()	Allows entry only if no security context is established for the given principal (that is, they're not logged in)
isAuthenticated()	Allows access for any authenticated user

You can also apply more arbitrary expressions in this configuration, but this list will do for simple security configurations.

You can also use Spring Security JSP tag library tags to control access to the elements (and to hide or show them) on the web page, as shown in the JSPX script snippet in the following listing.

Listing 8.3　Spring Security JSP tag library to control access to web page elements

```
<?xml version="1.0" encoding="UTF-8" standalone="no"?>
<div xmlns:sec="http://www.springframework.org/security/tags"          Spring
    xmlns:jsp="http://java.sun.com/JSP/Page"                           Security
  xmlns:menu="urn:jsptagdir:/WEB-INF/tags/menu"                        tag
    id="menu"                                                       ❶ library
    version="2.0">
    <jsp:output omit-xml-declaration="yes"/>
    <menu:menu id="_menu" z="nZaf43BjUg1iM0v70HJVEsXDopc=">
        <menu:category id="c_base" z="yTpmmNMm/hWoy3yf+aPcdUX2At8=">
            <menu:item id="i_base_new" messageCode="global_menu_new"
                url="/bases?form"
                z="+i6N/uFq65rRQkyN9G93ZSDxIec="/>
            <menu:item id="i_base_list" messageCode="global_menu_list"
                url="/bases?page=${empty param.page ? 1 :
                    param.page}&amp;
                size=${empty param.size ? 10 : param.size}"
                z="bztucYGCX6rDQ5LBvLu8c5Mn8mM="/>
        <sec:authorize ifAllGranted="ROLE_ADMIN">                    Control access
            <menu:item id="i_base_delete"                           to page
                messageCode="global_menu_delete"                  ❷ components
                url="/bases?delete"
                z="+i6N/uFq65rRQkyN9G93ZSDxIec="/>
        </sec:authorize>
```

```
        </menu:category>
    </menu:menu>
</div>
```

To use Spring Security tags detailed in the previous listing, you'll first specify the tag library namespace (`http://www.springframework.org/security/tags`) ❶ and then use security tags such as `authorize` ❷ with an attribute like `ifAllGranted` to specify the role or roles that will have access to the specific web page element (in this case, the `delete` menu item).

This will address the access control requirements in the view components, but what about the controller layer? You can restrict access to the `delete` and `update` use cases for a scaffolded entity by adjusting the `@RooWebScaffold` annotation (located in the `org.springframework.roo.addon.web.mvc.controller` package) in the specific controller class, adding `delete` and `update` attributes, and setting them to `false`. This will cause the Roo shell to automatically remove the delete and update methods from the controller class and update the corresponding JSPX view components:

```
@RooWebScaffold(path = "coursecatalog",
                automaticallyMaintainView = true,
                formBackingObject = CourseCatalog.class,
                delete=false, update=false
)
@RequestMapping("/coursecatalog")
@Controller
public class CourseCatalogController {
}
```

The next step is to define a more permanent authentication storage mechanism by persisting roles and principals into a database. Also, many real-world applications use a Lightweight Directory Access Protocol (LDAP)-based repository such as Microsoft Active Directory or Sun Directory Server Enterprise Edition (DSEE), or an open source LDAP product such as the OpenDS Directory Server, for storing user credentials. Later in this chapter, you'll also learn how to configure LDAP-based authentication in a Roo application.

8.2.2   *Storing roles and users in a database*

In a real system, you'd never configure security credentials within a configuration file, because you'd have to redeploy every time you needed to add a new user. Instead, you can use Roo to do this. First, you'll create entities and controllers to manage your security credentials. Figure 8.1 shows how your security model will look.

The database tables that these entities (`Principal`, `AuthorityPrincipal-Assignment`, and `Authority`) correspond to are `security_principals`, `security_authorities`, and `security_role_assignments`, respectively.

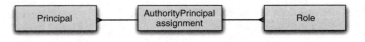

Figure 8.1   The Course Manager application security model

First, let's create the `Principal` entity:

```
entity jpa --class ~.model.security.Principal
    --table security_principals
field string  --fieldName username --notNull --sizeMax 50 --sizeMin 3
field string  --fieldName password --notNull --sizeMax 50 --sizeMin 3
field boolean --fieldName enabled
```

This Roo script defines a table, `security_principals`, with `username`, `password`, and `enabled` fields.

Next, you have to define your roles. Here's another entity that accomplishes the task:

```
entity jpa --class ~.model.security.Authority
    --table security_authorities
field string --fieldName roleId --notNull --sizeMax 10 --sizeMin 8
field string --fieldName authority --notNull --sizeMax 50
    --sizeMin 8 ➥ --regexp ^ROLE_[A-Z]*
```

And next, create your intersecting entity, `AuthorityPrincipalAssignment`:

```
entity jpa
    --class ~.model.security.AuthorityPrincipalAssignment <➥
    --table security_role_assignments
field reference --fieldName username --type ~.model.security.Principal
field reference --fieldName roleId --type ~.model.security.Authority
```

For all of these entities, let's define the controller classes using the `web mvc scaffold` command:

```
web mvc scaffold --class ~.web.security.UserController ➥
   --backingType ~.model.security.Principal --path /security/users
web mvc scaffold --class ~.web.security.RoleController ➥
   --backingType ~.model.security.Authority --path /security/roles
web mvc scaffold --class ~.web.security.RoleMappingController ➥
   --backingType ~.model.security.AuthorityPrincipalAssignment ➥
   --path /security/assignments
```

User-friendly field names

As discussed in chapters 5 and 6, you can improve the application's appearance by editing `application.properties` and changing the labels for menus and fields to more user-friendly names like Role, User, and Role Assignment.

You should also secure these new URLs so that only `ROLE_ADMIN` users can access them. Add the following `intercept-url` entry to protect all URLs below `/security`:

```
<intercept-url pattern="/security/**"
    access="hasRole('ROLE_ADMIN')" />
```

SECURITY PROTECTION BY PATH You'll note that it's easy to protect the whole set of security controllers by putting all of them under the same URL path.

You can do this by using the `--path /security/pathname` element in the `web mvc scaffold` Roo command, which automatically places controller request URLs and view paths in the `pathname` path, within the `/security` superpath.

It's important to note that the Roo add-on community is working on automating the steps required to use JDBC-based authentication configuration, which will make the job of enabling database-driven user authentication much easier in the future.

At this point, you've defined your database entities and the controllers to manipulate them. But, so far, you haven't attached them to the security system.

8.2.3   *Database-backed authentication*

Spring Security lets you define *user services* to access your user databases. Because the concept of a `principal` has been abstracted, you can plug in any kind of implementation: database-managed, LDAP, or flat-file. Spring Security also supports external single sign-on (SSO) systems such as Central Authentication Service (CAS), OpenSSO, and SiteMinder.

First, you'll configure your users using a relational database, accessing entities defined within the same Roo application. To do this, you'll have to update your Spring Security configuration file, applicationContext-security.xml. You'll add a real, data source–backed authentication database, as illustrated in the following listing, before the original `user-service` tag.

Listing 8.4   Database-backed authentication

```
<authentication-provider>
    <password-encoder hash="sha-256" />
        <salt-source user-property="username"/>
    </password-encoder>
  <jdbc-user-service data-source-ref="dataSource">

    users-by-username-query="
      SELECT username, password, enabled
      FROM security_principals WHERE username = ?"

    authorities-by-username-query="
      SELECT p.username, a.authority
      FROM security_principals p, security_authorities a,
          security_role_assignments ra
      WHERE p.username = ra.username
      AND a.roleId = ra.roleId
      AND p.username = ?"
   />

  <user-service>
    <user name="admin"
      password="8c6976e...2b448a918"
      authorities="ROLE_ADMIN" />
    <user name="user"
      password="04f8996...85b9df8fb"
      authorities="ROLE_STUDENT" />
  </user-service>
</authentication-provider>
```

1. JDBC user service and data source
2. Users query
3. Authorities query
4. Back door

The previous listing shows how to configure the database-backed authentication. You specify the SQL queries to retrieve user details and user roles in the users-by-user-name-query ❷ and authorities-by-username-query ❸ attributes of jdbc-user-service, respectively. Notice the second user service ❹ behind it is a "back door." If a user can't be found in the primary user service ❶, Spring Security will search the next one.

This approach is great for development-time databases, but you may want to consider making this an optional security configuration element, and leave it out when you get ready to move to a real production environment.

Note that the password values in the security_principals table should never be stored in plain text. They should be stored using a hash algorithm like SHA-256. The password-encoder element in the previous listing will authenticate the users by retrieving the password (which was stored after hashing the plain-text password value using the SHA-256 hash algorithm) from the table and un-hashing it to compare it with the password entered on the login screen. Also, when using the hashed passwords, it's a good security practice to use a salt value to protect against dictionary attacks. You'll want to use a randomly generated salt value for each user, which will allow you to use the username property for generating the salt. Then you'll configure all of this in the salt-source element in the Spring Security configuration file.

8.2.4 *LDAP-based authentication*

Spring Security provides support for LDAP-based authentication and authorization out of the box. To enable the LDAP authentication, you'll need to make a few minor edits to the applicationContext-security.xml file.

To use Spring Security LDAP authentication, you'll first need to add the following Spring LDAP dependencies in the Maven pom.xml file:

```
<dependency>
    <groupId>org.springframework.security</groupId>
    <artifactId>spring-security-ldap</artifactId>
    <version>${spring-security.version}</version>
</dependency>
<dependency>
    <groupId>org.springframework.ldap</groupId>
    <artifactId>spring-ldap-core</artifactId>
    <version>1.3.0.RELEASE</version>
</dependency>
<dependency>
    <groupId>org.springframework.ldap</groupId>
    <artifactId>spring-ldap-core-tiger</artifactId>
    <version>1.3.0.RELEASE</version>
</dependency>
```

Next, add the tags for the ldap-server and ldap-authentication-provider elements to the applicationContext-security.xml file, as shown in the following listing.

Listing 8.5 LDAP authentication configuration

```
<!-- Configure Authentication mechanism -->
    <!--   Real LDAP Server   -->
```

```
<ldap-server id="ldapServer"
        url="ldap://localhost:389"
        manager-dn="cn=Directory Manager"
        manager-password="LDAP_SERVER_PASSWORD"
/>
<authentication-manager alias="authenticationManager">
    <ldap-authentication-provider
            server-ref="ldapServer"
            user-dn-pattern="uid={0},dc=coursemanager,dc=com"
            user-search-filter="(uid={0})"
            user-search-base="dc=coursemanager,dc=com"
            group-search-base="dc=coursemanager,dc=com"
            group-role-attribute="dc=coursemanager,dc=com"
    />
</authentication-manager>
```

① LDAP server connection parameters

② LDAP authentication details

There are two main elements to review in the previous listing: the LDAP server connection details **①**, which include the server URL where the LDAP repository is running, the LDAP connection user id (manager-dn), and the password (manager-password); and the LDAP-based authentication manager **②**. In the authentication provider element, you specify the following attributes:

- User distinguished name (DN) pattern
- User and group search base values
- Group role attribute
- User search filter (in this case, the search filter is based on the user id that corresponds to the LDAP attribute uid)

You can use an open source LDAP server such as the OpenDS directory server for testing the previous LDAP user authentication configuration. The OpenDS server documentation (https://docs.opends.org/2.2) has instructions on how to install, configure, and launch the open source LDAP server. Refer to the readme.txt file in the sample application code provided with this book for instructions on how to configure and run the OpenDS server.

If your organization has a user data repository in a legacy system that doesn't support JDBC- or LDAP-based authentication, you can use a custom authentication provider for user authentication. In this scenario, the authentication configuration would look like the following:

```
<beans:bean id="customAuthenticationProvider"
    class="com.rooinaction.samples.security.authentication.➥
        MyCustomAuthenticationProvider">
    <beans:property name="adminUser" value="admin" />
    <beans:property name="adminPassword" value="test" />
</beans:bean>
<authentication-manager alias="authenticationManager">
    <authentication-provider ref="customAuthenticationProvider" />
</authentication-manager>
```

Your custom authentication provider `MyCustomAuthenticationProvider` class would extend the Spring Security framework's abstract class `Abstract-UserDetailsAuthenticationProvider` (located in the `org.springframework.security.authentication.dao` package).

As noted previously in this chapter, in Roo you have to manually configure and customize the security configuration to use a JDBC- or LDAP-based authentication. Roo's security setup command doesn't provide any customization options. Adding the ability to specify LDAP or JDBC options as additional command-line parameters when running Roo's security command makes for enhancement of the security command. These additional parameters can be used to specify the type of authentication (for example, JDBC, LDAP, or custom authentication) and other nondefault authentication details.

After you've updated the authentication provider configuration using either a JDBC-based or an LDAP-based authentication provider and you run the application, you'll see the authentication and authorization functionality in action.

In the next section, you'll find out how to handle the access denied errors by displaying a customized error page rather than the 403 error page.

8.2.5 *Handling access denied errors*

There are two more steps to take before you're ready to test your security configuration. First, if you try to log in as `user` to access a restricted URL (for example, http://localhost:8080/coursemanager/registrations/), you'll get the following error message:

```
HTTP Status 403 - Access is denied

description Access to the specified resource (Access is denied) ➥
has been forbidden.
```

To handle this error more gracefully, let's create a new view page called `AuthzError.jspx` with a user-friendly message, such as the one shown in the following code snippet:

```
<html>
    <head>
        <title></title>
        <meta http-equiv="Content-Type" content="text/html; ➥
            charset=UTF-8">
    </head>
    <body>
        <h2>Error:</h2>
        You are not authorized to execute this function.
    </body>
</html>
```

Let's also create a user-friendly error page (called `Error.jspx`) for handling the HTTP 404 errors.

```
<html>
    <head>
        <title></title>
        <meta http-equiv="Content-Type" content="text/html; ➥
            charset=UTF-8">
```

```
    </head>
    <body>
        <h2>Error Occurred.</h2>
        Please contact a technology support team member.
    </body>
</html>
```

Now you need to add these custom error pages to the web.xml file, as shown in the following:

```
<error-page>
        <error-code>403</error-code>
        <location>/AuthzError.jspx</location>
</error-page>
<error-page>
        <error-code>404</error-code>
        <location>/Error.jspx</location>
</error-page>
```

The last step in making your code example a complete web application is to add links in the footer section for the login URL.

8.2.6 *Adding login links*

Note that the links in the footer tile of the web page don't display the login link. The footer tile displays only the logout link when you're already logged in. You'll have to type the URL http://localhost:8080/coursemanager/login in the browser window to navigate to the login page of the Roo application. To add a new link for the login view in the footer section of each web page, you'll first need to add a new message code for the login link in the messages.properties file (located in src\main\webapp \WEB-INF\i18n folder):

```
# New spring message code for login
security_login=Login
```

Then you'll add the following JSTL code in the footer.jspx file (located in the src\main\webapp\WEB-INF\views folder) below the home link:

```
<!--  Login link in the footer tile.  -->
    <c:if test="${pageContext['request'].userPrincipal == null}">
        <c:out value=" | "/>
        <span>
            <spring:url value="login" var="login"/>
            <a href="${login}">
                <spring:message code="security_login"/>
            </a>
        </span>
    </c:if>
```

Now the login link will display next to the home link when the user isn't logged in.

8.3 Testing security setup

Now that you've completed all of the security configuration steps in this chapter, it's time to build the application running the `mvn package` command. After a successful build, launch the servlet container using the `mvn tomcat:run` command. Then navigate to the login page using the URL http://localhost:8080/coursemanager/login to authenticate into the Roo application.

Navigate to the main page of the web application and verify that the restricted menu items aren't visible. To do this, log in as `user` and make sure that only the menus that the `ROLE_STUDENT` role is allowed to view are visible. Log out and log back in as `admin` and you should now see all the menus that the `ROLE_ADMIN` role is authorized to access.

8.4 Adding security event logging

If you're interested in logging all of the security events (when a user logs in or logs out of the Roo application), you can do so by adding the `LoggerListener` Spring bean provided by the Spring Security framework. Security event logging is a requirement in several organizations, especially those that must be compliant with regulatory standards such as the Sarbanes-Oxley Act (SOX) or the Federal Information Security Management Act (FISMA).

The `LoggerListener` class (which is located in the `org.springframework .security.authentication.event` package) outputs authentication-related application events to the logger. All the authentication events are logged at the warning (`WARN`) logger level.

Note that this security event logger is part of Spring Security and not a Spring Roo feature, but it's included in the discussion here because most real-world applications require logging for troubleshooting as well as security compliance purposes. The following configuration snippet shows how to add the security event logging in the applicationContext-security.xml file:

```
<!-- Security event logging -->
<beans:bean id="loggerListener"
    class="org.springframework.security.authentication.event.➥
        LoggerListener" />
```

The following log output snippet shows the security event logger output messages after you enable `LoggerListener`:

```
2010-11-27 18:52:05,202 [http-8080-1] WARN
 org.springframework.security.authentication.event.LoggerListener -
 Authentication event AuthenticationSuccessEvent: user;
 details: org.springframework.security.web.authentication.
        WebAuthenticationDetails@380f4:
 RemoteIpAddress: 0:0:0:0:0:0:0:1; ➥
    SessionId: 74CAE479AA7B10ABAAB3155EAB14D53B

2010-11-27 18:52:05,206 [http-8080-1] WARN
 org.springframework.security.authentication.event.LoggerListener -
```

```
Authentication event InteractiveAuthenticationSuccessEvent: user;
details: org.springframework.security.web.authentication.
        WebAuthenticationDetails@380f4:
RemoteIpAddress: 0:0:0:0:0:0:0:1; ➥
    SessionId: 74CAE479AA7B10ABAAB3155EAB14D53B
```

The default logger level in the generated log4j.properties file is ERROR, so you'll need to modify the logger level to either WARN or INFO to be able to view the security event log messages. Run the following Roo commands to change logging level from the ERROR to the INFO level. Make sure that the ERROR log level is set for the application that's running in the production environment and set the INFO level to run only in nonproduction environments:

```
roo> hint logging
You can easily configure logging levels in your project.

Roo will update the log4j.properties file to control your logging.

Type 'logging setup' then hit TAB twice. Consider using 'DEBUG' level.
You may wish to specify the optional --package ➥
argument (defaults to 'ALL').

Remember to type 'hint' for further hints and suggestions.
roo> logging setup --level
logging setup --level
required --level: The log level to configure; no default value
roo> logging setup --level

DEBUG    ERROR    FATAL    INFO     TRACE    WARN
roo> logging setup --level INFO
Managed SRC_MAIN_RESOURCES\log4j.properties
roo>
```

The logging command shown in the previous example defaults to all packages in the web application, but you can use the optional --package argument to specify the package that you want to set the logging level. The following example provides the logging command again, but this time it specifies the package name for the classes in the Roo project (using the variable PROJECT, which maps to the org.rooinaction .coursemanager package):

```
logging setup --level DEBUG --package PROJECT
```

This will add the following line to the log4j.properties file:

```
log4j.logger.org.rooinaction.coursemanager=DEBUG
```

If you want to modify the log level for Spring Security Java classes, specify SECURITY as the value for the package argument in the setup command and it will add the DEBUG level to the org.springframework.security package. This is helpful for trouble-shooting any security-related bugs in the application.

The following listing shows the complete configuration with all of the custom changes discussed in this chapter for the applicationContext-security.xml security configuration file.

Listing 8.6 Security configuration for Course Manager application

```xml
<?xml version="1.0" encoding="UTF-8"?>
<beans:beans xmlns="http://www.springframework.org/schema/security"
    xmlns:beans="http://www.springframework.org/schema/beans"
    xmlns:xsi="http://www.w3.org/2001/XMLSchema-instance"
    xsi:schemaLocation="
      http://www.springframework.org/schema/beans
      http://www.springframework.org/schema/beans/spring-beans-3.0.xsd
      http://www.springframework.org/schema/security
      http://www.springframework.org/schema/security/
        spring-security-3.0.xsd">

    <http auto-config="true" use-expressions="true">
        <form-login login-processing-url="/resources/
            j_spring_security_check"
            login-page="/login"
            authentication-failure-url="/login?login_error=t"/>
        <logout logout-url="/resources/j_spring_security_logout"/>

        <intercept-url pattern="/coursecatalog/**" method="DELETE"
            access="hasRole('ROLE_ADMIN')" />
        <intercept-url pattern="/coursecatalog/**"
            access="hasAnyRole('ROLE_ADMIN', 'ROLE_STUDENT')" />
        <intercept-url pattern="/coursedetails/**" method="POST"
            access="hasRole('ROLE_ADMIN')" />
        <intercept-url pattern="/coursedetails/**" method="PUT"
            access="hasRole('ROLE_ADMIN')" />
        <intercept-url pattern="/coursedetails/**" method="GET"
            access="permitAll" />
        <intercept-url pattern="/coursedetails/**" method="DELETE"
            access="hasRole('ROLE_ADMIN')" />
        <intercept-url pattern="/coursedetails/**"
            access="hasAnyRole('ROLE_ADMIN','ROLE_STUDENT')" />
        <intercept-url pattern="/**" access="permitAll" />
    </http>

    <ldap-server id="ldapServer"
        url="ldap://localhost:389"
        manager-dn="cn=Directory Manager"
        manager-password="test123"
    />

    <authentication-manager alias="authenticationManager">
        <ldap-authentication-provider
            server-ref="ldapServer"
            user-dn-pattern="uid={0},dc=coursemanager,dc=com"
            user-search-filter="(uid={0})"
            user-search-base="dc=coursemanager,dc=com"
            group-search-base="dc=coursemanager,dc=com"
            group-role-attribute="dc=coursemanager,dc=com"
        />
```

```
</authentication-manager>

<beans:bean id="loggerListener"
    class="org.springframework.security.authentication.event.➥
    LoggerListener" />
```

```
</beans:beans>
```

As you can see in the previous listing, almost all of the application security aspects—such as the user authentication, the role-based access (RBAC) to different web pages (URLs) in the application, the expression language–based access control, and the security event logging—can be defined in the XML file without having to write a single line of Java code. This is the power the Spring Security framework brings to the table, and Roo takes complete advantage of this approach. The Spring Security framework makes the job of every application architect and developer easier, because they can spend their focus, time, and effort on the business logic part of the application instead of getting bogged down with all the security configuration details and other boiler-plate infrastructure tasks.

8.5   Summary

In this chapter, you learned how to implement security (which includes authentication and authorization aspects) in a Roo application. You reviewed the Spring Security concepts and the configuration details of application security in a Roo application. You also learned how to change the authentication provider configuration from the hardcoded username and password values that are used for testing purposes to a real-world user-credentialed data store like a relational database or an LDAP repository.

You looked at how to protect and restrict URLs and adjust the views for different web pages in the application based on what type of user is accessing that specific web page. Finally, you enabled the security event logging in the application to view the authentication event details as and when users log in to your web application.

In the next chapter, we'll switch gears a bit and discuss Roo's testing facilities. We'll review unit, integration, and web tests, and you'll learn how to test Roo services, entities, and web pages using JUnit and Selenium.

8.6   Resources

OpenDS directory server home page (http://www.opends.org)
OWASP Top Ten Project (http://mng.bz/yXd3)
Spring In Action, Third Edition, by Craig Walls (http://mng.bz/6xB2)
Spring LDAP project (http://mng.bz/759N)
Spring Security website (http://mng.bz/AWNl)

Part 4

Integration

In part 4, we focus on a couple of Java EE services that are critical parts of enterprise Java applications. You'll learn how to integrate enterprise services such as email and messaging with Roo applications. You'll also be introduced to another great feature of the Roo framework: support for add-ons.

But before we delve into these topics, we cover Roo's unit and integration testing support in chapter 9, "Testing your application." We look at the testing strategies for different tests like unit, integration, and functional tests. We also discuss DataOnDemand components—a useful test class to generate test fixtures. Mock objects are a great way to test a class with lots of dependencies. You'll learn how to mock entities and services as well as test Roo services and repositories inside the container. Finally, we explore web testing using the Selenium tool.

Chapter 10, "Enterprise services—email and messaging," shows you how to integrate a mail server and asynchronous messaging using the Java Message Service (JMS) API. You'll learn, with the help of sample application use cases, step-by-step details of implementing email notification and messaging using a JMS topic as well as a queue. You'll also learn how to monitor messaging activity using tools like VisualVM and Spring Insight.

In chapter 11, "Roo add-ons," and chapter 12, "Advanced add-ons and deployment," you'll learn both the basics and advanced topics in developing and deploying Roo add-ons. First, you'll learn how to find and install Roo add-ons from the central repository. You'll then build your own add-on to install jQuery and jQuery UI libraries.

In the advanced add-ons discussion, you'll learn how to install CoffeeScript language into your local development environment. You'll also learn how to publish the add-ons using the OSGi Bundle Repository (OBR) and the Roo add-on service.

Testing your application

This chapter covers

- Roo test creation commands
- Stubbing tests
- Mocking entities and collaborators
- Web-based testing challenges
- Testing with Selenium

Spring Roo helps you build your applications rapidly, but that doesn't mean you should skimp on your testing plans. Chances are, you're building the applications so fast that it would help to slow down a bit and write some useful tests. The more you test up front, the fewer surprises you'll find in production.

You've already learned that simple actions, such as using the `--test-Automatically` flag to create entities, help ensure you have a baseline of entity persistence tests for your application. But you can do more. As you saw in chapters 3 and 4, you can write your own tests, even reusing the DataOnDemand classes to create both persistent and transient versions of your entities. You can also write integration tests for your Spring beans and install Selenium for end-to-end testing.

In this chapter, you'll see how Roo makes it easy to set up your test environments and how you can test using Roo's integration and web testing technologies, such as the Spring test runner and Selenium.

9.1 *Roo testing philosophy*

A web-based application can be tested at several levels using isolated, method-level unit tests; more sophisticated, in-container integration tests; and live, externally executed website tests. Roo supports all three levels of testing, as shown in figure 9.1.

Think of these testing models as layers in a kind of testing cake. Without all of the layers, your tests are one-dimensional, and they look at your application from only a single viewpoint. You'll find different bugs at each level, so implementing each of these types of tests is key to finding all of the bugs hiding in your application.

9.1.1 *Layers of testing*

The review of the testing levels in this chapter follows the same order as depicted in the previous figure—you'll start with unit testing and finish with functional testing.

- *Unit tests*—Exercise single *units* of code, usually Java methods. Where necessary, other collaborating objects are either stubbed or mocked so that they can behave in predictable ways. For example, a Spring `CourseManager` bean may rely on a `TaxCalculator` bean. In a unit test, you'd test the `calculateCost()` method of `CourseManager`, but you'd want to generate a predictable result from the tax calculator bean reference, so you'd mock or stub it. JUnit is a popular testing API, and Roo uses it for all unit tests.

- *Integration tests*—Exercise methods in components such as Spring beans, but run the tests in a live container. You normally write integration tests to see how

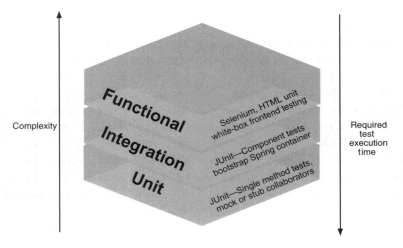

Figure 9.1   Testing levels in Roo, Spring, and most other frameworks. Note how complexity increases as the runtime environment is loaded or user interactions are posed, and how much faster tests run when isolated as unit tests.

the component behaves in its own environment, such as when connected to a database. Entities are best tested in integration tests. These tests are also written in JUnit, but using a special test runner that mounts the application server before running tests.

- *Functional tests*—Exercise the application using an external testing tool, such as a web browser emulator. Selenium is an open source web testing tool that can be used to test your application's web frontend.

Let's see how Roo provides access to these test frameworks.

9.1.2 Test-specific shell commands

Roo provides these tests using several key shell commands:

- `test stub` *and* `test mock`—Both of these commands create out-of-container unit tests.
- `test integration`—Creates in-container integration tests, which boot the Spring application context and execute all of the Roo entity API methods, such as `persist()`, `merge()`, `flush()`, and `remove()`. You can add your own tests to these as discussed in chapters 3 and 4.
- `selenium test --controller`—Installs and configures the Selenium web testing API if needed, and then generates a Selenium HTML test against a specific controller.

In this chapter, you'll learn about each of these commands in detail as well as the APIs of which you need to be aware, and how to approach specific testing scenarios. Before you get started with the commands, though, you need to review a key Roo testing feature that makes working with entity data easier: the DataOnDemand test framework component.

9.1.3 The DataOnDemand component

The DataOnDemand component is a useful test class that helps you generate test fixtures, the data required to set up your test case. You'll create these DataOnDemand classes in two ways: when you generate the automated entity integration tests,

```
roo> test integration --entity ~.model.Course
```

or when you create one as a standalone test component using the `dod` command:

```
roo> dod --entity ~.model.Course
```

The generated component is shown in figure 9.2.

The DataOnDemand component provides three key methods for test data generation: `getNewTransientEntityName`, `getSpecificEntityName`, and `getRandomEntityName`. Let's look at each of these methods in detail.

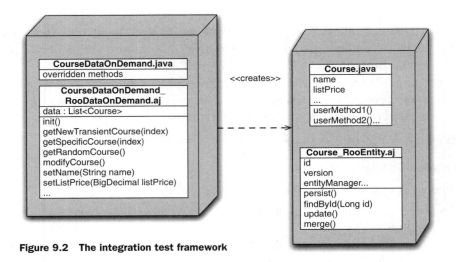

Figure 9.2 The integration test framework

Table 9.1 provides detail on the methods in the CourseDataOnDemand aspect.

Table 9.1 A sample of DataOnDemand methods, using the `Course` entity

Method	Test type(s)	Description
init()	Integration	Configures and persists ten instances of the Course entity, held in a member list variable, data. Entities created by this mechanism are used by getSpecificCourse(), getRandomCourse(), and other methods that take an index parameter. This method doesn't have to be called directly, because the other methods returning test entity instances will call it when necessary. If you call it after the elements are initialized, it returns without modifying the collection.
getNewTransientCourse (int index)	Unit, integration	Creates a new, legal instance of a course. This method doesn't persist the course; hence the name includes the term *transient*.
setFieldName(value)	Unit, integration	Used by getNewTransientCourse(), these setters generate legal values of each field. If your validations are too complex for a simple static definition of a field, you may push one of these methods in to the DataOnDemand class, and modify the behavior.
getRandomCourse()	Integration	Returns a random persistent course in the range of courses created by the init() command. If the list of courses isn't available, the init() command is executed automatically.

Table 9.1 A sample of DataOnDemand methods, using the `Course` entity *(continued)*

Method	Test type(s)	Description
`getSpecificCourse (int index)`	Integration	Returns a persistent course at the specified index. If the course index specified is too high, the method returns the course with the highest available index.

The DataOnDemand classes can be used for both unit entity tests and integration entity tests, as long as you use only methods such as `getNewtransientCourse` from the mock tests. Those methods create nonpersistent instances of the entity. All other methods work with a persistence context and must be called from within integration tests.

9.1.4 Key DataOnDemand methods

Let's dive into some detail on three key methods of the DataOnDemand framework. You need to understand them fully to take full advantage of them and write tests quickly.

FETCHING A TRANSIENT ENTITY

The `getNewTransientEntity` method returns an initialized, transient entity with sample data stored in each field. The entity is not persistent, so this method can be used by unit tests and integration tests.

A sample call:

```
CourseDataOnDemand dod = new CourseDataOnDemand();
Course course = dod.getNewTransientEntity(5);
```

The index helps to define the values for the data. The data returned holds to several predefined rules:

- All string-based fields hold the name of the field, an underscore, and the index value. For example, `description_5`.
- All numeric values return the value of the index.
- All date values return a randomized date, close to the value of the current date.
- All Boolean values return true.
- Relationships to single-sided entities, such as owners, may be initialized with values from other DataOnDemand components. For example, if the `Training-ProgramDataOnDemand` component exists, `CourseDataOnDemand` will call it to create an instance of the training program and set the value.

REFERENCED ENTITIES AND DATAONDEMAND WITH UNIT TESTS Currently, detection of referenced entities and their DataOnDemand instances can cause unit tests to fail. See https://jira.springsource.org/browse/ROO-2497 for more information. A quick workaround is to override the method that sets the entity, and create the referenced entity yourself using the referred to entity's DataOnDemand class.

For this chapter's sample course, the test data might look something like this:

```
name:  name_5
price: 5
description: description_5
...
```

The `getNewTransientEntity` method is useful anywhere you want to generate a simple entity instance. It's also used by the internal `init()` method to generate test entities for the other methods.

Use of this method to set up test fixtures saves you time and energy. Many of the tests in this book take advantage of this method.

FETCHING A PERSISTED ENTITY

The `getSpecificEntity` method returns an entity from the internal list of persisted entities. If the list is empty, it will be initialized automatically. Roo will initialize and persist ten instances in this list. If the user requests an out-of-range index value, it will return either the lowest or the highest element.

This method can be used only in a JPA environment, so it's useful only for integration tests. The entity has already been persisted and attached to the JPA entity manager, so you can modify and even delete the entity. Remember to define your integration test methods with `@Transactional` so the modifications are rolled back, or you may leave the DataOnDemand instances in an inconsistent state.

FETCHING A RANDOM ENTITY

If you don't care which persistent entity instance you work with, ask for a random one with `getRandomEntity()`. Repeated calls won't necessarily return unique instances because the sample range is only ten unique instances. If you truly need two different entities, use the `getNewTransientEntity()` method twice and persist each instance.

9.1.5 *Working with the DataOnDemand framework*

Let's look at some techniques you can use when working with the `DataOnDemand` components.

For example, when you write a unit test you'll use the transient getter, as in the following example, where you start with a generated entity, and set the list price to a value you prefer:

```
Course course = dod.getNewTransientCourse(0);
course.setListPrice(new BigDecimal(10.0d));
```

For working in an integration test, you can get a transient course and persist it, as in this code block that checks for a generated primary key after creating an instance of a course:

```
Course course = dod.getNewTransientCourse(0);
course.setListPrice(new BigDecimal(10.0d));
course.persist();
course.flush();
assertNotNull(course.getId());
```

Alternatively, you can grab a prepersisted instance and manipulate it, as you see in the next example, where this test asserts that an updated course has a different version number:

```
Course course = dod.getSpecificCourse(0);
Long oldVersion = course.getVersion();
course.setListPrice(new BigDecimal(103.0d));
course.update();
course.flush();
assertTrue(oldversion != course.getVersion());
```

In the previous example, you fetch the first generated course instance, capture the version of the course row when retrieved, and then modify the list price and update your entity. After a JPA flush, which guarantees that the data is written to the database, you can check the version, which should be incremented, allowing the assertion to pass.

> **INITIALIZING THE DOD DATA** You may be wondering if you have to initialize the data backing a DataOnDemad class. The answer is, no; instead, you construct a new instance. It'll initialize itself, provided a persistence context exists and you're running a Spring Integration test.

Using the `DataOnDemand` framework can speed up your test writing, making the creation of simple entity instances a trivial operation. Feel free to refactor the code as you see fit, pushing in methods that perhaps won't deal with your more complex validation rules or data persistence strategies. Remember to keep the core functionality in place for the three key methods mentioned previously in this chapter.

Now that you've seen how Roo approaches tests and how to generate test entity data, let's start looking at the various types of entity tests you can write, and how you can allow Roo to help you during the creation and execution of those tests. You'll review unit and integration tests with JUnit, and then perform some web testing with the Selenium API. Let's begin by looking at the Roo unit testing framework.

9.2   *Stubbed unit tests*

The `test stub` command creates a JUnit test that constructs an instance of a class, and creates test stubs for each of the public methods. You create the test by using the `test stub` command.

Let's look at a simple service that calculates a tax amount:

```
package org.rooina.coursemanager.service;

import java.math.BigDecimal;
import org.springframework.beans.factory.annotation.Autowired;

public class DefaultTaxCalcService implements TaxCalcService {

  private BigDecimal taxRate;

  @Autowired
  public DefaultTaxCalcService(BigDecimal taxRate) {
    this.taxRate = taxRate;
  }
```

```
@Override
public BigDecimal calculateTax(BigDecimal price) {
  return price.multiply(taxRate);
}
}
```

This class is initialized with a BigDecimal tax amount and calculates a simple tax based on an injected tax rate. This is injected into the component via the Spring container, either by annotation, JavaConfig, or XML injection. Now, let's create a unit test for this service:

```
roo> test stub --class ~.service.DefaultTaxService
```

This command creates `DefaultTaxServiceTest.java` in the src/test/java directory, stored within the same package as the `DefaultTaxCalcService` class. This assumes you'll be writing tests against the methods of the class. The following code lists the sample test, with the stubbed test method for the `calculateTax` service method:

```
package org.rooina.coursemanager.service;

import org.junit.Test;

public class DefaultTaxCalcServiceTest {

  private DefaultTaxCalcService defaultTaxCalcService = ➥
                              new DefaultTaxCalcService();

  @Test
  public void calculateTax() {
      org.junit.Assert.assertTrue(true);
  }
}
```

This class doesn't compile because the `DefaultTaxService` constructor requires a tax rate, injected as a BigDecimal. Let's update the test to pass:

```
package org.rooina.coursemanager.service;

import java.math.BigDecimal;

import junit.framework.Assert;

import org.junit.Test;

public class DefaultTaxCalcServiceTest {

  private DefaultTaxCalcService defaultTaxCalcService =
    new DefaultTaxCalcService(new BigDecimal("0.02"));

  @Test
  public void calculateTax() {
    BigDecimal price = new BigDecimal("50");
    BigDecimal taxAmount = defaultTaxCalcService.calculateTax(price);
    Assert.assertEquals("Tax rate invalid",
                    new BigDecimal("1.00"), taxAmount);
  }
}
```

FAIL THEM FIRST   For a real treat, why not set the stubbed tests to `assert-True(false)`, so that they fail? The correct order is red to green.

You can use the `test stub` command to quickly generate empty tests against controllers, services, and other beans, and quickly write simple JUnit tests.

Let's take a look at the next type of Roo test command, `test mock`, which is useful when you need to work with collaborating services and Roo entities.[1]

9.3   *Unit tests using mock objects*

Mock objects are objects that pretend to be instances of particular classes, but are completely controlled by the test developer. They appear to implement the specified interfaces, and you can configure them to return predictable values when their methods are called. You can use these mock objects instead of references to other Spring beans or collaborating classes.

There are a number of different mocking frameworks available for unit testing, including these:

- *Mockito* (http://mockito.org)—A popular unit test mocking library, well known for its easy-to-understand syntax and literate API, which uses method names such as when, then, answer, and other English language predicates. The Mockito API is great for mocking Spring bean and regular POJO collaborators with methods defined by an interface.
- *EasyMock* (http://easymock.org)—Mocks primarily based on interfaces. Uses a mock expectation recording and playback API, which can be a bit daunting to new users. In addition to Spring's interface-driven applications, it's a popular library.
- *JMock* (http://jmock.org)—Mocks based on interfaces as well. Developers define expected behavior and then execute their code.
- *PowerMock* (http://code.google.com/p/powermock)—An extension library that enhances the capabilities provided by EasyMock and Mockito. This mocking tool can mock static methods, interfaceless classes, constructors, final classes, and so on, which other APIs cannot.

Mock objects are often used when a layered application requires a particular Spring bean to collaborate with other beans, either in the same level or lower levels of the application. They take less time to create than a fully stubbed object, because you only have to create the mock object at runtime, define the specific behavior to mock, and ignore the rest of the methods in the class. Stubs require you to create a concrete class, and implement each of the methods of the object under test. That takes a lot of time, and unless you're able to exercise the entire stub across all of your test methods, it may be a waste of your time.

What if you want to see whether the entity can be validated appropriately, or if you need to stub the entity itself behind a service? Spring provides a feature to mock the

---

[1]   Refer to *JUnit in Action, Second Edition* for details on how to work with these APIs.

persistence layer enough to test your validations, without requiring a full JPA stack. This lets you perform basic unit tests against your entities, exercising logic you may have stashed away in `assertTrue` methods or methods that may contain business logic, and perform operations to generate derived data.

9.3.1   *Mocking services with Mockito*

Here's how you can use mocks to emulate collaborating objects:

- Create your mock objects and define expectations.
- Create an instance of your object under test, manually setting or injecting your mock collaborators.
- Exercise the method under test.
- Verify your test results.

If you were working within a traditional, layered Spring application, you'd likely have Spring service beans that would work with Data Access Objects. You could easily make a mock version of a DAO that returns a predefined list of students if the `getAllStudents()` method is called. A fragment of a test may look something like this example:

```
...
StudentDAO studentDAO = Mockito.mock(StudentDAO.class);
studentService.setStudentDAO(studentDAO);

Mockito.when(studentDAO.getAllStudents())
          .thenReturn(preDefinedListOfStudents);

List<Student> students = studentService.getAllStudents();
Assert.assertTrue(students.size() == predefinedListOfStudents.size());
```

In the previous fragment, you're testing a `StudentService` bean in isolation. It collaborates with a `Student` DAO, which you need to mock to provide that isolation. You'll use the `Mockito.mock(StudentDAO.class)` statement to provide the mock object, and then set the mock as your collaborating `Student` DAO. You then use the `Mockito.when` method to tell the mock object to respond with a predefined list of students (not shown) when the DAO's `getAllStudents()` method is called from the service.

As you can see, the Mockito framework makes it easy to define a mock object, such as `studentDAO` shown in the previous example. You can then manually inject the mock into `studentService` and tell the mock to return a prefabricated student list. After the service requests the `getAllStudents()` method on your mock, it automatically returns your predefined list of students.

> **LEARNING MORE**   For more information about the excellent Mockito mocking framework, visit the project website at http://mockito.org. You might also be interested in an API that layers on top of Mockito and its cousin EasyMock. Named *PowerMock*, this API allows you to mock static methods and implements a number of other helpful features. See the website at http://code.google.com/p/powermock.

Mockito does a great job with typical, interface-driven Spring beans. But it can't mock Roo entities, because Roo uses static methods within the entity to find entity instances from the database, and holds onto a private JPA entity manager to provide persistence logic.

All is not lost, though. Rod Johnson, the creator of Spring, contributed a testing framework element to help out: the static entity method mocking API.

9.3.2 *The entity mocking framework*

Spring provides a special mocking API to allow developers to write tests against static entity methods. To use it, you follow these steps:

1 Annotate your test class with `@MockStaticEntityMethods`.
2 Within a test method that requires collaboration with an entity, issue the method call that you'd like to mock. Because the annotation is in effect, the static method isn't executed, but is added to the list of methods to expect.
3 Use the `AnnotationDrivenStaticEntityMockingControl` (for brevity, let's abbreviate this as the acronym *ADSEMC*): call its `.expectReturn` method to define the result of the operation. You don't need to do this if the method has no return value.
4 Put the mock in playback mode with the `ADSEMC.playback()` method.
5 Exercise the mock.

Because of the static methods used by the entity finders, testing a Spring bean involving an entity requires use of the Spring entity mocking framework.

9.3.3 *Creating an entity mock test*

To set up a mock test case, you use the `test mock` command:

```
roo> test mock --entity ~.model.Course
```

Roo will then create a test class that looks like the example shown in the following listing.

Listing 9.1 A mock course test

```
package org.foo.model;

import org.junit.Test;
import org.junit.runner.RunWith;
import org.junit.runners.JUnit4;
import org.springframework.mock.staticmock.MockStaticEntityMethods;

@RunWith(JUnit4.class)
@MockStaticEntityMethods                                    Enable
 public class CourseTest {                                  mocking

  @Test
  public void testMethod() {
    int expectedCount = 13;
    Course.countCourses();                                  Record
                                                            expectation
```

```
    org.springframework.mock.staticmock.➥                        ◁┐ Expected
        AnnotationDrivenStaticEntityMockingControl ➥               │ result
            .expectReturn(expectedCount);

    org.springframework.mock.staticmock.➥                        ◁┐ Watch
        AnnotationDrivenStaticEntityMockingControl.playback();     │ for result

    org.junit.Assert.assertEquals(➥
        expectedCount, Course.countCourses());
  }
}
```

In the generated sample, the test is expected to call the `Course.countCourses()` method, returning the result of 13 rows. The `@MockStaticEntityMethods` annotation places the entity mock in expectation record mode. At this point, any calls to static methods, such as the `Course.countCourses()` method, won't execute, but will be added to the recording queue.

Next, you use the `AnnotationDrivenStaticEntityMockingControl` object to record an *expectation*: a definition of the behavior to trigger when calling the last method recorded. In this case, you want the `countCourses()` method invocation to return the value 13 when executed.

Finally, you put the mock in playback mode, and then call your `Course.count-Courses()` method, which now returns the value 13, which you can check against your assertion.

> **THIS SEEMS COMPLEX** While it's true that the setup for this test is a bit unwieldy, you benefit because you're able to test your validation assertions and plain business logic within a unit test, rather than booting the Spring container. Unit tests run in a fraction of the time.
>
> You'll need to decide whether to use integration tests for accuracy, or unit tests for speed, when testing validations and business logic attached to your entities.

You've examined the `test mock` command, and how to make use of it to write unit tests of Spring Roo entities. Now it's time to use this in a more complex example and test what happens when you try to validate data.

9.3.4 *Unit testing the completeRegistration() method*

A typical JUnit unit test will test a single "unit" of code, such as a method on a Spring bean. Everything else is either stubbed or mocked, so that you can focus your energies on exercising your method under test and verifying the result.

Now let's test an example Spring service method, `RegistrationService.completeRegistration(long offeringId, List<Long> studentIds)`. The implementation looks like this:

```
public class RegistrationServiceDefaultImplBean
                implements RegistrationService {
  @Override
```

```
@Transactional
public void completeRegistration(
    Long offeringId, List<Long> studentIds) {
  Offering offering = Offering.findOffering(offeringId);
  for (Long studentId : studentIds) {
    Student student = Student.findStudent(studentId);
    Registration registration = new Registration();
    registration.setStudent(student);
    registration.setOffering(offering);
    registration.setAttended(false);
    registration.setPaymentMade(false);
    offering.addRegistration(registration);
    registration.persist();
  }
 }
}
```

The method creates a number of `Registration` entities and associates them with the appropriate student and course offering. Figure 9.3 shows the order of operations.

The previous sequence diagram shows a fairly typical interaction with Roo's Active Record–based entities. Rather than relying on repositories or DAOs to wrap access to your entities, you use the static finder methods to locate them, and methods such as `persist()` and `merge()` to manipulate them. You also define transactionality on this

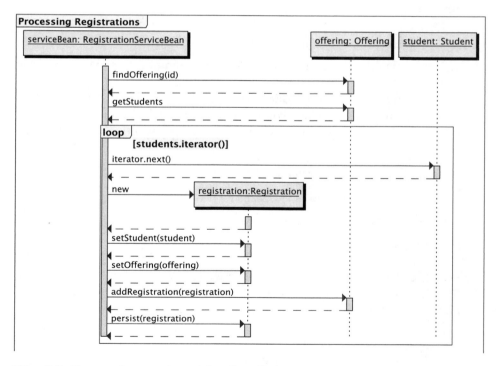

Figure 9.3 The `completeRegistration()` method

method, so that all operations against the entities are either committed or rolled back automatically.

Testing this method in the Spring container, as you'll see in section 9.4, is more involved and requires booting the application server. If you're purely testing application logic, and can emulate the data access routines rather than take the integration testing overhead, you can run the test as a unit test, and improve the speed of your build process as a result.

Now, let's implement the test using JUnit and Roo's own entity mocking framework.

9.3.5   *Mocking with the RegistrationServiceBean*

Let's write a test that exercises a bean that processes student registrations. The bean provides a `registerStudents` method that accepts a set of students and an offering, and then registers students for the provided course offering.

SETTING UP THE TEST

First, you'll create the unit test class, using the Roo Shell `test mock` command:

```
roo> test mock --entity ~.service.RegistrationServiceBeanImpl
```

Note that the term `--entity` can be any class definition. Let's open the bean definition for the newly created `RegistrationServiceBeanImplTest` and verify the class definition. Roo should define your test class with the `@MockStaticEntityMethods` annotation:

```
@MockStaticEntityMethods
public class RegistrationServiceDefaultImplBeanTest {
```

This annotation enables the entity mocking framework, as you'll see in the next example.

Now, you'll define three DataOnDemand class instances, one each for `Student`, `Offering`, and `Course`, which you'll use to decrease the amount of code in your test. Define them in the Roo console with the `dod` command if they're missing in your code:

```
private StudentDataOnDemand studentDod;
private OfferingDataOnDemand offeringDod;
private CourseDataOnDemand courseDod;
```

You'll also create the `Service` bean yourself, so hold onto a reference to that, too:

```
private RegistrationServiceDefaultImplBean
                               registrationServiceDefaultImplBean;
```

SETTING UP THE BEAN AND DATAONDEMAND CLASSES

Next, define a JUnit `@Before` method, `setup()`, which executes before each test. This method will create instances of all four of these objects:

```
@Before
public void setUp() {
  registrationServiceDefaultImplBean =
    new RegistrationServiceDefaultImplBean();
```

```
studentDod = new StudentDataOnDemand();
offeringDod = new OfferingDataOnDemand();
courseDod = new CourseDataOnDemand();
}
```

Now, for each method under test, JUnit will create a new instance of the Registration-
Service Bean, then reinitialize all three DataOnDemand instances.

RECORD TEST EXPECTATIONS

Define your test method, testRegisterStudents(). You'll annotate it with @Test:

```
@Test
  public void testRegisterStudents() {
    ...
  }
```

Now, let's write the code for the test. Referring back to the sequence diagram in
figure 9.3, you'll see that the first action of the method under test is to look up an
Offering based on the value of the offering key passed to it.

You'll use the OfferingDataOnDemand class to generate a test offering, and assign a
fake primary key value of 1:

```
Offering offering = offeringDod.getNewTransientOffering(1);
offering.setId(1L);
```

Now, you'll invoke the call you'd like to have your unit execute when it's under test,
and you'll follow that up with what you expect it to return:

```
Offering.findOffering(1L);
AnnotationDrivenStaticEntityMockingControl.expectReturn(offering);
```

You'll do this for every interaction you expect your unit to invoke.

For example, you can pass in ten Long primary key fields of students to register for
this class. To set up the condition, do the following:

```
List<Long> ids = new ArrayList<Long>();
List<Student> testStudents = new ArrayList<Student>();

// record expectations
for (int id = 0; id < 10; id++) {
  Student.findStudent((long)id);
  Student student = studentDod.getNewTransientStudent(id);
  student.setId(Long.valueOf(id));
  ids.add(Long.valueOf(id));
  AnnotationDrivenStaticEntityMockingControl.expectReturn(student);
}
```

By now we hope you're thinking that a straightforward integration test would be easier than this. You're right, but it'll run slowly and you'll have to run it against a live
database. If you're trying to make sure the actions in your sequence diagram are
called in the correct order, this test will do so at a fraction of the time.

TEST AND VERIFY

But you're not done yet. You have to run the test—like EasyMock, Spring's control doesn't do anything until you call the `playback()` method:

```
AnnotationDrivenStaticEntityMockingControl.playback();
```

Now you can perform the call, using the generated offering's primary key (`1L`) and the list of fake primary keys generated for each student mock call:

```
registrationServiceDefaultImplBean.
    completeRegistration(offering.getId(), ids);
```

If all is well, there'll now be ten registrations, which you'll fetch and assert, as shown in this next example:

```
Set<Registration> registrations = offering.getRegistrations();
Assert.assertEquals(10, registrations.size());
```

And that's that. About 30 lines of code, with appropriate white spacing. The main benefit of testing in this way is that it forces you to review the coupling of your entities and services. If you find you're mocking too many classes, you may have approached your design without thinking about the single responsibility principle (SRP).

9.4   Testing in-container with Roo

What if you need to spin up the Spring container to run your tests? Perhaps you want to verify that the database schema still operates against your entities and JPA code, or you want to make sure your Spring configuration is valid. Roo has two approaches for you—either you can use the Roo entity test framework and DataOnDemand classes, or build traditional Spring integration tests. Let's take a look at both approaches, starting with the entity test framework.

9.4.1   Creating entity integration tests

As you saw in chapters 3 and 4, you can create entity integration tests automatically in two ways, either during creation of the entities themselves,

```
roo> entity jpa --class ~.model.Course --testAutomatically
```

or later, as a separate action:

```
roo> test integration --entity ~.model.Course
```

In either case, Roo creates a scaffolded integration test, named `CourseIntegration-Test`, and places it within the same package structure as the entity in the Maven src/test/java directory. It also uses the DataOnDemand framework to scaffold the test data, and perform tests for all entity operations, as shown in figure 9.4.

The testing framework shown in the figure automatically exercises all methods in the Roo entity. The difference between this test and the ones discussed earlier in this chapter is that it runs within the Spring container. The funny thing is how short the Java class is:

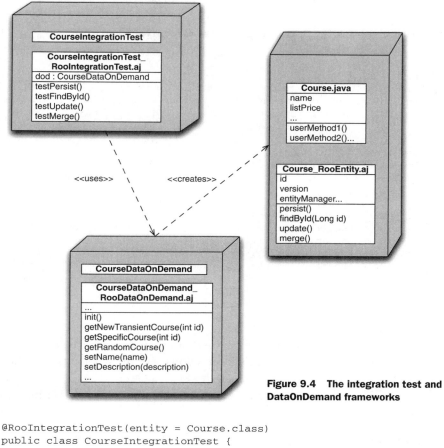

Figure 9.4 The integration test and DataOnDemand frameworks

```
@RooIntegrationTest(entity = Course.class)
public class CourseIntegrationTest {

@Test
  public void testMarkerMethod() {
  }
}
```

You'll do all of the work using the IntegrationTest aspect combined with the Data-OnDemand aspect. The following listing shows a portion of the CourseIntegrationTest _RooIntegrationTest.aj aspect.

Listing 9.2 The CourseIntegrationTest Roo aspect

```
privileged aspect CourseIntegrationTest_Roo_IntegrationTest {

  declare @type: CourseIntegrationTest:
    @RunWith(SpringJUnit4ClassRunner.class);

  declare @type: CourseIntegrationTest:
    @ContextConfiguration(
    locations = "classpath:/META-INF/spring/applicationContext.xml")
```

```
declare @type: CourseIntegrationTest: @Transactional;

@Autowired
private CourseDataOnDemand CourseIntegrationTest.dod;

...

@Test
public void CourseIntegrationTest.testFindCourse() {
  org.rooina.coursemanager.model.Course obj = dod.getRandomCourse();
  org.junit.Assert.assertNotNull(
     "Data on demand for 'Course' failed to initialize correctly",
     obj);
  java.lang.Long id = obj.getId();
  org.junit.Assert.assertNotNull(
     "Data on demand for 'Course' failed to provide an identifier",
     id);
  obj = org.rooina.coursemanager.model.Course.findCourse(id);
  org.junit.Assert.assertNotNull(
     "Find method for 'Course' illegally returned null for id '"
     + id + "'", obj);
  org.junit.Assert.assertEquals(
     "Find method for 'Course' returned the incorrect identifier",
     id, obj.getId());
}

...
}
```

As you saw in the previous listing, each method, such as findCourses(), is tested in a separate method, using some simple interactions with the DataOnDemand class and the entity's API.

Obviously, these tests may require you to do some leg work, pushing in various methods so you can change them.

9.4.2 Testing other Spring beans

For Roo-built services and repositories, any entity integration tests you define with test integration will automatically adjust between testing the entity directly and using the repository or service layer, if you've generated one for your entity. This means that you already know how to test Roo-built services and repositories.

Roo doesn't actually support the generation of freestyle tests from the shell. So, to build one, you can either create it using your IDE or use the class command to initialize it:

```
roo> class --class ~.web.BillingServiceSystemTest ➥
       --path SRC_TEST_JAVA
```

Roo uses Spring's annotation-driven JUnit 4 test runner in the automated integration tests. You configure this framework by hand as shown here:

```
import org.springframework.test.context.ContextConfiguration;
import org.springframework.test.context.junit4.SpringJUnit4ClassRunner;
import org.springframework.test.context.transaction.➥
       TransactionConfiguration;
```

```
import org.springframework.transaction.annotation.Transactional;

@ContextConfiguration(locations = ➥
    "classpath:/META-INF/spring/applicationContext*.xml")
@RunWith(SpringJUnit4ClassRunner.class)
public class BillingServiceSystemTest {

  @Autowired
  private BillingService service;

  long studentId;

}
```

The @ContextConfiguration annotation defines the Spring context files to search for to load your test. Roo stores these in META-INF/spring, so pull in the primary context file, applicationContext.xml. That file contains your JPA configuration settings. Next, you tell JUnit that it has to run under the Spring Framework with your @Run-With annotation.

The test will exercise the BillingService, verifying that an invoice can be created based on student registrations that haven't yet been paid. The JUnit initialization method initData() configures the test data for your service, so you can use it in multiple tests. It also captures the id of the student that you'll use to generate the invoice:

```
@Before
public void initData() {
  StudentDataOnDemand studentDod = new StudentDataOnDemand();
  Student student = studentDod.getRandomStudent();
  studentId = student.getId();
  CourseDataOnDemand courseDod = new CourseDataOnDemand();
  Course course1 = courseDod.getRandomCourse();
  course1.setListPrice(new BigDecimal("250.0"));
  course course2 = courseDod.getRandomCourse();
  course2.setListPRice(new BigDecimal("250.0"));
  OfferingDataOnDemand offeringDod = ➥
    new OfferingDataOnDemand();
  Offering offering1 = offeringDod.getRandomOffering();
  offering1.setCourse(course1);
  Offering offering2 = offeringDod.getRandomOffering();
  offering2.setCourse(course2);

  Registration reg = new Registration();
  reg.setOffering(offering1);
  reg.setAttended(true);
  reg.setOffering(offerings.get(0));
  reg.setPaymentMade(false);
  reg.setStudent(student);
  reg.persist();

  Registration reg2 = new Registration();
  reg.setOffering(offering2);
  reg.setCourse(course2);
  reg2.setAttended(true);
  reg2.setOffering(offerings.get(1));
  reg2.setPaymentMade(false);
  reg2.setStudent(student);
```

```
    reg2.persist();

    reg2.flush();
}
```

The `testGenerateInvoice()` test below exercises the generation of an invoice for the two course offerings the student took. The student should owe $500; you've created two courses, each with a list price of $250:

```
@Transactional
@Test
public void testGenerateInvoice() {
    Integer invoiceId = service.generateInvoice(➥
        studentId, startDate, endDate);

    Invoice invoice = Invoice.findInvoice(invoiceId);

    Assert.assertNotNull(invoice);
    Assert.assertEquals(new BigDecimal("500.00"),➥
        invoice.getAmount());

}
```

Now you've seen how you can write tests against live Spring beans such as Roo services and repositories. You can use this technique to test any Spring bean in your container; just autowire the bean into the test and exercise it as you would in your application code, using asserts to verify behavior.

Now that we've discussed how to write integration tests, we should mention that all of the tests introduced so far are rather invasive, looking at the system from the inside. Testers call these *white-box tests*.

Equally valuable are tests that look at the system as a *black box*: tests external to the application that exercise the application as a user would. For those tests, we'll look at Roo's support for web testing, using the Selenium automated web testing tool.

9.5   Web testing with Selenium

Testing shouldn't stop at the unit test or integration test level. These tests all exercise a particular component or set of components in compositions that you define yourself. But the best way to verify that the entire stack functions properly is to use some sort of external, black box test—meaning a test external to the application itself.

At a bare minimum, what you need is a mechanism to assert tests against the user interface, so that you can start testing at the level of a user interaction. Roo has support for this approach in the form of the Selenium web testing framework.

9.5.1   What is Selenium?

Selenium (http://seleniumhq.org) is a suite of web testing tools. It can exercise browser-based tests against an application, and has a Firefox-based IDE (Selenium IDE) for building tests interactively against a live application.

Selenium tests can be written in a number of languages, from HTML to the Java JUnit API to other languages such as Ruby or Python.

Selenium tests can be used in a number of ways, including

- *Feature testing*—Testing various use cases in your application, using a browser-based approach.
- *Monitoring*—Checking that a representative controller returns a valid result, which would indicate that the application is online.
- *Load testing*—Using Selenium's distributed testing engines, a heavy load can be placed on the application from a number of machines.

Selenium is widely adopted and there are a number of resources, such as *JUnit in Action, Second Edition,* that document it in detail. We'll focus on how to get Selenium up and running against a RESTful controller, and then we'll look at how to add JUnit-based Selenium tests for more sophisticated testing scenarios.

9.5.2 *Installing Selenium*

As with everything else in Roo, the Selenium framework is installed with a simple Roo shell command. The `selenium test` command takes several options, including the mandatory controller class to test:

```
selenium test --controller ~.web.TagController
```

The class must be a Roo-scaffolded controller. In response to this, Roo performs the following actions:

- Installs the Selenium dependencies and the Codehaus Maven Selenium plug-in in the Maven pom.xml file.
- Creates a WEB-INF/selenium directory to hold HTML tests.
- Builds a test-suite.xhtml master test suite file, which Roo will maintain whenever a new test is installed.
- Builds a test case for the entity scaffolded by the controller, with the name of test-*entity*.xhtml.

You'll see immediately that Roo's support for Selenium mostly focuses on *scaffolded* controllers. This may be a bit limiting, but later in this chapter we'll show you how to install support for any controller you want by using the JUnit API.

To run your tests, you first have to launch your web server. Open a new command prompt, switch to the project root directory and issue the following command to launch the Jetty web server:

```
mvn jetty:run
```

You'll need a running instance of your application in order to run Selenium tests. To trigger the tests, issue the following command from another operating system prompt to run your tests:

```
mvn selenium:selenese
```

This command launches the Selenium test runner, which should launch an instance of the Firefox browser and run your tests. After the tests are finished, the Selenium

Test suite results

result:	passed
totalTime:	1
numTestTotal:	1
numTestPasses:	1
numTestFailures:	0
numCommandPasses:	0
numCommandFailures:	0
numCommandErrors:	0
Selenium Version:	2.0
Selenium Revision:	a1

Suite Of Tests
Selenium test for TagController

http://localhost:8080/coursemanagertest/resources/selenium/test-tag.xhtml		
Selenium test for TagController		
open	http://localhost:8080/coursemanagertest/tags?form&lang=en_US	
type	_tag_id	someTag1
type	_description_id	someDescription1
clickAndWait	//input[@id='proceed']	

```
info: Starting test /coursemanagertest/resources/selenium/test-tag.xhtml
info: Executing: |open | http://localhost:8080/coursemanagertest/tags?form&lang=en_US |  |
info: onXhrStateChange(): xhr.readyState = 1 method = HEAD time = 1305756313620
info: onXhrStateChange(): xhr.readyState = 1 method = HEAD time = 1305756313620
info: onXhrStateChange(): xhr.readyState = 2 method = HEAD time = 1305756313631
info: onXhrStateChange(): xhr.readyState = 4 method = HEAD time = 1305756313631
info: Executing: |type | _tag_id | someTag1 |
info: Executing: |type | _description_id | someDescription1 |
info: Executing: |clickAndWait | //input[@id='proceed'] |  |
```

Figure 9.5   Successful Selenium report showing test run of the test-tag.xhtml test

Maven plug-in should declare the build a success. A test report will be generated in HTML format and placed in target/surefire-reports/selenium.html. The contents of this test are shown in figure 9.5.

Looking at the test report, you'll see that it contains counts of the number of tests, how many passes and failures, and the details for each test. Any failed test or test command is shown in red, successes are shown in green. You'll also see a detailed log of each test step underneath the pass or fail data. This is a comprehensive test report.

So now that you know how to install Selenium and generate and execute your tests, let's take a look at the test suite and the test that you initially generated on your Tag object.

9.5.3   *Autogenerated Selenium tests*

The generated tests are controlled by a master test suite file, test-suite.xhtml, located in src/main/webapp/. Let's review the contents of that file after you've generated the Tag test, as shown in the following listing.

Listing 9.3   test-suite.xhtml

```
<?xml version="1.0" encoding="UTF-8" standalone="no"?>
<html xmlns="http://www.w3.org/1999/xhtml" lang="en" xml:lang="en">
  <head>
    <title>Test suite for coursemanagertestproject</title>
```

```
    </head>
    <body>
      <table>
        <tr>
          <td>
            <b>Suite Of Tests</b>
          </td>
        </tr>

        <tr>
          <td>
            <a href="http://localhost:8080/coursemanagertest➥
                    /resources/selenium/test-tag.xhtml">
              Selenium test for TagController
            </a>
          </td>
        </tr>
      </table>
    </body>
</html>
```

The test suite is similar in concept to JUnit test suites—it contains a list of each Selenium test file you'll execute.

Roo maintains the test suite, adding to it every time a new Selenium test is generated from the Roo shell. You can write your own test suites, place them in the same directory, and add them to this test suite file.

Roo also generated your test case, based on the fields of your entity. Let's take a look at the test-tag.xhtml test file next.

Listing 9.4   test-tag.xhtml

```
<?xml version="1.0" encoding="UTF-8" standalone="no"?>
<html xmlns="http://www.w3.org/1999/xhtml" lang="en" xml:lang="en">
  <head profile="http://selenium-ide.openqa.org/profiles/test-case">
    <meta content="text/html; charset=UTF-8" http-equiv="Content-Type"/>
    <link href="http://localhost:8080/" rel="selenium.base"/>
    <title>Selenium test for TagController</title>
  </head>
  <body>
  <table border="1" cellpadding="1" cellspacing="1">
  <thead>
    <tr>
      <td colspan="3" rowspan="1">Selenium test for TagController</td>
    </tr>
  </thead>
  <tbody>
    <tr>
     <td>open</td>
     <td>http://localhost:8080/coursemanagertest/tags➥          ❶ Browse
        ?form&amp;lang=en_US</td>                                   to page
      <td> </td>
    </tr>
    <tr>
     <td>type</td>
```

```
      <td>_tag_id</td>
      <td>someTag1</td>
    </tr>
    <tr>
     <td>type</td>
       <td>_description_id</td>
      <td>someDescription1</td>
     </tr>
     <tr>
       <td>clickAndWait</td>
        <td>//input[@id='proceed']</td>
       <td> </td>
     </tr>
   </tbody>
   </table>
   </body>
</html>
```

❷ Type
into field

❸ Submit
form

The HTML-based Selenium test language was designed so that power users and advanced business experts could read and interpret it. You can see that the test starts by opening the URL to the tag controller ❶. Then, using the HTML ID of the field elements, the `type` command enters a value into each field ❷. Finally, the `clickAndWait` command ❸ tells Selenium to press the `proceed` button and wait for a valid response.

> **WHAT CAN YOU CHANGE?** This generated controller test file shouldn't be edited, because it's scaffolded like the controllers and entities themselves. Any change to the entity will also affect a change to the generated test file.
>   Roo will append only scaffolded tests to the test-suite.xhtml file, so you can add additional test files. Any additional entity will add an entry to the test suite. In this way, you can do some basic testing of the create method of the form.

But what if you're not scaffolding, or you want to take it a step further? You have two options: either you can add the additional test to the suite and write it in HTML semantics, or you can use the JUnit framework to generate test cases. Let's look at both approaches.

9.5.4   *Writing your own Selenium test*

The generated Selenium test submits form data based on legal values from the Bean Validation annotations, clicks the `proceed` button, and verifies that the next page is displayed. This isn't an in-depth test. What if the controller fails?

   Selenium tests can draw upon the full list of commands, collectively known as *Selenese*. These commands are documented at http://seleniumhq.org/docs/. Bear in mind, well-written tests attempt to perform a single activity and verify the result.

   The test opens an entity creation page, types data on the page, and submits the form. You can go a step farther and assert that the data submitted by the test is reflected in the new page. Here's a variation on the test that checks that the fields are shown in the `show` view, which is displayed after you submit. Copy your test-tag.jspx test to a test-tag-with-assertions.tagx, and add the lines in the following example to the end of the table:

```
<tr>
  <td>verifyText</td>
  <td>//div[@id='_s_org_rooina_coursemanager_model_Tag_tag_tag_id']</td>
  <td>someTag1</td>
</tr>
<tr>
  <td>verifyText</td>
  <td>//div[@id='_s_org_rooina_coursemanager_model_Tag↪
    _description_description_id']</td>
  <td>someDescription1</td>
</tr>
```

These commands verify that the `div` with the `id` specified in `@id` hold the value in the third table element. You can use the `assertText` command to fail the test and stop running further commands, but the `verifyText` command you're using marks the test as failed while it continues to run the rest of the commands in the test file.

If you want to know more about Selenium, we suggest you install the Selenium IDE, a Firefox plug-in that allows you to record, edit, and play back Selenium test cases. Figure 9.6 shows the IDE in action, reviewing a step in a test case.

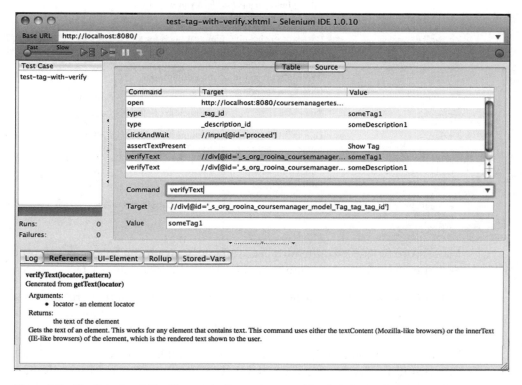

Figure 9.6 The Selenium IDE editor—note the context-sensitive help in the Reference tab

The Selenium IDE has full support for editing the commands generated by the tests you created in this chapter. Fire it up and import your HTML test case into the editor. You can run the test interactively, debugging and modifying the commands until you have the test you want. You can also save this test. Note: Don't save it with a preexisting generated test name, or it'll get overwritten when Roo adds another field to the entity.

KEY SELENESE COMMANDS

When you're working in the Selenium IDE, you'll see a drop-down list of commands. These commands are the language of Selenium, known as *Selenese*. There are a number of key commands that perform activities ranging from typing text into fields, to comparing values on forms, to verifying that text is, or is not, present, to submitting forms.

Table 9.2 shows a few common commands.

Table 9.2   Selenese commands

Selenium command	Usage	First parameter	Second parameter
type	Types the value of an input field. You can also use this command to select from an option field, using the data value, not the visible option.	locator	value
click[AndWait]	Clicks on a clickable element such as a button. If used with the suffix *AndWait*, assumes a server call has been made, and waits up to the configured timeout time for a response from the server.[a]	locator	value
check	Selects a radio button or checkbox field.	locator	none
open	Opens a URL in the frame under test. This is the first action in your scaffolded tests.	url	none
waitForPageToLoad	Pauses the script until a new page is fully loaded.	timeout (optional)	none

a. Many commands in the HTML Selenese dialect can be suffixed with *AndWait*. Consult the reference documentation for details.

Many more Selenese commands are available. Consult the Selenium reference guide, experiment with the Selenium IDE, and write your own tests.

> **MORE INFORMATION ON SELENIUM COMMANDS**   If you want to learn more about Selenese, you can refer to the excellent documentation online at http://seleniumhq.org, or review chapter 12 of *JUnit in Action, Second Edition*.

If you want to run an additional XHTML test, you'll have to add it to the Selenium test-suite.xhtml file. Assuming you named your new test test-tag-with-verify.xhtml in the same directory, you would add it to the test table, as shown in the following example:

```
<tr>
  <td>
    <a href="http://localhost:8080/coursemanagertest/⇒
            resources/selenium/test-tag-with-verify.xhtml">
      Better Selenium test for TagController
    </a>
  </td>
</tr>
```

You may look at this and think, "Wow, this is handy." If so, stop here and start collaborating with your subject matter experts on your tests, using this language as a kind of shared notation. But some of you may also think, "Ewwww. Writing code in HTML?" That's fine as well. For you, Selenium has an answer. Several, in fact.

9.5.5 *Adding JUnit semantics*

If it seems wrong to you to write test code in an HTML or XML markup language because you think, as we do, that code is code, and XML is configuration, you can rest easy. Selenium has language bindings for a number of higher-level languages, such as Java (JUnit 3 and JUnit 4, TestNG), Groovy (JUnit), C#, Ruby, RSpec, Perl, Python, and PHP. This means that APIs are available to a wide variety of programmers, and as such makes Selenium a go-to technology for many web testing efforts.

So, let's get started using Selenium with JUnit. You need to take several steps:

- Install the Selenium Java Client driver in your Maven pom.xml file.
- Write your JUnit tests, or convert them from HTML using the Selenium IDE.
- Optionally, configure Maven to run your tests in the integration test phase.

To install your Java Selenium API, add the following dependency to the pom.xml <dependency> section:

```
<dependency>
  <groupId>org.seleniumhq.selenium.client-drivers</groupId>
  <artifactId>selenium-java-client-driver</artifactId>
  <version>1.0.2</version>
  <scope>test</scope>
</dependency>
```

Now, to convert your test into JUnit, you'll use the helpful language translation feature of the Selenium IDE.[2] After you install the IDE in your Firefox browser, launch it using the Tools > Selenium IDE menu option. The IDE will appear. Clear any test text from the code window, and use the Options > Format menu to select the HTML code format, as shown in figure 9.7.

Note that all of the other formats also display in the drop-down menu in the previous figure. Paste your XHTML test code into the code editor on the right, and then switch the code to JUnit 4 by changing the format to JUnit 4 (Remote Control). Pretty

---

[2] The latest Selenium IDE has removed the Format menu option, and recommends cutting/pasting in a given language format. But you can bring the menu item back again. For more information, select Options > Format > Want the Formats Back? Click to read more.

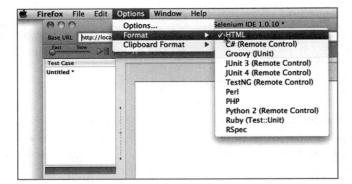

Figure 9.7 Selecting the code format

nifty. The following listing shows the generated code for your sample test, modified so that you can make it consistent with the rest of your application framework.

Listing 9.5 The generated JUnit test

```java
package org.rooina.coursemanager.web;

import com.thoughtworks.selenium.*;
import org.junit.After;
import org.junit.Before;
import org.junit.Test;
import java.util.regex.Pattern;

public class TagSeleniumTest extends SeleneseTestCase {
  @Before
  public void setUp() throws Exception {
      selenium = new DefaultSelenium("localhost", 4444,
                  "*chrome", "http://localhost:8080/");
      selenium.start();
  }

  @Test
  public void testAddTagAndVerify() throws Exception {
    selenium.open("http://localhost:8080/coursemanagertest/➥
                  tags?form&lang=en_US");
    selenium.type("_tag_id", "someTag1");
    selenium.type("_description_id", "someDescription1");
    selenium.click("//input[@id='proceed']");
    selenium.waitForPageToLoad("30000");
    assertTrue(selenium.isTextPresent("Show Tag"));
    verifyEquals("someTag1", selenium.getText(➥
      "//div[@id='_s_org_rooina_coursemanager_model_Tag_tag_tag_id']"));
    verifyEquals("someDescription1", selenium.getText(➥
      "//div[@id='_s_org_rooina_coursemanager_model➥
      _Tag_description_description_id']"));
  }

  @After
  public void tearDown() throws Exception {
      selenium.stop();
  }
}
```

This is a preferable test for most Java developers to use—for one thing, you can debug the code. Instead of using the XTML syntax, you can use real, honest-to-goodness compiled Java code to write your tests. You can also use [CTRL-SPACE] for code assistance in your favorite IDE. Now, that feels more like it! Let's inspect this code a little more.

In the setUp() method, the test creates a Selenium test runner client engine, which looks for a running Selenium server at port 4444. See the sidebar in this chapter on running a Selenium server to configure this. You'll also need to be running your web application; otherwise, the tests won't run, because they can't connect to the server.

Your test method contains calls to the selenium object, which communicates with the Selenium server to execute your tests. Now you can script tests to execute calls to your test web browser, typing data in fields, and clicking various buttons. Key methods include the selenium.open() function, which browses to a page; selenium.isText-Present(), which verifies that text is present within the resulting web page; and the combination of selenium.click(), which presses a form button, and selenium.waitForPageToLoad(), which will pause for a period of time to make sure a page is loaded in response to that button click.

Why do you have to fire up the Selenium server?

It may seem strange that the HTML-based Selenium tests don't require you to fire up your own server process, but the JUnit ones do. There's a simple reason: the mvn selenium:selenese goal does launch and stop the Selenium server, but when running normal JUnit tests, the Maven surfire test runner plug-in isn't aware of your Selenium test requirements.

You can configure Selenium, and even Jetty, to run your Selenium JUnit tests during the *integration test* phase of Maven, rather than the unit test phase. You can even start the Selenium server and Jetty web server when running your integration tests and execute the entire test suite automatically.

9.5.6   *The WebDriver API*

If you think starting a Selenium server in order to run tests seems complicated, and you'd like to try something more advanced, you can use the WebDriver API to write and execute Java Selenium tests in Selenium 2. This eliminates the need to fire up a Selenium server, and the API is more direct and simplified.

To use the WebDriver API, replace your Maven dependency on the Selenium Java client driver with this:

```
<dependency>
  <groupId>org.seleniumhq.selenium</groupId>
  <artifactId>selenium-java</artifactId>
  <version>2.16.1</version>
  <scope>test</scope>
</dependency>
```

With this API, you only need to boot the web server, not the Selenium driver. Web-Driver doesn't need a Selenium remote control server instance.

The sample coursemanager project in the chapter-09-testing folder uses the Web-Driver API for two tests: ITCourseSelenium.java and ItTagSelenium.java, located in the web test directory.

Let's take a quick look at the ItTagSelenium.java test to compare the API to the previous example:

```
public class ITTagSelenium {

  private WebDriver webDriver;

  @Before
  public void setUp() throws Exception {
    webDriver = new FirefoxDriver();
  }

  @Test
  public void testCreateTag() throws Exception {
    webDriver.get(
        "http://localhost:8080/coursemanager/tags?form&lang=en_US");
    webDriver.manage().timeouts().implicitlyWait(10, TimeUnit.SECONDS);
    webDriver.findElement(By.id("_name_id")).sendKeys("someTag1");
    webDriver.findElement(By.id("_description_id"))
                                        .sendKeys("someDescription1");
    webDriver.findElement(By.id("proceed")).click();
    Assert.assertEquals(true, 0 < webDriver.getPageSource()
                                        .indexOf("Show Tag"));
  }

  @After
  public void tearDown() throws Exception {
    webDriver.close();
  }
}
```

You can see some differences between the Selenium 1 API and the new WebDriver API used in Selenium 2. First, WebDriver has a more fluent, chained API, and second, the web drivers are created and used. No Selenium server needs to be configured to run WebDriver tests. To run this test, execute it in JUnit.

> **SEE IT IN ACTION** The sample coursemanager project in the chapter-09-testing folder has been written using the WebDriver API, and uses the Maven failsafe plug-in to fire off integration tests after the project is packaged. We've also configured the project so that the Jetty web server is booted before integration tests fire, and shut down after they've been run. To execute the tests, issue the mvn verify command.

You can find out more about the WebDriver at the Selenium project website, http://seleniumhq.org.

9.5.7   *Final thoughts on web testing*

There are a number of considerations we haven't discussed, and testing via the web is an enormous topic. Keep in mind that the most difficult part of web testing is getting to the right level of detail. You can certainly write web tests that dig deeply into validation rules and test service logic.

Many of those tests would be less brittle if built at the appropriate layer—for example, logic tests should be written as unit tests where possible because they won't change if somebody makes adjustments to the user interface.

9.6   *Improving your testing*

Here are other things you can do to improve your testing and overall code quality:

- Install the Maven Reporting plug-in, configuring the Cobertura code coverage report as well as the Surefire Testing report. These reports, when run with `mvn site`, can tell you the health of your unit and integration tests, and show you the code coverage of your application. More information about Maven-based tests can be found in chapter 10 of *JUnit in Action, Second Edition*, or at the Maven website, http://maven.apache.org.
- Configure a continuous integration tool, such as Jenkins (http://jenkins-ci.org), to run your build each time somebody checks in your code. Have it alert your users when activities fail.
- Look into other code-quality inspection tools that are compatible with Roo and Maven, such as Sonar (http://sonarsource.org).

Above all, your comfort level with changes to your application can only improve as your code coverage increases, because any change that breaks your software will instantly show up when you perform your unit testing and Spring container tests using `mvn test` and functional tests with Selenium, the Maven Surefire plug-in, and `mvn verify`.

9.7   *Summary*

In this chapter, you've learned how to test from a Roo perspective. You've reviewed all of the major testing approaches, from unit tests with stubs, mocks, and Roo's entity mocking support, to Spring container integration tests, to web testing with Selenium.

Testing is a key part of the development lifecycle, and you're encouraged to write tests against any of your coded logic. This chapter has only scratched the surface. Let's look at some other topics you may want to consider.

If you want to emulate more advanced features of your web tier, you can review Spring's built-in mock objects, included in the `spring-test.jar` and `spring-aspects.jar` artifacts, which include the mock web elements `MockHttpServlet`, `MockHttpServletRequest`, and `MockHttpServletResponse`.

You should also pay close attention to mock object frameworks. They're the best way to isolate your objects under test from other objects. Mockito is popular, but a lot of existing code is tested using EasyMock and JMock. Pick one mocking framework, as doing so makes it easy to read your tests without having to switch gears constantly.

Most real-world applications also have requirements for other functionality like sending emails to customers, or asynchronous offline data processing to lower the impact on the real-time application access. In the next chapter, you'll learn how to integrate enterprise application concerns into Roo applications, such as sending emails, asynchronous messaging (using the Java Messaging Service API), and enterprise application integration (EAI) requirements using the Spring Integration framework.

9.8   *Resources*

One chapter can't convey all of the nuances and issues you'll face when writing tests against your applications. You have a number of big topics yet to learn on testing in general.

Here are a few resources for further research.

BOOKS

Tachiev, Petar, et al. *JUnit in Action, Second Edition* (Manning Publications, 2010) is a great guide to unit and integration testing from the ground up, and includes a section on web testing with Selenium and other APIs.

Walls, Craig. *Spring in Action, Third Edition* (Manning Publications, 2011) covers Spring 3 and many topics, including how to configure tests in-container.

WEB

http://seleniumhq.org, the home of the Selenium web testing framework.

http://mockito.org, the Mockito mocking framework.

http://easymock.org, the EasyMock mocking framework.

http://www.springsource.org/spring-framework#documentation covers Spring's testing approach in chapter 9 of the Spring Framework documentation.

Enterprise services— email and messaging

10

This chapter covers

- Roo support for enterprise services
- Asynchronous messaging using a JMS topic
- Email service
- Asynchronous messaging using a JMS queue
- Monitoring messaging activity

In the previous two chapters, you secured your Roo application by adding the Spring Security API to the application architecture mix, and you learned how to enrich the web tier of the Roo application so it's functional from a business standpoint. In addition to robust security features and a rich user interface, a real-world application also requires services such as customer email notification and offline data processing that occurs outside of your main business operations, where your customers receive notifications about results at a later time.

In this chapter, we discuss the integration that the Roo framework provides for email and asynchronous messaging using the Java Message Service (JMS) API. We review three different use cases to demonstrate how to integrate email notifications

243

and asynchronous messaging into real-world software applications. We look at Roo commands to set up the infrastructure for email and JMS components. And we define Spring bean components to abstract the connection configuration parameters to communicate with these enterprise services. Finally, you'll generate the template code to send emails and post messages to a JMS topic and a queue.

By the end of this chapter, you'll understand how to implement enterprise application services like email and JMS messaging. You'll also be well versed on two design patterns: publish-subscribe (pub/sub) and point-to-point (PTP). With Roo's built-in support for email and JMS services, you'll also see why it's easier to implement these requirements within your application if you use Roo.

We start with a brief overview of email and JMS support that comes out of the box with the Spring Roo framework. We also cover how messaging works, the types of messaging, and the details of how Roo implements email and messaging components in enterprise Java applications.

10.1   Roo integration with enterprise services

Roo includes excellent support for several enterprise services as well as Java Enterprise Edition (Java EE) resources such as email and messaging. Roo also makes it easy to install the various components (configuration files as well as application code) that you need to enable email and messaging functionality in a Java application.

10.1.1 Email support

Roo provides the mail commands to set up the three components you'll need to implement the email notification capability. Let's look at these three components:

- *Mail sender*—This is the Spring Bean configuration for the `JavaMailSender-Impl` class and the SMTP mail server configuration parameters.
- *Email template*—This is the Spring Bean configuration for the `SimpleMail-Message` class.
- *Template field*—In a Java class (typically a controller or service class), the template field uses the template to send email messages.

Later in this chapter, you'll learn how to create these components using code examples. But first you'll need to become familiar with the asynchronous messaging paradigm and how it helps with offline processing requirements of Java applications.

10.1.2 Asynchronous messaging

Messaging is a communication method between software components where an application can send or receive messages to and from another application. Each application connects to a messaging agent (JMS broker) that provides facilities for creating, sending, receiving, and reading messages. Asynchronous messaging is based on a loosely coupled architecture in which the message sender and receiver don't know anything about each other, and they don't have to be available at the same time in order to communicate. This architecture is a core part of service-oriented architecture (SOA) and cloud computing (CC) architectures, both of which have been gaining more attention in recent years.

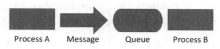

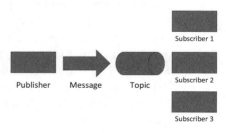

Figure 10.1   Asynchronous messaging architecture

Figure 10.1 shows the architecture for asynchronous messaging, which includes two processes: Process A for posting a message to a message queue, and Process B for consuming the message from the queue and continuing to the next step in the process flow.

JMS is a Java API that allows applications to create, send, receive, and read messages. The JMS API defines a common set of interfaces and associated semantics that allow Java applications to communicate with other messaging implementations.

In business use cases there are several advantages to using the asynchronous messaging architecture rather than a tightly coupled solution such as the Remote Procedure Call (RPC). These advantages include loose coupling, reliability, scalability, and message durability.

One of the use cases discussed later in this chapter (the course registration wait-list notification) is a good example of a use case that benefits from these advantages, and helps you implement JMS messaging using Roo commands.

The following sections briefly discuss the two messaging domains called *publish-subscribe* and *point-to-point*. The book *Java Message Service* by Mark Richards offers extensive coverage of the JMS topic. Another good resource is *ActiveMQ in Action* (http://www.manning.com/snyder/), which details messaging-oriented middleware application development using Apache's ActiveMQ container.

PUBLISH-SUBSCRIBE MESSAGING

In a publish-subscribe, or pub/sub, messaging scenario, a service component posts messages to a topic. Publishers and subscribers dynamically publish or subscribe to the topic. The messaging container takes care of distributing the messages arriving from a topic's multiple publishers to its multiple subscribers. Topics retain messages only as long as it takes to distribute them to current subscribers. In this messaging domain, each message may have one or more message consumers. The JMS destination you use for processing the pub/sub communication is topic (which is represented by the Java class `Topic` in the `javax.jms` package). The architecture for publish-subscribe messaging is shown in figure 10.2.

Figure 10.2   Publish-subscribe messaging architecture

In the scenario represented in figure 10.2, a single process (publisher) can post a message to a queue that can be consumed and used by multiple other processes (subscribers 1 through 3).

POINT-TO-POINT MESSAGING

The point-to-point pattern is built around the concept of message queues, senders, and receivers. Each message is addressed to a specific queue, and the receiving clients extract the messages from the queue or queues established to hold their messages. Queues retain all messages sent to them until the messages are consumed, or until the messages expire. In this domain, each message has only one consumer. The corresponding Java class for a JMS queue is the `javax.jms.Queue` class.

The JMS commands provided by Roo include the setup of JMS infrastructure components for the JMS container (with the ActiveMQ embedded broker, which makes it easier to unit test the asynchronous messaging logic in the application), JMS connection factory, and JMS destinations (topics or queues). Also included is a command for configuring the application-level JMS components and helper classes such as the JMS `Template` and the JMS `Listener` class.

If you have experience implementing asynchronous messaging using the JMS API in a Java application, you'll understand how many different objects you need to create in order to send a simple message. The steps include the following JMS constructs: connection factories, destinations, connections, sessions, message producers, and message consumers or listeners (for receiving messages). Roo makes it easier to create all these messaging components by running just a few commands without having to write a lot of Java code or XML configuration..

These commands are discussed in more detail, using code examples, later in this chapter. The example use cases include messaging patterns from the Enterprise Integration Patterns[1] website.

Let's get started by introducing the sample application. This application will include different use cases that use the asynchronous messaging paradigm.

10.2   *Defining the sample Course Manager use cases*

The business use cases for email and messaging services discussed in this chapter include course catalog distribution and course registration confirmation notification. The course catalog distribution use case involves publishing course catalog updates to a JMS topic, which trading partners subscribe to to get course updates. These trading partners can include institutions such as schools, community organizations, or other vendors. The course registration confirmation notification use case uses email and a JMS queue to notify customers who have successfully registered for a specific course.

The best way to see how these use cases work is to try them out in a sample application. Let's do that with a look at three use cases in the Course Manager application

---

[1]   If you're working on any messaging-related applications in your organization, an excellent resource for messaging design patterns is the *Enterprise Integration Patterns* book by Gregor Hohpe and Bobby Woolf. Srini met Gregor at a Java symposium in 2004 and attended one of his sessions on EIP patterns.

(the two we discussed previously and a third called the course registration wait-list notification use case) that use email functionality and asynchronous messaging to implement the business requirements. Asynchronous messaging uses JMS technology and covers both the pub/sub and PTP messaging scenarios.

10.2.1 Use case 1: course catalog distribution

The Course Manager application will broadcast the course catalog updates by posting a *course catalog message* to a JMS topic. Then the trading partners who subscribe to this topic will receive the message to process it and update their information systems. Roo uses the ActiveMQ messaging container as the default JMS provider.

ActiveMQ is an open source, lightweight asynchronous messaging and integration patterns provider from the Apache team. It supports the JMS 1.1 and Java EE 1.4 specifications with support for transient, persistent, transactional, and XA messaging. ActiveMQ also supports advanced messaging features such as message groups, virtual destinations, wildcards, and composite destinations.

Integration with the Spring framework is available out of the box, so you can embed ActiveMQ into Spring applications easily and configure it using Spring's XML configuration, which is what Roo does when you run the JMS commands. This feature benefits developers who follow test-driven development (TDD) techniques to test their application logic outside the container, without having to build and deploy the application every time they make a code change.

10.2.2 Use case 2: course registration confirmation notification

The second use case is the course registration confirmation notification. When students successfully register for a specific course, the requirement is that the Course Manager application immediately notifies them (via synchronous notification) that their registration has been successful, and provides a confirmation number.

10.2.3 Use case 3: course registration wait-list notification

The final use case you'll implement is the course registration wait-list notification. When a student tries to register for a course that's already full, the Course Manager program will capture the registration details and notify the student that their registration request has been placed on a waiting list. It will also notify the student again when someone else cancels their registration and there's an open spot available for the course.

Let's look more closely at each of these three use cases and implement them using Roo commands so you can see how the Roo framework supports enterprise services like email notification and asynchronous messaging.

10.3 Setting up JMS in the Course Manager

Your first step is to implement the course catalog distribution use case. In this section, you'll create all of the messaging components needed for the use case. You do this using Roo JMS commands.

10.3.1 *Course catalog updates*

The process flow diagram for the course catalog distribution use case is shown in figure 10.3.

You'll use Roo commands to create the JMS topic and the other messaging components needed to implement this use case. All the JMS commands are contained in the `org.springframework.roo.addon.jms.JmsCommands` class.

Figure 10.3 Course catalog distribution process flow

JMS PROVIDER

The first step to enabling JMS capability is to install a JMS provider in your Roo project. Similar to the `persistence setup` command, the `jms setup` command requires you to specify the provider details such as the JMS provider type (a required argument), the `destinationType` (an optional argument; specify `QUEUE` or `TOPIC`), and the `destinationName` (also an optional argument). The following command is for the provider setup, where you'll create a new JMS topic called `CourseCatalogUpdate-Alerts` to post the course catalog details:

```
jms setup --provider ACTIVEMQ_IN_MEMORY --destinationType TOPIC
    --destinationName jms.topic.CourseCatalogUpdateAlerts
```

The following example shows the console output for this command:

```
Created SRC_MAIN_RESOURCES\META-INF\spring\applicationContext-jms.xml
Managed SRC_MAIN_RESOURCES\META-INF\spring\applicationContext-jms.xml
Managed ROOT\pom.xml [Added dependency org.springframework:➥
    spring-beans:${spring.version}]
Managed ROOT\pom.xml [Added dependency org.springframework:➥
    spring-jms:${spring.version}]
Managed ROOT\pom.xml [Added dependency org.apache.geronimo.specs:➥
    geronimo-jms_1.1_spec:1.1]
Managed ROOT\pom.xml [Added dependency org.apache.activemq:➥
    activemq-core:5.3.2]
Managed ROOT\pom.xml [Added dependency org.apache.xbean:➥
    xbean-spring:3.6]
roo>
```

In the previous example Roo added dependencies to the Maven build file (pom.xml). These dependencies are required to implement the JMS-related code in your application. These dependencies are shown in the following listing.

Listing 10.1 Maven dependencies for JMS-related code

```
<dependency>
        <groupId>org.springframework</groupId>
        <artifactId>spring-beans</artifactId>
```

```xml
                    <version>${spring.version}</version>
        </dependency>
<dependency>
            <groupId>org.springframework</groupId>
            <artifactId>spring-jms</artifactId>
             <version>${spring.version}</version>
        </dependency>
<dependency>
            <groupId>org.apache.geronimo.specs</groupId>
            <artifactId>geronimo-jms_1.1_spec</artifactId>
             <version>1.1</version>
        </dependency>
<dependency>
            <groupId>org.apache.activemq</groupId>
            <artifactId>activemq-core</artifactId>
             <version>5.3.2</version>
            <exclusions>
                <exclusion>
                    <groupId>commons-logging</groupId>
                    <artifactId>commons-logging</artifactId>
                </exclusion>
                <exclusion>
                    <groupId>commons-logging</groupId>
                    <artifactId>commons-logging-api</artifactId>
                </exclusion>
            </exclusions>
        </dependency>
<dependency>
            <groupId>org.apache.xbean</groupId>
            <artifactId>xbean-spring</artifactId>
             <version>3.6</version>
            <exclusions>
                <exclusion>
                    <groupId>commons-logging</groupId>
                    <artifactId>commons-logging</artifactId>
                </exclusion>
            </exclusions>
        </dependency>
</dependency>
```

❶ Spring JMS JAR file

❷ JAR file with JMS API

❸ ActiveMQ library

❹ XBean library

The main JMS libraries you'll need are the JMS API ❷ and the ActiveMQ API ❸, respectively. The XBean library ❹ included in the Maven application build file in the previous listing allows you to run the ActiveMQ messaging broker by referencing an XML configuration file located in the classpath. The XBean URI points to an XML document, which can be parsed via the XBean API. You'll need the Spring JMS JAR file ❶ to use Spring JMS classes, such as org.springframework.jms.core.JmsTemplate and org.springframework.jms.connection.CachingConnectionFactory, which simplify the JMS code in the application.

Roo also creates a new Spring configuration file called applicationContext-jms.xml, which contains the Spring bean configuration details for all of the messaging components used in the application. The following listing shows this configuration.

Listing 10.2   The Spring context configuration file with JMS components

```
<?xml version="1.0" encoding="UTF-8" standalone="no"?>
<beans xmlns="http://www.springframework.org/schema/beans"          ❶ ActiveMQ
    xmlns:amq="http://activemq.apache.org/schema/core"                  namespace
     xmlns:aop="http://www.springframework.org/schema/aop"
    xmlns:jms="http://www.springframework.org/schema/jms"            ❷ JMS
     xmlns:xsi="http://www.w3.org/2001/XMLSchema-instance"              namespace
    xsi:schemaLocation="http://www.springframework.org/schema/beans
http://www.springframework.org/schema/beans/spring-beans-3.0.xsd
http://www.springframework.org/schema/aop
    http://www.springframework.org/schema/aop/spring-aop-3.0.xsd
http://activemq.apache.org/schema/core
    http://activemq.apache.org/schema/core/activemq-core-5.2.0.xsd
http://www.springframework.org/schema/jms
    http://www.springframework.org/schema/jms/spring-jms-3.0.xsd">

    <amq:broker persistent="false" useJmx="true">                    ❸ Embedded
        <amq:transportConnectors>                                        ActiveMQ
            <amq:transportConnector uri="tcp://localhost:61616"/>        broker
        </amq:transportConnectors>
    </amq:broker>

    <amq:connectionFactory brokerURL="vm://localhost"                ❹ JMS
        id="jmsFactory"/>                                                connection
                                                                         factory
    <bean class="org.springframework.jms.connection.
        CachingConnectionFactory" id="cachingConnectionFactory">
         <property name="targetConnectionFactory">                   ❺ Caching JMS
            <ref local="jmsFactory"/>                                    connection
         </property>                                                      factory
    </bean>

    <bean class="org.springframework.jms.core.JmsTemplate"           ❻ Spring JMS
            id="jmsTemplate">                                            template

        <property name="connectionFactory"
            ref="cachingConnectionFactory"/>
        <property name="defaultDestination"                          ❼ JMS topic to
            ref="courseCatalogUpdateAlerts"/>                           broadcast
    </bean>                                                              course catalog
    <amq:topic id="courseCatalogUpdateAlerts"                           distribution
        physicalName="jms.topic.CourseCatalogUpdateAlerts"/>
    <jms:listener-container connection-factory="jmsFactory"
        destination-type="topic"/>
</beans>
```

Note that the previous configuration file uses the ActiveMQ namespace (amq) ❶, which simplifies the configuration syntax for defining the JMS components. Similarly, the Spring JMS namespace ❷ simplifies the configuration for Spring JMS classes (like jms:listener-container, shown in the previous configuration). The ActiveMQ messaging broker ❸ and the JMS connection factory ❹ beans are used to configure the infrastructure details of the JMS container.

The JMS connection factory used for the Spring JMS template is an instance of the CachingConnectionFactory class (located in the org.springframework.jms

.connection package) ❺. The advantage of using the `CachingConnectionFactory` class is to avoid creating a connection for each request to post a message to the JMS destination. In the next section you'll see how Spring's JMS template ❻ works. The JMS topic you'll use for this use case is defined by the `amq:topic` element ❼ with a JNDI name of `jms.topic.CourseCatalogUpdateAlerts`.

JMS TEMPLATE

The next step is to add a `JmsTemplate` attribute into an existing class (usually a controller or a service class). The JMS template creation command requires two parameters: `fieldName` for the name of the field to add (default is `jmsTemplate`), and `class`, which is the name of the class to receive this field. Let's type in the command `field jms template`, which creates the template attribute and shows the following output:

```
Managed SRC_MAIN_JAVA\com\rooinaction\coursemanager\web\⟿
    CourseCatalogController.java
~.web.CourseCatalogController roo>
```

The JMS template field and a new method called `sendMessage` have been added to the controller class, as shown in the following code.

Listing 10.3 Controller class with JMS logic

```
public class CourseCatalogController {

    @Autowired
    private transient JmsTemplate jmsTemplate;

    public void sendMessage(Object messageObject) {
        jmsTemplate.convertAndSend(messageObject);
    }
}
```

❶ JMS template attribute

❷ JMS message send logic

In the previous code example, the new variable `jmsTemplate` ❶ is used for injecting the instance of `JmsTemplate` into the controller class. The `sendMessage` method ❷ is where you add your custom business logic for posting the message into the JMS destination (topic).

JMS LISTENER

The third step in the JMS setup is to create a JMS consumer class. You'll use the command `jms listener class` for this step. The command takes three parameters: `class` (mandatory parameter to specify the name of the class to create the JMS listener), `destinationName` to specify the name of the destination (default value for this parameter is `myDestination`), and `destinationType`, which is used to define the type of the destination (default is `QUEUE`).

Type in the following command specifying the custom names you want for your JMS components:

```
jms listener class --class ~.messaging.⟿
    JmsCourseCatalogUpdateTopicListener --destinationType TOPIC ⟿
    --destinationName jms.topic.CourseCatalogUpdateAlerts
```

Here's the output of this command:

```
Created SRC_MAIN_JAVA\com\rooinaction\coursemanager\messaging
Created SRC_MAIN_JAVA\com\rooinaction\coursemanager\messaging\
    JmsCourseCatalogUpdateTopicListener.java
Managed SRC_MAIN_RESOURCES\META-INF\spring\applicationContext-jms.xml
~.web.CourseCatalogController roo>
```

Roo adds the JMS configuration in the applicationContext-jms.xml file, as shown in the following listing.

Listing 10.4   Configuration for JMS listener components

```
<jms:listener-container connection-factory="jmsFactory"            ➊ JMS listener
    destination-type="topic"/>                                        container

<jms:listener destination="jms.topic.CourseCatalogUpdateAlerts"
    method="onMessage" ref="jmsCourseCatalogUpdateTopicListener"/>
 </jms:listener-container>
<bean class="org.rooinaction.coursemanager.messaging.
    JmsCourseCatalogUpdateTopicListener"                            ➌ Message-driven
    id="jmsCourseCatalogUpdateTopicListener"/>                         POJO class
```

Plain Java
(POJO) class
as a JMS
listener ➋

The JmsCourseCatalogUpdateTopicListener class ➌ is where you'll write the logic on how to process the message received from the CourseCatalogUpdateAlerts JMS topic. The Spring JMS module makes it easier to expose a POJO as a message-driven component ➋ with the help of the JMS listener container ➊ component.

There's also a new Java class, JmsCourseCatalogUpdateTopicListener, added in the package you specified (org.rooinaction.coursemanager.messaging). This new class has a placeholder method called onMessage that you can use to add your business logic to do the processing when a message is posted in the CourseCatalog-UpdateAlerts JMS topic, as shown in the following example:

```
package org.rooinaction.coursemanager.messaging;

public class JmsCourseCatalogUpdateTopicListener {

    public void onMessage(Object message) {
        System.out.println("JMS message received: " + message);
    }
}
```

NOTE   Because this JMS destination is the same Topic where you post the message from the controller class, make sure the destinationName parameter in step 3 has the same value as the destinationName parameter specified in the JMS provider setup (step 1).

10.3.2 *Testing the course catalog distribution use case*

With the required JMS setup complete, you're ready to test and validate the JMS broadcast functionality in the Course Manager application. But if you want to do this testing using the web application inside an application server container, you'll have to compile, build, and deploy the web application to the container before you can do any testing. You'll also need to launch the application, navigate to the home page, update the course catalog, and publish it. All of these steps take time, which could impact your development time and progress. So, in the spirit of agile software development and unit testing, you'll create few test client classes to make your job easier and your testing faster.

You'll post the message to the JMS topic using Spring's JMS template class in the test client. This gives you an easy way to publish and intercept the events that you can use to unit test the JMS functionality from within the IDE, without having to build and deploy the web application to the container.

The following listing shows the code for the JUnit test class, `CourseCatalog-UpdateEventPublisherTest`, that you'll create to test JMS functionality.

Listing 10.5   JUnit test class for testing course catalog distribution event

```
@RunWith(SpringJUnit4ClassRunner.class)
@ContextConfiguration(locations = {
        "classpath:/META-INF/spring/applicationContext.xml",
        "classpath:/META-INF/spring/applicationContext-jms.xml"
    })
public class CourseCatalogUpdateEventPublisherTest {

    private static final Log log = LogFactory.getLog(➥
        CourseCatalogUpdateEventPublisherTest.class);

    @Autowired
    private transient JmsTemplate jmsTopicTemplate;

    @Test
    public void verifyCourseCatalogUpdateEventIsSuccessful() {

        String courseCatalogEvent = "Test CourseCatalogEvent Message.";
        log.debug("CourseCatalogEvent: " + courseCatalogEvent);

        // Post the message to JMS Destination
        sendMessage(courseCatalogEvent);
    }

    private void sendMessage(Object messageObject) {
        jmsTopicTemplate.convertAndSend(messageObject);
    }
}
```

When you run the unit test class, you'll see that when the `CourseCatalogUpdateEvent` occurs, the message listener (`JmsCourseCatalogUpdateTopicListener`) will get the program control and process the JMS message.

That's all of the steps required to enable the publish-subscribe messaging feature for the course catalog distribution use case. We'll come back to the point-to-point messaging domain later in the chapter, but next we'll look at how to integrate the email notification feature in a Roo application. This is covered in the following section as part of the course registration confirmation notification use case.

10.4   *Adding email support for course registration*

The course registration confirmation notification use case involves a synchronous process, so you want to ensure that all steps in the process are successfully completed before a confirmation email is sent to a student. The process flow details for this use case are shown in figure 10.4.

There are three main steps to implement the course registration confirmation notification use case, which we'll cover in detail in the following section. These steps include defining the SMTP server configuration, the email message template, and the email template attribute.

10.4.1 *Registration confirmation via email*

Similar to the JMS configuration, the main steps to enable the SMTP configuration using Roo mail commands include setting up the SMTP server and email message template, and adding the mail template attribute in a Java class (usually controller or service). For your sample application, you'll also create a custom Java class to encapsulate the email processing application logic so any class in the application can use this helper class for the notification requirements, without having to duplicate the same logic in multiple classes. The next few sections show the different mail commands you'll use to enable the email feature in your sample application. Roo's mail commands are contained in the org.springframework.roo.addon.email.MailCommands class.

JAVA CLASS FOR EMAIL PROCESSING

Before you set up the email configuration, you need to create an interface and an implementation class for encapsulating the email processing logic to decouple it from the application logic.

The Roo shell supports creating new Java interfaces or classes from the command line using interface or class commands, respectively. You first create an interface called NotificationService. Type in the following command on the Roo shell:

```
interface --class ~.email.NotificationService
```

Roo creates the Java interface in the specified package and displays the following output:

```
Created SRC_MAIN_JAVA\org\rooinaction\coursemanager\email
Created SRC_MAIN_JAVA\org\rooinaction\coursemanager\email\⟹
   NotificationService.java
~.email.NotificationService roo>
```

Now, run the class command to create the skeleton for the implementation class called NotificationServiceImpl:

```
class --class ~.email.NotificationServiceImpl
```

Figure 10.4   Course registration confirmation notification use case

Here's the output of the `class` command:

```
Created SRC_MAIN_JAVA\org\rooinaction\coursemanager\email\➥
    NotificationServiceImpl.java
~.email.NotificationServiceImpl roo>
```

Now that you have the helper class (and its interface that the client classes can use to delegate the email processing logic), you're ready to build the infrastructure components of the email configuration. First among these components is the email sender (SMTP server).

EMAIL SENDER

The email sender setup command installs Spring's `JavaMailSender` in this project. This command takes several parameters with the information required to configure the Spring bean configuration for the `JavaMailSenderImpl` class. Here's a list of these parameters and what information they provide to the command.

- `hostServer`—SMTP host server (required parameter)
- `protocol`—Used by the mail server (for example, SMTP)
- `port`—Number used by mail server
- `encoding`—Used for sending mail messages
- `username`—For the SMTP account
- `password`—For the SMTP account

To set up the SMTP server configuration, use the following command:

```
roo> email sender setup --hostServer smtp.gmail.com --protocol SMTP ➥
    --port 587 --username rooinaction --password yourpassword
```

And here's the output on the Roo console:

```
Managed SRC_MAIN_RESOURCES\META-INF\spring\applicationContext.xml
Managed ROOT\pom.xml [Added dependency org.springframework:➥
    spring-context-support:${spring.version}]
Managed ROOT\pom.xml [Added dependency javax.mail:mail:1.4.1]
Managed ROOT\pom.xml [Added dependency javax.activation:➥
    activation:1.1.1]
Created SRC_MAIN_RESOURCES\META-INF\spring\email.properties
```

This command creates a new properties file called email.properties to store the SMTP server connection parameters. It also adds the `mailSender` Spring bean configuration to the applicationContext.xml file. The following listing shows the SMTP configuration details.

Listing 10.6 SMTP provider configuration

```
<bean class="org.springframework.mail.javamail.JavaMailSenderImpl" ➥
        id="mailSender">
    <property name="host" value="${email.host}"/>
    <property name="protocol" value="${email.protocol}"/>
    <property name="port" value="${email.port}"/>
    <property name="username" value="${email.username}"/>
    <property name="password" value="${email.password}"/>
```

```
    <property name="javaMailProperties">
        <props>
            <prop key="mail.smtp.auth">true</prop>
            <prop key="mail.smtp.starttls.enable">true</prop>
        </props>
    </property>
</bean>
```

In a real-world application, you should define the SMTP server as a JNDI resource. For example, to configure an SMTP session as a JNDI object in a Tomcat container, you'd add a new `Resource` element in the configuration to Tomcat's context.xml file. This configuration is shown in the following listing.

Listing 10.7   In-container JNDI resource configuration for SMTP provider

```
<?xml version="1.0" encoding="UTF-8"?>

<Context path="/myapp" docBase="myapp" debug="5" crossContext="false">

    <Resource name="mail/Session"
              auth="Container"
              type="javax.mail.Session"
              username="smtp_user_name"
              password="smtp_password"
              mail.debug="true"
              mail.user="username"
              mail.password="password"
              mail.transport.protocol="smtp"
              mail.smtp.host="SMTP_HOST_NAME"
              mail.smtp.auth="true"
              mail.smtp.port="25"
              mail.smtp.starttls.enable="true"/>
</Context>
```

The previous configuration will create a new SMTP resource in the Tomcat container and will be available for all web applications running on the servlet container. This configuration is straightforward, but let's look at how to view and modify the SMTP properties in the file generated by Roo.

VIEW AND MODIFY SMTP PROPERTIES

You can use the Roo shell command called `properties` to view and modify the contents of properties files like the email.properties file created in the previous step. Let's check the contents and modify one of the properties in this file. First, to view the email.properties file contents, type in the following command:

```
properties list --name email.properties --path SPRING_CONFIG_ROOT
```

The output of this command is shown in the following example:

```
email.host = smtp.gmail.com
email.password = yourpassword
email.port = 587
email.protocol = smtp
email.username = rooinaction
roo>
```

Let's modify the password property in this file. You can do this by using the `properties` command with the `set` argument. Here's the example:

```
properties set --name email.properties --path SPRING_CONFIG_ROOT ➥
    --key email.password --value newpassword
```

It shows the following message, which says that the properties file has been updated:

```
Managed SRC_MAIN_RESOURCES\META-INF\spring\email.properties
roo>
```

You can call the `properties list` command again to view an update. A different command will display all of the properties of the Roo shell. This command is `system properties`, which displays the following output (abbreviated to show only the first few entries).

Listing 10.8   Command output for system properties

```
awt.toolkit = sun.awt.windows.WToolkit
developmentMode = false
felix.auto.deploy.dir = C:\dev\frameworks\Roo\spring-roo-1.2.0.➥
    RELEASE\bundle
felix.config.properties = file:C:\dev\frameworks\Roo\spring-roo-1.2.0.➥
    RELEASE\conf\config.properties
file.encoding = Cp1252
file.encoding.pkg = sun.io
file.separator = \
flash.message.disabled = false
java.awt.graphicsenv = sun.awt.Win32GraphicsEnvironment
java.awt.printerjob = sun.awt.windows.WPrinterJob
....
```

After you've modified the SMTP properties to fit your application requirements, you're ready to create the SMTP message template.

EMAIL MESSAGE TEMPLATE

You need to create the email template that the Spring framework will use to send the email messages. The command `email template setup` configures a template for the `SimpleMailMessage` class using two parameters: `from` and `subject`. Type in the following command:

```
email template setup --from rooinaction@rooinaction.com --subject ➥
    "Course Registration Confirmation"
```

The output of the previous command looks like this:

```
Managed SRC_MAIN_RESOURCES\META-INF\spring\applicationContext.xml
Managed SRC_MAIN_RESOURCES\META-INF\spring\email.properties
roo>
```

This command adds the following two additional properties to the email.properties file:

```
email.from=rooinaction@rooinaction.com
email.subject=Course
```

This command also adds a new Spring bean definition in the applicationContext.xml file for the `MailMessage` template class with the `from` and `subject` attributes set to the specified values in the command line:

```
<bean class="org.springframework.mail.SimpleMailMessage" ⇥
        id="templateMessage">
    <property name="from" value="${email.from}"/>
    <property name="subject" value="${email.subject}"/>
</bean>
```

EMAIL TEMPLATE ATTRIBUTE IN SERVICE CLASS

In this last step, you set up the email template attribute in the newly created custom `NotificationService` class. Type in the following command:

```
field email template --fieldName mailTemplate ⇥
    --class ~.email.NotificationServiceImpl
```

Here's the command output:

```
Managed SRC_MAIN_JAVA\org\rooinaction\coursemanager\email\⇥
    NotificationServiceImpl.java
```

The `NotificationServiceImpl` class will now look like that shown in the following listing.

Listing 10.9   Notification service implementation class

```
@Component
public class NotificationServiceImpl implements NotificationService {

    private static final Log log = LogFactory.getLog(⇥
            NotificationServiceImpl.class);

    @Autowired
    private transient MailSender mailTemplate;                    ❶ Email sender

    @Autowired
    private transient SimpleMailMessage simpleMailMessage;        ❷ MailMessage
                                                                    implementation
    public void sendMessage(String mailTo, String message) {       class
        log.debug("NotificationServiceImpl::⇥
            sendMessage() called.");
        simpleMailMessage.setTo(mailTo);                          ❸ Email
        simpleMailMessage.setText(message);                         send
        mailTemplate.send(simpleMailMessage);                       logic
    }
}
```

This class has the attributes for the SMTP mail server ❶ and Spring's `MailMessage` implementation class ❷ to abstract the email send logic. The `sendMessage` method ❸ has the email notification code.

You can now run the Eclipse command, `perform eclipse`, to refresh the project contents so the Roo project is refreshed with all of the code and configuration changes you've made so far.

10.4.2 Testing the course registration confirmation notification use case

You'll create a test client class similar to the way you tested the JMS functionality to verify the registration notification functionality. The following listing shows the code example of the test class RegistrationNotificationEventPublisherTest.

Listing 10.10 JUnit test class for course registration confirmation notification

```
@RunWith(SpringJUnit4ClassRunner.class)
@ContextConfiguration(locations = {
        "classpath:/META-INF/spring/applicationContext.xml"
    })
public class RegistrationNotificationEventPublisherTest {

    @Autowired
    private NotificationService notificationService;

    @Test
    public void verifyThatRegistrationNotificationIsSuccessful() {
        // Send e-mail notification
        String mailTo = "test-user@gmail.com";
        String message = "Registration Successful.";
        notificationService.sendMessage(mailTo, message);
    }
}
```

Now that we've covered the first two use cases in the Course Manager sample application, you know how to enable the JMS (pub/sub) and email features in Roo applications. Let's look at the step-by-step details for implementing point-to-point asynchronous messaging, which involves a queue (as opposed to a topic).

10.5 Asynchronous messaging for registration confirmation

The course registration wait-list notification use case involves asynchronous messaging, where the main business process stops when a customer's registration request is placed on the waiting list. After this step, the offline (asynchronous) processing takes over. The offline processing includes a JMS queue-based messaging solution, which uses a CourseRegistrationCancellationEvent to unregister a customer who wants to cancel a registration. The program then notifies the first customer on the waiting list that there's an open spot in the course and their registration has now been confirmed.

Let's look at how you would implement this use case in a Roo application.

10.5.1 JMS configuration

Similar to the first use case covered in this chapter, the JMS configuration for the course registration wait-list notification use case includes steps for setting up the JMS queue, called CourseRegistrationWaitListQueue. You'll use the same JMS provider (ActiveMQ messaging server) you created in that use case and create a message queue on that JMS container. This use case requires three steps, which include creating a new message queue, a JMS template, and a message listener class.

MESSAGE QUEUE

The first step in the JMS configuration for this use case is to create a message queue that will be used to post the course registration wait-list notification details. Here's the JMS command to add the configuration for a JMS Queue with the name jms.queue .CourseRegistrationWaitListQueue:

```
jms setup --provider ACTIVEMQ_IN_MEMORY --destinationType QUEUE ➥
    --destinationName jms.queue.CourseRegistrationWaitListQueue
```

The message queue configuration step adds a new amq:queue Spring bean in the JMS Spring configuration file. As shown in the following snippet, a JMS queue (amq:queue) and a JMS listener container (jms:listener-container) for mapping the queue to the JMS provider are added to the applicationContext-jms.xml file:

```
<amq:queue id="jms.queue.CourseRegistrationWaitListQueue" ➥
    physicalName="jms.queue.CourseRegistrationWaitListQueue"/>
<jms:listener-container connection-factory="jmsFactory" ➥
    destination-type="queue"/>
```

JMS TEMPLATE FIELD

After you configure the message queue component, the next step is to add a JMS template to the helper Java class, which in this case is the CourseRegistration-NotificationHelper class. Here's the command for this configuration:

```
field jms template --fieldName jmsTemplate --class ➥
    ~.web.CourseRegistrationNotificationHelper
```

As the following command-line output shows, Roo added the JMS template attribute (jmsTemplate) to the CourseRegistrationNotificationHelper Java class:

```
Updated SRC_MAIN_JAVA\org\rooinaction\coursemanager\web\➥
        CourseRegistrationNotificationHelper.java
~.web.CourseRegistrationNotificationHelper
roo>
```

JMS LISTENER

Now for the final step: you need to add a listener class that acts as an asynchronous message consumer. The following is the Roo command for the message listener configuration:

```
jms listener class --class ~.messaging.JmsCourseRegistrationWaitList➥
    QueueListener --destinationType QUEUE --destinationName ➥
    jms.queue.CourseRegistrationWaitListQueue
```

Roo creates a new Java class called JmsCourseRegistrationWaitListQueueListener with a stub for the onMessage() method. It also updates the applicationContext-jms.xml file, as shown in the following output:

```
Created SRC_MAIN_JAVA\org\rooinaction\coursemanager\messaging\➥
    JmsCourseRegistrationWaitListQueueListener.java
Managed SRC_MAIN_RESOURCES\META-INF\spring\applicationContext-jms.xml
```

The following Spring bean element for the JmsCourseRegistrationWaitListQueue-Listener class is added to the XML configuration file:

```
<bean class="org\rooinaction\coursemanager.messaging.➥
    JmsCourseRegistrationWaitListQueueListener" ➥
    id="jmsCourseRegistrationWaitListQueueListener"/>
```

With the configuration steps complete, you're now ready to test the new Java classes and configuration changes for the course registration wait-list notification use case.

10.5.2 Testing JMS setup for wait-list notification

To test the course registration wait-list notification functionality, you need to post a message to the JMS queue and process the message using the listener class. Let's write a new unit test class (called RegistrationNotificationWaitListEventPublisherTest) to test the wait-list scenario. The following listing shows the code for this unit test.

Listing 10.11   JUnit test class for course registration wait-list notification

```
@RunWith(SpringJUnit4ClassRunner.class)
@ContextConfiguration(locations = {
        "classpath:/META-INF/spring/applicationContext.xml",
        "classpath:/META-INF/spring/applicationContext-jms.xml"
    })
public class RegistrationNotificationWaitListEventPublisherTest {

    private static final Log log = LogFactory.getLog(➥
            RegistrationNotificationWaitListEventPublisherTest.class);

    @Autowired
    private transient JmsTemplate jmsQueueTemplate;

    @Test
    public void verifyRegistrationWaitListNotificationIsSuccessful() {

        String regNotifyWaitListEvent = "Test regNotifyWaitList Message.";

        log.debug("regNotifyWaitListEvent: " + regNotifyWaitListEvent);

        // Post the message to JMS Destination
        sendMessage(regNotifyWaitListEvent);
    }

    private void sendMessage(Object messageObject) {
        jmsQueueTemplate.convertAndSend(messageObject);
    }
}
```

10.5.3 Course completion certificate use case

Another good case for using JMS messaging is the certificate completion use case. Let's say the Course Manager application organization outsources the process of printing the course completion certificates and mailing them to the students. You can use the Trading Partner user role (ROLE_TRADING_PARTNER), for example, to notify of the course completion event and provide the student details. This allows the course completion certificate with the student's information to be generated and sent to the student.

As previously discussed in this chapter, there are several different components that are working together in a typical enterprise messaging application to send, receive, and process the various business message objects. This is why it's important to monitor these JMS components to see what's going on behind the scenes of the application to be able to respond to any production problems and troubleshoot the messaging-related issues. This is what we'll look at in the next section on how to monitor the Course Manager application using tools like VisualVM.

10.6   *Monitoring messaging activity*

Now that you've implemented all of the use cases, let's look at how to monitor your application to ensure that the various JMS resources you've installed and configured (JMS container, JMS topic, and JMS queue) are up and running, as well as how many messages they're processing.

The Java standard for application and system or server monitoring is the Java Management Extensions (JMX). For JMS message activity monitoring purposes, Roo provides a JMS add-on that enables monitoring (JMX) support by default. So you can check the JMS message activity using tools such as JConsole, VisualVM, or any other JMX client.

To turn on the monitoring capability in the ActiveMQ messaging broker, you'll use the useJmx parameter (with a value of true) in the amq:broker element. After you make this change and restart the messaging server, you can use the following URL to connect to the ActiveMQ Broker JMX MBean server: service:jmx:rmi:///jndi/rmi://localhost:1099/jmxrmi.

After you've enabled the JMX feature in the ActiveMQ broker, you can use a JMX client to monitor the messaging activity in the application in a server runtime environment.

10.6.1 *Application monitoring using VisualVM JConsole*

The VisualVM tool comes bundled with the JDK installation, with the jvisualvm and jconsole executable files located in the %JAVA_HOME%/bin directory. Note that JAVA_HOME is the folder where you installed JDK on your machine. The JConsole module in VisualVM can be used for monitoring the MBean components.

Open a new command prompt and run the following commands to launch the VisualVM tool:

```
set JAVA_HOME="C:\Program Files\Java\jdk1.6.0_22"

set PATH=%PATH%;%JAVA_HOME%\bin;

cd %JAVA_HOME%\bin

jconsole service:jmx:rmi:///jndi/rmi://localhost:1099/jmxrmi
```

Figure 10.5 shows the MBean screen in the JConsole JMX client tool.

Another monitoring tool you can use in nonproduction environments is the new Spring Insight product from the SpringSource group (http://www.springsource.org/insight).

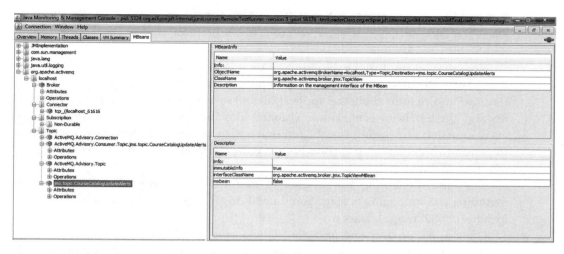

Figure 10.5 Messaging activity details using the JConsole JMX client

10.6.2 *Application monitoring using Spring Insight*

Spring Insight provides a graphical look at an application's performance, response-time charts, and histograms, providing developers with a dashboard view into the application's runtime environment to find where it's spending most of its time in the program flow.

Spring Insight gives visibility into the application performance for each web request made in the web application. You can see all of the JDBC requests made, how much time it took to render the web pages, or the initialization times for any of the Spring beans. Also, the Application Health screen shows which Spring MVC control-lers are taking considerable time and allows you to drill down into the details of the requests that took longer times. You can also navigate to specific remote web service calls that were made.

Spring Insight uses the AspectJ load-time weaving feature to add the tracing and monitoring statistics to web applications. This means your sample application doesn't require any additional code or configuration changes to use Spring Insight. Also, Spring Insight collects the response data in memory and doesn't require a backend database or a persistent data store.

VMware vFabric tc Server, Developer Edition (formerly known as SpringSource tc Server: http://mng.bz/LDGg) includes the Spring Insight monitoring module. The SpringSource Tool Suite (STS) IDE tool also bundles with Spring Insight. If you're using the STS tool, you already have Spring Insight available for you to monitor your application's performance and other server metrics.

At the time of this writing, Spring Insight doesn't have a plug-in for JMS, but it's on the feature list to be added in a future release. You can still see the components that were triggered by a JMS message. For example, if the JMS message listener calls any

Spring bean component (such as a Java class that uses one of these annotations: @Service, @Repository, or @Controller), it will be displayed on the Spring Insight dashboard.

Note that Spring Insight shouldn't be used in a production environment because it displays a detailed view of all of your application's performance details, including sensitive information about the application and server settings. It's meant for developers and QA testers to get runtime visibility into the applications in nonproduction environments. The Spring Insight reference manual (see the "Resources" section at the end of this chapter) is a good resource for learning more about this application monitoring framework.

Let's use the Spring Insight tool to monitor the activity in your application, including JMS messaging activity. You'll need this URL to view the dashboard: http://localhost:8080/insight/traces.

Open a web browser and navigate to the Spring Insight dashboard page using the previously mentioned URL. Click on the Browse Resources tab and expand the web application node in the Resources pane under the application's root node.

When you run the Course Manager application and test the course registration functionality, you can see the details of the controller classes being called, and the messages being sent to JMS destinations (CourseCatalogUpdateAlerts topic and CourseRegistrationWaitListQueue queue) and consumed by the corresponding JMS listener objects. These details are shown in figure 10.6.

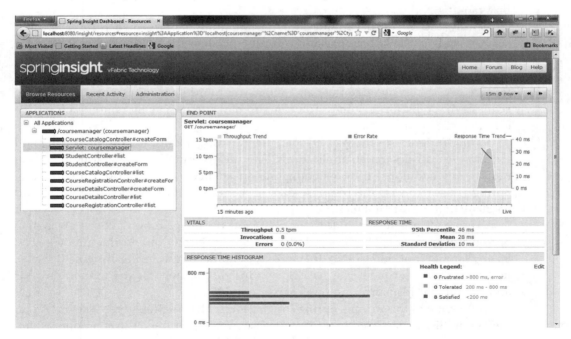

Figure 10.6   Spring Insight's application monitoring dashboard

As you can see, it's a straightforward process to enable the monitoring of messaging components in the Course Manager application using the JMX monitoring technology. You can view the attributes of various JMS components as well as invoke the operations (methods) of these components to dynamically change the JMS configuration parameters.

10.7 Summary

In this chapter, you learned how to send email notifications to your Course Manager application customers (students) from within the Spring Roo application, without having to write or configure the setup for the email provider, email processing logic, and so on. Roo's email add-on makes it easier because it requires only a few commands to set up the SMTP provider and add Spring's email template classes into your application.

You've also learned how to implement asynchronous messaging for business use cases that require offline processing capability, such as the course catalog distribution and the course registration wait-list notification use cases. You were able to do this by leveraging another Roo add-on, the JMS add-on, provided by the Roo framework. You also reviewed the publish-subscribe pattern (use case 1: course catalog distribution) as well as the point-to-point messaging pattern (use case 3: course registration wait-list notification) in this chapter.

At this point in the book, all of the chapter discussions on the Roo application have been based on it being deployed on a server hosted by an organization's internal server environment. What if you want to deploy the same Roo application on a third-party server (or servers, in the case of a server cluster) hosted outside of an organization, at an external third-party site, on what's called a *cloud*? With the cloud computing paradigm gaining attention over the last few years, cloud hosting has become a popular choice for software implementations.

We discuss cloud computing in chapter 13, where we'll deploy the Course Manager application to the Cloud Foundry server environment. Roo once again provides excellent support for moving the Course Manager application to an externally hosted server environment. But before that, in the next two chapters, we'll look at how to create custom add-on components using the Roo framework.

10.8 Resources

ActiveMQ Messaging/JMS Container (http://activemq.apache.org/)

Apache Velocity Framework (http://velocity.apache.org/)

Enterprise Integration Patterns (http://www.eaipatterns.com/)

Java Management Extensions (JMX) Technology (http://mng.bz/3k5z)

Java Message Service (JMS) (http://mng.bz/vEJP)

JMS (Java Message Service), for information about message-driven POJOs in Spring (http://mng.bz/ni05)

Spring Insight main page (http://www.springsource.org/insight)

Using JConsole (http://mng.bz/4LPo)

Using Spring Insight (reference manual) (http://mng.bz/hHFU)

VisualVM (http://visualvm.java.net/)

11

Roo add-ons

This chapter covers

- Using Roo add-ons
- Writing your own add-ons
- Modifying your project configuration
- Providing Roo shell commands
- Learning Felix and OSGi terminology

In the previous chapter, you learned how to process email notifications to the customers of your sample Course Manager application. You also took steps to implement an asynchronous processing solution based on Java Message Service technology using two different JMS destinations (topic and queue).

In this and the next chapter, we explain how to install existing Roo add-ons from the central Roo add-on repository. Then we show you how to write and install your own add-ons, beginning with the somewhat confusingly named *simple add-on*. Finally, we discuss the *advanced add-on* and related infrastructure features woven into Roo.

When you write Spring Roo applications you use a modular add-on architecture. Many of the core Roo components were written as add-ons, including the entity and field management commands, interactions with Maven, Java `toString()` and Java-Bean method constructions, Spring MVC configurations, email, JMS, and more.

All of these add-ons are OSGi components, so if you're confused by the terminology, you may wish to do a little extra research. Manning's *OSGi in Action* (Hall et al., 2011) contains a thorough overview of all things OSGi, and we used it as a reference when we wrote these chapters. Expect some of the material in this chapter to be complex, because the Roo add-on API hasn't had the rigorous refinement from hundreds of developers as have the APIs from Grails, Rails, or Maven. Our goal in these chapters is to demystify Roo's complexity, so we can encourage more developers to contribute to the current pool of Roo add-ons.

Without further ado, let's roll up our sleeves and dig into Roo add-ons.

11.1 Extending Roo with add-ons

Roo was designed from the ground up to be extremely extensible. All of the Roo features we discuss in this book are interrelated modules known as *add-ons*. Each add-on can define a set of Roo commands, manipulate project configurations, and listen for changes in the file system, such as the addition or removal of a @RooToString annotation.

Roo developers can define their own add-ons and even publish them to the main Roo add-on repository. There are add-ons in place to support web frameworks such as JSF, Vaadin, and Wicket (a recently introduced service-and-repository data mapping technology from SpringSource); automatic JAXB and JSON data conversion; building executable WARs; and so on.

Roo's extensibility allows you to easily add to the set of commands and features by installing additional add-ons. If you don't see Roo support for your favorite feature or framework, you can write an add-on, install it, and have those capabilities in your projects. Much like other agile development tools, Roo is only as powerful and rich as the features the community puts into it, so open source developers have the power to shape the future direction of this tool.

11.2 How add-ons work

Roo add-ons are "tool-time" features—they're wired into the shell as OSGi bundles, which are special JAR files that can be loaded and unloaded at will from an OSGi-compliant application. You already use OSGi bundles in many different software products, including tools such as ServiceMix, Mule, and the Eclipse IDE. All Eclipse plug-ins are implemented as OSGi bundles, and you can even expose an OSGi command line by appending the -console flag to the eclipse binary.

The Roo shell environment runs atop an OSGi implementation from Apache, the Felix container. Roo has distributed more than 37 add-on bundles that make up the base of the Roo platform. You've already used a few. The following list of add-ons comprises the base Roo install. These add-ons may change as the Roo team continues to update the project and add new features:

```
addon-backup              addon-cloud-foundry
addon-configurable        addon-creator
addon-dbre                addon-dod
```

```
addon-email                      addon-equals
addon-finder                     addon-git
addon-gwt                        addon-javabean
addon-jdbc                       addon-jms
addon-jpa                        addon-jsf
addon-json                       addon-layers-repository-jpa
addon-layers-repository-mongo    addon-layers-service
addon-logging                    addon-op4j
addon-oscommands                 addon-plural
addon-property-editor            addon-propfiles
addon-roobot-client              addon-security
addon-serializable               addon-solr
addon-test                       addon-tostring
addon-web-flow                   addon-web-mvc-controller
addon-web-mvc-embedded           addon-web-mvc-jsp
addon-web-selenium               classpath
```

Add-ons provide features in the form of specific shell commands. For example:

- *addon-jpa*—Provides the `entity jpa` command to create Roo entities, which we detailed in chapters 3 and 4.
- *classpath*—Although not prefixed with `addon-`, the commands provided in this project include `class`, `interface`, `enum`, and `field` because they create Java classes, interfaces, and enums.
- *addon-web-mvc-controller*—Provides the `web mvc all` and `web mvc controller` commands, as well as the `web mvc setup` and `web mvc scaffold` commands to set up and optionally generate scaffolded web pages, as discussed in chapter 5.
- *addon-web-selenium*—Installs the Selenium web testing engine and allows for scaffolding of HTML-based web tests.

You can also install other add-ons to provide support for new features and frameworks. Let's review the add-on management system and some third-party add-ons.

11.3   *Working with published Roo add-ons*

Like other rapid development platforms, Roo has a number of add-ons available for installation over the internet, because its development team hosts a live directory of components that automatically downloads on startup. You may see the download process occurring on the top right of your console window, finishing with

```
Downloaded 100% of roobot.xml.zip
```

The downloaded file contains a list of all Roo add-ons registered with *Roo-bot*, a service available to Roo developers that exposes published add-ons to all Roo users. We'll experiment with this directory, and we'll start by learning how to search for add-ons; then we'll install and test an add-on; and, finally, we'll remove an add-on.

The key thing to remember is that, unlike Grails or Rails, where the add-on is used at runtime, our add-ons are merely Roo shell extensions. After we compile the project code, all effects of the add-on will result in standard Java EE code and web artifacts.

11.3.1 *Finding the Roo repository add-ons*

Let's get started. Use the `addon list` command to show a list of add-ons in the repository, which we have excerpted in the following example:

```
roo> addon list

65 found, sorted by rank; T = trusted developer; R = Roo 1.2 compatible
ID T R DESCRIPTION -------------------------------------------------------
01 Y Y 3.0.5.RELEASE
02 - Y 1.0.0.0001 This bundle wraps the standard Maven artifact:
      google-collections-1.0.0.
...
08 - Y 0.7.0 JasperReport support for Spring MVC based projects. With
      JasperReport support you give to the project the feature of
      create...
...
42 Y Y 1.2.0.M1 Offers GIT integration in the project. Each
      successfully executed command will be automatically committed to
      a local GIT...
...
57 - - 1.0.0 The Executable WAR Addon configures the Maven project
      to makes it possible to create web applications that can be
      run from the command
...
```

You'll get a full list of the add-ons in the repository, whether or not they are compatible with your version of Roo. The fields returned are

- `ID`—The search result # of the add-on.
- `(T)rusted`—Whether the team member deploying the add-on is a trusted or approved Roo developer. These add-ons must be approved by the Roo team to gain the `T` code.
- `(R)oo 1.2 Compatible`—These add-ons are compatible with the add-on system as of version 1.2 or later.
- `Description`—The description of each add-on. It starts with the version of the add-on.

The `addon list` command has several options, including

- `--compatibleOnly`—Show only compatible add-ons.
- `--trustedOnly`—Show only add-ons by trusted developers.
- `--communityOnly`—Show only add-ons contributed to the system by the outside community. Some of the add-ons available include upgrades of key Roo components and optional JARs, so this option weeds out internal JARs from the list.
- `--linesPerResult`—By default, Roo shows only two comment lines. If an add-on has more documentation, you can expand the number of rows to read the result.
- `--refresh`—The list of add-ons are loaded on startup. Use this option to force a reload of the list.

You can also use the search command to locate a specific add-on. The `--requires-Description` option searches text within the description:

```
roo> addon search --requiresDescription git

1 found, sorted by rank; T = trusted developer; R = Roo 1.2 compatible
ID T R DESCRIPTION ----------------------------------------------------
01 Y Y 1.2.0.M1 Offers GIT integration in the project. Each
        successfully executed command will be automatically committed to
        a local GIT...
```

The `--requiresCommand` option searches for the commands provided by the add-on:

```
roo> addon search --requiresCommand git

1 found, sorted by rank; T = trusted developer; R = Roo 1.2 compatible
ID T R DESCRIPTION ----------------------------------------------------
01 Y Y 1.2.0.M1 Offers GIT integration in the project. Each
        successfully executed command will be automatically committed to
        a local GIT...
```

For all of the add-on commands, you can type two dashes (`--`) and use the `[TAB]` completion key to see additional options.

More than one way to install a Roo add-on

There are four ways to install an add-on to your Roo configuration:

- Use the `addon install` command to install it from the central Roo add-on repository.
- Use the `osgi start` command to install add-ons from a URL or a file. You'll use this technique later in this chapter when you write your own add-ons.
- Use the `osgi obr` repository commands to mount an OSGi repository and install the add-on from that repository. Useful in a corporate environment where your team needs to share company-wide add-ons.
- Copy the add-on JAR file to the Roo installation's `bundles` directory.

We discuss the `osgi start` and `osgi obr` commands in the next chapter.

The report format is a bit basic, but we hope to soon see an add-on portal website that displays this information in a more useful way.

The `addon info` command shows details about your add-on. The following example assumes `roo-equals-roo-addon` was search result 01:

```
Name.........: Spring Roo - Addon - GIT
BSN..........: org.springframework.roo.addon.git
Version......: 1.2.0.M1 [available versions: 1.1.1.RELEASE,
               1.1.2.RELEASE, 1.1.3.RELEASE, 1.1.4.RELEASE,
               1.1.5.RELEASE, 1.2.0.M1]
Roo Version..: 1.2
Ranking......: 0.0
JAR Size.....: 14278 bytes
PGP Signature: 0xEC67B395 signed by Alan Stewart (stewarta@vmware.com)
```

```
OBR URL......: http://spring-roo-repository.springsource.org/repository
             .xml.zip
JAR URL......: httppgp://spring-roo-repository.springsource.org/release
             /org/springframework/roo/org.springframework.roo.addon.g
             it/1.2.0.M1/org.springframework.roo.addon.git-1.2.0.M1.j
             ar
Commands.....: 'git revert commit' [Roll project back to a specific com
             mit]
Commands.....: 'git revert last' [Revert last commit]
Commands.....: 'git log' [Commit log]
Commands.....: 'git push' [Roll project back to a specific commit]
Commands.....: 'git setup' [Setup Git revision control]
Commands.....: 'git commit all' [Trigger a commit manually for the proj
             ect]
Commands.....: 'git config' [Git revision control configuration (.git/c
             onfig)]
Commands.....: 'git reset' [Reset (hard) last (x) commit(s)]
Description..: Offers GIT integration in the project. Each successfully
             executed command will be automatically committed to a lo
             cal GIT repository. Tags: #git, #scm, #wrappedCoreDepend
             ency
```

The Roo add-on system is a great way to find and experiment with published and contributed add-ons. You can also install your own add-on to this repository, further contributing to the Roo platform. We'll show you how in chapter 12.

11.3.2 Installing with add-on install

Now that you've learned how to search for add-ons, it's time to install one and experiment. Let's install the Roo Git add-on. There are two ways to do this.

The first is to use the search ID of a previously executed search:

```
roo> addon search --requiresCommand git

1 found, sorted by rank; T = trusted developer; R = Roo 1.2 compatible
ID T R DESCRIPTION -------------------------------------------------
01 Y Y 1.2.0.M1 Offers GIT integration in the project. Each
        successfully executed command will be automatically committed to
        a local GIT...

roo> addon install id --searchResultId 01
```

The second is to use the bundle symbolic name, abbreviated as BSN in the previous addon info command:

```
roo> addon install bundle --bundleSymbolicName ⇒
    org.springframework.roo.addon.git
```

This method works well when you're putting together Roo script files for your developers to use in the future, and don't want to rely on a search result ID.

WATCH THOSE SEARCH IDS Each time you perform an addon search or addon list command, the search result IDs change. They aren't permanent numbers.

It's time to use your add-on to set up a git repository.

11.3.3 *Using the Git add-on*

You can check your shell to see the new command by hitting [TAB]:

```
roo> [TAB]
*/                /*              //              ;             addon
backup            class           controller      date          dependency
development       download        email           enum          equals
exit              field           flash           focus         git
 gwt               help            hint            interface     jms
json              logging         metadata        osgi          perform
persistence       pgp             poll            process       properties
proxy             quit            reference       script        system
test              version         web
```

Now the git command appears alongside the rest of the Roo shell commands.

You can set up a Git repository from a Roo project. This add-on provides a series of shell commands that configure and automatically manage changes to the repository with each shell command. To set up the Git repository, you can issue this one-line command:

```
roo> git setup
Git commit 4c655f6c43eb4e76e1cfa13919f213ca3466a5a7 [git setup]
```

This command will issue a git init command in your project directory, if needed, and otherwise use your existing Git configuration. It will then issue a git commit to record the change you've made.

Now, any change you make to your project configuration in the Roo shell will be followed by a commit to the Git repository:

```
roo> entity jpa --class ~.model.StudentSurvey --testAutomatically
Created SRC_MAIN_JAVA/.../model/StudentSurvey.java
Created SRC_TEST_JAVA/.../model/StudentSurveyDataOnDemand.java
Created SRC_TEST_JAVA/.../model/StudentSurveyIntegrationTest.java
Created SRC_MAIN_JAVA/.../model/StudentSurvey_Roo_Configurable.aj
Created SRC_MAIN_JAVA/.../model/StudentSurvey_Roo_ToString.aj
Created SRC_MAIN_JAVA/.../model/StudentSurvey_Roo_Jpa_Entity.aj
Created SRC_MAIN_JAVA/.../model/StudentSurvey_Roo_Jpa_ActiveRecord.aj
Created SRC_TEST_JAVA/.../model/StudentSurveyIntegrationTest_Roo_Config
        urable.aj
Created SRC_TEST_JAVA/.../model/StudentSurveyDataOnDemand_Roo_DataOnDem
        and.aj
Created SRC_TEST_JAVA/.../model/StudentSurveyIntegrationTest_Roo_Integr
        ationTest.aj
Created SRC_TEST_JAVA/.../model/StudentSurveyDataOnDemand_Roo_Configura
        ble.aj
Git commit 87f7126c44029e99ed9345d8884cde47d43d545c
  [entity jpa --class ~.model.StudentSurvey --testAutomatically]
```

Pretty handy. You can also force a commit right from the shell:

```
roo> git commit all --message "configured the big one"
```

And you can also revert to your last commit:

```
git revert last --message "undid the entity create - not needed."
Revert of commit HEAD~0 successful.
```

Finally, you can also review your Git log:

```
~.model.StudentSurvey roo> git log
---------- Start Git log ----------
commit id: dc95fbfcb94c528ec7846e95fe4b34b0157f66ca
message:   Revert "entity jpa --class ~.model.StudentSurvey
   --testAutomatically"

This reverts commit 87f7126c44029e99ed9345d8884cde47d43d545c


commit id: 87f7126c44029e99ed9345d8884cde47d43d545c
message:   entity jpa --class ~.model.StudentSurvey
   --testAutomatically

commit id: 4c655f6c43eb4e76e1cfa13919f213ca3466a5a7
message:   git setup
```

There are more features of this add-on, so consult your `addon info` output and experiment.

11.3.4 Upgrading Roo add-ons

You can use the `addon upgrade` command to search for and automatically install upgrades to Roo add-ons:

```
roo> addon upgrade available
The following add-ons / components are available for ➥
upgrade for level: ANY
----------------------------------------------------------------
[level: ANY] ...roo.addon.property.editor;1.1.4.RELEASE > ➥
             1.2.0.BUILD-SNAPSHOT
[level: ANY] ..roo.addon.gwt;1.1.4.RELEASE > 1.2.0.BUILD-SNAPSHOT
[level: ANY] ..roo.addon.propfiles;1.1.4.RELEASE > 1.2.0.BUILD-SN..
[level: ANY] ..roo.addon.web.selenium;1.1.4.RELEASE > ➥
             1.2.0.BUILD-SNAPSHOT
[level: ANY] ..roo.addon.solr;1.1.4.RELEASE > 1.2.0.BUILD-SNAPSHOT
[level: ANY] ..roo.addon.json;1.1.4.RELEASE > 1.2.0.BUILD-SNAPSHOT
[level: ANY] ..roo.addon.backup;1.1.4.RELEASE > 1.2.0.BUILD-SNAPSHOT
...
```

BEWARE OF UPDATING THE INTERNAL ROO ADD-ONS In the previous example, the add-ons from Roo 1.1.4 are upgradable to a build snapshot version of Roo 1.2.0. Due to a missing add-on, however, when we upgraded to 1.2.0, the Roo shell detected a problem and was no longer functional. If you accidentally upgrade your Roo artifacts and the shell won't start properly, you can go back to the original installed version by deleting the contents of the cache directory in your Roo installation directory.

You'll also lose any additional add-ons you've installed previously, so it's a good idea to store your third-party add-on installation scripts in your version control system and update them whenever you add a new approved add-on.

By default, the upgrade engine searches for any version, including releases, release candidates, and milestone releases. You can customize this, for example, by limiting to only release-level add-ons:

```
roo> addon upgrade settings --addonStabilityLevel RELEASE
Add-on Stability Level: RELEASE stored
```

Or you can list only available add-ons for your Roo shell release level:

```
roo> addon upgrade available
No add-ons / components are available for upgrade for level: RELEASE
```

This setting is stored between restarts, so if you want to experiment, make sure to reset it before searching for upgrades.

11.3.5 *Trusting PGP keys*

When a user installs add-ons using the addon command, Roo verifies whether or not the user trusts the add-on developer by checking whether they have trusted the developer's PGP key.

You can see the following list of trusted keys that are installed into your Roo environment by issuing the pgp key command:

```
roo> pgp list trusted keys

>>>> KEY ID: 0xBB0371CE <<<<
    More Info: http://keyserver.ubuntu.com/pks/lookup? ➥
               fingerprint=on&op=index&search=0xBB0371CE
    Created: 2010-Jul-11 17:29:06 +0000
    Fingerprint: eb25ea09869e3be5def83c43a9cb702ebb0371ce
    Algorithm: RSA_GENERAL
    User ID: Spring Roo <s2-roo@vmware.com>
      Signed By: Key 0x00B5050F (Ben Alex <balex@vmware.com>)
      Signed By: Key 0xBB0371CE (Spring Roo <s2-roo@vmware.com>)
    Subkey ID: 0x90BDE537 [RSA_GENERAL]
>>>> KEY ID: 0x6163CB9E <<<<
    More Info: http://keyserver.ubuntu.com/pks/lookup? ➥
               fingerprint=on&op=index&search=0x6163CB9E
    Created: 2010-Jun-09 06:07:56 +0000
    Fingerprint: 868df24600c3c8e4d999ea3584f200286163cb9e
    Algorithm: RSA_GENERAL
    User ID: Stefan Schmidt <schmidts@vmware.com>
      Signed By: Key 0x00B5050F (Ben Alex <balex@vmware.com>)
      Signed By: Key 0xEC67B395 (Alan Stewart <stewarta@vmware.com>
                 )
      Signed By: Key 0x6163CB9E (Stefan Schmidt <schmidts@vmware.co
                 m>)
    Subkey ID: 0x411B8828 [RSA_GENERAL]
...
```

You can permanently trust the keyholder of this key by issuing the pgp trust command:

```
roo> pgp trust --keyId 0x0E5BA660

Added trust for key:
```

```
>>>> KEY ID: 0x0E5BA660 <<<<
     More Info: http://keyserver.ubuntu.com/pks/lookup? ➥
               fingerprint=on&op=index&search=0x0E5BA660
     Created: 2010-Aug-05 14:43:59 +0000
     Fingerprint: f2b858c56bcbada85df77995c74ccbff0e5ba660
     Algorithm: DSA
     User ID: Stefan Bley <stefan.bley@saxsys.de>
        Signed By: Key 0x0E5BA660 (Stefan Bley <stefan.bley@saxsys.d
                   e>)
     Subkey ID: 0xB14BD4B7 [ELGAMAL_ENCRYPT]
```

This command, unlike `pgp automatic trust`, is a permanent decision and is kept within Roo's configuration. If you upgrade to a new version of Roo, you may have to redo your trust relationships. You can also untrust a PGP key:

```
roo> pgp untrust --keyId 0xACB27429
Revoked trust from key:
>>>> KEY ID: 0xACB27429 <<<<
     More Info: http://keyserver.ubuntu.com/pks/lookup? ➥
          fingerprint=on&op=index&search=0xACB27429
     Created: 2010-Jun-13 15:14:48 +0000
     Fingerprint: 8f19905b317143e44bd28ba83fec2947acb27429
     Algorithm: RSA_GENERAL
     User ID: Christian Tzolov <christian@tzolov.net>
          Signed By: Key 0xACB27429 - not locally trusted
     Subkey ID: 0xD9D8D1C2 [RSA_GENERAL]
```

11.3.6 Removing add-ons

To remove an add-on, use the `addon remove` command. This command is tab-completion aware, so if you aren't sure which add-on you want to remove, keep hitting [TAB] to autocomplete the `bundleSymbolicName` command-line property:

```
roo> addon remove --bundleSymbolicName ➥
   org.springframework.roo.addons.git
Successfully removed add-on:
org.springframework.roo.addons.git
```

> **ADD-ON REMOVAL DOESN'T ALWAYS REMOVE CODE** Code contributed by the add-on generally stays put. But nothing will keep it up to date, so you may want to use push-in refactoring to put the code under developer control again. As the add-on developer, you may wish to provide a `remove` command so that you can clean up after yourself before developers uninstall your add-on.

This command removes the artifact from the Roo installation's bundle cache directory.

11.4 Enough OSGi to be dangerous

Because all add-ons are written as OSGi bundles, it may help you to learn enough OSGi to be dangerous. For the bold, a trip into the OSGi specification, or Manning's *OSGi in Action*, is a good diversion, but you can also get started with merely a basic understanding of OSGi.

OSGi is a dynamic module system for Java. It allows Java applications to load, start, stop, update, and unload artifacts such as JARs and WARs on the fly, without stopping and restarting. Think of it as a dynamic, class-loading system that's smart enough to resolve complex dependencies. You use OSGi in many applications today, including Eclipse, which the SpringSource Tool Suite is based on, and which runs with a small application core under the Equinox OSGi container. The ServiceMix and Mule integration platforms have OSGi at their core so they can configure new integration services at runtime. The platform has been around for years and was originally developed to manage the modularity of applications on mobile devices.

We'll begin this investigation of OSGi with a little terminology.

11.4.1 *OSGi bundles and manifests*

OSGi bundles are JAR, WAR, or EAR files that contain a special file, META-INF/MANIFEST.MF, with some well-defined headers. To see these headers, open a Roo shell and type in

```
roo> osgi headers
```

You'll see a ton of output, broken up into sections by information about each bundle. Here's an excerpt of the contents of Roo's entity OSGi bundle:

```
...
Spring Roo - Addon - Entity (15)
--------------------------------
Bnd-LastModified = 1314712639731
Build-Jdk = 1.6.0_23
Built-By = roobuild
Bundle-Copyright = Copyright VMware, Inc. All Rights Reserved.
...
Bundle-Description = Support for the creation and management ⇒
    of domain entities.
Bundle-ManifestVersion = 2
Bundle-Name = Spring Roo - Addon - Entity
Bundle-SymbolicName = org.springframework.roo.addon.entity
Bundle-Vendor = VMware, Inc
Bundle-Version = 1.2.0.BUILD-SNAPSHOT
Created-By = Apache Maven Bundle Plugin
Export-Package = org.springframework.roo.addon.entity...
...
Import-Package = org.osgi.service.component;version="[1.1,2)",..
Manifest-Version = 1
Service-Component = OSGI-INF/serviceComponents.xml
Tool = Bnd-1.43.0
...
```

OSGi components export certain Java packages, using the `Export-Package` header. They also require other packages to function, as detailed by the `Import-Package` header. Every Roo add-on contains a manifest that describes the exposed packages, and is identified by both a human-readable `Bundle-Name`, and an identifier known as a `Bundle-SymbolicName`. You'll refer to the symbolic name wherever Roo asks you for a bundle's ID.

ACCESSING THE FELIX OSGI CONSOLE   For those OSGi experts among you, try to access the underlying Felix shell directly using the Roo shell command `osgi framework command` **felix-command**. All valid Felix command activities are valid here as well. Keep in mind that you're using OSGi only to expose and use components, so the utility of this command is limited.

11.4.2 Bundle lifecycle

OSGi bundles go through several lifecycle phases, including `resolved`, `installed`, `started`, and `stopped`. You start a bundle with the `osgi start` command. You stop one with `osgi stop`. You'll learn how to use these commands when you create an OSGi bundle.

Roo *activates* a bundle when you start it. At the time of activation, OSGi loads the component into memory. The Apache SCR feature exposes OSGi components marked with the `@Component` annotation, and injects any components into other OSGi components with the `@Reference` annotation. In this way, SCR-based OSGi components behave like the dependency injection model in Spring beans. However, OSGi components are stateful, whereas Spring's beans are stateless by default.

11.4.3 Viewing bundles in the OSGi container

You can use the `osgi ps` shell command to show the status of the bundles and add-ons installed in the container. For example, type in

```
roo> osgi ps
```

to bring back a list of all OSGi "processes" or active bundles. The following shows some example output:

```
roo> osgi ps
START LEVEL 99
  ID   State      Level  Name
[ 0] [Active ] [   0] System Bundle (3.0.7)
[ 1] [Active ] [   1] jansi (1.5)
[ 2] [Active ] [   1] Apache Felix Bundle Repository (1.6.4)
[ 3] [Active ] [   1] Apache Felix iPOJO (1.6.8)
[ 4] [Active ] [   1] Apache Felix Log Service (1.0.0)
[ 5] [Active ] [   1] Apache Felix Declarative Services (1.6.0)
[ 6] [Active ] [   1] Apache Felix Shell Service (1.4.2)
[ 7] [Active ] [   1] Spring Roo - Addon - Backup (1.1.4.RELEASE)
[ 8] [Active ] [   1] Spring Roo - Addon - @Configurable Support
                      (1.1.4.RELEASE)
[ 9] [Active ] [   1] Spring Roo - Addon - Creator (1.1.4.RELEASE)
[10] [Active ] [   1] Spring Roo - Addon - Database Reverse
                      Engineering (1.1.4.RELEASE)
...
```

Each OSGi bundle is listed in the previous output, along with an ID, state, starting level, and name. You can install any OSGi JAR file, and you may need to if your Roo shell commands have to interact with a Java library that's not already installed in your Roo shell, such as a JDBC driver.

11.4.4 *Starting and uninstalling a bundle*

To start an OSGi module, use the `osgi start` command, passing it the URL of an OSGi-ified JAR file. If you've developed an add-on and have access to the JAR file, you may mount it in this way:

```
roo> osgi start --url file:///Users/kenrimple/[...]/ ➥
     org.sillyweasel.maven.reports.addon-0.1.0.BUILD-SNAPSHOT.jar
```

If your OSGi bundle happens to be configured as a Roo add-on, the shell will initialize it when started and add any configured commands. The add-on's JAR file and configuration settings will be installed in the `cache` directory of the Roo installation, and will be available until removed from the system.

You can use the `osgi uninstall` command to unload the same Roo add-on bundle. You'll need to type in the bundle's symbolic name:

```
roo> osgi uninstall --bundleSymbolicName ➥
   org.sillyweasel.maven.reports.addon
```

This will remove the bundle from your Roo shell. If you'd rather update it from the latest source file, use `osgi update`, and tell it which bundle and what location to reload it from:

```
roo> osgi update --bundle org.sillyweasel.maven.reports.addon ➥
     --url file:///path..to../org.sillyweasel.maven.reports....jar
```

> **WHY NOT USE THE OSGI INSTALL COMMAND?** This command loads only an OSGi bundle into your shell—it doesn't start it. You'll have to issue the `osgi start` command afterward. It's easier to load and start in one step with `osgi start`. If you accidentally installed a bundle using the install variant, you can start it by issuing the `osgi start` command. Roo doesn't currently provide an `osgi stop` command—see Issue ROO-2734 in https://jira.springsource.org for details on a potential fix.

That's enough OSGi to be dangerous now. You're ready to write your own add-ons with Roo.

11.5 *Types of Roo add-ons*

Roo lets you create your own add-ons, using projects built using the Roo shell `addon create` command. There are four variants. Table 11.1 outlines the differences between them, and their pros and cons.

Table 11.1   Roo add-ons: using the `addon create` command

Add-on type	Features	Pros and cons
`simple`	Installs commands. Performs operations such as file manipulation and installation of tag libraries and other files.	*Pros:* Easy to understand; contains simple example code to get a minimal example working quickly. *Cons:* Limited features, and managing dependencies requires use of more services and features.

Table 11.1   Roo add-ons: using the addon create command *(continued)*

Add-on type	Features	Pros and cons
advanced	Installs commands. Performs operations. Manipulates build configuration. Installs annotations and ITDs. Watches code for changes and reacts when annotations are added or deleted.	*Pros:* Extremely powerful; the sky is the limit. *Cons:* Complicated, and uses a number of non-integrated APIs and services. Developer needs to understand OSGi, Felix, and Aspect-J ITDs to get the most out of the add-on.
wrapper	Installs a Maven artifact as an OSGi module. Installs features needed by other plug-ins, such as a database driver for the reverse engineering add-on.	*Pros:* Simple to configure. Command can also pull in transitory dependencies with some adjustments to the Maven POM file. *Cons:* None. If you're installing a Roo shell command that needs a feature in a Java library, such as a JDBC driver or an email service provider, this is the one option for installing the library.
i18n	Defines an installable language for your applications. This artifact defines a language name, flag, locale, and a message source properties file to install a language into your Roo shell.	*Pros:* Allows for bundling of additional languages into your application, which then can be assumed into your user interface, if working with the Roo scaffolded web template design. *Cons:* Useful when paired with the scaffolded user interface, but may have less utility than adding the locale to your current message source.

All four add-on types will be covered in this two-chapter series. The wrapper add-on type creates JARs such as those used in chapter 4, section 4, "Reverse engineering your database," for installing a database driver into the Roo shell.

It's time to start experimenting with your own add-ons. In this chapter, we'll get you started by covering how to wrap a standard JAR and provide it to the Roo shell using the OSGi wrapper add-on. We'll create an i18n add-on to provide a Norwegian translation of the Roo scaffold labels. Then we'll build a simple add-on that installs jQuery, jQuery UI, and some replacement tags in the Roo tag library. Finally, in the next chapter, we'll branch out and create an add-on to provide access to the Coffee-Script language, which we'll use to simplify some of the JavaScript files.

11.6 Roo wrapper add-ons

A wrapper add-on takes a given Maven artifact and wraps it with the proper OSGi MANIFEST.MF entries, delivering it as a new JAR to be used by the Roo shell. The JAR may then be started as an OSGi bundle with osgi start and accessed by other Roo add-ons. For example, to wrap the Apache math library, you can search for the proper Maven artifact information on http://search.maven.org, as shown in figure 11.1.

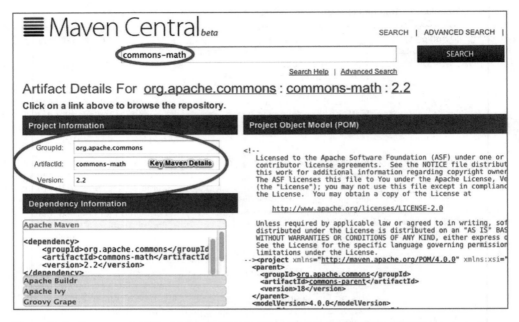

Figure 11.1   You can use https://search.maven.org to search for any public artifact. In our search, we found version 2.2 of Apache's `commons-math` and will use it to construct our wrapper class.

Now, let's use the `groupId`, `artifactId`, and `version` from the Maven repository search to create a `wrapper` add-on. Create an empty directory named `commons-math-wrapper`, navigate to it, and open a Roo shell. Issue the following add-on project creation command:

```
roo>   addon create wrapper --groupId org.apache.commons ➥
        --artifactId commons-math --version 2.2 ➥
        --topLevelPackage org.rooinaction.bundles ➥
        --vendorName "Apache Software Foundation" ➥
        --licenseUrl "http://www.apache.org/licenses/LICENSE-2.0" ➥
        --projectName commons-math-wrapper
```

Roo creates a new project that you can use to build your add-on. The final artifact name will be the provided `topLevelPackage` parameter, coupled with the `artifactId` and `version` parameters, plus ".0001." Now, you'll create the wrapper artifact. To do this, issue this Roo shell command:

```
roo> perform command --mavenCommand bundle:bundle
```

Once Roo completes the bundling process, the wrapper will be built in `target`, and the previous example becomes `org.rooinaction.bundles.commons-math-2.2.0001.jar`. You can now install this bundle into the Roo shell:

```
roo> osgi start --url file:///path-to-project/target/ ➥
        org.rooinaction.bundles.commons-math-2.2.0001.jar
```

The `commons-math` API is available to all Roo add-ons that need it. You can use this technique to expose new JDBC drivers to the Roo shell, which you can use to run the database reverse engineering command discussed in chapter 4.[1]

11.7 Adding a language to Roo with i18n

You can define a special project, known as a *Roo localization add-on*, that contains the standard Roo web framework localization file, messages.properties, which you can translate for your required language. You'll need to supply a fully translated properties file, an icon for the language, and the details[2] for the locale to support, such as the language name.

For this application, you'll create a language localization add-on to support Norwegian, which isn't provided out of the box. You can create a new localization project by localizing your language file, providing your icon PNG, creating a new directory, and issuing the following Roo command in the empty directory:

```
roo> addon create i18n ➡
--topLevelPackage org.rooinaction.addons.i18n.norwegian ➡
--locale no ➡
--messageBundle messages_no.properties ➡
--language norwegian ➡
--projectName rooinaction-norwegian-language-addon ➡
--flaggraphic norway.png
```

In this example, Roo was able to look up the flag for Norway using a web service and download the `norway.png` file itself. For unknown flags, you'll have to find a legally distributable flag image, convert it to PNG format with a size of 16-by-11 pixels, and place it in the project root directory.

From this point on, the project files will be contained in the src/main/resources directory of this project, under the package specified by the `topLevelPackage` parameter. You can then build the application with `mvn package`. If the add-on builds properly, you can install it into your Roo shell with this command:

```
roo> osgi start --url file:///path-to-target-dir/ ➡
      org.rooinaction.addons.i18n.norwegian-0.1.0.BUILD-SNAPSHOT.jar
```

To use your add-on, switch back to your web project and issue this Roo command:

```
roo> web mvc language --code no
```

Before you create your own language add-on, use the public add-on searching feature to see if someone else has already provided one.

---

[1] Supporting Oracle's JDBC drivers requires you to create a wrapped OSGi library, because Oracle currently restricts downloads of its drivers from anywhere other than Oracle itself. Review the issue at http://mng.bz/ 26am.

[2] For this section, we used http://translatify.appspot.com/ to translate the properties file into Norwegian. We had to manually extract the HTML table of translated code because the zip file returned was incomplete. This application no longer functions in the way it was used, so you'll need to find your own translation service.

11.8   *A simple add-on: jQuery UI*

Roo uses the Dojo form library for all client-side form validation and widgets, as we discussed in chapter 7. Many developers have embraced the more widely adopted jQuery library and a wide variety of components contained within it. The Dojo form library poses a challenge for these developers, because it chooses both a JavaScript library and a widget library for them.

Roo allows add-on developers to modify files in the installation, so it's easy to modify the platform to suit your needs. Let's build an add-on to set up a jQuery-based frontend. You'll focus on several major tasks:

- Installing the jQuery JavaScript library
- Installing the jQuery UI component library, styles, and images
- Adjusting the `load-scripts.tagx` tag to load each of the libraries and the stylesheet

All of these tasks can be accomplished easily using a Roo add-on. You can create an add-on project to hold your customizations and test them with a simple MVC project. Let's start by creating the add-on project.

11.8.1   *Creating the jQuery UI add-on*

You develop add-ons using the `add-on create` command, which generates a new project. First you'll create the directory to hold your project:

```
$ mkdir jquery-addon
$ cd jquery-addon
```

Next, create the add-on project. You'll use the simple add-on command:

```
$ roo
roo> addon create simple
    --topLevelPackage org.rooinaction.addons.jqueryui ➥
    --projectName jqueryui ➥
    --description "An add-on to install jQuery UI"
```

The output will indicate that the simple add-on has been generated as a Maven project, and organized by the usual directories, src/main/java, src/main/resources, src/test/java, and others. The generated add-on contains a sample component, named `Jqueryaddon`, which will need to be replaced. It includes

- An interface-driven `Operations` class, `JqueryuiOperationsImpl`, and its base interface `JqueryuiOperations`. This component defines methods that are executed in response to Roo shell commands.
- A commands class, `JqueryuiCommands`, which implements the `CommandMarker` interface and defines the commands exposed by the add-on. This class contains methods annotated with two annotations, `@CliAvailabilityIndicator` and `@CliCommand`, which define whether your add-on commands are available, and which methods to call in your add-on operations class.

- An enum, `JqueryuiPropertyName`, which is an example of an enumerated property that can be sent to a command. Commands such as `persistence setup` use this component for the `--database` options, such as `HYPERSONIC _PERSISTENT` and `ORACLE`.
- A set of tags, located in the src/main/resources directory, for potential inclusion into the consuming project.
- A legal license agreement file, which you can replace with the license your project will use.
- An assembly.xml file, which provides the ability to package the entire project, including dependencies, into a zip file.

You'll need to customize these files for your purposes, so that you install the proper commands to set up the add-on.

But before you do this, you have to do some cleanup, because Roo delivers more code than you need. You'll need to remove some files you aren't using to clean up the library. Delete the tag files in the org/rooinaction/jqueryaddon directory of src/ main/resources, leaving the directory there for use by your new tags. Also, delete the `JqueryaddonPropertyName.java` enum class; you won't be using that one either:

```
$ rm src/main/resources/org/rooinaction/addons/jqueryui/*.tagx
$ rm src/main/java/org/rooinaction/addons/jqueryui/➥
                            JqueryuiPropertyName.java
```

Now, take a moment to define your goals for the add-on.

11.8.2 *The jQuery UI add-on goals*

You'll want your Roo add-on to provide two commands:

- `jquery api install`—Installs the jQuery JavaScript library in a JavaScript library directory, /js, within the web application, and adds a reference to it to the JSPX tag, `load-script.tagx`, which adds the library to the Roo page layout.
- `jquery ui install`—Installs the jQuery UI library, graphics, and stylesheet, and edits the `load-script.tagx` library to add the framework to the Roo page layout.

After executing these commands, developers can use the jQuery and jQuery UI JavaScript libraries in their applications.

To develop this add-on, you'll need to create the proper components in your add-on project, and copy the appropriate file resources to the src/main/resources directory, under the project package directory, org/rooina/jqueryaddon. Let's start by defining the operations that the add-on will perform.

11.8.3 *Defining the jQuery install operations*

First, you'll set up your operations interface. You'll start by editing the existing `JqueryaddonOperations.java` interface. Replace the contents with the following:

```
package org.rooinaction.jqueryaddon;

public interface JqueryaddonOperations {

  boolean isInstalljQueryCommandAvailable();
  boolean isInstalljQueryUICommandAvailable();
  void installjQueryApi();
  void installjQueryUIApi();
}
```

You've defined two command methods, one for each of the Roo shell commands: installjQueryApi(), which installs the jQuery API, and installjQueryUIApi(), which installs the jQuery UI API. You also defined two Boolean methods, installj-QueryApi() and installjQueryUIApi(), which are executed by the Roo shell when it checks whether to make each of the commands available.

Next, edit the JqueryaddonOperationsImpl.java implementation class. As you'll see in the following listing, you'll gut everything but the first two lines of the class, and change them to extend the Roo support class AbstractOperations, which provides a few helper methods you'll take advantage of during implementation.

> **Listing 11.1   Setting up your operations implementation**

```
package org.rooinaction.jqueryaddon;

import org.apache.felix.scr.annotations.Component;
import org.apache.felix.scr.annotations.Reference;
import org.apache.felix.scr.annotations.Service;
import org.springframework.roo.classpath.operations.AbstractOperations;
import org.springframework.roo.project.Path;
import java.io.*;

@Component                                              ❶ Adds
@Service                                                  helper
public class JqueryuiOperationsImpl extends AbstractOperations    methods
        implements JqueryuiOperations {

  @Reference
  private ProjectOperations projectOperations;         ❷ Injects
                                                          Roo
  @Reference                                              services
  private PathResolver pathResolver;

}
```

When building this class, let your IDE find the imports for you to save time.

You added two annotations, @Component and @Service. But these aren't the Spring annotations; they're from the Service Component Registry (SCR) API, which is part of the Apache Felix OSGi container, on which Roo is based. Your add-on operations class is an OSGi service, which makes it visible to Roo for inclusion into the system.

The class now extends AbstractOperations ❶, a helpful abstract class that provides some project management facilities. You also injected references to two Roo OSGi services: instances of ProjectOperations and PathResolver, which you'll use to access components that change your project configuration ❷.

ROO AND OSGI: CONFIGURING ROO AT RUNTIME Remember, Roo add-ons are OSGi bundles—they can be added and removed from running Roo shell environments at will, and these annotations identify this class as an OSGi component that exports OSGi services, which can be consumed by other OSGi components, such as the Roo shell.

Unless you have to add a class or a library to the Roo runtime path, such as a JDBC driver, you won't need to restart after installing new Roo add-ons. Consult your add-on's home page for details.

Let's build the first Roo add-on command method—the one that installs jQuery itself.

11.8.4 Copying jQuery to the web application

It's time to write the `installjQueryApi()` method, which copies jQuery to your project. Add the following method to the `JqueryuiOperations` class. The following listing shows your implementation.

Listing 11.2 The `installjQueryApi()` method

```
public void installjQueryApi() {
  String pathIdentifier = pathResolver.getFocusedIdentifier(
      Path.SRC_MAIN_WEBAPP, "/js");
  copyDirectoryContents("js/jquery/jquery-1.5.1.min.js",         ❶ Get full
      pathIdentifier, true);                                          path

  String targetDirectory = pathResolver.getFocusedIdentifier(
      Path.SRC_MAIN_WEBAPP, "WEB-INF/tags/util");

  String loadScriptsTagFile = targetDirectory + "/load-scripts.tagx";

  InputStream loadScriptsTagFileStream = fileManager
      .getInputStream(loadScriptsTagFile);

  Document document =
      XmlUtils.readXml(loadScriptsTagFileStream);
                                                                  ❷ No
  buildAndAddJSNode(document, "/js/jquery-1.5.1.min.js");            cleanup

  fileManager.createOrUpdateTextFileIfRequired(loadScriptsTagFile,
      XmlUtils.nodeToString(document), false);
  }
```

This method first copies the `jquery-1.5.1.min.js` file from the `org/rooina/jqueryaddon/js/jquery` directory of `src/main/resources`. You'll use the `pathResolver` you set up at the top of your class to find the absolute path to the web application's `/js` directory. This will be created if it doesn't already exist.[3] You then use the `copyDirectoryContents` method ❶, which comes from the `AbstractOperations` Roo add-on class. It uses Roo's `FileManager` component to perform the copy operation.

---

[3] You'll need to download the jQuery library from http://jquery.org and place it in the previously mentioned directory for this to work.

Note that the method `XmlUtils.readXml(InputStream)` will automatically close the stream, so you don't need to do any cleanup. The same holds for the `fileManager` method `createOrUpdateTextFileIfRequired` ❷, as it performs bulk operations to stream the file and is responsible for its own cleanup.

> **USE THE FILEMANAGER FOR FILE ACCESS**   Because the `FileManager` can automatically undo operations if your command throws an exception, it makes it easier to roll back your changes to the file system. Use it whenever you have to manipulate files.

To properly refer to the destination path, which must be absolute, you use the `Path-Resolver` ❶, a helper object from the Roo `projectOperations` helper, injected into your class as a `@Reference` earlier in section 11.8.3. This component has visibility into the currently running Roo shell, which gives you the proper OS path to the file.

This class will not compile yet; you must define a helper method next, `buildAnd-AddJSNode`, to install your JavaScript tags.

11.8.5 *Installing jQuery in JavaScript*

Next, you need to edit the load-script.tagx JSPX tag file, and use the HTML `<script>` tag to install the command. You loaded the XML source for this file into a DOM `Document` instance in the previous `installjQueryApi()` method.

You'll add a new `<script>` tag to the end of the document, which you access via the document's DOM method `getFirstChild()`. The `buildAndAddJSNode(document, path, var)` method does the work for you:

```
private void buildAndAddJSNode(Document doc, String var) {
  XmlElementBuilder builder = new XmlElementBuilder("script", doc);
  builder.addAttribute("type", "text/javascript");
  builder.addAttribute("src", var);
  addComment(doc, builder);
  Element springJSTag = builder.build();
  doc.getDocumentElement().appendChild(springJSTag);
}
```

Some HTML browsers can't deal with bodiless script tags, so you have to add a comment to the tag using the helper `addComment(document, builder)` method:

```
private void addComment(Document document, XmlElementBuilder builder) {
  Comment comment = document.createComment("required for FF3, Opera");
  builder.addChild(comment);
}
```

This method emits the following tags to the end of the script tag file:

```
<script src="/js/jquery-1.5.1.min.js" type="text/javascript">
  <!--required for FF3 and Opera-->
</script>
```

You're almost finished. But there's one more task for this command—defining whether it's available or not at the time the user hits [TAB].

11.8.6 *Defining the availability of the jquery setup*

Each time someone uses tab completion, or the Roo shell changes the configuration in some way, all Roo components are asked whether their commands are available. The add-on can conditionally expose their commands and hide them when they don't make sense, such as when trying to add a web feature before the web framework is installed.

You need to determine when to show your `jquery` commands. To do so you'll implement the `isInstalljQueryCommandAvailable()` method, which returns a Boolean result:

```
public boolean isInstalljQueryCommandAvailable() {
  String jsLocation = pathResolver.getFocusedIdentifier(
      Path.SRC_MAIN_WEBAPP, "/js");

  return fileManager.findMatchingAntPath(
      jsLocation + "**/jquery-1.*.min.js").isEmpty();
}
```

You use the injected Roo `pathResolver` to determine the proper path to a file starting with jquery-1, and ending with .min.js. You could have searched for your exact version, but then you wouldn't be able to detect a user-upgraded jQuery library. Obviously, this issue will come up when someone mounts a future 2.x jQuery library, or names it differently.

> **WHAT IS THE *FOCUSED* IDENTIFIER?** You may wonder what the `focused` fragment in the `pathResolver` method refers to. Back in chapter 2, we discussed how you can create multimodule Roo projects. Asking for the focused project or identifier scopes your request for the module you're working on, or the top-level module if you either don't have modules or aren't focused on one. There are also methods to ask for the top-level project so you can affect changes at that level.

Now, if the shell user has installed jQuery before, the script file will be available in the 'js' directory of the web application, so it should return `false`. Otherwise, it should return `true`, which will allow the command to become visible in the shell.

> **THAT'S HOW THEY HIDE COMMANDS** Add-ons can provide visibility (or invisibility) of shell commands. For example, the Spring MVC add-on is always present, but doesn't make itself active until you have a valid Roo project. The entity add-on doesn't allow you to create an entity until you have a persistence context configured in your application. Take a good look at the existing Roo add-ons from the Roo project itself to learn how you can take advantage of this.

Now let's look at the second level of JavaScript enhancements: installing the jQuery UI.

### 11.8.7	*Installing the jquery UI setup command*

Some developers are happy working with Dojo for their user interface widgets, but they want jQuery for other purposes. Others may want it all and will choose to install both. Your add-on gives developers a choice. You'll configure another command, jquery UI setup, to install the UI library as well as assets such as stylesheets and graphics.

First, you'll detect whether you're able to install the command itself. You have to check whether the application is a web application and then verify that you've installed the jQuery library itself. This is a variant of the check for jQuery in section 11.8.6 earlier in this chapter:

```
public boolean isInstalljQueryUICommandAvailable() {

  String jsLocation = pathResolver.getFocusedIdentifier(
      Path.SRC_MAIN_WEBAPP, "/js");
  if (projectOperations.isFocusedProjectAvailable()) {
    boolean hasJqueryUI = !fileManager.findMatchingAntPath(
        jsLocation + "/jquery-ui-*.min.js").isEmpty();

    return !isInstalljQueryCommandAvailable() && !hasJqueryUI;
  } else {
    return false;
  }
}
```

Check whether the /js directory in your src/main/webapp project folder contains a jQuery UI main JavaScript file. If it does, and you can't install the jQuery library (referring back to the jQuery detection method), you can install the jQuery UI.

Installing the jQuery UI is a little tricky. It comes with multiple JavaScript files, a number of images, and a stylesheet. So your installjQueryUIApi method in the following listing is a bit longer, but not more complex.

**Listing 11.3	Installing the jQuery UI**

```
public void installjQueryUIApi() {
    copyDirectoryContents("js/jqueryui/*.js",
        pathResolver.getFocusedIdentifier(Path.SRC_MAIN_WEBAPP, "/js"),
        true);
    copyDirectoryContents("images/*.png",
        pathResolver.getFocusedIdentifier(Path.SRC_MAIN_WEBAPP,
            "/images"), true);
    copyDirectoryContents("styles/*.css",
        pathResolver.getFocusedIdentifier(Path.SRC_MAIN_WEBAPP,
            "/styles"), true);

    String targetDirectory = pathResolver.getFocusedIdentifier(
        Path.SRC_MAIN_WEBAPP, "/WEB-INF/tags/util");

    String loadScriptsTagFile = targetDirectory + "/load-scripts.tagx";

    InputStream loadScriptsTagFileStream = fileManager
        .getInputStream(loadScriptsTagFile);
```

```
Document document = XmlUtils.readXml(loadScriptsTagFileStream);

buildAndAddJSNode(document,
    "/js/jqueryui/jquery-ui-1.8.14.custom.min.js");
buildAndAddJSNode(document,
    "/js/jqueryui/jquery.validate.min.js");
buildAndAddJSNode(document,
    "/js/jqueryui/additional-methods.min.js");
buildAndAddCSSNode(document,
    "/styles/jquery-ui-1.8.14.custom.css");

IOUtils.closeQuietly(loadScriptsTagFileStream);

fileManager.createOrUpdateTextFileIfRequired(loadScriptsTagFile,
    XmlUtils.nodeToString(document), false);
}
```

You also need to add another helper method to this class—one that adds a CSS node to the load-script.tagx file:

```
private void buildAndAddCSSNode(Document document, String fileName) {
  XmlElementBuilder builder = new XmlElementBuilder("link", document);
  builder.addAttribute("href", fileName);
  builder.addAttribute("rel", "stylesheet");
  builder.addAttribute("type", "text/css");
  addComment(document, builder);
  Element springCSSTag = builder.build();
  document.getDocumentElement().appendChild(springCSSTag);
}
```

You need to take one more step: you have to tell the Roo shell that these commands exist. That's where the JqueryuiCommands.java class comes in.

11.8.8 *Installing your commands*

To make your commands visible to the shell, you need to define your add-on to the Roo shell system. The JqueryuiCommands.java class does this for you. This class must

- Implement the CommandMarker interface.
- Inject an instance of the JqueryuiOperations class via the OSGi @Reference annotation. This is similar to the Spring @Autowired annotation, but works in an OSGi container. Because you have an implementation of this class, Felix will find it and inject the instance, which in this case is JqueryuiOperations-Impl.java.
- Provide at least one Boolean method annotated with @CliAvailability-Indicator, which will return whether a method, or a set of methods, is available to the Roo shell.
- Provide at least one method annotated with @CliCommand, which defines the method to execute in your command component for a given Roo shell command. This ties the two components together.

The following listing defines your commands class, JqueryuiCommands.

Listing 11.4   The commands definition: JqueryuiCommands

```
package org.rooinaction.addons.jqueryui;

import org.apache.felix.scr.annotations.Component;
import org.apache.felix.scr.annotations.Reference;
import org.apache.felix.scr.annotations.Service;
import org.springframework.roo.shell.CliAvailabilityIndicator;
import org.springframework.roo.shell.CliCommand;
import org.springframework.roo.shell.CommandMarker;

import java.util.logging.Logger;

@Component
@Service
public class JqueryuiCommands implements CommandMarker {

  @Reference private JqueryuiOperations operations;

  @CliAvailabilityIndicator("jquery api setup")
   public boolean isApiInstallCommandAvailable() {
     return operations.isInstalljQueryCommandAvailable();
     }

  @CliAvailabilityIndicator("jquery ui setup")
   public boolean isInstalljQueryUIAvailable() {
     return operations.isInstalljQueryUICommandAvailable();
   }

  @CliCommand(value = "jquery api setup", help="provide jquery API")
   public void installjQueryApi() {
     operations.installjQueryApi();
   }

  @CliCommand(value = "jquery ui setup", help="provide jqueryui")
   public void setupjQueryUIApi() {
     operations.setupjQueryUIApi();
   }
}
```

❶ Inject delegate

This class is used by the Roo shell every time a user attempts the tab completion mechanism, or types in the name of a command directly. Roo calls any @CliAvailbilityIndicator methods exposed in running add-ons to see whether they respond to the provided command. If a user executes a command, and the indicator method returns true, Roo executes the method annotated with @CliCommand with the same text.

This CommandMarker class forwards the command request to the Operations class, which OSGi injects for you using the @Reference annotated operations variable. For the setupjQueryApi() method, you delegate to the same method name in the JqueryuiOperationsImpl implementation. You'll see that you refer to the injected class ❶ via the interface, JqueryuiOperations, as you would using Spring's dependency injection features.

DO YOU NEED A COMMANDMARKER AND AN OPERATIONS CLASS? No, you don't. But your class will be bloated with methods for both types of operations, so unless the add-on is small, we recommend you separate the implementation of the add-on from exposure to commands by the add-on.

You'll install your add-on and put it through its paces next.

11.8.9 Building and installing the add-on

You can build your add-on the usual way, using `mvn package` to compile and turn it into a JAR file. Any JUnit tests you write will be executed, as usual. Please note that, at this time, Spring Roo doesn't have explicit support for writing any sort of Roo integration tests in the Felix OSGi container. The way you test add-ons is to install them in a test project.

You're ready to build your add-on:

```
roo> perform package
```

Roo has attached additional steps to your Maven packaging stage, including the generation and installation of OSGi entries in the META-INF/MANIFEST.MF file contained within the JAR, as shown in the next listing.

> **Listing 11.5 The META-INF/MANIFEST.MF file**

```
Manifest-Version: 1.0
Export-Package: org.rooinaction.addons.jqueryui;uses:="org.springframew
 ork.roo.shell,org.springframework.roo.classpath.operations,org.springf
 ramework.roo.project,org.springframework.roo.support.util,org.springfr
 amework.roo.process.manager,org.w3c.dom"
Built-By: krimple
Tool: Bnd-1.15.0
Bundle-Name: jqueryui
Created-By: Apache Maven Bundle Plugin
Bundle-Copyright: Copyright Your project/company name goes here (used
 in copyright and vendor information in the manifest). All Rights Rese
 rved.
Bundle-Vendor: Your project/company name goes here (used in copyright
 and vendor information in the manifest)
Build-Jdk: 1.6.0_26
Bundle-Version: 0.0.1.BUILD-SNAPSHOT
Bnd-LastModified: 1311435382474
Bundle-ManifestVersion: 2
Bundle-License: http://www.gnu.org/copyleft/gpl.html
Bundle-Description: Installs jQuery UI
Bundle-DocURL: http://www.rimple.com/sillyweasel
Bundle-SymbolicName: org.rooinaction.addons.jqueryui
Import-Package: org.springframework.roo.classpath.operations;version="
 [1.2,2)",org.springframework.roo.process.manager;version="[1.2,2)",or
 g.springframework.roo.project;version="[1.2,2)",org.springframework.r
 oo.shell;version="[1.2,2)",org.springframework.roo.support.util;versi
 on="[1.2,2)",org.w3c.dom
```

How did Roo know to build an OSGi bundle here? Because add-ons aren't standard JAR or WAR projects; rather, they're defined in the pom.xml file with the packaging type of `bundle`, and are configured using a Maven plug-in, `maven-bundle-plugin`, which sets up the appropriate entries in the manifest. Let's take a look at the relevant sections in the pom.xml file:

```xml
<?xml version="1.0" encoding="UTF-8" standalone="no"?>
<project ...>
...
  <artifactId>org.rooinaction.addons.jqueryui</artifactId>
...
  <packaging>bundle</packaging>
...
  <build>
    <plugins>
      <plugin>
        <groupId>org.apache.felix</groupId>
        <artifactId>maven-bundle-plugin</artifactId>
        <version>2.3.4</version>
        <extensions>true</extensions>
        <configuration>
          <instructions>
            <Bundle-SymbolicName>
              ${project.artifactId}
            </Bundle-SymbolicName>
            <Bundle-Copyright>
              Copyright ${project.organization.name}.
              All Rights Reserved.</Bundle-Copyright>
            <Bundle-DocURL>${project.url}</Bundle-DocURL>
          </instructions>
          ...
        </configuration>
      </plugin>
    </plugins>
  </build>
...
</project>
```

Anyone who's experimented with OSGi modules in the past will welcome Roo's use of BND tool (see http://mng.bz/D593). Although you didn't write the OSGi manifest file yourself, Roo used BND to put it together for you. OSGi expects you to explain which libraries you're making available to consumers of the add-on (`Export-Package:`); which ones you'll need to mount the add-on (`Import-Package:`); and other information, such as the `Bundle-Name`, a human-readable name, and the `Bundle-SymbolicName`, the name used to uniquely identify the bundle in the Roo shell.

You'll note that the packages from libraries used in the source code, such as `org.w3c.dom` and `org.springframework.roo.support.util`, are listed in both the import and export entries. If you'd like to customize these settings, you can adjust them in the pom.xml file, in the build/plugins/plugin section.

For example, to exclude the export of `org.w3c.dom` from your add-on so that it doesn't get installed in the container automatically, change the bundle to use the `Export-Package` tag:

```
<Export-Package>!org.w3c.dom</Export-Package>
```

This becomes important in more complex add-ons, because the Roo shell will take BND's defaults and export all packages found in the source code.

To install your add-on, you'll use the `osgi start` command:

```
roo> osgi start --url path-to-target-dir/ ➥
    org.rooinaction.addons.jqueryui-0.0.1.BUILD-SNAPSHOT.jar
```

You can verify the installation by using the `osgi ps` command; your add-on will appear at the bottom of the list:

```
roo> osgi ps
...
[  72] [Active      ] [    1] jqueryui (0.0.1.BUILD-SNAPSHOT)
```

You'll also see your add-on in the `[TAB]` completion in the Roo shell, because it exposes the `jquery` commands.

11.8.10 Installing jQuery in your project

Now for the piece de resistance: you'll need to define a new application and install the add-on in the Roo shell for your `jquery` commands to appear. You'll start by creating a `jqueryui-test` Roo application:

```
$ mkdir jqueryui-test
$ cd jqueryui-test
$ roo
...
roo> project
    --topLevelPackage org.rooinaction.addons.demo.jqueryuitest ➥
    --projectName jqueryui-test
```

Now you'll add persistence and web support:

```
jpa setup --database HYPERSONIC_PERSISTENT --provider HIBERNATE
web mvc setup
```

Finally, tell the shell to set up your jQuery API and jQuery UI library:

```
roo> jquery api setup
Created SRC_MAIN_WEBAPP/js
Created SRC_MAIN_WEBAPP/js/jquery-1.5.1.min.js
Updated SRC_MAIN_WEBAPP/WEB-INF/tags/util/load-scripts.tagx
roo> jquery ui setup
Created SRC_MAIN_WEBAPP/js/additional-methods.min.js
Created SRC_MAIN_WEBAPP/js/jquery-ui-1.8.14.custom.min.js
... [images, css files]
Updated SRC_MAIN_WEBAPP/WEB-INF/tags/util/load-scripts.tagx
roo>
```

To verify, take a look at the `load-scripts.tagx` script in src/main/webapp/WEB-INF/ tags. You'll see that jQuery and jQuery UI JavaScript entries have been added, and that the jQuery UI theme stylesheet has been mounted. Your add-on worked, and it not only installed jQuery support, it also reconfigured the application to support it.

Finally, review the contents of src/main/webapp/js, src/main/webapp/images, and src/main/webapp/styles to see the new artifacts.

11.8.11   *Using the jQuery UI in your application*

Let's modify a tag in the generated Roo tag libraries to use a jQuery UI widget, instead of a Dojo one. You'll edit the tag library file tags/util/panel.tagx, replacing the Dojo `TitlePane` widget with a jQuery UI `Accordion`. Replace the DIV section and the Dojo install script with the following code:

```
<div id="_title_${sec_id}_id">
  <h3>${sec_title}</h3>
  <div>
    <jsp:doBody />
  </div>
</div>
<script type="text/javascript">
  $(document).ready(function() {
      $("#_title_${sec_id}_id").accordion();
    });
</script>
```

The jQuery `$(document).ready()` method executes the script after the page loads, in a manner similar to Dojo's initializing method, `dojo.addOnLoad()`. The elegance of jQuery is evident here: the $ method on the next line selects the DIV in the previous example by its id, and then applies the jQuery UI `accordion` function to it, which styles the component with a border. Figure 11.2 shows the effect.

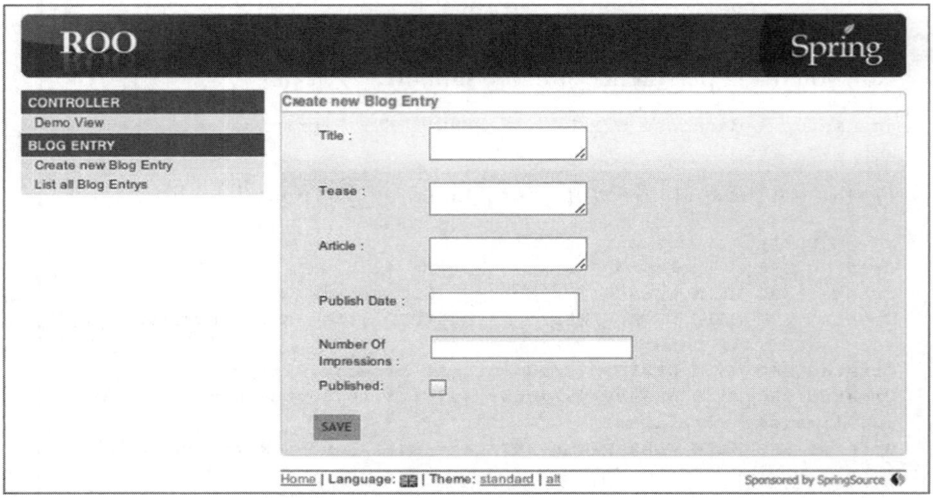

Figure 11.2   A jQuery UI–styled page

UPDATING YOUR ADD-ON   To update your add-on, follow the parameters in the `osgi update` command:

```
osgi update --bundleSymbolicName org.rooinaction.addons.jqueryui ➥
    --url path..to..jar../
```

You can take this add-on further. For example, using the previous technique, you could replace all of the Roo standard tags with jQuery UI widgets, or even install other commands to provide and use other jQuery plug-ins. You could then install those tags with a separate Roo shell command, such as the `jquery tags setup`. The possibilities are endless.

11.9   Summary

In this chapter, we've looked at how to find and install Roo add-ons, and we've discussed how they are built on top of OSGi. We used the `pgp trust` command to allow installation of signed add-ons, which let us verify their source and identity. You then built your own add-on to install jQuery and the jQuery UI, from which you could manipulate configuration files, generate supporting tag library and JavaScript library files, and expose the commands to the shell. You also learned how to install, update, and remove your add-ons using the various `osgi` Roo commands, such as `osgi start`.

In the next chapter, we'll show you how to write advanced add-ons. We'll build an add-on to install the CoffeeScript language into your Maven build, and show you how to install it using an OSGi Bundle Repository and the Roo add-on service.

11.10 Resources

Here are some helpful links for the tools and technologies we discussed in this chapter:

For information about jQuery and jQuery UI, visit http://jquery.org.

Apache Felix, the OSGi container for Roo, is documented at http://felix.apache.org.

Though you probably won't need it, for background information the OSGi specification (Roo uses 4.2) can be downloaded at http://www.osgi.org/Release4/Download.

Advanced add-ons and
deployment

12

This chapter covers

- Writing advanced add-ons
- Surveying key Roo infrastructure components
- Generating a GPG key
- Deploying add-ons to the RooBot and an OBR repository

Now that you've learned how to install add-ons to customize your projects, you may be thinking, "So what? Normally I update my Maven POM and install these frameworks myself." True, but add-ons can be much more powerful than a code-generation mechanism. Mastering the Roo add-on system is key to providing a wealth of productivity enhancements for your development team.

In this chapter, we'll take a look at how to build advanced Roo add-ons. We'll delve into Roo's key infrastructure beans such as the `fileManager` and `project-Operations` components, how to accept parameters, and how to register for and react to changes in class definitions. We'll wrap up by showing you how to deploy your add-on to the Roo add-on repository, also known as the *RooBot*.

Let's begin by learning how to create an advanced add-on.

12.1 Advanced add-ons

Advanced add-ons are generated from a template that provides an extra level of customization. You still have the ability to create and expose commands to the shell, but in addition you can now create annotations that generate ITDs, watch for and act on changes in classes in the Roo package path (such as adding a `@RooToString` annotation to a bean), and manipulate the Maven configuration.

The advanced add-on template generates a few other key files:

- *src/assembly/assembly.xml*—This is a Maven assembly file, which can be used to deliver the final add-on as a ZIP or JAR file. The assembly file will include Javadoc and source JARs. You create the assembly by issuing the `mvn assembly :assemble` command.
- *configuration.xml (in src/main/resources, under the add-on's top-level package)*—This file is a template that allows you to use XML to load configuration elements, such as Maven dependencies and plug-ins.
- A `Roo` *annotation class*—Used to install features such as ITDs.
- `Metadata` *and* `MetadataProvider` *implementations (in src/main/java, under the add-on's top-level package)*—These files are used to define and deliver the metadata to the Roo shell. This metadata can add and remove methods and properties from classes and generate ITDs.

With the advanced add-on, you can manipulate your entire project. Let's dive in and create an advanced add-on right now—one that will enable a feature to simplify your JavaScript programming.

12.2 To create an advanced add-on, you need Coffee(Script)

CoffeeScript, a language created by Jeremy Ashkenas, was designed to make JavaScript code using a simple Ruby- or Python-like syntax. Billed as a cross-compiler, CoffeeScript takes this simple language and turns it into a more complex JavaScript equivalent.

Don't let the name fool you; building an advanced add-on isn't as hard as it seems, especially if what you're looking to do is configure additional Maven artifacts and plug-ins. That's all you have to do to install CoffeeScript, so let's go.

12.2.1 What is CoffeeScript?

CoffeeScript is a JavaScript simplification language. It can make your scripts more readable and concise. For example, a data grid loading function in the Dojo JavaScript Toolkit API, which Roo uses to decorate standard HTML controls with client-side validation and rich internet features, may look something like this:

```
function loadGrid(dataGrid) {
    dojo.xhrGet({
        url: "${mydatasource}",
        load: function(data, ioArgs) {
            dataGrid.setStore(
                new dojo.data.ItemFileReadStore(
                    {data: {items : data}})
```

```
            );
        },
    error: function(error) {
        console.log("Grid data loading failed.", error);
    }
    });
}
```

Using the CoffeeScript language, you can reduce the syntax and make it more read-able. The same function looks like this:

```
loadGrid = (datagrid) -> dojo.xhrGet
  url: -> "${mydatasource}"
  load: (data, ioArgs) ->
    dataGrid.setStore(new dojo.data.ItemFileReadStore {
      data: { items: data }
    })
  error: (error) ->
    console.log("Grid data loading failed.", error)
```

The syntax is more concise: functions can be defined anonymously with `(params) ->` body, rather than the wordy `function() { ... }` syntax. Semicolons are optional, and passing JavaScript object literals to functions requires a set of indented parameters, such as the `url:`, `load:`, and `error:` parameters to the `xhrGet` function in the previous example.

There are CoffeeScript compilers and interpreters available for a wide variety of languages, including a Maven plug-in. Getting interested? Then let's set up an add-on that installs a Maven CoffeeScript compiler plug-in into your application.

12.2.2 *Creating a CoffeeScript add-on*

To create your add-on, you'll use the advanced add-on creation command. Create a directory named `coffeescript-addon`, switch to it, and fire up the Roo shell. Then create your add-on application:

```
roo> add-on create advanced ➥
    --topLevelPackage org.rooina.addons.coffeescript ➥
    --projectName coffeescript-addon ➥
    --description "Adds the coffeescript maven compiler"
```

You'll define two add-on shell commands: `coffeescript setup` and `coffeescript remove`, which will add and remove the Maven CoffeeScript compiler to your project.

First, you'll define the add-on capabilities. Open the project in the SpringSource Tool Suite, and replace the contents of `CoffeeScriptOperations` with the following four method signatures:

```
package org.rooina.addons.coffeescript;

public interface CoffeescriptOperations {

  boolean isSetupCommandAvailable();
  boolean isRemoveCommandAvailable();
  void setup();
  void remove();
}
```

The `CoffeescriptOperations` interface is self-documenting—it provides both a setup and a tear-down command, as well as availability indicator methods for each. Next, let's define the Maven configuration setting changes so you can tell the add-on how to install the Maven CoffeeScript compiler.

12.2.3 Configuring the Maven plug-in

Roo defines a configuration.xml file in org/rooinaction/addons/coffeescript that you can use to define the Maven artifacts you'll be adding. The format is arbitrary; you fetch what you want using an XML parser. Replace the contents of this file with the Maven plug-in definition, as shown in the next listing.

Listing 12.1 The CoffeeScript plug-in settings in configuration.xml

```xml
<?xml version="1.0" encoding="UTF-8" standalone="no"?>
<configuration>
  <coffeescript>
    <plugins>
      <plugin>
        <groupId>com.theoryinpractise</groupId>
        <artifactId>coffee-maven-plugin</artifactId>
        <version>1.1.3</version>
          <executions>
            <execution>
                <id>compile-coffeescript</id>              Hook into
              <phase>compile</phase>                       lifecycle
              <goals>
                 <goal>coffee</goal>
              </goals>
            </execution>
          </executions>
        <configuration>
         <coffeeDir>
            src/main/webapp/scripts
         </coffeeDir>
         <targetDirectory>
            src/main/webapp/scripts
         </targetDirectory>
        </configuration>
      </plugin>
    </plugins>
  </coffeescript>
</configuration>
```

Maven users will immediately recognize the `plugin` instruction, which is how Maven installs additional build features.

The Maven CoffeeScript plug-in installs a Java-based CoffeeScript compiler and will automatically compile any file ending in .coffee in the src/main/webapp/scripts directory, placing the JavaScript version of the file in the final /webapp/scripts directory as a JavaScript file. Now you're ready to define some of your command methods.

12.2.4 *Creating the setup command*

To set up your `CoffeescriptOperationsImpl` class, which will install your Maven plug-in, open up the `CoffeeScriptOperationsImpl` class and remove the existing methods. Next, create and stub out the `isSetupCommandAvailable()`, `isRemoveCommand-Available()`, and `remove()` methods, returning `true` from the Booleans and, for now, doing absolutely nothing inside of the `remove()` method:

```
@Component
@Service
public class CoffeescriptOperationsImpl
  implements CoffeescriptOperations {

  public void remove() { }
  public boolean isSetupCommandAvailable() { return true; }
  public boolean isRemoveCommandAvailable() { return true; }

}
```

Next, create the `setup()` method. This method will parse your XML configuration file and feed the defined plug-ins to your Roo add-on for addition to your pom.xml file. The following listing shows your approach.

Listing 12.2   Setting up the CoffeeScript plug-in

```
public void setup() {
    List<Plugin> pluginsToAdd = getPluginsFromConfigurationXml();
    projectOperations.addBuildPlugins(pluginsToAdd);          ◁┐ Install
  }                                                          ❶ plug-ins

private List<Plugin> getPluginsFromConfigurationXml() {
    Element configuration = XmlUtils.getConfiguration(this.getClass());
    Collection<Element> configPlugins = XmlUtils.findElements(
              "/configuration/coffeescript/plugins/plugin",
              configuration);
    List<Plugin> plugins = new ArrayList<Plugin>();             ◁┐ Extract
    for (Element pluginXml : configPlugins) {                 ❸ plug-ins
        plugins.add(new Plugin(pluginXml));
    }

    return plugins;
}
```

 Load config XML ❷

You've placed the code for pulling the plug-ins in the `getPluginsFromConfiguration-Xml()` method. In this method, you're using the `XmlUtils` class again, this time to read your new `configuration.xml` descriptor ❷. You'll use this file to install the plug-ins, located in the XPath of /configuration/coffeescript/plugins/plugin.

Construct a list of the plug-ins you find ❸, adding each one to the list using the Roo `Plugin` class, which takes an XML DOM `Element` from the `XmlUtils.findElements` method. This automatically turns the XML DOM `Element` into a form that the `project-Operations` instance can accept. Although you're adding only one plug-in this time, you can go back and add others by adding them to the configuration.xml file. This makes managing the plug-in more flexible for more work in the future.

Finally, in the `setup()` method, call the `projectOperations.addBuildPlugins` method ❶, which will install the new `plugin` node(s) in the pom.xml file.

You're almost ready to test this add-on. One final step remains before you can make the add-on run—defining your commands to the Roo shell.

12.2.5 *Setting up the CoffeescriptCommands*

Open up the `CoffeescriptCommands.java` file, which will define and delegate the available commands for your add-on. Replace the body of the class with the implementation defined in the following listing.

Listing 12.3 `CoffeescriptCommands.java`

```java
package org.rooina.addons.coffeescript;

import org.apache.felix.scr.annotations.Component;
import org.apache.felix.scr.annotations.Reference;
import org.apache.felix.scr.annotations.Service;
import org.springframework.roo.shell.CliAvailabilityIndicator;
import org.springframework.roo.shell.CliCommand;
import org.springframework.roo.shell.CommandMarker;

@Component
@Service
public class CoffeescriptCommands implements CommandMarker {

  @Reference private CoffeescriptOperations operations;           ◁┐ Inject
                                                                  ❶ delegate
  @CliAvailabilityIndicator({ "coffeescript setup" })
  public boolean isSetupCommandAvailable() {
    return operations.isSetupCommandAvailable();
  }

  @CliAvailabilityIndicator({ "coffeescript remove" })
  public boolean isRemoveCommandAvailable() {
      return operations.isRemoveCommandAvailable();
  }

  @CliCommand(value = "coffeescript setup",
      help = "Install the CoffeeScript compiler")
  public void setup() {
    operations.setup();
  }

  @CliCommand(value = "coffeescript remove",
      help = "Remove the coffeescript compiler")
  public void remove() {
    operations.remove();
  }
}
```

By now the `CommandMarker` class in the previous code should be more familiar. Just as Spring injects beans into other beans using `@Autowired`, an OSGi SCR service such as this class injects the `CoffeescriptOperations` instance, `operations`, into this object using the SCR `@Reference` annotation ❶. You then delegate all calls for checking command availability and performing commands to the `operations` delegate.

12.2.6 *Accessing parameters*

You may pass parameters to your Roo add-on commands. For example, adding a `compileIndividualFiles` option to the `coffeescript setup` command:

```
@CliCommand(value = "coffeescript setup",
    help = "Install the CoffeeScript compiler")
public void setup(
  @CliOption(key="compileIndividualFiles", mandatory=false,
    unspecifiedDefaultValue = "false",
    optionContext = "true, false",
    help = "Compile individual files into separate JS files.")
    boolean compileIndividualFiles) {
operations.setup(compileIndividualFiles);
```

This option is then sent to the operation method for use by your add-on code. Note that you can specify a default value if the option isn't passed, and hints for correct options such as `true` and `false`.

Although you could finish out the add-on implementation, let's first take it for a spin. You'll build your add-on, install it in the Roo shell, and test it with a sample project.

12.2.7 *Building and installing the CoffeeScript add-on*

To build your add-on, you drop to the command line and issue a Maven command:

```
$ mvn package
```

Your target OSGi bundle is located in `target` as the JAR artifact. If it was built successfully, copy the full path, including the root of the file path.

To install the add-on, use the same `osgi start` command you used with the simple add-on (the ellipsis [. . .] represents the full path to the JAR file):

```
osgi start --url ▶
   file:///...org.rooina.addons.coffeescript-0.1.0.BUILD-SNAPSHOT.jar
```

> **YOU'RE NOT INSTALLING THE ADD-ON FOR A SINGLE PROJECT**   Unlike a lot of other frameworks, Roo holds the add-ons within the shell itself, rather than at the project level. Because your add-on adds commands to the Roo shell itself, the installation needs to occur at that level. Once you *use* an add-on, you benefit from the operations it performs, regardless of the project you're working on.
>
> If an add-on misbehaves, you'll need to remove it from the entire Roo shell using `osgi uninstall`.

If the start command worked, hit `[TAB]` and you should see both the `coffeescript setup` and `coffeescript remove` commands in your tab completion list.

12.2.8 *Using the CoffeeScript add-on*

Now, create an empty project directory, such as `test-coffeescript`, and fire up the Roo shell. When inside the shell, create a simple project with a web application. You can use this short script:

```
project --topLevelPackage org.rooina.projects.test.coffeescript ➡
    --projectName test-coffeescript
jpa setup --database HYPERSONIC_PERSISTENT --provider HIBERNATE
web mvc setup
controller class --class ~.web.FooController
```

Try the add-on by issuing the `coffeescript setup` command:

```
roo> coffeescript setup
Updated ROOT/pom.xml [added plugin ➡
  com.theoryinpractise:coffee-maven-plugin:1.1.3]
...
```

Open the project's pom.xml file in your editor. If you search for the `coffee-maven-plugin` entry, you'll find your `plugin` definition, complete from the configuration .xml file.

12.2.9 *Testing the CoffeeScript add-on*

You can test the plug-in with a simple CoffeeScript script. Create `src/main/webapp/hello.coffee` with the following contents:

```
alert message for message in ['Coffeescript', 'Is', 'Fantastic']
```

CoffeeScript compiles into native JavaScript. To test it, add a reference to the script in your home page, src/main/webapp/WEB-INF/views/index.jspx, near the end of the file, just before </util:panel/>:

```
<spring:url value="/scripts/hello.js" var="hello_js" />
<script type="text/javascript" src="${hello_js}"> ➡
    <!-- comment required --></script>
```

You're ready to test. To build and test your application from the operating system prompt, execute

```
mvn coffee:coffee
```

The `coffee:coffee` command executes the CoffeeScript compiler. Next, start your Jetty web server to test the script:

```
mvn jetty:run
```

The `jetty:run` command, which depends on the Maven `package` command, will build the rest of the project and launch the Jetty plug-in.

Browse to your project's home page. You'll see three alert boxes displayed in succession. This proves that you're running the compiled CoffeeScript file, `hello.coffee`, which was transformed into the following JavaScript code in `/scripts/hello.js`:

```
(function() {
  var message, _i, _len, _ref;
  _ref = ['Coffeescript', 'Is', 'Fantastic'];
  for (_i = 0, _len = _ref.length; _i < _len; _i++) {
    message = _ref[_i];
    alert(message);
  }
}).call(this);
```

Use your browser's View Source command to view the script. Pretty nifty. The more advanced Mavenites among this book's readers will quickly begin to customize the plug-in, including adding steps to attach the `coffee` goal to a Maven lifecycle step, such as `prepare-resources`.

Now, let's wrap up this section by adding implementations of the script detection methods and the removal command.

12.2.10 Removing CoffeeScript from a project

The first step is the easy one—remove the add-on. This is the inverse of the add command, so you'll refactor, extracting the common code, and adding or removing the plug-ins based on the operation. You can review the refactored code in the following listing.

> **Listing 12.4   Removing the CoffeeScript plug-in from Maven**

```
public void remove() {
    List<Plugin> pluginsToRemove =                                   Removes
        findCoffeescriptPluginsFromMavenBuild();                     from Maven
    projectOperations.removeBuildPlugins(pluginsToRemove);   ⊲┘      build
}

private List<Plugin> findCoffeescriptPluginsFromMavenBuild() {       Defines
    Plugin pluginDefinition = new Plugin(                            search
        "com.theoryinpractise", "coffee-maven-plugin", "unused");  ⊲┘ criteria

    Set<Plugin> plugins = projectOperations.getProjectMetadata().
      getBuildPluginsExcludingVersion(pluginDefinition);

    return new ArrayList<Plugin>(plugins);
}
```

The `remove()` method delegates to a private method, `findCoffeescriptPlugins-FromMavenBuild()`, which uses a method on the `projectMetaData` object, `getBuild-PluginsExcludingVersion`, to search for any add-ons in the project's Maven pom.xml file. The `projectOperations` object method, `removeBuildPlugins`, takes this list and uses it to remove any plug-ins defined in the file. This removes the CoffeeScript compiler feature from the project.

Let's test the remove feature. Build the add-on using `mvn package` and then run the Roo shell `osgi update` command to replace the currently installed `CoffeeScript` add-on:

```
$ mvn package
...
$ roo
roo> osgi update
      --bundleSymbolicName org.rooina.addons.coffeescript ➥
      --url:///...target/ ➥
          org.rooina.addons.coffeescript-0.1.0.BUILD-SNAPSHOT.jar
```

The command takes a `bundleSymbolicName` to reference the installed add-on, which is defined from the Maven `artifactId` of the CoffeeScript add-on's pom.xml file.

Finally, try to issue the CoffeeScript remove method. If it works, you'll see that the pom.xml file no longer contains the CoffeeScript plug-in.

A better implementation would also allow for an optional parameter, such as `--removeScripts` or `--convertAndRemoveScripts`, which would remove the Coffee-Script files. This should be an optional method. Experiment with your own add-on and see what additional features you might provide.

12.2.11 Detecting setup and remove command availability

You need to provide commands that manipulate the visibility of your commands. You'll start with detecting the `setup` command feature. Expose the `coffeescript setup` command only if

- You haven't installed the CoffeeScript Maven plug-in
- Your project is defined as a web application

That seems to be a straightforward pair of instructions. You'll start by defining two private helper methods in the class, `isCoffeeScriptAddOnInstalled()` and `isProject-War()`, to help figure this out. The following listing shows your approach.

Listing 12.5 Detecting project features

```
private boolean isProjectWar() {
  return projectOperations.isProjectAvailable() &&          Get full
    fileManager.exists(                                      path
      projectOperations.getPathResolver()
        .getIdentifier(Path.SRC_MAIN_WEBAPP,
                        "WEB-INF/web.xml"));                 Is this a
  }                                                          webapp?

private boolean isCoffeeScriptPluginInstalled() {
  List<Plugin> plugins =
    findCoffeescriptPluginsFromMavenBuild();

    if (plugins.size() > 0) {                                Plug-in
      return true;                                         ❶ installed?
    } else {
      return false;
    }
  }
}
```

To find out what project type is attempting to access the `coffeescript setup` command, the `isProjectWar()` method fetches the web.xml file path for your project. You then check whether this file exists, which would confirm that the project is a WAR.

You'll express the next operation (checking that the CoffeeScript Maven plug-in is not installed) as a positive-logic check. The check `isCoffeeScriptPluginInstalled` lets you use it in both a positive and negative manner. You need to ask the `project-Operations` object for all installed Maven plug-ins and iterate through them, looking for a hit ❶.

You also need to inject another support class, the `FileManager`, which you can do via another class-level member variable:

```
@Reference private FileManager fileManager;
```

Now, you'll define the isSetupCommandAvailable() method, which is almost identical, making sure that the project is a valid WAR but does *not* have the CoffeeScript add-on installed:

```
public boolean isSetupCommandAvailable() {
  if (!projectOperations.isProjectAvailable() ||
      !isProjectWar()) {
    return false;
  }

  return !isCoffeeScriptPluginInstalled();
}
```

This step will only allow access to the command if the project is a WAR, and if the add-on isn't installed. You also protect the command from appearing if the Roo shell hasn't created a project yet.

The isRemoveCommandAvailable() method is the inverse of this method:

```
public boolean isRemoveCommandAvailable() {
  if (!projectOperations.isProjectAvailable() ||
      !isProjectWar()) {
    return false;
  }
  return isCoffeeScriptPluginInstalled();
}
```

Again, you don't allow access to the command unless you're working within a defined Roo project, and the project has to be set up as a WAR. In addition, the project must contain an installed Maven CoffeeScript plug-in, so that you can then remove it. Your removal method looks like this:

```
public void remove() {
  List<Plugin> pluginsToRemove =
    findCoffeescriptPluginsFromMavenBuild();
  projectOperations.removeBuildPlugins(pluginsToRemove);
}
```

Update your add-on, and remember the command to update it is osgi update:

```
roo> osgi update
     --bundleSymbolicName org.rooina.addons.coffeescript ➥
     --url:///...target/➥
         org.rooina.addons.coffeescript-0.1.0.BUILD-SNAPSHOT.jar
```

Experiment with tab completion in your test project—if the add-on is already installed, you'll see only the coffeescript remove command. Conversely, if it's not yet installed, you'll see only the coffeescript setup command. Run each command and check your pom.xml file. You'll see the plug-in added and removed each time you run the relevant command.

Now we'll review some of the services and beans made available to add-on developers.

12.3   Key add-on beans and services

To get the most from your add-on system, you have to learn each of the OSGi services that Roo provides. The following section details some of the major services and some snippets that you can experiment with in your own add-ons.

12.3.1 ProjectOperations

You can use the `ProjectOperations` service to manipulate your project in a number of ways. It's injected via

```
@Reference private ProjectOperations projectOperations;
```

There are a number of features in this service. Let's start by reviewing the ones that affect your Maven build.

CONFIGURING YOUR MAVEN BUILD

Here are a few methods that let you manipulate your pom.xml file. As with the rest of these examples, they'll be written after the add-on command completes using a transactional file manager, so your projects won't get damaged by incomplete configuration changes in the case of a bug. You can adjust these features:

- Maven build plug-ins:
  ```
  addBuildPlugin(Plugin),
  addBuildPlugins(List<Plugin>)
  updateBuildPlugin(Plugin)
  removeBuildPlugin(Plugin)
  removeBuildPlugins(List<Plugin>)
  ```

- Maven dependencies:
  ```
  addDependency(Dependency)
  addDependencies(List<Dependency>)
  removeDependency(Dependency)
  removeDependencies(List<Dependency>)
  ```

- Maven properties:
  ```
  addProperty(Property)
  removeProperty(Property)
  ```

- Maven filters:
  ```
  addFilter(Filter)
  removeFilter(Filter)
  ```

- Maven resources (properties files, XML descriptors, and the like):
  ```
  addResource(String moduleName, Resource resource)
  removeResource(String moduleName, Resource resource)
  ```

There are more commands you can issues as well, although you need to cast to a more specific type of `ProjectOperations` to do so.

ADDITIONAL MAVEN OPERATIONS

Your reference to `ProjectOperations` also implements the `MavenOperations` interface, which gives you the ability to create a project yourself using the `createProject()` method.

You also expose whether you're able to create a project with the `isCreate-ProjectAvailable()` method:

```
if (((MavenOperations)projectOperations).isCreateProjectAvailable()) {
  ...
}
```

You could also create a project on your own within your add-on, potentially using a separate configuration:

```
((MavenOperations)projectOperations).createProject(
    new JavaPackage("com.foo.bar.project"),
      "FooBarBaz", 6));
```

The snippet above creates a new project named "FooBarBaz" with the top-level package of `com.foo.bar.project`, and using Java version 6.0.

You can also execute any valid Maven command with `executeMvnCommand(String)`. For example:

```
try {
  ((MavenOperations)projectOperations).executeMvnCommand("jetty:run");
} catch (IOException e) {
  //handle error
  ...
}
```

12.3.2 The PathResolver

The `PathResolver` is a service that properly accesses your project files for you. It provides complete file paths for your root project and any modules associated with it. It can be injected as well:

```
@Reference private PathResolver pathResolver;
```

You can use the resolver to fetch various file path roots:

```
String warRoot = pathResolver.getFocusedRoot(Path.SRC_MAIN_WEBAPP);
String javaRoot = pathResolver.getFocusedRoot(Path.SRC_MAIN_JAVA);
```

This would equate to the file path on your file system for the src/main/webapp and src/main/java directories of your currently focused module. You can also concatenate a subpath, such as

```
String indexFilePath = pathResolver.
    getFocusedPath(Path.SRC_MAIN_WEBAPP, "index.jspx");
```

This points to the index file at the root of your web application.

12.3.3 The file manager

You used the file manager to copy files in chapter 11, so it's not completely foreign to you. All writes go through an implementation of this service. You can gain access to it from your `ProjectOperations` instance using injection as well:

```
@Reference private FileManager fileManager;
```

The file manager is a transactional engine that writes files after an add-on task has been committed. If any `RuntimeException` is thrown, such as one thrown by the Apache `commons-lang3` project's `Validate` annotation, the writes for all files manipulated via this manager won't be performed.

As in chapter 11, you can also use it indirectly. The `AbstractOperations` base class contains a handy `copyDirectoryContents` method that you used to copy the jQuery JavaScript files in chapter 11:

```
copyDirectoryContents("js/jqueryui/*.js",
  pathResolver.getFocusedIdentifier(Path.SRC_MAIN_WEBAPP, "/js"), true);
```

The `copyDirectoryContents` method uses the `FileManager`, as well.

You'll also notice the use of the `pathResolver` in this fragment. The `PathResolver` is frequently used along with the `FileManager` to pull together the proper source or destination paths for a given operation.

12.3.4 *Manipulating files transactionally*

Let's put this together with a simple file writing example. Let's say you want to create a new JavaScript file in the project's src/main/webapp/js directory:

```
String jsLocation = pathResolver.getFocusedIdentifier(
  Path.SRC_MAIN_WEBAPP, "/js/myscript.js");

MutableFile file = fileManager.createFile(jsLocation);

try {
  PrintWriter writer = new PrintWriter(file.getOutputStream());
  writer.println("var myvar = 10; alert (myvar);");
catch (IOException e) {
  throw new IllegalStateException("file cannot be written to");
} finally {
  IOUtils.closeQuietly(writer);
}
```

You'll use the `pathResolver` to look up the proper path for the /js/myscript.js file within the webapp directory. Then, instead of creating a standard Java file structure and writing to it directly, you ask the `fileManager` to create a reference to a *mutable file*, which is a virtual buffer for the file you wish to write.

You then write your information to the file and use the Apache Commons `IOUtils` class's `closeQuietly()` method to properly close the file. Because the `PrintWriter` can throw an `IOException` during the write process, you have to catch it and rethrow as a runtime exception, here the `IllegalStateException`, to handle it properly.

Roo doesn't write this file right away. It waits until the Roo shell command that issued the changes completes, and then tells the file manager to write all of the file create, update, and delete operations at once. While not 100% fail-safe, it will generally stop an add-on from half-modifying a given file. For the curious, browse the Roo source code for `DefaultFileManager.commit()` to see the operations performed.

12.3.5 *Services wrap-up*

You're only scratching the surface of the key services and beans provided by Roo. We haven't even discussed the ITD services and type system, and unfortunately, space doesn't allow it here. We could write an entire book on Roo add-ons, so stay tuned for that. Because the framework is under heavy refactoring for version 1.2, we decided that documenting the internal Roo services wouldn't be useful at this time.

> **THIS API UNDERGOES CONSTANT TWEAKING**   The code we're showing you is valid as of Roo 1.2.1. One significant (albeit small) change is that the Roo team removed their own IOUtils class, and are now using the Apache Commons IO library's IOUtils methods instead.
>
> The team also removed their own Assert class in 1.2.1, replacing it with the Apache Commons Lang project's Verify method.
>
> In the future, more tweaks should be expected. The general add-on development process should remain the same; however, expect to need to adjust your add-ons once deployed every time Roo is updated.

We encourage you to read the Roo source code, which is easily digestible, and review the various built-in add-ons. The project is available at http://github.com/springsource/spring-roo.

12.4 *Publishing your add-ons*

When you've finished writing your add-on, and you've tested it with your team, it's time to publish it. Roo gives you several options: the manual installation via a URL, deployment to a Maven repository as part of an OBR repository, and indexing with the SpringSource RooBot as part of the public Roo add-on repository. Table 12.1 shows the approaches and their respective pros and cons.

Table 12.1   Roo add-on publication options

Option	Approach	Pros	Cons
Manual distribution	Distribute the binary JAR file through a web download or other means. Developers can use the osgi install command to install it.	■ Good for initial testing, experimentation. ■ Good for corporate, closed-source add-ons. ■ No hosting setup required.	■ Developers need to know URLs for each add-on you provide. ■ You'll have to publicize instructions for each add-on.
Using an OSGi Bundle Repository (OBR)	Host your own bundle repository and expose your add-on through that service.	■ Allows you to curate the add-ons you'll provide. ■ One OBR can provide many add-ons. ■ Great choice for internal, corporate, or private team add-ons.	■ Needs a Maven repository to deploy to. ■ Not listed in the public Roo add-on repository.

Table 12.1   Roo add-on publication options *(continued)*

Option	Approach	Pros	Cons
Host on Roo's add-on service	Contribute your add-on to the Roo add-on repository list as a publicly available add-on.	■ Contributes to the Roo add-on community and enriches Roo developers. ■ Gives your add-on maximum exposure.	■ Your add-on will get lots of exposure, so be prepared to support bug fixes, and communicate with the community. ■ Not a good solution for corporate add-ons.

Let's take a look at each of these approaches in detail.

12.4.1 *Manual distribution*

You've used this approach with the `osgi start` command. There are few requirements placed on you for this deployment option, so it's the logical place to start. You need to package your artifact and publish the JAR file in a publicly available location, such as a web server or a network share.

Because you don't use a key signing process to authenticate these add-ons, they should only be installed this way for development purposes, or inside your own organization.

Table 12.2 summarizes the commands used to publish and consume the add-on.

Table 12.2   Manual add-on distribution command summary

Roo command (single-line)	Notes
`perform maven package`	Executes the Maven 'package' command, which will build and deliver the artifact in the `target` directory.
`osgi start --url url`	Loads and starts the Roo add-on.
`osgi update` `  --bundleSymbolicName name`	Updates an existing add-on, using the name defined in the `MANIFEST.MF` file header `Bundle-SymbolicName:`. Roo defines this variable using the `${project.groupId}` and the `${project.artifactId}` values.
`osgi uninstall` `  --bundleSymbolicName name`	Stops and removes the add-on.
`osgi ps [--format format ]`	Similar to a Unix 'ps' command, shows the running OSGi bundles and add-ons. You can use the `--format` parameter with the values of `BUNDLE_NAME`, `LOCATION_PATH`, `SYMBOLIC_NAME`, and `UPDATE_PATH` to show different information by bundle.
`osgi headers` `  [--bundleSymbolicName name ]`	Shows the headers for all bundles, or a selected bundle.

Table 12.2   Manual add-on distribution command summary *(continued)*

Roo command (single-line)	Notes

`osgi log [`
`  --maximumEntries max`
`  --level`
`[INFO|WARNING|DEBUG|ERROR| ]`
	Displays the Felix OSGi container log. Useful when deployment has failed due to an unexpected problem, such as a missing dependency or Java package.

You learned about using the OSGi commands `osgi start` and `osgi uninstall` during your `jQueryUI` add-on installation in chapter 11, so we can skip that technique and move on to deploying artifacts to an `OBR Repository`. Remember, all Roo add-ons are `OSGi` bundles, so these commands will come in handy on a regular basis.

12.5   Deploying to an OBR

You're probably thinking, "What's an OBR?" It stands for OSGi Bundle Repository, which is a standard format for defining a collection of OSGi artifacts on a central server. OBR provides commands for clients to search and download artifacts from a repository via a special, publicly available file, repository.xml. This file contains entries for all resources provided by the `repository`.

Let's deploy your CoffeeScript Roo add-on to an OBR on the Google Code project hosting service. The first step involves digitally signing your artifacts.

12.5.1   Generating and using your PGP keys

To sign your OBR bundle, you'll first need to set up a secure key, known as a `PGP` key pair. An open source tool exists to do this: `GPG`, which stands for GnuPG. GPG is an open source implementation of the PGP key signing standard, and can be downloaded at http://gnupg.org. When configured, you create a new public/private keypair using the `gpg` command:

```
gpg --gen-key
```

We won't cover the process here, because it's documented in a number of places, including the informative Roo manual reference instructions available at https://help.ubuntu.com/community/GnuPrivacyGuardHowto.

> **PRETTY GOOD PRIVACY**   PGP stands for *pretty good privacy*, and is based on the open source Open PGP standard RFC-4880, documented at http://tools.ietf.org/html/rfc4880.

After you've generated your keypair, write down your passphrase; you'll need it every time you configure another machine.

You'll also need to set the default passphrase when running the Maven build, and possibly your default GPG key. To do this, you'll create or edit a file named ~/.m2/settings.xml. (The '~' symbol refers to your home directory, which you're referencing in Unix format.) This file provides settings for your Maven builds. You'll add a `profiles` section, which injects Maven properties into one or more builds, based on an activation strategy:

```
<settings>
  ...
  <profiles>
    <profile>
      <id>gpg</id>
      <properties>
        <gpg.passphrase>thegpgpassphrase</gpg.passphrase>
      </properties>
    </profile>
  </profiles>
  <activeProfiles>
    <activeProfile>gpg</activeProfile>
  </activeProfiles>
  ...
</settings>
```

The profile you installed, with the `id` of gpg, adds a property named `gpg.passphrase`. You activate it using the `activeProfiles` tag, which turns the profile on by default. This injects the property into your Maven build.

To list your keys, you can use the `gpg --list-keys` command. The results we saw on Ken's system were as follows:

```
$ gpg --list-keys

/Users/krimple/.gnupg/pubring.gpg
---------------------------------
pub   2048R/E96FE35F 2010-06-11
uid                  Ken Rimple <krimple@chariotsolutions.com>
sub   2048R/68520BEB 2010-06-11

pub   2048R/9EC1BFA3 2010-12-07
uid                  Ken Rimple (Geek.) <krimple@chariotsolutions.com>
sub   2048R/F986D076 2010-12-07

pub   2048R/B6F65A34 2011-06-01
uid                  Ken Rimple (Silly Weasel) <ken.rimple@gmail.com>
sub   2048R/5C1EF315 2011-06-01

pub   2048R/CA57AD7C 2004-12-06
uid                  PGP Global Directory Verification Key
uid                  [jpeg image of size 3400]
uid                  DNR KS1 <do-not-reply@keyserver1.pgp.com>
uid                  DNR-KS2 <do-not-reply@keyserver2.pgp.com>
```

Because our system has a number of keys, to make one the default, such as the Silly Weasel key, we edited the GPG configuration file, also located off of the home directory in the path ~/.gnupg/gpg.conf. We set up the default key using the value of 9EC1BFA3 as the `default-key` property in that file:

```
default-key 9EC1BFA3
```

The next step for you is to configure the settings that define your version control system in the Maven pom.xml file.

12.5.2   *Using a version control system*

Each time you release an update to your add-on, you'll need to upload a build to a source code repository. We use Google Code, a cloud-based project hosting system, to host a Subversion repository at http://code.google.com/p/sillyweasel-coffeescript-addon. You can choose any cloud-based hosting provider as long as pubic viewing of files is available.

> **HOW DO I CREATE A GOOGLE CODE PROJECT?**   To create a free, open source project on Google Code, sign up for an account through your Google Mail or Google Apps account. The URL for Google Code is http://code.google.com. You'll need to follow the sign-up instructions, and you can choose between SVN and GIT hosting models. As an alternative to this process, you can create a public repository on GitHub.

Next, you have to supply the proper SVN URL settings in the Maven pom.xml file.

First, we edited the <scm> section to set the Maven connection and URL variables:

```
<scm>
   <connection>
scm:svn:https://sillyweasel-coffeescript-addon.googlecode.com/svn/trunk
   </connection>

   <developerConnection>
scm:svn:https://sillyweasel-coffeescript-addon.googlecode.com/svn/trunk
   </developerConnection>

   <url>
    http://code.google.com/p/sillyweasel-roo-addons/source/browse
   </url>
</scm>
```

Next, we modified the distributionManagement section to tell Maven where to deliver our add-on:

```
<distributionManagement>
  <repository>
    <id>Google Code</id>
    <url>
     dav:https://sillyweasel-roo-addons.googlecode.com/svn/repo
    </url>
  </repository>
</distributionManagement>
```

Finally, we edited the Maven settings.xml file again (in ~/.m2) to add our credentials for the Google Code server:

```
<settings>
...
  <servers>
    <server>
      <id>Google Code</id>
      <username>MYUSERNAME</username>
      <password>MYPASSWORD</password>
```

```
    </server>
  </servers>
  ...
</settings>
```

After making these changes, you're ready to develop and release your add-on. During development, point your add-on developer team to the source tree and let them work with it using standard Subversion (or Git if you choose) commands. At some point in the cycle, you'll be ready to release your add-on.

12.5.3 Releasing the add-on

The release of an add-on is generally performed by a designated member of the team. This member will coordinate all check-ins, ensure that all unit and integration tests run properly, perform tests by installing and using the add-on, and ensure that none of the artifacts used by the Maven POM of the add-on are using unreleased (snapshot) versions of the libraries referenced.

> **DON'T USE SNAPSHOT VERSIONS OF DEPENDENCIES**   Because Maven releases are meant to be 100% reproducible, all dependencies to your project need to be *released* versions. For example, if the dependent library version is `1.0.2-SNAP-SHOT`, it's considered unstable, and under development. Versions such as `1.0.2-RELEASE`, `1.0.2`, or `1.0.2-BETA` are releases, and therefore can be checked out and built as of the time that release was marked in the source control system. If you're testing your add-on and want to run through the release process without having to check for snapshots, you can *temporarily* issue your `mvn release:prepare` command using the flag `-Dignore-Snapshots=true`. Do *not* use this for typical releases.

Deployment in Maven uses the somewhat complex but useful `maven-release-plugin`. You should read the Maven documentation on the plug-in for the most up-to-date details, but the general process involves two steps:

- *Prepare your release*—Check to make sure you haven't left uncommitted code in your local repository copy, and that you haven't used any snapshot dependencies (which means they can change and are not released versions). You do this via the `mvn release:prepare` command.
- *Release the artifact*—Perform the release. You use the `mvn release:release` command.

The release prepare process asks for three pieces of information: the name of the release version, the SCM tag for the release, and the new development version of the project (including the version of the release to deploy, the label to use for the release in the version control tag, and the next development version):

```
$ mvn release:prepare

What is the release version for
   "sillyweasel-coffeescript-addon"?
   org.rooinaction.addons.coffeescript:
```

```
        org.rooinaction.addons.coffeescript) 0.1.2: : 0.1.2
What is SCM release tag or label for
    "sillyweasel-coffeescript-addon"?
    (org.rooina.addons.coffeescript:
     org.rooina.addons.coffeescript)
org.rooina.addons.coffeescript-0.1.2-SNAPSHOT: : 0.1.2-SNAPSHOT
        org.rooina.addons.coffeescript-0.1.2
What is the new development version for
    "sillyweasel-coffeescript-addon"? (
    org.rooina.addons.coffeescript:
    org.rooina.addons.coffeescript)
    0.1.3-SNAPSHOT: : 0.1.3-SNAPSHOT
```

After answering these questions, Maven will build the code, tag the release with the release tag, and commit the tag to the version control system. This marks the time of the release so that you can then perform the release itself:

```
$ mvn release:perform
```

Maven checks out the code tagged by the release:prepare step, which was tagged at the time the development coordinator felt the team was ready to release the code:

```
[INFO] --- maven-release-plugin:2.2:perform (default-cli) @ ➡ >
            org.rooina.addons.coffeescript ---
[INFO] Checking out the project to perform the release ...
```

Maven then executes the deploy goal, which does a full build, deploying the final target artifact to your defined target repository, which is defined in this case as dav:https://sillyweasel-roo-addons.googlecode.com/svn/repo. This artifact includes the source, Javadoc, and release JARs. It also writes a pom.xml file in the release directory:

```
...
[INFO] Executing goals 'deploy'...
...
[INFO] Loading source files for package org.rooina.addons.coffeescript
    Constructing Javadoc information...
[INFO] Building jar: /.../sillyweasel-coffeescript-addon/target/ ➡
checkout/target/org.rooina.addons.coffeescript-0.1.2-javadoc.jar
[INFO] Installing ➡
        org/rooina/addons/coffeescript/org.rooina.addons.coffeescript ➡
        /0.1.2/org.rooina.addons.coffeescript-0.1.2.jar
[INFO] Writing OBR metadata
[INFO] Uploading: ➡
    dav:https://sillyweasel-coffeescript-addon.googlecode.com ➡
    /svn/.../addons/coffeescript/org.rooina.addons.coffeescript ➡
    /0.1.2/org.rooina.addons.coffeescript-0.1.2.jar
[INFO] Uploading: ➡
        dav:https://sillyweasel-coffeescript-addon.googlecode.com ➡
    /svn/.../addons/coffeescript/org.rooina.addons.coffeescript ➡
    /0.1.2/org.rooina.addons.coffeescript-0.1.2-sources.jar
[INFO]Uploading: ➡
        dav:https://sillyweasel-coffeescript-addon.googlecode.com ➡
    /svn/.../addons/coffeescript/org.rooina.addons.coffeescript ➡
    /0.1.2/org.rooina.addons.coffeescript-0.1.2-javadoc.jar
...
```

```
-/stuff $ ls -l sillyweasel-coffeescript-addon-read-only/repo/org/rooina/addons/coffeescript/org.rooina.addons.coffeescript/0.1.4/
total 336
-rw-r--r--  1 krimple  staff  45161 Sep 16 10:46 org.rooina.addons.coffeescript-0.1.4-javadoc.jar
-rw-r--r--  1 krimple  staff    487 Sep 16 10:46 org.rooina.addons.coffeescript-0.1.4-javadoc.jar.asc
-rw-r--r--  1 krimple  staff     32 Sep 16 10:46 org.rooina.addons.coffeescript-0.1.4-javadoc.jar.asc.md5
-rw-r--r--  1 krimple  staff     40 Sep 16 10:46 org.rooina.addons.coffeescript-0.1.4-javadoc.jar.asc.sha1
-rw-r--r--  1 krimple  staff     32 Sep 16 10:46 org.rooina.addons.coffeescript-0.1.4-javadoc.jar.md5
-rw-r--r--  1 krimple  staff     40 Sep 16 10:46 org.rooina.addons.coffeescript-0.1.4-javadoc.jar.sha1
-rw-r--r--  1 krimple  staff   9433 Sep 16 10:46 org.rooina.addons.coffeescript-0.1.4-sources.jar
-rw-r--r--  1 krimple  staff    487 Sep 16 10:46 org.rooina.addons.coffeescript-0.1.4-sources.jar.asc
-rw-r--r--  1 krimple  staff     32 Sep 16 10:46 org.rooina.addons.coffeescript-0.1.4-sources.jar.asc.md5
-rw-r--r--  1 krimple  staff     40 Sep 16 10:46 org.rooina.addons.coffeescript-0.1.4-sources.jar.asc.sha1
-rw-r--r--  1 krimple  staff     32 Sep 16 10:46 org.rooina.addons.coffeescript-0.1.4-sources.jar.md5
-rw-r--r--  1 krimple  staff     40 Sep 16 10:46 org.rooina.addons.coffeescript-0.1.4-sources.jar.sha1
-rw-r--r--  1 krimple  staff  14750 Sep 16 10:46 org.rooina.addons.coffeescript-0.1.4.jar
-rw-r--r--  1 krimple  staff    487 Sep 16 10:46 org.rooina.addons.coffeescript-0.1.4.jar.asc
-rw-r--r--  1 krimple  staff     32 Sep 16 10:46 org.rooina.addons.coffeescript-0.1.4.jar.asc.md5
-rw-r--r--  1 krimple  staff     40 Sep 16 10:46 org.rooina.addons.coffeescript-0.1.4.jar.asc.sha1
-rw-r--r--  1 krimple  staff     32 Sep 16 10:46 org.rooina.addons.coffeescript-0.1.4.jar.md5
-rw-r--r--  1 krimple  staff     40 Sep 16 10:46 org.rooina.addons.coffeescript-0.1.4.jar.sha1
-rw-r--r--  1 krimple  staff  10010 Sep 16 10:46 org.rooina.addons.coffeescript-0.1.4.pom
-rw-r--r--  1 krimple  staff    487 Sep 16 10:46 org.rooina.addons.coffeescript-0.1.4.pom.asc
-rw-r--r--  1 krimple  staff     32 Sep 16 10:46 org.rooina.addons.coffeescript-0.1.4.pom.asc.md5
-rw-r--r--  1 krimple  staff     40 Sep 16 10:46 org.rooina.addons.coffeescript-0.1.4.pom.asc.sha1
-rw-r--r--  1 krimple  staff     32 Sep 16 10:46 org.rooina.addons.coffeescript-0.1.4.pom.md5
-rw-r--r--  1 krimple  staff     40 Sep 16 10:46 org.rooina.addons.coffeescript-0.1.4.pom.sha1
-/stuff $
```

Figure 12.1 Artifacts deployed in a release

The repository has both signatures as well as copies of the artifacts, as shown in figure 12.1.

Because add-on projects include the `maven-bundle-plugin`, Maven sets up the OBR entry and adds your new release properly to the right location as part of the release process. In our project, that file is located at `https://sillyweasel-coffeescript-addon.googlecode.com` under the directory /svn/repo/repository.xml.

Now you've got an official release, deployed on a Maven repository, which is OBR-enabled. Time to use it.

12.5.4 Using the OBR to fetch your add-on

To use this repository, you can use the `osgi obr` commands to attach to the OBR and install an add-on from it. You will install the add-on for the Roo shell, not for a specific project. Here's an example, using our `sillyweasel-coffeescript-addon` (please type on one line):

```
roo> osgi obr url add --url ➥
    https://sillyweasel-coffeescript-addon.googlecode.com/ ➥
    svn/repo/repository.xml
```

And to start the add-on, we have the bonus feature of [TAB] completion:

```
roo> osgi obr start --bundleSymbolicName org.rooina.addons.coffeescript
```

The fun part is having to trust your own Roo encryption key before you install the add-on. Now is a good time to refer back to the trust section in chapter 11 and install your key.

The key OSGi OBR commands are shown in table 12.3.

Now that you've seen how to build, sign, upload, and release your OBR-based Roo add-on, it's time to consider 'going public' and publishing it to the Roo central repository.

Table 12.3   OSGi OBR commands

Command	Notes
`osgi obr info --bundleSymbolicName name [;version]`	Shows the Roo add-on information about this add-on bundle. Without specifying the version of the bundle, it displays all versions found. Appending a version, such as `;0.1.1`, displays information about an individual version.
`osgi obr list [--keywords 'keywords']`	Shows all add-ons, optionally matching the text in the `keywords` option.
`osgi obr add --url url`	Adds an OSGi OBR to your repository list. The URL must point to the location of a repository.xml file stored in your repository, and that file must be visible to the developers accessing the repository.
`osgi obr refresh --url url`	Updates your copy of the OBR by again fetching and parsing the OBR file. Use this when checking for updated versions of your add-on.
`osgi obr remove --url url`	Removes this OBR directory from the list of managed OBRs in your Roo shell.

12.6   *Submitting your add-on*

It's easy to upload an artifact to the Roo add-on repository, as of the time of this publication. In the future this may change, but provided your artifact exists in a proper OBR, you only need to send an email to s2-roobot@vmware.com, with the full URL to the OBR's repository.xml file. In the case of the Silly Weasel Roo add-on, the URL is

```
http://sillyweasel.coffeescript-addon.googlecode.com/ ➥
  svn/repo/repository.xml
```

Using a GMail client, the email you send would look something like figure 12.2.

After you send this email, the RooBot will wake up and process the request. Any errors will be shown on the RooBot monitoring page, which at the time of publication resides at http://spring-roo-repository.springsource.org/roobot/roobot-log.txt. This URL may change in the future if the add-on submission procedure is adjusted. The

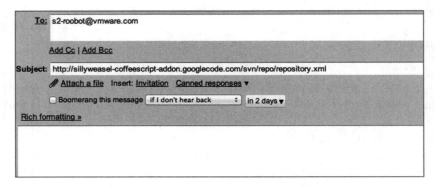

Figure 12.2   Email to the RooBot, which contains the OBR repository URL

gist of this process, however, is to submit your repository URL so that your add-ons get incorporated into the Roo add-on central repository.

The following code is an example of what you can get from the RooBot when submitting an erroneous add-on request. In this example, we used the httppgp:// URL syntax in our email request, which is incorrect procedure. The source control repository needs to support PGP signed keys and URLs, but the repository itself must be a clear http: or https: URL:

```
2011-09-16 02:46:50.889 -
    org.springframework.integration.MessageHandlingException:
    java.net.MalformedURLException: unknown protocol: httppgp
    org.springframework.integration.transformer.
    MessageTransformationException:
      org.springframework.integration.MessageHandlingException:
       java.net.MalformedURLException: unknown protocol: httppgp
       ...
       lengthy Java stack trace ensues...
```

If you get no messages in this URL, don't worry. It's possible that your add-on is already accepted. Try restarting the Roo shell, and use the add-on search command:

```
roo> addon search coffee
1 found, sorted by rank; T = trusted developer; R = Roo 1.2 compatible
ID T R DESCRIPTION -------------------------------------------------
01 - Y 0.1.4 Adds the coffeescript maven compiler
-----------------------------------------------------------------
```

Yep, it's there. Now you can install it, provided you've removed the prior version with osgi uninstall. You'll use the search ID from the last search:

```
roo> addon install id 01
```

That's it. This process may change as Roo finds wider adoption, and if an approval process is put in place. The basic concept of exposing a Roo repository and downloading it is a nifty way to use an OSGi framework extension. This exposes a large number of developers to software automatically. This is a use case for OSGi we can certainly get behind.

12.7 Summary

As you've seen in this chapter, Roo has a powerful add-on API, capable of completely transforming the stock Roo platform into any type of development environment you can imagine. With Roo, you can create add-ons to support different persistence models, frontend APIs, and integration tools, and even to customize your team's development platform.

Add-ons are a complex topic, worthy of their own book. We suggest that add-on developers learn the basics of OSGi bundle development, get cozy with the stock Felix shell, understand as much as they can about the OBR and SCR technologies, and above all, read other add-on code, particularly the built-in Roo add-ons from the Roo source tree. As the add-on framework continues to evolve and becomes more useful with each release, developers should download and keep up to date with the Roo source code. It's located on GitHub at https://github.com/SpringSource/spring-roo.

12.7.1 Resources

The following books and articles may be useful to you as you continue your journey.

BOOKS

Castro Alves, Alexandre. *OSGi in Depth* (Manning Publications, 2011)

Hall, Richard S. et al. *OSGi in Action* (Manning Publications, 2011)

WEB

"Introducing Spring Roo, Part 3: Developing Spring Roo add-ons" by Shekhar Gulati. On IBM developerWorks: http://www.ibm.com/developerworks/opensource/library/os-springroo3/index.html

"Developing Spring Roo Addons" on Marc Schweiterman's Weblog: http://marcschwieterman.com/blog/developing-spring-roo-addons/

Details on the Apache Felix Maven bundler plug-in, which is used to assemble Roo add-ons in to OSGi bundles: http://felix.apache.org/site/apache-felix-maven-bundle-plugin-bnd.html

Part 5

Roo in the cloud

In this final part of the book, we show you how to deploy Roo applications in the cloud where your application will run on a third-party hosting provider. Cloud computing solutions offer flexibility in deploying applications without requiring any internal server infrastructure.

Chapter 13, "Cloud computing," explores the cloud computing paradigm and focuses on one of the cloud computing service models called *platform as a service (PaaS)*. We look at one particular cloud service offering from VMware called *Cloud Foundry*. You'll learn about the Roo add-on for Cloud Foundry and how to install the add-on. Then you'll use the add-on commands to deploy your Roo application to a Cloud Foundry instance. We also look at the ways to view application logs and memory settings to monitor an application running in the cloud.

Spring Integration is a framework for implementing event-based messaging applications. In chapter 14, "Workflow applications using Spring Integration," we look at adding Spring Integration support in a Roo application. You'll see how the new Spring Integration add-on helps with creating and managing various enterprise integration components you can use to simplify the design of the course registration use case. You'll do some design refactoring of the use case discussed in chapter 10—email and messaging—to take advantage of Spring Integration framework components.

Cloud computing

This chapter covers

- Defining cloud computing
- Using the platform as a service model
- Understanding Cloud Foundry
- Deploying a Roo add-on to Cloud Foundry

In the previous two chapters, you learned how to write and install custom Roo add-on components, both simple and advanced add-on types.

In this chapter, you'll learn how to package and deploy the sample Roo application to an external hosting service using a new web application deployment paradigm called *cloud computing (CC)*. We'll discuss this new paradigm and the cloud service offering from VMware[1] called *Cloud Foundry*.

Roo includes an add-on component for Cloud Foundry to help developers with the tasks of deploying Roo applications to the cloud. We'll show you how to configure and deploy your Roo applications using the Cloud Foundry add-on.

Why are organizations turning to cloud computing? Scalability (for scaling up as well as down on demand) is one reason. Another is that using cloud computing means no equipment, maintenance, or operational costs.

---

[1] The parent company of the SpringSource team who created the Spring Roo framework.

Interest in cloud computing has steadily increased over the last few years, as companies discover that hosting applications on an external network provider is a cost-effective method of deploying an application without having to invest in the operational infrastructure. Let's look at the different service and deployment models offered by cloud computing; but first we'll define CC.

13.1 *What is cloud computing?*

Cloud computing (or cloud hosting) has moved up the chart of software implementation options to become the third most popular choice for developers, just behind *build* and *buy*. Organizations are attracted to the option of hosting their applications on the cloud because it offers them a low-cost and highly scalable implementation.

There are three types of service models in cloud computing.

The *infrastructure as a service (IaaS)* model helps organizations to outsource the whole infrastructure used to support their operations (including storage, hardware, servers, and networking components). The cloud service provider owns and maintains the equipment and charges the clients on a per-use basis (see http://mng.bz/DR1h). Amazon's Elastic Computing Cloud (EC2) is an example of an IaaS model.

In a *platform as a service* or *PaaS* model, web applications are developed in-house and deployed to an external hosting site to be hosted on the cloud. Google App Engine (GAE), Microsoft's Azure, VMware's Cloud Foundry, and Heroku are examples of PaaS cloud computing offerings.

In the third cloud architecture model, called *software as a service*, or *SaaS*, applications are developed, hosted, and maintained as third-party programs by an external vendor. SalesForce.com and Google's GMail are examples of SaaS solutions.

In this chapter, you'll learn how to deploy the Roo sample Course Manager application you've developed to the Cloud Foundry server environment. Here again, Roo provides excellent support to perform the steps necessary to run the Roo application in the externally hosted server environment.

13.1.1 *Platform as a service*

The National Institute of Standards and Technology (NIST) defines[2] *cloud computing* as follows:

> *Cloud computing as a model for enabling ubiquitous, convenient, on-demand network access to a shared pool of configurable computing resources (for example, networks, servers, storage, applications, and services) that can be rapidly provisioned and released with minimal management effort or service provider interaction. This cloud model promotes availability and is composed of five essential characteristics, three service models, and four deployment models.*

For more information on these characteristics refer to NIST Special Publication 800-145 that defines cloud computing and describes the different cloud computing models.

---

[2] NIST Special Publication 800-145: The NIST Definition of Cloud Computing (Draft).

NIST defines the *platform as a service model* as follows:

The capability provided to the consumer is to deploy onto the cloud infrastructure consumer-created or acquired applications created using programming languages and tools supported by the provider. The consumer does not manage or control the underlying cloud infrastructure including network, servers, operating systems, or storage, but has control over the deployed applications and possibly application hosting environment configurations.

Several PaaS cloud providers can deploy Java-based web applications to the cloud infrastructure, including Heroku, CloudBees, and Cloud Foundry.

HEROKU

Heroku started as a cloud provider for Ruby on Rails–based web applications, but now it also supports Java applications. Its architecture is based on isolated processes called *Dynos*, which receive web requests from a routing (load balancer) component, connect to application resources via environment variables, and write output to a logging component called *LogPlex*. There are two types of Dynos: A *web dyno* is a web process running the application code and responding to HTTP requests. More web dynos provide more concurrency to access the web application. The second type is a *worker dyno*, which is a background process that runs the application code and processes jobs from a queue.

Heroku's architecture model also includes a routing component, fine-grained control of DNS, custom domains, and SSL features. Heroku has logging and visibility capability to monitor the application's operations with real-time logging and auditing, process status inspection, and an audit trail. To deploy and manage the Java applications and their operations, Heroku provides the following interfaces:

- Command-line interface
- Web console
- REST API

Heroku supports databases like PostgreSQL, and the add-on features include support for NoSQL databases like Redis, MongoDB, and Neo4J; scheduling support; caching frameworks like memcached; and messaging products like RabbitMQ.

CLOUDBEES

The CloudBees PaaS lets developers build, test, and deploy Java web applications in the cloud. CloudBees allows development teams to move their development and production activities to the cloud without infrastructure costs or overhead. It provides integration with the Jenkins continuous integration (CI) tool for application builds, and it also offers a private cloud option if organizations prefer to install a cloud infrastructure within their network.

Cloud Foundry, the third cloud provider we mentioned earlier in this section, will get more attention later in this chapter. For information on other available PaaS cloud providers, review the list of websites in the Resources section at the end of this chapter.

First, we'll look at how the Cloud Foundry product is different from other cloud solutions and what it offers to application developers and operations teams.

13.2   *Cloud Foundry*

Cloud Foundry is an open source PaaS cloud solution from SpringSource, the same organization behind the Spring Roo framework. It allows the deployment of applications written using Spring, Rails, and other modern frameworks. Cloud Foundry supports different programming models and services from VMware and third parties.

The Cloud Foundry application platform includes an application execution engine, an automation engine for application deployment and lifecycle management, and a scriptable command-line interface. It provides integration with development tools like Spring Tool Suite (STS) to help with development and deployment processes.

Figure 13.1 shows the open PaaS application architecture model of Cloud Foundry described by VMware's Rod Johnson in his blog post (http://mng.bz/G8Sk) that announced the release of the Cloud Foundry product. It shows all of the programming models, application services, and deployment options that Cloud Foundry brings to the table.

As you can see from the architecture model diagram, the Cloud Foundry platform offers diverse services in the areas of cloud deployment models, programming languages, and enterprise application services. In the deployment area, Cloud Foundry currently has three offerings:

- *CloudFoundry.com*—This is the VMware-hosted, manage-and-support service. It provides a multitenant PaaS that runs on the vSphere cloud platform.
- *CloudFoundry.org*—This is the open source community site for developers to collaborate and contribute to the Cloud Foundry project.
- *Micro Cloud Foundry*—The Micro Cloud Foundry (http://mng.bz/LCcz) is a local version of the Cloud Foundry service. It runs in a virtual machine on a developer's Mac or PC. Developers can use Micro Cloud Foundry to run a cloud on their own computers for development and testing purposes. You can build cloud applications locally and deploy them to Cloud Foundry without changing the code.

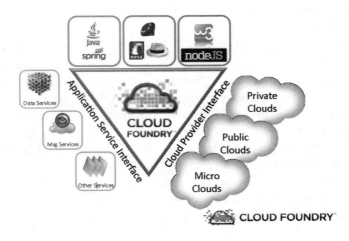

Figure 13.1   Cloud Foundry's open PaaS architecture model

13.2.1 Hosting

Cloud Foundry supports the following program models for developing cloud-based applications:

- Spring and Java
- Ruby (Rails and Sinatra)
- Node.js
- Other JVM languages and frameworks, including Groovy, Grails, and Scala

13.2.2 Database support

As you can see, Cloud Foundry supports a diverse set of programming languages and runtime environments. It also supports the following databases for data storage and persistence requirements:

- MongoDB
- MySQL
- Redis
- PostgreSQL

MongoDB is one of the NoSQL databases (also known as nonrelational databases or NRDBMS), and it's gaining in popularity for storing document-based, unstructured data.

PostgreSQL database support was added in Spring Roo 1.2 to provide another choice (in addition to MySQL) of open source relational database services offered by Cloud Foundry.

13.2.3 Messaging

Messaging services such as RabbitMQ are also offered as part of the Cloud Foundry service infrastructure. Messaging patterns play a significant role in developing loosely coupled application architectures, which is a big part of cloud computing models. You can expect to see more integration and innovation in this area in future versions of cloud computing architectures.

The deployment process of moving a web application to Cloud server instances involves several steps. These steps include uploading the web application to the server and binding various services—like database, messaging, scheduling, and monitoring services—to the application. Performing these steps manually takes a great deal of time and effort because there are many environment variables that need to be set up correctly for the application to function as expected on remote servers.

It would be nice to take these steps in a more automated manner using simple commands. Here is where the Cloud Foundry Roo add-on comes to the rescue. The add-on makes it easy to deploy Java applications from the Roo console.

In the next section, you'll learn how to install and use the Cloud Foundry Roo add-on component. You'll also deploy and manage the cloud services from the Roo command shell using the add-on.

13.3 *Roo add-on for Cloud Foundry*

The Cloud Foundry add-on[3] is well integrated with Cloud Foundry services. Using the Roo add-on commands, you can perform various Cloud Foundry tasks, such as logging in to Cloud Foundry, viewing the already deployed applications, binding to services, and deploying new applications. There are several Cloud Foundry commands added to the Spring Roo shell to make it easy to view, deploy, and monitor your cloud applications.

Let's look at how to install the Cloud Foundry add-on so you can start issuing the commands provided by the add-on component.

13.3.1 *How to install the Cloud Foundry add-on*

Before you start developing Roo applications to deploy to the cloud, you need to create an account on Cloud Foundry. You can do this by signing up for a Cloud-Foundry.com account at http://www.cloudfoundry.com/. Using the new credentials you receive from the Cloud Foundry team, you can log in to the website to deploy applications to the cloud. You can also download the virtual image of Micro Cloud Foundry to test the applications locally on your PC or Mac.

To get started, you need to run the `pgp automatic trust` command to enable automatic PGP key trusting, and ensure that the signed bundles needed by the Cloud Foundry add-on can be installed on your system. Because you don't want to leave the system with this setting, as soon as the add-on files are installed, you should disable the automatic PGP trusting by running the same command again:

```
pgp automatic trust
```

Here's the output of the `pgp` command:

```
roo> pgp automatic trust
Automatic PGP key trusting enabled (this is potentially unsafe); ⇥
disable by typing 'pgp automatic trust' again
roo>
```

Then you run the `addon install` command to instruct Roo to download and install the Cloud Foundry support. When you see the "Deploying...done. Successfully installed add-on: Spring Roo - Addon - Cloud Foundry [version: 1.1.5.RELEASE]" message on your screen, you'll know you've successfully installed Cloud Foundry support:

```
addon install bundle --bundleSymbolicName org.springframework.roo. ⇥
addon.cloud.foundry
```

This command takes a few minutes to download all of the required JAR files. Here's the output of the add-on install command:

```
roo> addon install bundle --bundleSymbolicName org.springframework. ⇥
roo.addon.cloud.foundry

Target resource(s):
```

---

[3] Available since the Roo 1.1.3 release.

```
------------------
Spring Roo - Addon - Cloud Foundry (1.1.5.RELEASE)

Required resource(s):
---------------------
Spring Beans (3.0.5.RELEASE)
jcl-over-slf4j (1.6.1)
slf4j-nop (1.6.1)
Spring AOP (3.0.5.RELEASE)
Servlet Specification API (2.5.0)
Spring Core (3.0.5.RELEASE)
Jackson JSON processor (1.6.2)
Data mapper for Jackson JSON processor (1.6.2)
Spring Context (3.0.5.RELEASE)
Spring Roo - Wrapping - aopalliance (1.0.0.0010)
Spring Web (3.0.5.RELEASE)
slf4j-api (1.6.1)
Spring Roo - Wrapping - Cloud Foundry API (0.0.1.0010)

Optional resource(s):
---------------------
Spring Expression Language (3.0.5.RELEASE)
Spring ASM (3.0.5.RELEASE)

Deploying...done.

Successfully installed add-on: Spring Roo - Addon - Cloud Foundry ⇥
[version: 1.1.5.RELEASE]
[Hint] Please consider rating this add-on with the following command:
[Hint] addon feedback bundle --bundleSymbolicName org.springframework.⇥
roo.addon.cloud.foundry --rating ... --comment "..."
roo>
```

Now, type the pgp automatic trust command again to disable key trusting. Here's the output of this command showing the PGP key trusting is now disabled:

```
roo> pgp automatic trust
Automatic PGP key trusting disabled (this is the safest option)
roo>
```

You're ready to execute the Cloud Foundry commands. Type in the command cloud foundry and press TAB twice. You'll see displayed the available Cloud Foundry commands, as shown in the following snippet:

```
roo> cloud foundry

cloud foundry clear      cloud foundry login
```

Now that you've installed Cloud Foundry support, you can begin to issue any of the 30-plus Cloud Foundry Roo add-on commands to perform various tasks in the cloud application development lifecycle. In the next section, you'll find more details about some of these commands and learn how to use them to deploy and run your application in the Cloud Foundry server environment.

13.3.2 *Add-on commands*

As you can see in the following example, the Cloud Foundry add-on offers various commands to manage the applications on the cloud server instances. These commands are used for different tasks to deploy and monitor cloud applications:

```
cloud foundry bind service
cloud foundry clear login details
cloud foundry create service
cloud foundry delete app
cloud foundry delete service
cloud foundry deploy
cloud foundry files
cloud foundry info
cloud foundry list apps
cloud foundry list instances
cloud foundry list services
cloud foundry login
cloud foundry map url
cloud foundry restart app
cloud foundry start app
cloud foundry stop app
cloud foundry unbind service
cloud foundry unmap url
cloud foundry update app memory
cloud foundry view app memory
cloud foundry view app stats
cloud foundry view crashes
cloud foundry view crash logs
cloud foundry view logs
```

You'll use the key commands required to deploy your sample application. You'll use commands to log in to Cloud Foundry website, deploy the new application, and verify that the application has been deployed correctly. You'll also test the application from the Cloud Foundry site using the application URL you specify during the deployment step. The following section provides a step-by-step approach to all of the add-on commands you'll use in the application deployment process.

Cloud Foundry also offers a command-line interface (CLI) called vmc, which allows you to interact with the Cloud Foundry instance from the command shell.

13.3.3 *Cloud Foundry command-line interface*

With the vmc tool you can deploy Java-, Ruby-, and Node.js-based web applications to the Cloud Foundry servers. You can also configure the deployed applications to use the built-in services provided by the Cloud Foundry platform.

The interface is written in Ruby, so you'll need Ruby and Ruby Gem installed before you can use the CLI commands. The following list contains the vmc commands you can use to deploy and manage the applications in Cloud Foundry:

```
vmc info
vmc apps
vmc services
```

```
vmc frameworks
vmc runtimes

cd myapp
vmc push <appname>
vmc instances <appname>
vmc instances <appname> 3

vmc create-service <service> <name> <app>
bind-service <servicename> <appname>
update <appname>
map <appname> <url>
logs <appname>
stats <appname>
target <url>
```

For more information on the vmc tool, check the support page (http://mng.bz/SfWG) on the Cloud Foundry community website.

You now have the add-on installed and ready for use. Let's see how to deploy the sample application using the new Cloud Foundry add-on commands.

13.4 Deploying the Course Manager application to the cloud

You'll use the Cloud Foundry credentials sent to you to log in to the Cloud Foundry site and deploy the Roo application using the Roo commands from the shell, or from the STS IDE tool, or using the command-line tool vmc.

13.4.1 Cloud Foundry login

To deploy the Roo application to the cloud, first log in to the Cloud Foundry site, which you can do by running the following command on the Roo command shell:

```
cloud foundry login --email CLOUD_FOUNDRY_EMAIL_ADDRESS --password ➥
CLOUD_FOUNDRY_PASSWORD
```

This command takes in three arguments: email, password, and cloudControllerUrl. When logging in to Cloud Foundry for the first time, the email and password arguments are mandatory parameters. Roo will store the login credentials locally for subsequent logins so you aren't required to enter the email and password every time you log in. The cloudControllerUrl parameter is optional. It defaults to the cloud service provided by VMware (http://api.cloudfoundry.com). You can change it to point to other private Cloud Foundry server instances. Here's the console output for the login command:

```
Credentials saved.
Logged in successfully with email address CLOUD_FOUNDRY_EMAIL_ADDRESS
roo>
```

If you want to clear the login credentials stored in memory, you can run the command cloud foundry clear login details, which will remove the email and password values from the cache and will prompt for user account credentials the next time you try to log in.

Now you can type commands like `cloud foundry info` to get the usage details of your user account at VMware's cloud application platform. You can also run the command `cloud foundry list` with one of three options (apps, instances, or services) to get the details on deployed applications, the number of instances where an application is deployed to, and the list of system services available to use in your cloud applications. For example, type the command `cloud foundry list apps` and you should see the following output on the console:

```
==================================== Applications ====================

Name           Status      Instances   Services    URLs
----           ------      ---------   --------    ----
hello          STARTED     1                       hello.cloudfoundry.com
hellotest      STARTED     1                       hellotest.cloudfoundry.com
```

Alternatively, you can type the command `cloud foundry list services` to see the following output on the console. The services command shows the name, description, and version of each system service available in the current release of Cloud Foundry:

```
======================= System Services ========================

Service        Version     Description
-------        -------     -----------
redis          2.2         Redis key-value store service
mongodb        1.8         MongoDB NoSQL store
rabbitmq       2.4         RabbitMQ messaging service
postgresql     9.0         PostgreSQL database service (vFabric)
mysql          5.1         MySQL database service
```

13.4.2 *Deploying the Course Manager application*

The command you use to deploy applications to the Cloud Foundry instances is `cloud foundry deploy`. The deploy command has a number of command-line parameters:

- `appName`
- `path`
- `urls`
- `instances`
- `memory`

The parameters `appName` and `path` are required. Here's the command for deploying the Course Manager application:

```
cloud foundry deploy --appName coursemanager --path CREATE
```

The CREATE option in the previous example will trigger the Maven build commands to clean, compile, and package the application. The deploy command will also move the WAR file to the Cloud Foundry instance. If all of these steps complete successfully, you should see the following message at the end of the Maven build process:

```
The application
coursemanager
 was successfully pushed
```

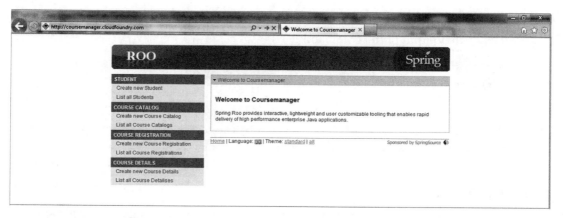

Figure 13.2   Course Manager Roo application running on Cloud Foundry

Now, to verify that the `coursemanager` Roo application has been successfully deployed, let's run the `cloud foundry list apps` command again to view all of the applications currently deployed. Here's the output of this command, which shows that the new application, `coursemanager`, has been deployed with a web URL of `coursemanager.cloudfoundry.com` and with a status of `STOPPED`:

```
===================================== Applications ====================

Name            Status      Instances  Services   URLs
----            ------      ---------  --------   ----
hello           STARTED     1                     hello.cloudfoundry.com
hellotest       STARTED     1                     hellotest.cloudfoundry.com
coursemanager   STOPPED     1                     coursemanager.cloudfoundry.com
```

Let's start the application by issuing the command `cloud foundry start app --appName coursemanager`. If you run the `cloud foundry list apps` command one more time, you'll see that `coursemanager` has been started and is ready to receive web requests.

You can access Course Manager application running on the cloud by using the specified URL (http://coursemanager.cloudfoundry.com) as shown in figure 13.2.

After you've deployed the application, you'll need to check runtime statistics like the JVM-related information, add new services like a database, and bind them to your web application. The following section covers these topics and shows how to perform them using the add-on commands.

13.5   Managing cloud services

Let's take a look at the add-on command to get statistics, such as number of cores, memory, disk space, and uptime of the application.

13.5.1   Application statistics

The following command displays the resource information such as number of CPUs (1), cores (4), memory, disk (30 MB), and the application uptime:

```
cloud foundry view app stats --appName coursemanager
```

Here's the output of the command:

```
============================= App. Stats =============================

Instance    CPU (Cores)    Memory (limit)    Disk (limit)    Uptime
--------    -----------    --------------    ------------    ------
0           0.9 (4)        231.58M (256M)    30.0M (2048M)   1d:
```

The next step is to bind services provided by Cloud Foundry to your application. As you saw earlier with the command cloud foundry list services, these services include databases (both relational and NoSQL databases) and messaging services.

13.5.2 *Binding services*

To provision a new service, you use the following command by specifying the name and the type of the service. Let's create a new service to store and retrieve MongoDB from the NoSQL database, which is used to store document-based, unstructured data. In this example, these values are mymongodb and mongodb, respectively:

```
cloud foundry create service
```

Here's the command output on the Roo console:

```
roo> cloud foundry create service --serviceName mymongodb ➥
    --serviceType mongodb
The service 'mymongodb' was successfully created
```

Now you need to look at the list of available and provisioned services by running the list services command you ran before (cloud foundry list services). Here's the new output of this command showing the new MongoDB service you created:

```
======================= System Services =======================

Service       Version    Description
-------       -------    -----------
rabbitmq      2.4        RabbitMQ messaging service
mongodb       1.8        MongoDB NoSQL store
redis         2.2        Redis key-value store service
postgresql    9.0        PostgreSQL database service (vFabric)
mysql         5.1        MySQL database service


= Provisioned Services =

Name          Service
----          -------
mymongodb     mongodb
```

To bind your application coursemanager to this new service, use the following command:

```
cloud foundry bind service --serviceName mymongodb --appName coursemanager
```

After the application is bound to a service, you can start using the service in the application functionality.

```
cloud foundry restart app --appName coursemanager
```

If you need to delete an existing service, you can use the following command specifying the service name:

```
cloud foundry delete service --serviceName mymongodb
```

Let's do a quick check on what you've accomplished so far. You've deployed the application to the Cloud Foundry environment and created a new service to bind the application. Your application is up and running now, so the next step is to monitor the application running in the cloud. Since the application isn't hosted in the organization's network boundaries, it's critical to monitor its status and respond to any production problems as and when they occur.

13.6   *Application monitoring in the cloud*

The Cloud Foundry add-on provides some monitoring commands to keep an eye on how the application is performing, if it's up and running, and other aspects.

13.6.1 *View application logs*

The application log information can be obtained by running the command `cloud foundry view logs --appName coursemanager --instance 0`.

If you want to see if your application had any crashes, you can run the command `cloud foundry view crashes`. Here's this command and its console output:

```
roo> cloud foundry view crashes --appName coursemanager
The application 'coursemanager' has never crashed
roo>
```

You can use the command `cloud foundry view crash logs` to view the log information about when application crashes happened. This gives operations and developer teams the ability to check the availability and uptime of their applications in the cloud and troubleshoot any outages (crashes) that may occur during the application usage.

13.6.2 *Provisioning memory*

You can view the current memory setting of a cloud application, and update memory if you need to, from the `cloud foundry view app memory --appName coursemanager` command. This command allows you to see the memory used by the application (256MB).

To change the allocated memory you can run `cloud foundry update app memory --appName coursemanager` with the new memory setting.

As you can see, the Cloud Foundry add-on commands are extensive and useful in deploying and monitoring cloud applications.

13.7   *The road ahead*

Cloud Foundry is a relatively new technology and is growing in terms of new features with every product release. You can expect to see more integrations with popular technologies and application frameworks such as the Neo4J graph database (there's already a Roo add-on for Neo4J database integration in the works) and other frameworks in the areas of messaging, workflow, enterprise application integration, security, and social computing.

Heroku recently released beta support for Scala (http://mng.bz/4zb5) and Play (http://mng.bz/QXEx) frameworks and its roadmap for the future includes polishing support and the general release of the feature. There'll be some additional Heroku tooling needed for Spring Roo applications. The Heroku team is also working on aligning the cloud computing framework with continuous delivery. They are working on creating a deployment platform that supports continuous delivery, while allowing developers to use a framework of their choice among the supported frameworks, with few changes to developer experience and workflow.

13.8   *Summary*

In this chapter, you learned about Cloud Foundry, the cloud computing product from VMware, and how to install the Cloud Foundry add-on in Roo. You used the add-on commands to deploy to a Cloud Foundry instance. You found out how to view the application logs, memory settings, and information on system crashes.

You also used the other add-on commands to perform tasks such as starting and stopping applications and binding services.

Cloud Foundry is based on the open source PaaS cloud computing model and has great potential to innovate in the cloud computing space. It allows developers to increase their productivity without getting bogged down with infrastructure setup and maintenance overhead. Cloud Foundry's integration with Roo gives you the ability to develop applications on your local development environment (which should be easier when you use Micro Cloud Foundry), and the means to deploy and manage applications, all from within the Roo command shell.

The next chapter builds on discussions from previous chapters and focuses on the integration Roo provides when working with Spring Integration. This framework is used for Enterprise Service Bus (ESB) and workflow-based use cases.

13.9   *Resources*

Amazon Elastic Computing Cloud (http://aws.amazon.com/ec2/)

CloudBees (http://www.cloudbees.com/)

Cloud Foundry (http://www.cloudfoundry.com/)

Google App Engine (http://code.google.com/appengine/)

Heroku (http://www.heroku.com)

Micro Cloud Foundry (http://mng.bz/LCcz)

Microsoft Azure (http://www.windowsazure.com/en-us/)

Platform as a service—the NIST definition (http://mng.bz/4LQu)

SalesForce.com (http://www.salesforce.com/)

Workflow applications using Spring Integration

This chapter covers

- Workflow applications
- Enterprise application integration
- Spring Integration
- Spring Integration add-on for Roo
- Course registration implementation using Spring Integration

In the previous chapter, you learned how to deploy Java applications to the cloud. Using the Roo framework made it easier and faster to package and migrate your application from a local environment to the cloud server instance.

In this chapter, we discuss the support for the Spring Integration framework that Roo provides for workflow-based applications. The Spring Integration framework is a SpringSource project that's been grabbing the spotlight recently. The framework implements the popular *enterprise integration patterns*, a set of common components in applications involving some type of workflow, where multiple steps in the business process are executed either sequentially or in parallel.

Because Spring Integration is an add-on like the JMS and email add-ons, this chapter is similar from a content flow standpoint to previous chapters where we covered those two add-ons, and our discussion focuses mainly on Roo commands and how each command works.

By the end of this chapter, you'll know how to use enterprise integration patterns to implement the advanced types of use cases in enterprise Java applications. You'll also be comfortable using the Spring Integration framework as well as its add-on for Roo, which will let you implement Spring Integration components using Roo commands in less time than it would take if you were to manually configure the Spring Integration workflow components.

Let's get started with a discussion of workflow applications and the enterprise integration patterns (EIPs).

14.1 *Workflow applications*

Workflow-based applications include business processes that consist of multiple steps, with each step requiring a different type of trigger mechanism (time-based versus event-based), a different interaction model (synchronous versus asynchronous), or a different type of order for execution (sequential versus parallel). This type of architecture provides a great deal of flexibility and extensibility to application design and offers several advantages over traditional asynchronous messaging.

An ideal architecture solution to implement workflow requirements should manage the messaging and integration concerns and let the application architects and developers focus on the business components, without having to worry about the complex infrastructure and integration plumbing code. Enterprise integration patterns help in this space by providing a set of messaging architecture and design patterns to successfully implement your workflow requirements.

14.1.1 *Enterprise application integration*

Enterprise application integration (see http://mng.bz/u7is) helps software architects and developers design and implement integration requirements in their applications. These patterns are based on asynchronous messaging architectures that make the application design more modular and loosely coupled from other components within the application.

These EAI patterns are driven by design principles such as loose coupling, event-driven architectures, and synchronous and asynchronous interaction models.

Two types of dependencies (or couplings) are involved—a component-level dependency and a system-level dependency. A component- or type-level dependency deals with associating between various components in the application. For example, a controller class may depend on a service class, which may in turn depend on a data access object (DAO) class. These component-level dependencies can be reduced using the dependency injection (DI) principle.

Conversely, a system-level dependency refers to the coupling between two systems, whether they're two internal systems within the same organization, or systems that are hosted in an external organization. By limiting one system level of coupling to another you can evolve and implement any changes in one system without adversely impacting the other system. Minimizing the system-level coupling also ensures that one system can function when the other system it relies on isn't available. The communication and interaction between these systems can happen based on business events that trigger the subsequent processing in the main system.

Event-driven architecture (EDA) is another important component of enterprise application integration. We'll look at this component next.

14.1.2 *Event-driven architecture*

The architectural pattern known as *event-driven architecture* explains how complex applications are broken down into a set of components or services that interact via events. One of the primary advantages of this is a loosely coupled application architecture, which helps to simplify the implementation of the component by eliminating concern about how to communicate with other components. *Staged event-driven architecture (SEDA)* is an architectural pattern where the events are communicated via channels that act as buffers during high throughput in the system. SEDA-based architectures are more scalable than are standard multithreaded applications. They're also tunable at runtime, allowing optimization for the current load being experienced.

Event-driven, message-based architecture centers on two main components: events and messages. The message-based interaction operates through a structure of channels and endpoints, through which the messages are sent to carry out the functionality of the application.

With this big-picture view of event-driven, message-based architecture understood, you're ready to see how the Spring Integration framework implements this architecture style.

14.2 *Using the Spring Integration framework*

Spring Integration is a framework for implementing event-based messaging applications. It provides a simple model for building enterprise integration solutions while maintaining the separation of concerns between business logic and integration logic.

Spring Integration is an extension of the Spring programming model to support enterprise integration patterns, taking advantage of the inversion of control (dependency injection) capability provided in the Spring core framework. Its architecture is based on lightweight messaging and integration with external systems using declarative adapters that provide a higher-level abstraction for functionality like remoting and messaging.

For more information on this topic, refer to *Spring Integration in Action* (http://www.manning.com/fisher/) from Manning. The book was coauthored by Spring

Integration project lead Mark Fisher and offers a wealth of resources. The Spring Integration website (http://mng.bz/br9v) is another helpful resource, providing documentation on how to use the framework in Spring applications.

Another framework that works nicely with Spring Integration is Spring Batch, which can be used to design and implement batch (offline) applications.

14.2.1 Spring Batch

Spring Batch enables the development of batch-based use cases that are common in the operations of enterprise systems. A POJO-based framework, it provides reusable functions that are essential in processing large volumes of records, such as transaction management, job processing statistics, job restart, and resource management.

The Spring Batch and Spring Integration frameworks complement each other well and produce sophisticated event-driven, high-volume, high-performance batch applications. One scenario where using a Spring Integration and Spring Batch combination adds value to the solution architecture is when a batch job needs to be launched based on a business event. An example of this is when a data file is uploaded to an FTP server from an internal application or an external system. It's also a good solution if any of the steps in the workflow need to be run as a batch with job restart or skip capabilities, which are available out of the box in Spring Batch.

Currently, Roo has no add-on available for Spring Batch, making it a good add-on candidate because there are several commands in the batch framework and it would be easier to set up the jobs and other batch components using Roo commands.

If you're interested in learning more about Spring Batch framework's features and API, refer to these additional resources: *Spring Batch in Action* (http://manning.com/templier/), and the Spring Batch project website (http://mng.bz/F66T).

14.3 Adding Spring Integration to your Roo application

In this section, we'll discuss the design details of the course registration use case with EIP patterns and Spring Integration in the mix.

You implemented the course registration use case in chapter 10. In that solution design, the messaging infrastructure you set up didn't allow the flexibility to add other steps in the process flow. If you need the flexibility to add (or modify or remove) any components without having to write a lot of code to change the order of tasks, you can take advantage of the Spring Integration framework. This alternative implementation of the course registration use case is the main focus of this chapter.

14.3.1 Course registration: a workflow-based approach

Let's revisit the course registration use case, which includes multiple steps to process the course registration request before the last step of sending a confirmation email notification. This is a good use case for a workflow-based solution. The beauty of this solution is that you can implement a successful registration and a wait-list scenario within the same workflow. This is one of the advantages to using a workflow approach and the Spring Integration framework in enterprise Java applications. It allows you to design a solution with different branches (forks) and subprocesses in the process flow.

You'll re-architect the solution you created for the wait-list notification use case covered earlier in this book. This time you'll take advantage of the workflow capabilities the Spring Integration framework provides.

The course registration process, using the Spring Integration solution, includes the following steps:

1 When a student submits the course registration request, you post a message with the course registration details in a message queue.

2 A channel adapter component receives the message and performs a data transformation to filter out the data in the message that's not required for your course registration process. Because the request data can come from different systems including external business partners, you need the transformation step to ensure that the input data to the next step is Course Manager domain friendly and doesn't contain any unknown or invalid data.

3 The next step in the process is to check course availability. If the course is available, the program will route the course registration request to the branch to continue processing the request. This processing can be done offline without consuming any resources in the main business process. If the course isn't available, the request will be routed to another branch in the program flow where the wait-list processing occurs. This also can happen outside the main process.

4 The Course Manager program performs all of the required updates and processing.

5 The final step is to notify the student with either the course registration confirmation or that the registration request has been placed on the wait list.

The diagram in figure 14.1 shows the various steps of the course registration process flow with two different scenarios—one for successfully registering for a course the user finds available, and the other for the wait-list scenario.

You'll use some of the integration patterns in the implementation of the course registration use case. Let's take a look at these patterns in more detail.

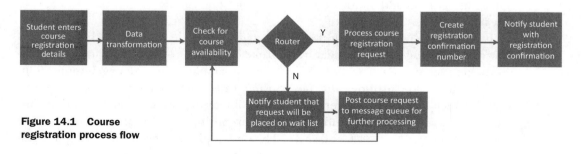

Figure 14.1 Course registration process flow

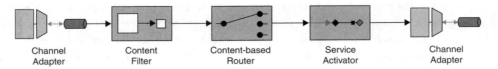

Figure 14.2   Course registration workflow with integration components

14.3.2   Integration patterns used in the solution

As you can see, you're using a few different integration patterns, listed on the EAI patterns catalog site (http://mng.bz/U87T), to implement the components in the workflow process. Here's the list of design patterns used in the solution and what they're responsible for:

- *Inbound Channel Adapter*—This component in the workflow receives the course registration details from a message queue.
- *Content Filter*—This component removes the data elements from the course registration message that aren't necessary for processing the course registration.
- *Content-Based Router*—This component routes the registration request to the course registration confirmation or the wait-list step in the process, based on course availability.
- *Outbound Channel Adapter*—This component sends an email notification to the customer after processing the course registration request.

The EAI patterns site uses special modeling (UML) notations for each of these patterns. Figure 14.2 shows the integration patterns using the UML notations.

By now, you must be itching to start testing, so let's get to it. In the next section, we'll dive into the installation, configuration, and use of the new Roo add-on component in the sample application.

14.4   Spring Integration add-on for Roo

Fortunately, an add-on component exists to create and manage Spring Integration components using Roo commands without having to write the code from scratch. The Spring Integration add-on for Roo provides quick and simple configuration of Spring Integration flows.

In this chapter, we'll look at the course registration use case that includes a workflow with a message queue, a data transformation step, a routing step, and a notification step to send an email to the customer of the sample Course Manager application.

The discussion includes the new Spring Integration add-on (http://mng.bz/VX0h), which is not yet in general release. We'll look at how to install the add-on and then how to run Roo commands for setting up Spring Integration components like SERVICE_ACTIVATOR, ROUTER, and so on. The design philosophy of the Spring Integration add-on aligns with the enterprise application integration patterns and their implementation in enterprise applications.

Another helpful tool when you need to add the various Spring Integration components into the application is the SpringSource Tool Suite (http://mng.bz/k0jd), or STS. This Eclipse-based IDE tool makes the job of adding different components easier, without having to configure them manually from scratch. STS also provides a good context-sensitive help feature.

Spring Integration Scala DSL[1] is another new project from the Spring Integration team that makes it easy to configure Spring Integration components using a domain-specific language (DSL) approach. This project is also in the early stages of development.

The Spring Integration add-on's current status is that of a work in progress, and at the time of this writing, it's not in GA release. The current version's support is not comprehensive in that the add-on doesn't persist the Spring configuration files after issuing the Roo commands. But it does have good support for setting up the various Spring Integration components in the workflow.

We'll start this discussion by running different add-on commands to show you how to set up the Spring Integration workflow and associate the components to one another. Then you'll create the required Spring configuration files to test the workflow setup. You'll also write the Java classes needed to capture the business logic of the use case. Finally, you'll write a JUnit test in order to test the different course registration scenarios.

The add-on also provides a `focus` command, similar to the Roo focus command, but it works on integration patterns rather than on Java classes.

14.4.1 How to install the Roo add-on for Spring Integration

You'll perform the following steps to install the Spring Integration add-on:

1 Download the source from its Git repository location.
2 Compile the Java classes and package the JAR files.
3 Deploy the JAR files to the Roo runtime environment (which is based on OSGi technology).
4 After completing the installation process, you're ready to use the Spring Integration add-on.

Let's look at each of these steps in more detail.

GETTING THE SPRING INTEGRATION ADD-ON SOURCE CODE

Let's first check out the add-on source code from its Git repository location to a local directory on your machine. You can use a Git client tool like SmartGit (http://mng.bz/n5pg) to work with the Git repository, using a graphical user interface tool. Figure 14.3 shows the SmartGit client tool window, with the SpringIntegrationRoo-Addon Git project folders (in the left pane) and files (in the right pane).

---

[1] See http://blog.springsource.org/2012/03/05/introducing-spring-integration-scala-dsl/.

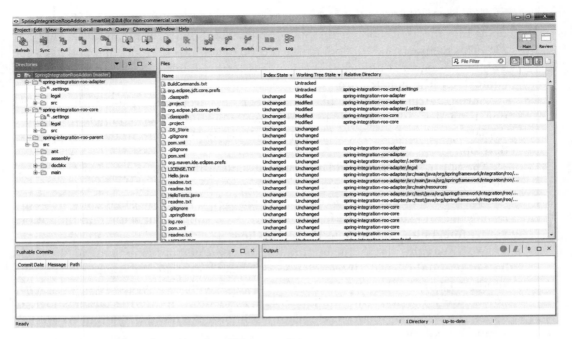

Figure 14.3   Spring Integration add-on SmartGit screenshot

Now you need to clone the project using the add-on component's Git repository URL.[2] It includes three subprojects (or Maven modules):

- spring-integration-roo-parent
- spring-integration-roo-core
- spring-integration-roo-adapter

The spring-integration-roo-parent module includes the common dependency JAR files for the other modules in the project. And the spring-integration-roo-core module contains all the Roo commands for setting up a new project, creating various Spring Integration pipeline components, and configuring each component in the workflow.

BUILD THE ADD-ON

To compile and package the add-on JAR files, run Maven `clean` and `install` commands, as shown in this example:

```
REM First, set JAVA_HOME and MAVEN_HOME variables to point to JDK
REM and Maven home directories respectively. Add these two variables
REM to the PATH system environment variable.

set PROJECT_HOME=C:/dev/projects/SpringRooProjects/ ➥
    SpringIntegrationRooAddon
cd %PROJECT_HOME%

mvn clean install
```

---

[2] See git://git.springsource.org/spring-integration/roo-addon.git.

This will create two JAR files for the core and adapter modules, which you can deploy to the Roo environment, as discussed in the next section.

DEPLOY THE ADD-ON

The Spring Integration add-on depends on the following four libraries:

- Apache Commons Logging
- Spring Core
- Spring Beans
- Spring ASM

If you try to deploy the Roo add-on without having these libraries installed first, the framework will throw the error shown in the following listing.

Listing 14.1 Error when deploying without the dependent Java libraries

```
ERROR: Error starting file:/C:/dev/frameworks/Roo/v1.2.0/ ⇒
    spring-roo-1.2.0.M1/bundle ⇒
    spring-integration-roo-core-1.0.0.BUILD-SNAPSHOT.jar
(org.osgi.framework.BundleException: Unresolved constraint in bundle
spring-integration-roo-core [71]: Unable to resolve 71.0: ⇒
    missing requirement [71.0] package;
(&(package=org.springframework.util)(version>=3.0.0)) ⇒
    [caused by: Unable to resolve 69.0:
missing requirement [69.0] package; (&(package=org.apache. ⇒
    commons.logging)(version>=1.1.1)
(!(version>=2.0.0)))])]org.osgi.framework.BundleException: ⇒
    Unresolved constraint in bundle
spring-integration-roo-core [71]: Unable to resolve 71.0: ⇒
    missing requirement [71.0] package;
(&(package=org.springframework.util)(version>=3.0.0)) ⇒
    [caused by: Unable to resolve 69.0:
missing requirement [69.0] package; (&(package=org.apache. ⇒
    commons.logging)(version>=1.1.1)
(!(version>=2.0.0)))]
```

You have two options to resolve this error. You can copy the required JAR files to the target folder in the PROJECT_HOME directory, or you can install these libraries using the OSGi commands. To do this, first you create a new directory under target called RooAddOnLibraries and copy the zip file contents into this new folder.

There are five JAR files under the bundles subdirectory:

- spring-asm-3.0.4.RELEASE.jar
- spring-beans-3.0.4.RELEASE.jar
- spring-core-3.0.4.RELEASE.jar
- spring-integration-roo-adapter-1.0.0.BUILD-SNAPSHOT.jar
- spring-integration-roo-core-1.0.0.BUILD-SNAPSHOT.jar

Install these JAR files to the bundle folder under Roo's installation directory using the osgi start command for each JAR file, as shown in this example:

```
osgi start --url file:///C:/dev/projects/SpringRooProjects/ ➥
    SpringIntegrationRooAddon/spring-integration-roo-core/ ➥
    target/spring-integration-roo-core-1.0.0.BUILD-SNAPSHOT.jar
osgi start --url file:///C:/dev/projects/SpringRooProjects/ ➥
    SpringIntegrationRooAddon/spring-integration-roo-adapter/ ➥
    target/spring-integration-roo-adapter-1.0.0.BUILD-SNAPSHOT.jar
```

If you need to uninstall a library, you can use the following command:

```
osgi uninstall --bundleSymbolicName spring-integration-roo-core
```

Let's install the Apache Commons Logging library now. The OSGi version of the Commons Logging JAR file can be downloaded from the SpringSource Enterprise Bundle Repository (http://mng.bz/PpyY), which hosts OSGi-ready versions of hundreds of open source enterprise libraries commonly used to develop Spring applications.

You can download the Apache Commons Logging (version 1.1.1) library (`com .springsource.org.apache.commons.logging-1.1.1.jar`) from the bundle repository (http://mng.bz/ad5d).

After installing the required libraries, type the following command to view all of the installed libraries and their current status (for example, whether they're active or not):

```
osgi ps
```

The output of this command is shown in the next listing.

Listing 14.2   `osgi ps` command output showing all active OSGi bundles

```
[ 67] [Active ] [ 1] Spring ASM (3.0.4.RELEASE)
[ 68] [Active ] [ 1] Spring Beans (3.0.4.RELEASE)
[ 69] [Active ] [ 1] Spring Core (3.0.4.RELEASE)
[ 70] [Active ] [ 1] Spring Integration ROO add-on ADAPTER module ➥
    (1.0.0.BUILD-SNAPSHOT)
[ 71] [Active ] [ 1] Spring Integration ROO add-on CORE module ➥
    (1.0.0.BUILD-SNAPSHOT)
[ 74] [Active ] [ 1] Apache Commons Logging (1.1.1)
```

Another way to verify that the Spring Integration add-on components are installed correctly is to use the `osgi log` command.

The following listing shows the output of this command.

Listing 14.3   `osgi log` output showing current status of OSGi bundles

```
2011.04.19 20:24:34 INFO - Bundle: spring-integration-roo-core - ➥
    BundleEvent STARTED
2011.04.19 20:24:34 INFO - Bundle: spring-integration-roo-core - ➥
    [org.springframework.roo.shell.Converter] - ServiceEvent REGISTERED
2011.04.19 20:24:34 INFO - Bundle: spring-integration-roo-core - ➥
    [org.springframework.roo.shell.Converter] - ServiceEvent REGISTERED
2011.04.19 20:24:34 INFO - Bundle: spring-integration-roo-core - ➥
    [org.springframework.roo.shell.Converter] - ServiceEvent REGISTERED
2011.04.19 20:24:34 INFO - Bundle: spring-integration-roo-core - ➥
    [org.springframework.roo.shell.Converter] - ServiceEvent REGISTERED
2011.04.19 20:24:34 INFO - Bundle: spring-integration-roo-core - ➥
2011.04.19 20:24:34 INFO - Bundle: spring-integration-roo-core - ➥
```

```
    [org.springframework.integration.roo.addon.IntegrationOperations] ➨
    - ServiceEvent REGISTERED
2011.04.19 20:24:34 INFO - Bundle: spring-integration-roo-core - ➨
    [org.springframework.roo.shell.CommandMarker] - Service
Event REGISTERED
2011.04.19 20:24:34 INFO - Bundle: spring-integration-roo-core - ➨
    [org.springframework.roo.shell.CommandMarker] - Service
Event REGISTERED
2011.04.19 20:24:34 INFO - Bundle: spring-integration-roo-core - ➨
    [org.springframework.integration.roo.addon.IntegrationContext] - ➨
    ServiceEvent REGISTERED
2011.04.19 20:24:34 INFO - Bundle: spring-integration-roo-adapter - ➨
    BundleEvent STARTED
2011.04.19 20:24:34 INFO - Bundle: spring-integration-roo-adapter - ➨
    BundleEvent RESOLVED
2011.04.19 20:24:34 INFO - Bundle: org.springframework.core - ➨
    BundleEvent STARTED
2011.04.19 20:24:34 INFO - Bundle: org.springframework.beans - ➨
    BundleEvent STARTED
2011.04.19 20:24:34 INFO - Bundle: org.springframework.beans - ➨
    BundleEvent RESOLVED
2011.04.19 20:24:34 INFO - Bundle: org.springframework.asm - ➨
    BundleEvent STARTED
```

So far, you've downloaded, compiled, packaged, and deployed the Spring Integration add-on component source code along with the libraries on which the add-on depends. Now you can start using the add-on to implement the course registration use case. Before you do that, you need to quickly verify that you successfully installed the add-on and that there were no errors during deployment.

14.4.2 *Verifying the add-on installation*

To verify success of the add-on installation, run the `help` command in the Roo command shell window. This will display all of the Spring Integration commands. The following listing is the partial output of this command that shows Roo's Spring Integration commands.

> **Listing 14.4 Spring Integration Roo commands to verify the add-on installation**

```
* integration flow delete - Allows you to delete an existing ➨
    Integration flow
* integration flow edit - Allows you to edit an existing ➨
    Integration flow
* integration flow fold - Allows you to fold an existing ➨
    Integration flow to be exposed via convenient namespace support
* integration flow list - Lists available flows
* integration flow read - Allows you to read an existing ➨
    Integration flow
* integration flow start - Starts the new Integration flow
* integration project - Focuses the Command Line context on the ➨
    component specified
```

If you want context-sensitive help, you can type `integration` and press TAB:

```
roo> integration flow
integration flow read        integration flow start
```

Note that the exact syntax of these commands may change in more recent releases of the Spring Integration add-on, because the version of the add-on component is not in GA release at the time of this writing.

Now you're ready to use the new add-on for your use case implementation. In the next section, we'll discuss the implementation of the course registration confirmation use case step by step using Roo commands to define and configure the Spring Integration components you need in the use case.

14.5   Course registration workflow components

Before you can start creating the workflow components required for implementing the use case, you first need to set up the Spring Integration flow.

14.5.1   Spring Integration flow setup

Let's create a new project to see how the add-on sets up a Spring Integration project. Change your directory to a new folder called coursemanager-spring-int and run the following command to set up the project:

```
integration project --name coursemanager-spring-int --rootDomain ⇒
    org.rooinaction.coursemanager
```

This creates a new project called `coursemanager-spring-int` that's similar to how Roo creates a new Java project when you run the `project` command.

You can now type `integration flow` and press TAB twice to see what command options are available. It will show the following output on the command shell window:

```
integration flow read    integration flow start
```

Because you didn't create an existing Spring Integration flow yet, you need to use the start option with the `integration flow` command:

```
roo> integration flow start --name course-mgmt-int
```

The output should say

```
Started new flow: course-mgmt-int
```

If you want to edit an existing Spring Integration workflow, use the command `integration flow edit`, specifying the name of the flow, as this example shows:

```
roo> integration flow edit --name course-mgmt-int
```

The output will say that the flow is ready for edits:

```
Flow 'course-mgmt-int' is ready for modification
```

To see all of the available Spring Integration commands at this time, you can press TAB twice and it will display the following list of commands:

```
coursemanager-spring-int[course-mgmt-int] roo>

aggregate    enrich      filter      produce     route        ⇒
    send     service
stop         transform   validate
```

As you can see in the previous output example, there are several commands to create the different Spring Integration components that you need in your use case.

Note that the available commands are context sensitive, meaning that you see only the commands that are relevant to the Spring Integration component that's currently in focus.

Another interesting feature to note is that the new add-on has support for maintaining the state of the project between Roo restarts.

14.5.2 Configuring Spring Integration components

Now that the base Spring Integration flow is set up, you're ready to start adding the integration components you need to implement the course registration use case requirements. These components include the following:

- Input channel adapter (message queue)
- Transformer
- Router
- Output channel adapter

Let's look at how to implement each of these components using Roo commands. First, start with the input channel adapter, which is based on a JMS queue. Post the course registration details to the message queue and the channel adapter helps with receiving the message from the queue for further processing in the subsequent steps of the workflow.

INPUT CHANNEL ADAPTER

The input channel adapter in this case is acting as a producer, so you need to run the `produce` command to set up the adapter component. Type `produce` and press TAB twice to see the available options for the `produce` command. If you do this a couple of times, you'll see the command for setting up the channel adapter. Here's the example of this command:

```
coursemanager-spring-int[course-mgmt-int] roo> produce via ➥
    channel-adapter
```

As you can see from the output in the following listing, a number of different adapter options are available, from `ftp`, `jdbc`, and `jms` to some new adapters that were added in recent releases of Roo, such as `twitter` and `xmpp`.

Listing 14.5 Variations of `produce` command for creating channel adapter component

```
produce via channel-adapter bean      produce via channel-adapter event
produce via channel-adapter feed      produce via channel-adapter file
produce via channel-adapter ftp       produce via channel-adapter http
produce via channel-adapter jdbc      produce via channel-adapter jms
produce via channel-adapter mail      produce via channel-adapter sftp
produce via channel-adapter tcp       produce via channel-adapter ➥
    twitter
produce via channel-adapter udp       produce via channel-adapter xmpp
```

You'll use the `jms` option for your requirements. Here's the full command to configure the JMS channel adapter:

```
coursemanager-spring-int[course-mgmt-int] roo> produce via channel-adapter jms
```

You can now use the previously mentioned `focus` command to switch to a specific component in the workflow. Let's run the `focus` command with the `--name` parameter to see the list of different components available. Here's the output of this command:

```
channel_fffa           channel_valueA           channel_valueB  ⟹
    inbound-adapter_e57b
```

The channel adapter's ID is `inbound-adapter_e57b`. You can now use the `focus` command with the component ID to switch the focus to the inbound channel adapter. After running the `focus` command, if you press TAB twice, it will display the list of available commands:

```
coursemanager-spring-int[course-mgmt-int] ...inbound-adapter_e57b roo>

aggregate    config      diagram      enrich       filter       focus  ⟹
    produce      route       send
service      stop         transform    validate
```

TRANSFORMER

One of the commands listed is `transform`, which can be used to define a transformer component in the workflow. It's useful for data transformation requirements. Let's run the `transform` command, which creates a data transformer and sets the focus to this new component. Here's output of the command after a transformer component has been added to the workflow:

```
coursemanager-spring-int[course-mgmt-int] ...trnsfmr_6054 roo>

aggregate    config      diagram      enrich       filter  ⟹
    focus    produce
route        send        service      stop         transform  ⟹
    validate
```

Another command that's available is the `diagram` command, which you can use for viewing Spring Integration workflow details, such as what Spring Integration components are defined and assembled so far in your use case. Type the `diagram` command and press Enter. The output of the `diagram` command showing the FLOW details with the channel adapter, message channel, and transformer components is shown here:

```
========================================
 FLOW: -> inbound-adapter_e496(JMS) -> channel_6054 -> trnsfmr_6054
========================================
```

You only have two components defined so far in the process, so the diagram doesn't have a lot of components. You'll run this command again later in this section after creating all of the components to show how the FLOW diagram will look after all of the workflow components are in place.

ROUTER

The next workflow component you need to define is a router that can be used to send the incoming messages to different steps in the process based on the predefined business rules. The command to define a router component is route. After you create the router component, you can run another command, validate, to perform a validation of the Spring Integration flow you've created so far. Here's the output of the validate command:

```
Validating Flow: course-mgmt-int
```

The last component you'll create for your use case is the output channel adapter. It'll send the email notifications to customers after performing all of the steps in the course registration workflow.

OUTPUT CHANNEL ADAPTER

Similar to the produce command you used earlier in this section to create an inbound adapter, now you'll run the send command to define the outbound channel adapter. You'll also specify that you need an email-based adapter by including the mail parameter in the send command. Here's the command for defining the output channel adapter component:

```
coursemanager-spring-int[course-mgmt-int] ...router_9a29 roo> send via ➥
    adapter mail --name course-reg-email
```

When the final workflow component has been defined, you can run the diagram command one more time to see the final version of the Spring Integration flow details. Here's the command output:

```
========================================
 FLOW: -> inbound-adapter_302d(JMS) -> channel_302d -> ➥
     trnsfmr_33b4 -> channel_9a29 -> router_9a29(HVR)[channel_valueB,
channel_valueA] -> channel_course-reg-email -> course-reg-email(MAIL)
 FLOW: -> channel_valueA
 FLOW: -> channel_valueB
========================================
coursemanager-spring-int[course-mgmt-int] ...course-reg-email roo>
```

Also, when you're finished creating and configuring all of the Spring Integration components you need for your use case, you can run the stop command to exit the course-mgmt-int workflow.

14.5.3 *Spring Integration configuration details*

Let's add the Spring configuration file and Maven dependencies to test the Spring Integration components.

First you start with the Spring configuration file. The following listing shows the contents of the applicationContext-integration.xml file.

> **Listing 14.6 Configuration details for JMS components in course registration use case**

```
<?xml version="1.0" encoding="UTF-8"?>
<beans xmlns="http://www.springframework.org/schema/beans"
  xmlns:xsi="http://www.w3.org/2001/XMLSchema-instance"
  xmlns:integration="http://www.springframework.org/schema/integration"
  xsi:schemaLocation="http://www.springframework.org/schema/beans
```

```
        http://www.springframework.org/schema/beans/spring-beans.xsd
        http://www.springframework.org/schema/integration
        http://www.springframework.org/schema/integration/ ➡
          spring-integration.xsd">

  <bean id="connectionFactory" class="org.springframework.jms. ➡
        connection.CachingConnectionFactory">
        <property name="targetConnectionFactory">
            <bean class="org.apache.activemq. ➡
                    ActiveMQConnectionFactory">
                <property name="brokerURL" value="vm://localhost"/>
            </bean>
        </property>
        <property name="sessionCacheSize" value="10"/>
        <property name="cacheProducers" value="false"/>
    </bean>

    <bean id="courseRegistrationRequestQueue" class="org.apache. ➡
        activemq.command.ActiveMQQueue">
        <constructor-arg value="jms.queue. ➡
            CourseRegistrationRequestQueue"/>
    </bean>

    <integration:poller id="poller" default="true" fixed-delay="1000"/>

</beans>
```

This configuration file defines the JMS queue-related Spring beans using the ActiveMQ
server as the messaging container. A second configuration file, coursemanager-spring-
int-config.xml, contains the Spring bean configuration for the integration components. This is shown in the following listing.

Listing 14.7   Spring configuration for course registration workflow components

```
<?xml version="1.0" encoding="UTF-8"?>
<beans:beans xmlns="http://www.springframework.org/schema/integration"
    xmlns:xsi="http://www.w3.org/2001/XMLSchema-instance"
    xmlns:beans="http://www.springframework.org/schema/beans"
    xmlns:context="http://www.springframework.org/schema/context"
    xmlns:jms="http://www.springframework.org/schema/integration/jms"
    xmlns:jmx="http://www.springframework.org/schema/integration/jmx"
    xmlns:stream="http://www.springframework.org/schema/➡
        integration/stream"
    xsi:schemaLocation="http://www.springframework.org/schema/beans
        http://www.springframework.org/schema/beans/spring-beans.xsd
        http://www.springframework.org/schema/context
        http://www.springframework.org/schema/context/➡
            spring-context.xsd
        http://www.springframework.org/schema/integration
        http://www.springframework.org/schema/integration/➡
            spring-integration.xsd
        http://www.springframework.org/schema/integration/jms
        http://www.springframework.org/schema/integration/jms/➡
            spring-integration-jms.xsd
        http://www.springframework.org/schema/integration/jmx
        http://www.springframework.org/schema/integration/jmx/➡
            spring-integration-jmx.xsd
```

```
        http://www.springframework.org/schema/integration/stream
        http://www.springframework.org/schema/integration/stream/➡
            spring-integration-stream.xsd">

<!--  Test Outbound Adapter for Unit Testing  -->
<channel id="stdinToJmsoutChannel"/>
<stream:stdin-channel-adapter id="stdin" ➡
    channel="stdinToJmsoutChannel"/>

<jms:outbound-channel-adapter
    id="jmsout"
    channel="stdinToJmsoutChannel"
    destination="courseRegistrationRequestQueue"/>


<!--  Inbound Adapter  -->
<jms:message-driven-channel-adapter
    id="coursemanager-jms-input-adapter"
    destination="courseRegistrationRequestQueue"
    channel="jmsInToTransformerChannel"/>

<channel id="jmsInToTransformerChannel"/>
<!--  Transformer  -->
<transformer input-channel="jmsInToTransformerChannel"
    output-channel="transformerToRouterChannel"
    expression="payload.toUpperCase() + '- [' + ➡
        T(java.lang.System).currentTimeMillis() + ']'"/>

<channel id="transformerToRouterChannel"/>

<recipient-list-router id="coursemanager-router" input-channel=➡
    "transformerToRouterChannel">
    <recipient channel="jmsinToStdoutChannel"
        selector-expression=➡
        "payload.contains('12345')"/>
    <recipient channel="jmsinToWaitListChannel" ➡
        selector-expression="payload.contains('99999')"/>
</recipient-list-router>

<channel id="jmsinToStdoutChannel"/>
<channel id="jmsinToWaitListChannel"/>

<stream:stdout-channel-adapter id="courseRegSuccess" ➡
    channel="jmsinToStdoutChannel" append-newline="true"/>

<stream:stdout-channel-adapter id="courseRegWaitList" ➡
    channel="jmsinToWaitListChannel" append-newline="true"/>

    <!--  Mail Output Channel Adapter  -->
<!-- replace 'userid and 'password' wit the real values -->
<mail:inbound-channel-adapter id="pop3ShouldDeleteTrue"
    store-uri="pop3://[userid]:[password]@pop.gmail.com/INBOX"
    channel="routerToOutputAdapterChannel"
    should-delete-messages="true"
    auto-startup="true"
    java-mail-properties="javaMailProperties">

    <poller fixed-rate="20000"/>
</mail:inbound-channel-adapter>

<util:properties id="javaMailProperties">
```

```
            <beans:prop key="mail.pop3.socketFactory.fallback">
                false</beans:prop>
            <beans:prop key="mail.debug">true</beans:prop>
            <beans:prop key="mail.pop3.port">995</beans:prop>
            <beans:prop key="mail.pop3.socketFactory.class">
                javax.net.ssl.SSLSocketFactory</beans:prop>
            <beans:prop key="mail.pop3.socketFactory.port">
                995</beans:prop>
    </util:properties>
</beans:beans>
```

There are some additional Maven build dependencies for the Spring Integration classes. These dependencies are shown in the next listing. We're using Spring Integration framework version 2.0.5 in this code example. The version is specified as `<spring.integration.version>2.0.5.RELEASE</spring.integration.version>` in the Maven pom.xml file.

Listing 14.8   Maven build dependencies for Spring Integration

```
<!--    Spring Integration Dependencies   -->
        <dependency>
            <groupId>org.apache.activemq</groupId>
            <artifactId>activemq-core</artifactId>
            <version>${activemq.version}</version>
        </dependency>
        <dependency>
            <groupId>org.springframework.integration</groupId>
            <artifactId>spring-integration-jms</artifactId>
            <version>${spring.integration.version}</version>
        </dependency>
        <dependency>
            <groupId>org.springframework.integration</groupId>
            <artifactId>spring-integration-jmx</artifactId>
            <version>${spring.integration.version}</version>
        </dependency>

        <dependency>
            <groupId>org.springframework</groupId>
            <artifactId>spring-jms</artifactId>
            <version>${spring.version}</version>
            <scope>compile</scope>
        </dependency>

        <dependency>
            <groupId>org.springframework.integration</groupId>
            <artifactId>spring-integration-core</artifactId>
            <version>${spring.integration.version}</version>
        </dependency>
        <dependency>
            <groupId>org.springframework.integration</groupId>
            <artifactId>spring-integration-stream</artifactId>
            <version>${spring.integration.version}</version>
        </dependency>

        <dependency>
            <groupId>org.springframework.integration</groupId>
```

```
        <artifactId>spring-integration-mail</artifactId>
        <version>${spring.integration.version}</version>
    </dependency>
```

14.5.4 Testing Spring Integration flow

To test the course registration use case with Spring Integration, you'll write a test client class called CourseRegistrationSpringIntegrationTestClient. Because most of the workflow details are captured in the configuration file, all you need to do in the test client is to post a course registration request message to the JMS queue, course-RegistrationRequestQueue. To make it easier to test, use the stream support provided by the Spring Integration framework. Instead of writing the code to create and post a message to the JMS queue, use a stdout-channel-adapter component, which allows you to type in the course registration test message at the console to trigger the course registration workflow. The following listing shows the test client class.

Listing 14.9 Test client for testing course registration with Spring Integration

```
package org.rooinaction.coursemanager.integration;

import java.io.File;

import org.apache.commons.logging.Log;
import org.apache.commons.logging.LogFactory;
import org.springframework.context.support.➥
    ClassPathXmlApplicationContext;

/**
 * @author
 *
 * Test Data:
 * Successful Registration Text Message:
 * Test Course Registration # 12345
 *
 * Waitlist Registration Text Message:
 * Test Course Registration # - 99999
 *
 */
public class CourseRegistrationSpringIntegrationTestClient {

    private static final Log log = LogFactory.➥
        getLog(CourseRegistrationSpringIntegrationTestClient.class);

    private final static String[] configFiles = {
        "/META-INF/spring/integration/➥
            applicationContext-integration.xml",
        "/META-INF/spring/integration/coursemanager-spring-int-config.xml"
    };

    public static void main(String[] args) {
        CourseRegistrationSpringIntegrationTestClient client = ➥
            new CourseRegistrationSpringIntegrationTestClient();
        client.verifyThatCourseRegistrationIsSuccessful();
    }
```

```
public void verifyThatCourseRegistrationIsSuccessful() {
    log.debug("verifyThatCourseRegistrationIsSuccessful() ⇥
        method is called.");
    log.debug("Cleaning up the ActiveMQ Test Data.");
    File tmpDirAMQ = new File("activemq-data");
    cleanupActiveMQDatabase(tmpDirAMQ);
    log.debug("Loading Spring Application Context.");
    new ClassPathXmlApplicationContext(configFiles, ⇥
        CourseRegistrationSpringIntegrationTest.class);
    log.debug("[For testing purposes, Successful Registration ⇥
        message should contain " +
            "the number 12345 and the Waitlist should ⇥
            contain 99999].");
    System.out.println("Type the Course Registration Test ⇥
        Message and press the Enter key.");
}

private void cleanupActiveMQDatabase(File dirAMQ) {
    if (dirAMQ.exists()) {
        String[] children = dirAMQ.list();
        if (children != null) {
            for (int i = 0; i < children.length; i++) {
                cleanupActiveMQDatabase(new File(dirAMQ, ⇥
                    children[i]));
            }
        }
    }
    dirAMQ.delete();
}
}
```

14.6   Summary

In this chapter, you learned how to implement a workflow solution using the Spring Integration framework and the Roo add-on. Using the Roo add-on makes the implementation process easier, without having to write a lot of code. Following Roo's philosophy, the Spring Integration add-on allows you to easily create and manage integration components.

As you've seen, the Spring Roo framework has a good ecosystem in areas of application development, with common use cases such as data access (CRUD) and user interface development, as well as advanced use cases such as asynchronous messaging, Spring Integration, and support for emerging technologies like cloud computing.

14.7   Resources

Enterprise integration patterns (http://www.eaipatterns.com)
Spring Integration add-on source repository (http://mng.bz/VX0h)
Spring Integration framework website (http://mng.bz/7377)
SpringSource Tool Suite (http://www.springsource.com/developer/sts)

index

Spring in Action, Third edition
by Craig Walls

> ISBN: 978-1-935182-35-1
> 424 pages
> $49.99
> June 2011

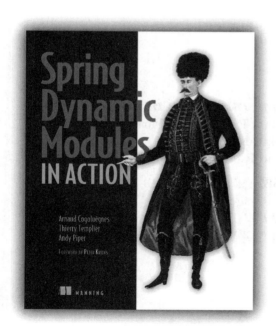

Spring Dynamic Modules in Action
by Arnaud Cogoluègnes, Thierry Templier,
  and Andy Piper

> ISBN: 978-1-935182-30-6
> 548 pages
> $59.99
> September 2010

For ordering information go to www.manning.com

Spring Batch in Action
by Arnaud Cogoluègnes,
    Thierry Templier, Gary Gregory,
    Olivier Bazoud

ISBN: 978-1-935182-95-5
504 pages
$59.99
October 2011

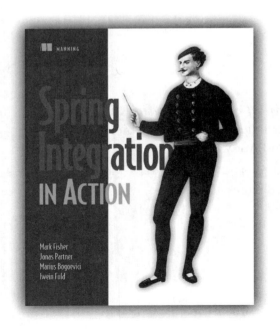

Spring Integration in Action
by Mark Fisher, Jonas Partner,
    Marius Bogoevici,
    and Iwein Fuld

ISBN: 978-1-935182-43-6
400 pages
$49.99
April 2012

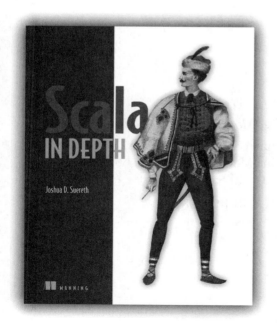

MORE TITLES FROM MANNING

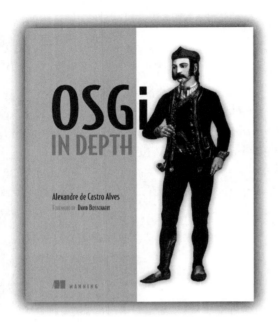

OSGi in Depth
by Alexandre de Castro Alves

  ISBN: 978-1-935182-17-7
  392 pages
  $75.00
  December 2011

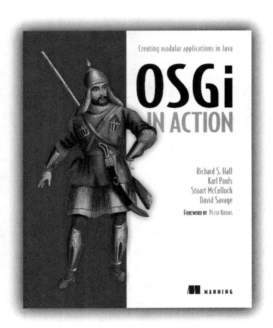

OSGi in Action
Creating Modular Applications in Java

by Richard S. Hall, Karl Pauls,
   Stuart McCulloch,
   and David Savage

  ISBN: 978-1-933988-91-7
  576 pages
  $49.99
  April 2011